Readings from
American Scientist

Use and Misuse of Earth's Surface

Edited by

Brian J. Skinner

Yale University

Member, Board of Editors

American Scientist

WILLIAM KAUFMANN, INC.   LOS ALTOS, CALIFORNIA

Front cover: A giant smelter and surrounding landscape at Morenci, Arizona, one of the world's largest copper-producing complexes. The mill and smelter, which make up the group of buildings surrounding the smokestacks, receive ore from an open pit mine (out of view at left), separate the valuable copper minerals from the rock, and smelt the copper-rich concentrate down to copper metal. Photograph by Brian J. Skinner.

Library of Congress Cataloging in Publication Data

Main entry under title:

Use and misuse of Earth's surface.

   Bibliography: p.
   Includes index.
   1. Man—Influence on nature—Addresses, essays, lectures.   2. Human ecology—Addresses, essays, lectures. I. Skinner, Brain J., 1928–   .II. American Scientist.
GF75.U83   304.2   81-6043

ISBN 0-913232-95-5

Contents

Introducing

Earth and Its Inhabitants

A new series of books containing readings originally published in *American Scientist*.

The 20th century has been a period of extraordinary activity for all of the sciences. During the first third of the century the greatest advances tended to be in physics; the second third was a period during which biology, and particularly molecular biology, seized the limelight; the closing third of the century is increasingly focused on the earth sciences. A sense of challenge and a growing excitement is everywhere evident in the earth sciences—especially in the papers published in *American Scientist*. With dramatic discoveries in space and the chance to compare Earth to other rocky planets, with the excitement of plate tectonics, of drifting continents and new discoveries about the evolution of environments, with a growing human population and ever increasing pressures on resources and living space, the problems facing earth sciences are growing in complexity rather than declining. We can be sure the current surge of exciting discoveries and challenges will continue to swell.

Written as a means of communicating with colleagues and students in the scientific community at large, papers in *American Scientist* are authoritative statements by specialists. Because they are meant to be read beyond the bounds of the author's special discipline, the papers do not assume a detailed knowledge on the part of the reader, are relatively free from jargon, and are generously illustrated. The papers can be read and enjoyed by any educated person. For these reasons the editors of *American Scientist* have selected a number of especially interesting papers published in recent years and grouped them into this series of topical books for use by nonspecialists and beginning students.

Each book contains ten or more articles bearing on a general theme and, though each book stands alone, it is related to and can be read in conjunction with others in the series. Traditionally the physical world has been considered to be different and separate from the biological. Physical geology, climatology, and mineral resources seemed remote from anthropology and paleontology. But a growing world population is producing anthropogenic effects that are starting to rival nature's effects in their magnitude, and as we study these phenomena it becomes increasingly apparent that the environment we now influence has shaped us to be what we are. There is no clear boundary between the physical and the biological realms where the Earth is concerned and so the volumes in this series range from geology and geophysics to paleontology and environmental studies; taken together, they offer an authoritative modern introduction to the earth sciences.

Volumes in this Series

The Solar System and Its Strange Objects Papers discussing the origin of chemical elements, the development of planets, comets, and other objects in space; the Earth viewed from space and the place of man in the Universe.

Earth's History, Structure and Materials Readings about Earth's evolution and the way geological time is measured; also papers on plate tectonics, drifting continents and special features such as chains of volcanoes.

Climates Past and Present The record of climatic variations as read from the geological record and the factors that control the climate today, including human influence.

Earth's Energy and Mineral Resources The varieties, magnitudes, distributions, origins and exploitation of mineral and energy resources.

Paleontology and Paleoenvironments Vertebrate and invertebrate paleontology, including papers on evolutionary changes as deduced from paleontological evidence.

Evolution of Man and His Communities Hominid paleontology, paleoanthropology, and archaeology of resources in the Old World and New.

Use and Misuse of Earth's Surface Readings about the way we change and influence the environment in which we live.

Introduction: Use and Misuse of Earth's Surface

In the closed ecosystem of Earth, every organism interacts with and is dependent in some way on other organisms. Disturb some interactions and the rest of the system must change and adjust—just as surgery causes reactions throughout a human body. In a beautifully written essay printed in *The Medusa and the Snail,* Lewis Thomas likens Earth to an enormous, developing embryo that is, "for all its stupendous size and the numberless units and infinite variety of its life forms, coherent. Every tissue is linked for its viability to every other tissue; it gets along by symbiosis." He further points out that while we have learned a great deal about the way individual species have evolved, we are nevertheless still neophytes in our comprehension of the way Earth works and survives as a single entity. "And now human beings have swarmed like bees over the whole surface, changing everything, meddling with all other parts, making believe we are in charge, risking the survival of the entire magnificent creature."

Fortunately we seem at last to have become aware of the changes we have wrought, and with awareness has come the emerging field of environmental studies. One's perceptions of just what environmental studies encompass are necessarily colored by experience and interest. To some, problems of local pollution or the scars of strip mining are paramount, but to others the extinction of an animal species or the rapidly changing carbon dioxide content of the atmosphere seem more worthy of investigation and action. But regardless of where one places the emphasis, human-induced changes of the natural world are involved—alterations that are both animate and inanimate. The articles reprinted in this volume have been selected to demonstrate the kinds of environmental changes we know best; a complete list would be virtually impossible because new ones are being discovered almost every day.

The root and cause of all artificially-induced environmental change is the human population, and the first two papers address this issue. Citing the rising per capita consumption of natural resources as well as a growing global population, Holdren and Ehrlich point out that civilization has become a massive new ecological force, one that changes climates, restructures the land surface, and distributes synthetic chemicals around the world. But as massive as this ecological force already is, it continually grows larger, apparently without causing much alarm. Many people have a false sense of security derived from three dangerous misconceptions: (1) the size and growth of the human population bears no relation to escalating ecological problems; (2) environmental deterioration consists solely of pollution that is localized and reversible; and (3) science and technology can support continuous growth and perpetual use of natural resources.

The second paper, by James R. Echols, examines the central tenet of the classic Malthusian dilemma—that unchecked growth must eventually outrun supplies. While no thoughtful person can deny the mathematical correctness of the argument, there remains the question as to when the equation becomes unbalanced and whether the moment can be predicted in time for populations to be controlled in such a way as to forestall the evil day. Some experts believe it is already too late. James Echols views the high population growth rates of less developed countries and draws the conclusion that their fertility will outrun food production by the year 2000.

Should all of our actions be justified solely in terms of human needs—economic, social, ecological? Western culture tends to argue "yes," but Ehrenfeld suggests that more reliable criteria exist, criteria centered on the values of all species and all communities. He uses a seemingly unimportant—but endangered—animal, the Houston toad, to prove his point that the extinction of this strange fellow would be a loss for us all.

Pollution is the accumulation of unwanted materials at various places in the environment. It is one of the most obvious and least pleasant aspects of environmental decay. But is pollution necessary? Bohn and Cauthorn argue that most resources are taken from the lithosphere while most wastes are put into the atmosphere or hydrosphere. A stable pattern, they argue, would put more of the waste back in the lithosphere. But not all pollution comes from old tires, chemical waste, and other trash. Some comes from the wide dispersal of materials once believed to be harmless but now known to be slowly-ticking time bombs. Two such issues have attracted a great deal of attention during the last decade. The first is chemical pollution, of which lead poisoning is an example. Lead poisoning is widespread, continuing, and underestimated according to Wessel and Dominski, but it is a preventable danger. The second concerns one of the great social and political issues of the day, radiation pollution. How do we decide what constitutes an acceptable risk? Bernard Cohen compares the potential health hazards of all-nuclear generation of electricity to other health hazards such as smoking. The risk of nuclear power for a large population, he calculates, is equivalent to smoking six cigarettes in one's lifetime, or one every 10 years.

Unpleasant though local pollution may be, large-scale and global changes pose the greatest dangers. Four papers discuss problems of air pollution. John T. Middleton, Acting Commissioner of the Air Pollution Control Office in 1971, discusses the major sources and controls of air pollution, using the region of East St. Louis and Granite City, Illinois, and St. Louis, Missouri, as an example. Fennelly, by contrast, focuses on a single aspect of air pollution—the increase of small solid and liquid particles in the atmosphere. Aerosol particles vary widely in composition; as a result they can cause local changes that have deleterious effects on human health as well as regional changes in the climate. Toon and Pollack discuss how the climatic changes are brought about. But even though many questions surrounding aerosols remain unanswered, probably the biggest question regarding the atmosphere concerns the slow increase in its carbon dioxide content. We burn fossil fuels and add CO_2 to the atmosphere faster than the natural system (fixation by plants and solution in the ocean) can respond. Baes and coauthors discuss the possible effects of CO_2 buildup on the global climate. Like it or not, we are all pawns in this giant, uncontrolled experiment.

The disruption of bodies of water is perhaps the best understood of all environmental effects. But it is also one of the most difficult to deal with. A giant among the founders of environmental studies, G. Evelyn Hutchinson discusses eutrophication in lakes, a natural effect that can be greatly enhanced, often disastrously, by human activities. Walter E. Westman follows with a short paper discussing the practical problems of regulating effluents and the cost involved in cleaning up the mess. But can changes in a lake or river ever be reversed? Dolan and his coauthors quote Emory C. Kolb to the effect that "no one will ever know the Colorado River as it really was. It's too late." The Grand Canyon, they argue, is being affected both by the vastly changed flow of the Colorado River and the increased presence of people. The changes are irreversible and a new state of equilibrium is being reached.

Every farmer's furrow, every house, shopping center, or post hole changes the land surface in some way. They influence how the wind blows, how plants grow, how water flows, how sediment is transported—in short, how nature shapes the surface of the land by erosion. Individual actions are minuscule, but in sum they are enormous. Sheldon Judson points out that erosion never ceases, and because our actions have increased its rate, human endeavor has the dubious honor of being a major geological factor. A case study demonstrates our actions. Lockeretz discusses the great Dust Bowl—that portion of the Great Plains ravaged by dust storms because of inadequate farming practices. Of course, the Dust Bowl years happened before air pollution was recognized as a problem. Lockeretz remarks on this fact and illustrates the way environmental concerns have grown by remarking that given our present concerns "about air pollution measured in parts per billion, it is hard to picture dust so thick that pedestrians could literally bump into each other in the middle of the day." But that's the way it was 45 years ago.

Seven papers discuss the impacts of environmental changes on plant and animal communities. We tend to think of all changes as being necessarily bad, but two of the papers present evidence of beneficial changes. Bormann and Likens look at the role of natural disturbance in the development of forest ecosystems. Nature's effects are random; those involving people, they argue, might "be thought of as an organizing force imposing synchrony on the previous asynchronous patches of presettlement steady-state ecosystems." Rhoads, McCall, and Yingst offer an aquatic example. Dredge spoils from estuaries like those around the edge of Long Island Sound can be dumped and managed in such a way that seafloor productivity is enhanced rather than diminished.

By contrast with the northern hardwood forests of North America studied by Bormann and Likens, Berwick's paper discusses the Gir Forest in India. Considering the major competing and interacting forces—people, wild and domestic animals, and plants—he suggests ways to preserve the ecological integrity of the forest. The problems of the Gir, and the solutions, are not exclusively local. Rather, they are typical of a set of land-use problems found throughout the semi-arid regions from which 19 percent of the total terrestrial primary food production is derived. Thayer, Wolfe, and Williams offer another aquatic example by focusing on the seagrasses that grow in estuarine environments, pointing out how they interact with other elements of the estuarine trophic zone and how ever-increasing human use of the coast is disrupting the system.

Does all this evidence add up to proof that we can disrupt a natural system so completely that entire faunas are sent to extinction? Two papers, one by Krantz and the other by Mosimann and Martin, argue that this is indeed the case. Nothing more complex than Paleoindians hunting with their primitive weapons, argue Mosimann and Martin, caused the extinction of the giant mammalian fauna of the New World. But hunting is not the only way animals disappear. Krantz points out that indirect means such as competition for a particular food supply or changes in ecological relationships from agricultural practices are just as effective. Will the large-mammal fauna of Africa suffer a similar fate to its now extinct relatives of Europe and North America?

Suggestions for Further Reading

Belloli, R.C., *Contemporary Physical Science: Our Impact on Our World* (New York: Macmillan, 1978).

Chanlett, E.T., *Environmental Protection* (New York: McGraw-Hill, 1973).

Colinvaux, Paul, *Why Big Fierce Animals Are Rare* (Princeton, New Jersey: Princeton University Press, 1978).

Committee on Atmospheric Sciences, N.R.C., *Weather and Climate Modification* (Washington, D.C.: National Academy of Sciences, 1973).

Committee on Geological Sciences, N.R.C., *The Earth and Human Affairs* (San Francisco: Canfield Press, 1972).

Down, C.G. and J. Stocks, *Environmental Impact of Mining* (New York: John Wiley and Sons, 1977).

Ehrlich, Paul R., Anne H. Ehrlich and John P. Holdren, *Human Ecology: Problems and Solutions* (San Francisco: W. H. Freeman and Co., 1973).

Garrels, Robert M., Fred T. Mackenzie and Cynthia C. Hunt, *Chemical Cycles and the Global Environment: Assessing Human Influences* (Los Altos, California: William Kaufmann, 1975).

Goldman, C.R., James McEvoy III and P.J. Richerson, *Environmental Quality and Water Development* (San Francisco: W. H. Freeman and Co., 1973).

Martin, P.S. and H.E. Wright Jr., *Pleistocene Extinctions: The Search for a Cause* (New Haven, Connecticut: Yale University Press, 1967).

McKenzie, G.D. and R.O. Utgard, editors, *Man and His Physical Environment. Readings on Environmental Geology* (Minneapolis: Burgess Publishing Co., 1972).

Moore, J.W. and E.A. Moore, *Environmental Chemistry* (New York: Academic Press, 1976).

Pickering, W.F., *Pollution Evaluation: The Quantitative Aspects* (New York: Marcel Dekker, 1977).

Schneider, S.H., *The Genesis Strategy: Climate and Global Survival* (New York: Dell Publishing, 1976).

Singer, S.F., editor, *Global Effects of Environmental Pollution* (Dordrecht, Holland: D. Reidel Publishing Co., 1970).

Singer, S.F., editor, *The Changing Global Environment* (Dordrecht, Holland: D. Reidel Publishing Co., 1975).

Strahler, A.N. and A.H. Strahler, *Environmental Geoscience: Interaction Between Natural Systems and Man* (Santa Barbara, California: Hamilton Publishing Co., 1973).

PART 1 *Population and Attitudes*

John P. Holdren
Paul R. Ehrlich

Human Population and the Global Environment

Population growth, rising per capita material consumption, and disruptive technologies have made civilization a global ecological force

Three dangerous misconceptions appear to be widespread among decision-makers and others with responsibilities related to population growth, environmental deterioration, and resource depletion. The first is that the absolute size and rate of growth of the human population has little or no relationship to the rapidly escalating ecological problems facing mankind. The second is that environmental deterioration consists primarily of "pollu-

Dr. Holdren is Assistant Professor in the Energy and Resources Program, University of California, Berkeley, holding the only professorial appointment on that campus not associated with a department. His training has been in engineering and plasma physics, with B.S. and M.S. degrees from M.I.T. (1965 and 1966) and the Ph.D. from Stanford (1970). His research interests include the comparative environmental impact of advanced energy technologies, and regional and global environmental problems. Dr. Ehrlich is Professor of Biological Sciences at Stanford University. He received his A.B. from the University of Pennsylvania in 1953 and his Ph.D. from the University of Kansas in 1957. His research in theoretical and experimental population biology includes studies of coevolution and the dynamics and genetics of natural populations. This paper is adapted from "Man as a Global Ecological Force," by Dr. Holdren (in Population: Perspective 1973, *H. Brown, J. Holdren, A. Sweezy, and B. West, eds., Freeman-Cooper, 1974) and "Human Population and the Global Environment," by Drs. Ehrlich and Holdren, which was presented at the U.N. Symposium on Population, Resources and Environment, Stockholm, 24 Sept.–5 Oct. 1973. Dr. Holdren's contributions to these studies were made while he was Senior Research Fellow in the Caltech Population Program and the Environmental Quality Laboratory, California Institute of Technology. Copyright © 1974 by John P. Holdren and Paul R. Ehrlich. Addresses: Dr. Holdren, Energy and Resources Program, University of California, Berkeley, CA 94720; Dr. Ehrlich, Department of Biological Sciences, Stanford University, Stanford, CA 94305.*

tion," which is perceived as a local and reversible phenomenon of concern mainly for its obvious and immediate effects on human health. The third misconception is that science and technology can make possible the long continuation of rapid growth in civilization's consumption of natural resources.

We and others have dealt at length with the third misconception elsewhere (*1*). In this paper, we argue that environmental deterioration is a much more subtle, pervasive, and dangerous phenomenon than is implied by the narrow view of "pollution" alluded to above. We show further that population size and the rate of population growth, in rich countries as well as in poor ones, have been and continue to be important contributing factors in the generation of environmental disruption.

Environmental problems can be classified according to the nature of the damage to human beings:

1. Direct assaults on human welfare, including obvious damage to health (e.g. lead poisoning or aggravation of lung disease by air pollution), damage to goods and services (e.g. the corrosive effects of air pollution on buildings and crops), social disruption (e.g. displacement of people from their living areas by mining operations and hydroelectric projects), and other direct effects on what people perceive as the "quality of life" (e.g. congestion, noise, and litter).

2. Indirect effects on human welfare through interference with services provided for society by natural biological systems (e.g. diminution of ocean productivity by filling estuaries and polluting coastal waters, crop failure caused by pests whose natural enemies have been exterminated by civilization, and acceleration of erosion by logging or overgrazing).

Most of the attention devoted to environmental matters by scientists, politicians, and the public alike has been focused on the *direct* effects and, more particularly, on their acute rather than their chronic manifestations. This is only natural. It would be wrong, however, to interpret limited legislative and technical progress toward ameliorating the acute symptoms of environmental damage as evidence that society is on its way to an orderly resolution of its environmental problems. The difficulty is not merely that the discovery, implementation, and enforcement of treatment for the obvious symptoms is likely to be expensive and difficult, but also that the long-term human consequences of chronic exposure to low concentrations of environmental contaminants may be more serious—and the causes less amenable to detection and removal—than the consequences of exposure to acute pollution as it is perceived today.

The most serious threats of all, however, may well prove to be the indirect ones generated by mankind's disruption of the functioning of the natural environment—the second category listed above, to which we will devote most of our attention here.

Natural services

The most obvious services provided for humanity by the natural environment have to do with food production. The fertility of the soil is maintained by the plants, animals, and microorganisms that participate in the great nutrient cycles—nitrogen, phosphorus, carbon, sulfur. Soil itself is produced from plant debris and weathered rock by the joint action of bacteria, fungi, worms, soil mites, and insects. The best protection against erosion of soil and flooding is natural vegetation.

At many stages of the natural processes comprising the nutrient cycles, organisms accomplish what humans have not yet learned to do —the complete conversion of wastes into resources, with solar energy captured by photosynthesis as the driving energy source. Human society depends on these natural processes to recycle many of its own wastes, from sewage to detergents to industrial effluents (reflect on the term "biodegradable"). In the course of the same cycles, the environmental concentrations of ammonia, nitrites, and hydrogen sulfide—all poisonous—are biologically controlled (2, 3).

Insects pollinate most vegetables, fruits, and berries. Most fish—the source of 10 to 15 percent of the animal protein consumed by mankind—are produced in the natural marine environment, unregulated by man. (As is well known, animal protein is the nutrient in shortest supply in a chronically malnourished world.) Most potential crop pests—one competent estimate is 99 percent—are held in check not by man but by their natural enemies and by characteristics of the physical environment such as temperature, moisture, and availability of breeding sites (3). Similarly, some agents of human disease are controlled principally not by medical technology but by environmental conditions, and some carriers of such agents are controlled by a combination of environmental conditions and natural enemies (4).

Finally, the natural environment in its diversity can be viewed as a unique library of genetic information. From this library can be drawn new food crops, new drugs and vaccines, new biological pest controls. The loss of a species, or even the loss of genetic diversity

Table 1. Productivity of various ecosystems (in kilocalories of energy per square meter per year)

Ecosystem	Net primary productivity	Net community productivity
Alfalfa field	15,200	14,400
Pine forest	5,000	2,000
Tropical rain forest	13,000	little or none
Long Island Sound	2,500	little or none

Source: Odum (5)

within a species, is the loss forever of a potential opportunity to improve human welfare.

These "public-service" functions of the global environment cannot be replaced by technology now or in the foreseeable future. This is so in some cases because the process by which the service is provided is not understood scientifically, in other cases because no technological equivalent for the natural process has yet been devised. But in the largest number of cases, the sheer size of the tasks simply dwarfs civilization's capacity to finance, produce, and deploy new technology.

The day is far away when food for billions is grown on synthetic nutrients in greenhouses free of pests and plant diseases, when the wastes of civilization are recycled entirely by technological means, and when all mankind lives in surroundings as sterile and as thoroughly managed as those of of an Apollo space capsule. Until that improbable future arrives—and it may never come—the services provided by the orderly operation of natural biological processes will continue to be irreplaceable as well as indispensable.

Some elements of ecology

How many of these natural services are actually threatened by human activities? Any of them? All of them? These questions call for a closer look at the operation of the biological systems that provide the services.

Productivity. Plant communities are at the base of all food webs and are thus the basis of all life on earth. The fundamental measure of performance of a plant community is the rate at which solar energy is captured by photosynthesis to be stored in chemical bonds. In this context, *gross primary productivity* refers to the total rate of energy capture; *net primary productivity* is the total minus the rate at which captured energy is used to sustain the life processes of the plants themselves. Thus, net primary productivity measures the rate at which energy is made available to the remainder of the food web. *Net community productivity* is what remains after the other organisms in the biological community have used part of the net primary productivity to sustain their own life processes. The net community productivity may be exported (for example, in the form of grain from a wheat field) or it may remain in the community in the form of an enlarged standing crop of plants and animals. A community in balance may have no net community productivity at all—that is, the net primary productivity may be entirely burned up by the animals and microorganisms within the community. The productivities of various kinds of ecosystems are shown in Table 1 (5).

A critical point concerning energy flow in ecosystems is that each step in a food chain results in the eventual loss (as heat) of a substantial fraction of the energy transferred. A good rule of thumb for the loss is 90 percent. This means it takes 10,000 kilocalories of corn to produce 1,000 kcal of steer and, more generally, that available energy diminishes 10-fold at each higher trophic level. Thus, the food web is often described as an energy pyramid.

Gains in production of animal protein come at high cost in primary calories, and the yield of prized food fishes such as cod and tuna is limited by their position on the fourth or fifth trophic level of the oceanic food web.

Complexity and stability in ecosystems. The intricate interlacing of most biological food webs provides a form of insurance against some kinds of disruptions. If one species of herbivore in a complex community is eradicated by disease or drought, the primary carnivores in the community may survive on other kinds of herbivores that are less susceptible to the disease. If a population of predators dwindles for one reason or another, an outbreak of the prey species is unlikely if there are other kinds of predators to fill the gap. Species diversity is one of a number of forms of biological complexity believed by many ecologists to impart stability to ecosystems.

Exactly what is meant by ecological stability? One definition is the ability of an ecosystem that has suffered an externally imposed disturbance to return to the conditions that preceded the disturbance. A more general meaning is that a stable ecosystem resists large, rapid changes in the sizes of its constituent populations. Such changes (called fluctuations or instabilities, depending on the circumstances) entail alteration of the orderly flow of energy and nutrients in the ecosystem. Usually this will mean disruption of the "public-service" functions of the ecosystem, whether or not the instability is severe enough to cause any extinctions of species.

What kinds of complexity can influence stability, and how? Species diversity, already mentioned, presumably imparts stability by providing alternative pathways for the flow of nutrients and energy through the ecosystem. Another possible advantage of a large number of species in a community is that there will then be few empty niches—and thus few opportunities for invasion by a new species from outside the community, with possible disruptive effect. Sheer number of species is not the only determining factor in this type of complexi-

ty, however: a degree of balance in population sizes among the species is also required if the capacity of the alternative pathways is to be adequate and the niches solidly occupied. Measures of complexity exist at the population level as well as at that of the community. One is genetic variability, which provides the raw material for resistance against new threats. Another is physiological variability, in the form of a mixed age distribution. (Here the advantage of complexity manifests itself when threats appear that are specific to a particular stage in the organism's life cycle—say, a disease that strikes only juveniles.) There are other forms of complexity as well, including physical complexity of habitat and variety in the geographic distribution of a given species.

The causal links between complexity and stability in ecological systems are by no means firmly established or well understood, and exceptions do exist (6). The evidence of a general correlation between these properties is growing, however, and consists of theoretical considerations of the sort summarized above, general observations of actual ecosystems of widely varying complexity (the relatively simple ecosystem of the boreal coniferous forest—the "north woods"—is observed to be less stable than the complex tropical rain forest), and a limited number of controlled laboratory and field experiments.

Time scales of ecological change. Ecological stability does not mean constancy or stagnation, and ecological change can take place over much longer time spans than the month-to-month or year-to-year time scale of fluctuations and instabilities. Ecological *succession* refers to the orderly replacement of one community in an area with other communities over periods often measured in decades. *Evolution* refers to changes in the genetic characteristics of species, brought about by natural selection over time periods ranging from a few generations to hundreds of millions of years. Note that, in terms of human beings, evolution is not the solution to pollution. When significant evolutionary change does take place on the short time scale of a few generations, it is necessarily at

the expense of the lives of a large fraction of the population.

History of human ecological disruption

Ecological disruption on a large scale by human beings is not a new phenomenon. Even before the advent of agriculture, man as a hunter is thought to have contributed to a reduction in the number of species of large mammals inhabiting the earth (7). Much more significant, however, was the era of abuse of soils and habitat that was initiated by the agricultural revolution about 10,000 years ago and has continued up to the present.

One of the best known early examples is the conversion to desert of the lush Tigris and Euphrates valleys, through erosion and salt accumulation resulting from faulty irrigation practices (8). In essence, the downfall of the great Mesopotamian civilization appears to have been the result of an "ecocatastrophe." Overgrazing and poor cultivation practices have contributed over the millennia to the expansion of the Sahara Desert, a process that continues today; and the Rajasthan desert in India is also believed to be partly a product of human carelessness and population pressure (9).

Much of Europe and Asia were deforested by preindustrial men, beginning in the Stone Age; heavy erosion, recurrent flooding, and nearly permanent loss of a valuable resource were the result. Overgrazing by the sheep of Navajo herdsmen has destroyed large tracts of once prime pastureland in the American Southwest (10). Attempts to cultivate too intensively the fragile soils of tropical rain-forest areas are suspected of being at least in part responsible for the collapse of the Mayan civilization in Central America and that of the Khmers in what today is Cambodia (11). (The famous temples of Angkor Wat were built partly of laterite, the rock-like material that results when certain tropical soils are exposed to the air through cultivation.)

The practice of agriculture—even where quality of soils, erosion, or salt accumulation do not pose problems—may encounter ecological difficulties. The most basic is that agriculture is a simplifier of ecosystems, replacing complex natural biological communities with relatively simple man-made ones based on a few strains of crops. Being less complex, agricultural communities tend to be less stable than their natural counterparts: they are vulnerable to invasions by weeds, insect pests, and plant diseases, and they are particularly sensitive to extremes of weather and variations in climate. Historically, civilization has attempted to defend its agricultural communities against the instabilities to which they are susceptible by means of vigilance and the application of "energy subsidies"— for example, hoeing weeds and, more recently, applying pesticides and fungicides. These attempts have not always been successful.

The Irish potato famine of the last century is perhaps the best-known example of the collapse of a simple agricultural ecosystem. The heavy reliance of the Irish population on a single, highly productive crop led to 1.5 million deaths when the potato monoculture fell victim to a fungus. To put it another way, the carrying capacity of Ireland was reduced, and the Irish population crashed.

Contemporary man as an ecological force

Agriculture. Advances in agricultural technology in the last hundred years have not resolved the ecological dilemma of agriculture; they have aggravated it. The dilemma can be summarized this way: civilization tries to manage ecosystems in such a way as to maximize productivity, "nature" manages ecosystems in such a way as to maximize stability, and the two goals are incompatible. Ecological succession proceeds in the direction of increasing complexity. Ecological research has shown that the most complex (and stable) natural ecosystems tend to have the smallest *net* community productivity; less complex, transitional ecosystems have higher net community productivity; and the highest net community productivities are achieved in the artificially simplified agricultural ecosystems of man (see Table 1). In short, productivity is achieved at the expense of stability.

Table 2. World land use, 1966 (in millions of km²)

	Total	Tilled	Pasture	Forest	Other*
Europe	4.9	1.5	0.9	1.4	1.1
U.S.S.R.	22.4	2.3	3.7	9.1	7.3
Asia	27.8	4.5	4.5	5.2	13.7
Africa	30.2	2.3	7.0	6.0	15.0
North America	22.4	2.6	3.7	8.2	7.9
South America	17.8	0.8	4.1	9.4	3.5
Oceania	8.5	0.4	4.6	0.8	2.7
Total†	134.2	14.3	23.6	40.2	51.2
Percentage	100%	10.6%	21.3%	29.9%	38.2%

* Deserts, wasteland, built-on land, glaciers, wetlands
† Less Antarctica

Source: Borgstrom (*12*)

Of course, mankind would have to practice agriculture to support even a fraction of the existing human population. A tendency toward instability in agricultural ecosystems must be accepted and, where possible, compensated for by technology. However, the trends in modern agriculture—associated in part with the urgent need to cope with unprecedented population growth and in part with the desire to maximize yields per acre for strictly economic reasons—are especially worrisome ecologically. There are four major liabilities.

1. As larger and larger land areas are given over to farming, the unexploited tracts available to serve as reservoirs of species diversity and to carry out the "public-service" functions of natural ecosystems become smaller and fewer (see Table 2) (*12*).

2. Pressure to expand the area under agriculture is leading to destructive attempts to cultivate land that is actually unsuitable for cultivation with the technologies at hand. For example, the expansion of agriculture to steep hillsides has led to serious erosion in Indonesia (*13*), the increasing pressure of slash-and-burn techniques is destroying tropical forests in the Philippines (*14*), and attempts to apply the techniques of temperate-zone agriculture to the tropical soils of Brazil and Southern Sudan have led to erosion, loss of nutrients, and laterization (*15*). Overlogging of tropical forests has had similar effects.

3. Even in parts of the world where land area under agriculture is constant or (for economic reasons) dwindling, attempts to maximize yields per acre have led to dramatic increases in the use of pesticides and inorganic fertilizers, which have far-reaching ecological consequences themselves (*2*).

4. The quest for high yields has led also to the replacement of a wide range of traditional crop varieties all over the world with a few, specially bred, high-yield strains. Unprecedented areas are now planted to a single variety of wheat or rice. This enormous expansion of monoculture has increased the probability and the potential magnitude of epidemic crop failure from insects or disease (*16*).

Effects of pollution on ecosystems. The expansion and intensification of agriculture has been accompanied by a continuing industrial revolution that has multiplied many times over both the magnitude and variety of the substances introduced into the biological environment by man. It is useful to classify these substances as *qualitative pollutants* (synthetic substances produced and released only by man) and *quantitative pollutants* (substances naturally present in the environment but released in significant additional amounts by man).

Well-known qualitative pollutants are the chlorinated hydrocarbon pesticides, such as DDT, the related class of industrial chemicals called PCB's (polychlorinated biphenyls), and some herbicides. These substances are biologically active in the sense of stimulating physiological changes, but since organisms have had no experience with them over evolutionary time the substances are usually not easily biodegradable. Thus, they may persist in the environment for years and even decades after being introduced and may be transported around the globe by wind and water (17). Their long-term effects will be discovered only by experience, but their potential for disruption of ecosystems is enormous.

Within the category of quantitative pollutants, there are three criteria by which a contribution made by mankind may be judged significant.

1. Man can perturb a natural cycle with a large amount of a substance ordinarily considered innocuous, in several ways: by overloading part of the cycle (as we do to the denitrifying part of the nitrogen cycle when we overfertilize, leading to the accumulation of nitrates and nitrites in ground water) (18); by destabilizing a finely tuned balance (as we may do to the global atmospheric heat engine, which governs global climate, by adding CO_2 to the atmosphere via combustion of fossil fuels); or by swamping a natural cycle completely (as could happen to the climatic balance in the very long term from man's input of waste heat).

2. An amount of material negligible compared to natural global flows of the same substance can cause great damage if released in a sensitive spot, over a small area, or suddenly (for example, the destruction of coral reefs in Hawaii by silt washed from construction sites).

3. *Any* addition of a substance that can be harmful even at its naturally occurring concentrations must be considered significant. Some radioactive substances fall in this category, as does mercury.

The most general effect of pollution of all kinds on ecosystems is the loss of structure or complexity (19). Specifically, food chains are shortened by pollution via the selective loss of the predators at the top, because predators are more sensitive to environmental stresses of all

kinds—pesticides, industrial effluents, thermal stress, oxygen deficiency—than are herbivores. This increased sensitivity results from several mechanisms: the predator populations are usually smaller than those of the prey species, so the predator populations tend to have a smaller reservoir of genetic variability and, hence, less probability of evolving a resistant strain; top predators are often exposed to higher concentrations of toxic substances than organisms at lower trophic levels, owing to the phenomenon of biological concentration of pollutants as they move up the food chain; and, finally, the direct effects of pollution on predators are compounded by the fact that pollutants may reduce the size of the prey population to the point where the predator population cannot be supported. Loss of structure may also occur at lower trophic levels when, for a variety of reasons, one species of herbivore or lower carnivore proves especially sensitive to a particular form of environmental stress. The food web does not have to be eradicated from top to bottom to show significant differential effects.

The adverse effects of loss of structure on the "public-service" functions performed by ecosystems are varied and serious. The vulnerable top predators in marine ecosystems are generally the food fishes most highly prized by man. The loss of predators on land releases checks on herbivorous pests that compete with man for his supply of staple crops. Damaging population outbreaks of these pests—the classic "instability"—are the result. (A good example of the outbreak phenomenon is the experience with pesticides and cotton pests in Peru's Canete Valley (20).) The loss of structure of ecosystems also increases the load on the aquatic food webs of decay, which are already heavily stressed by the burden of mankind's domestic and agricultural wastes. The resulting overload precipitates a vicious progression: oxygen depletion, a shift from aerobic to less efficient anaerobic bacterial metabolism, the accumulation of organic matter, and the release of methane and hydrogen sulfide gas (19).

Vulnerability of the sea. The ocean,

presently indispensable as a source of animal protein, may be the most vulnerable ecosystem of all. Its vast bulk is deceiving. The great proportion of the ocean's productivity—over 99%—takes place beneath 10% of its surface area, and half of the productivity is concentrated in coastal upwellings amounting to only 0.1% of the surface area (21). The reason is that productivity requires nutrients, which are most abundant near the bottom, and sunlight, available only near the top. Only in the coastal shelf areas and in upwellings are nutrients and sunlight both available in the same place.

The coastal regions, of course, also receive most of the impact of man's activities—oil spills, fallout from atmospheric pollutants generated on the adjacent land, and river outflow bearing pesticide and fertilizer residues, heavy metals, and industrial chemicals. Almost perversely, the most fertile and critical components in the ocean ecosystem are the estuaries into which the rivers empty; estuaries serve as residence, passage zone, or nursery for about 90% of commercially important fish (3). To compound the problem of pollution, the salt marshes that are an integral part of estuarine biological communities are being destroyed routinely by landfill operations.

Overfishing is almost certainly also taking a heavy toll in the ocean, although it is difficult to separate its effect from that of pollution and destruction of the estuarine breeding grounds and nurseries. The combined result of these factors is clear, however, even if the blame cannot be accurately apportioned. Since World War II, the catches of the East Asian sardine, the California sardine, the Northwest Pacific salmon, the Scandinavian herring, and the Barents Sea cod (among others) have entered declines from which there has been no sign of recovery (2).

The 1972 world fisheries production of somewhat over 60 million metric tons was already more than half of the 100 million that some marine biologists consider to be the maximum sustainable yield (21). But recent interruptions in the pattern of continuously increasing yields since

World War II (22), declining catches per unit effort, and increasing international friction over fishing rights make it seem unlikely that theoretical maximum yields will even be approached.

Flows of material and energy. Many people still imagine that mankind is a puny force in the global scale of things. They are persuaded, perhaps by the vast empty spaces visible from any jet airliner in many parts of the world, that talk of global ecological disruption is a preposterous exaggeration. The question of the absolute scale of man's impact, however, is amenable to quantitative investigation. Natural global flows of energy and materials can be reasonably calculated or estimated, and these provide an absolute yardstick against which to measure the impact of human activities.

The results are not reassuring. As a global geological and biological force, mankind is today becoming comparable to and even exceeding many natural processes. Oil added to the oceans in 1969 from tanker spills, offshore production, routine shipping operations, and refinery wastes exceeded the global input from natural seepage by an estimated 20-fold; the minimum estimate for 1980, assuming all foreseeable precautions, is 30 times natural seepage (23). Civilization is now contributing half as much as nature to the global atmospheric sulfur burden, and will be contributing as much as nature by the year 2000 (24). In industrial areas, civilization's input of sulfur (as sulfur dioxide) so overwhelms natural removal processes that increased atmospheric concentrations and acidic surface water are found hundreds to thousands of kilometers downwind (25). Combustion of fossil fuels has increased the global atmospheric concentration of carbon dioxide by 10% since the turn of the century (26). Civilization's contribution to the global atmospheric burden of particulate matter is uncertain: estimates range from 5 to 45% of total annual input (26). Roughly 5% of all the energy captured by photosynthesis on earth flows through the agricultural ecosystems supporting the metabolic consumption of human beings and their domestic animals—a few

Table 3. Mankind's mobilization of materials (in thousands of metric tons per year)

Element	Geological rate (river flow)	Man's rate (mining and consumption)
Iron	25,000	319,000
Nitrogen	3,500	30,000
Copper	375	4,460
Zinc	370	3,930
Nickel	300	358
Lead	180	2,330
Phosphorus	180	6,500
Mercury	3	7
Tin	1.5	166

Source: Institute of Ecology (2), SCEP (3)

out of some millions of species (27). The rates at which mankind is mobilizing critical nutrients and many metals (including the most toxic ones) considerably exceeds the basic geological mobilization rates as estimated from river flows (see Table 3) (3). Such figures as these do not prove that disaster is upon us, but, combined with the ecological perspective summarized above, they are cause for uneasiness. In terms of the scale of its disruptions, civilization is for the first time operating on a level at which global balances could hinge on its mistakes.

Some of the forms of disruption just described are, of course, amenable in principle to elimination or drastic reduction through changes in technology. Civilization's discharges of oil, sulfur dioxide, and carbon dioxide, for example, could be greatly reduced by switching to energy sources other than fossil fuels. In the case of these pollutants, then, the questions involve not whether the disruptions *can* be managed but whether they *will* be, whether the measures will come in time, and what social, economic, and new environmental penalties will accompany those measures. At least one environmental problem is intractable in a more absolute sense, however, and this is the discharge of waste heat accompanying all of civilization's use of energy. We refer here not simply to the well-publicized thermal pollution at the sites of electric generating plants, but to the fact that all the

energy we *use*—as well as what we waste in generating electricity—ultimately arrives in the environment as waste heat. This phenomenon may be understood qualitatively by considering the heat from a light bulb, the heat from a running automobile engine and the heat in the exhaust, the heat from friction of tires against pavement and metal against air, or the heat from the oxidation of iron to rust—to name a few examples. Quantitatively, the ultimate conversion to heat of all the energy we use (most of which occurs near the point of use and almost immediately) is required by the laws of thermodynamics; the phenomenon cannot be averted by technological tricks.

The usual concern with local thermal pollution at power plants is that the waste heat, which is usually discharged into water, will adversely affect aquatic life. Most of the waste heat from civilization's energy use as a whole, by contrast, is discharged directly into the atmosphere, and the concern is disruption of climate. Again, it is instructive to compare the scale of human activities with that of the corresponding natural processes, in this case the natural energy flows that govern climate. One finds that the heat production resulting from (and numerically equal to) civilization's use of energy is not yet a significant fraction of the solar energy incident at the earth's surface on a global average basis (see Table 4); even if the present 5% per annum rate of increase of global energy use

Table 4. Energy flows (in billion thermal kilowatts)

Civilization's 1970 rate of energy use	7
Global photosynthesis	80
15 billion people at 10 thermal kilowatts/person	150
Winds and ocean currents	370
Poleward heat flux at 40° north latitude	5,300
Solar energy incident at earth's surface	116,000

Sources: Woodwell (27), Sellers (29), Hubbert (29)

persists, it will take another century before civilization is discharging heat equivalent to 1% of incident solar energy at the surface worldwide (28).

Considerably sooner, however, as indicated in Table 4, mankind's heat production could become a significant fraction of smaller natural energy transfers that play a major role in the determination of regional and continental climate (e.g. the kinetic energy of winds and ocean currents and the poleward heat fluxes) (29). It is especially important in this connection that civilization's heat production is and will continue to be very unevenly distributed geographically. Human heat production already exceeds 5% of incident solar radiation at the surface over local areas of tens of thousands of square kilometers, and will exceed this level over areas of millions of square kilometers by the year 2000 if present trends persist (26). Such figures could imply substantial climatic disruptions. In addition to the effects of its discharge of heat, civilization has the potential to disrupt climate through its additions of carbon dioxide and particulate matter to the atmosphere, through large-scale alteration of the heat-transfer and moisture-transfer properties of the surface (e.g. agriculture, oil films on the ocean, urbanization), through cloud formation arising from aircraft contrails, and, of course, through the combined action of several or all of these disruptions.

Much uncertainty exists concerning the character and imminence of inadvertent climate modification through these various possibilities. It is known that a global warming of a few degrees centigrade would melt the icecaps and raise sea level by 80 meters, submerging coastal plains and cities. A few degrees in the opposite direction would initiate a new ice age. Although such global warming or cooling is certainly possible in principle, a more complicated alteration of climatic *patterns* seems a more probable and perhaps more imminent consequence of the very unevenly distributed impacts of civilization's use of energy. It is particularly important to note that the consequences of climatic alteration reside not in any direct sensitivity of humans to moderate changes in temperature or moisture, but rather in the great sensitivity of food production to such changes (30) and, perhaps, in the possible climate-related spread of diseases into populations with no resistance against them (4).

The effect of climate on agriculture was once again dramatically demonstrated in early 1973. Because of "bad weather," famine was widespread in sub-Saharan Africa and was starting in India. Southeast Asia had small rice harvests, parts of Latin American were short of food, and crops were threatened in the United States and the Soviet Union. If there is another year of monsoon failure in the tropics and inclement weather in the temperate zones, the human death rate will climb precipitously. A telling symptom of overpopulation is mankind's inability to store sufficient carry-over food supplies in anticipation of the climatic variations that are a regular feature of the planet Earth.

Role of population

It is beyond dispute that a population too large to be fed adequately in the prevailing technological and organizational framework, as is the case for the globe today, is particularly vulnerable to environmental disruptions that may reduce production even below normal levels. More controversial, however, are the roles of the size, growth rate, and geographic distribution of the human population in *causing* such environmental disruptions, and it is to this issue that we now turn.

Multiplicative effect. The most elementary relation between population and environmental deterioration is that population size acts as a multiplier of the activities, consumption, and attendant environmental damages associated with each individual in the population. The contributing factors in at least some kinds of environmental problems can be usefully studied by expressing the population/environment relation as an equation:

environmental disruption = population × consumption per person × damage per unit of consumption

Needless to say, the numerical quantities that appear in such an equation will vary greatly depending on the problem under scrutiny. Different forms of consumption and technology are relevant to each of the many forms of environmental disruption. The population factor may refer to the population of a city, a region, a country, or the world, depending on the problem being considered. (This point, of course, raises the issue of population *distribution*.) The equation, therefore, represents not one calculation but many.

For problems described by multiplicative relations like the one just given, no factor can be considered unimportant. The consequences of the growth of each factor are amplified in proportion to the size and the rate of growth of each of the others. Rising consumption per person has greater impact in a large population than in a small one—and greater impact in a growing population than in a stationary one. A given environmentally disruptive technology, such as the gasoline-powered automobile, is more damaging in a large, rich population (many people own cars and drive them often) than in a small, poor one (few people own cars, and those who do drive them less). A given level of total consumption (population times consumption per person) is more damaging if it is provided by means of a disruptive technology, such as persistent pesticides, than if provided by means of a relatively nondisruptive one, such as integrated pest control.

The quantitative use of the population/environment equation is best illustrated by example. Suppose we take as an index of environmental impact the automotive emissions of lead in the United States since World War II. The appropriate measure of "consumption" is vehicle-miles per person, which increased twofold between 1946 and 1967. The impact per unit of consumption in this case is emissions of lead per vehicle-mile, which increased 83%, or 1.83-fold, in this period (31). Since the U.S. population increased 41%, or 1.41-fold, between 1946 and 1967, we have,

relative increase in
emissions =
$1.41 \times 2.0 \times 1.83 = 5.16$ or 416%

Note that the dramatic increase in the total impact arose from rather moderate but simultaneous increases in the multiplicative contributing factors. None of the factors was unimportant—if population had *not* grown in this period, the total increase would have been 3.66-fold rather than 5.16-fold. (Contrast this result with the erroneous conclusion, arising from the assumption that the contributing factors are additive rather than multiplicative, that a 41% increase in population "explains" only one-tenth of 416% increase in emissions.)

Calculations such as the foregoing can be made for a wide variety of pollutants, although with frequent difficulty in uncovering the requisite data. Where data are available, the results show that the historical importance of population growth as a multiplicative contributor to widely recognized environmental problems has been substantial (32).

Between 1950 and 1970, for example, the world population increased by 46%. By regions, the figures were: Africa, 59%; North America, 38%; Latin America, 75%; Asia, 52%; Europe, 18%; Oceania, 54%; Soviet Union, 35% (33). On the as-

Table 5. Percentage increases in population and energy consumption per capita between 1950 and 1970

	Population (%)	Energy/person (%)
World	46	57
Africa	59	73
North America	38	43
Latin America	75	122
Asia	52	197
Europe	18	96
Oceania	54	54

Source: United Nations (33, 34)

sumption (which will be shown below to be too simplistic) that the patterns of technological change and rising consumption per capita that were experienced in this period would have been the same in the absence of population growth, one can conclude that the absolute magnitudes of damaging inputs to the environment in 1970 were greater *by these same percentages* than they would have been if population had remained at its 1950 value. Another way of saying this is that, under our simplistic assumption, the magnitude of damaging inputs to the global environment in 1970—a very large figure—would have been only 68% as large if population had not grown between 1950 and 1970. (This follows from the relation: 1970 inputs in absence of population growth equal actual 1970 inputs times 1950 population divided by 1970 population.)

Not only has population growth been important in *absolute* terms as a contributor of environmental damage, but it has been important *relative* to other sources of such damage. Perhaps the best way to illustrate this fact is with statistics for energy consumption per person, probably the best aggregate measure of both affluence and technological impact on the environment. One finds that energy consumption per person worldwide increased 57% between 1950 and 1970 (33, 34). By this measure then, and under our simple assumption that population growth and trends in af-

fluence and technology were independent, one finds that population growth in the period 1950–1970 was almost equal to the *combined* effect of rising affluence and technological change as a contributor of damaging inputs to the environment. (The comparison of population growth and energy consumption broken down by major geographical regions is given in Table 5.) We shall argue, moreover, that the effect of the simplistic assumption of independence of population and other factors is more probably to *underestimate* the role of population than to overestimate it.

Nonlinear effects. While it is useful to understand what proportion of the historical increase in specific environmental problems has been directly attributable to the multiplier effect of population growth, there is a more difficult and perhaps more important question than this historical/arithmetical one. Specifically, under what circumstances may nonlinear effects cause a small increase in population to generate a disproportionately large increase in environmental disruption? These effects fall into two classes. First, population change may *cause* changes in consumption per person or in impact upon the environment per unit of consumption. Second, a small increase in impact upon the environment—generated in part by population change and in part by unrelated changes in the other multiplicative factors—may stimulate a disproportionately large environmental change.

An obvious example in the first category is the growth of suburbs in the United States at the expense of central cities, which has had the effect of increasing the use of the automobile. Another is the heavy environmental costs incurred in the form of large water projects when demand (population times demand per person) exceeds easily exploited local supplies. Still another example is that of diminishing-returns phenomena in agriculture, in which increases in yield needed to feed new mouths can be achieved only by disproportionate increases in inputs such as fertilizer and pesticides.

Many phenomena that have the effect of generating disproportionate consequences from a given change in demographic variables cannot easily be expressed in the framework of a single equation. One such class of problems involves technological change—the substitution of new materials or processes for old ones that provided the same types of material consumption. Obvious examples are the substitution of nylon and rayon for cotton and wool, of plastics for glass and wood and metals, of aluminum for steel and copper. Such substitutions may be necessitated by increasing total demand, or they may be motivated by other factors such as durability and convenience. Substitutions or other technological changes that are motivated by the pressure of increased total demand, and that lead to increases in environmental impact per unit of consumption, should be considered as part of the environmental impact of population growth.

Environmental disruption is not, however, measured strictly by man's inputs *to* the environment— what *we* do to *it*. Equally important is how the environment responds to what we do to it. This response itself is often nonlinear: a small change in inputs may precipitate a dramatic response. One example is the existence of thresholds in the response of individual organisms to poisons and other forms of "stress." Fish may be able to tolerate a 10° rise in water temperature without ill effect, whereas a 12° rise would be fatal. Carbon monoxide is fatal to human beings at high concentrations but, as far as we know, causes only reversible effects at low concentrations. Algal blooms in overfertilized lakes and streams are examples of exceeding a threshold for the orderly cycling of nutrients in these biological systems.

Another nonlinear phenomenon on the response side of environmental problems involves the simultaneous action of two or more inputs. A disturbing example is the combined effect of DDT and oil spills in coastal waters. DDT is not very soluble in sea water, so the concentrations to which marine organisms are ordinarily exposed are small. However, DDT is very soluble in oil. Oil spills therefore have the ef-

surface layer of the ocean, where much of the oil remains and where many marine organisms spend part of their time (23). These organisms are thus exposed to far higher concentrations of DDT than would otherwise be possible, and as a result, the combined effect of oil and DDT probably far exceeds their individual effects. Many other synergisms in environmental systems are known or suspected: the interaction of sulfur dioxide and particulate matter in causing or aggravating lung disease; the interaction of radiation exposure and smoking in causing lung cancer; the enhanced toxicity of chlorinated hydrocarbon pesticides when plasticizers are present (35).

The exact role of population change varies considerably among the various forms of nonlinear behavior just described. A nonlinearity in the environment's response to growing total input—such as a threshold effect—increases the importance of all the multiplicative contributors to the input equally, whether or not population and the other contributors are causally related. Some other forms of nonlinearity, such as diminishing returns and certain substitutions, would occur eventually whether population or consumption per capita grew or not. For example, even a constant demand for copper that persisted for a long time would lead eventually to increasing expenditures of energy per pound of metal and to substitution of aluminum for copper in some applications. In such instances, the role of population growth—and that of rising consumption per capita—is simply to accelerate the onset of diminishing returns and the need for technological change, leaving less time to deal with the problems created and increasing the chances of mistakes. With respect to other phenomena, such as the effects of population concentration on certain forms of consumption and environmental impact, population change is clearly the sole and direct cause of the nonlinearity (e.g. additional transportation costs associated with suburbanization).

Time factors

The pattern of growth. All rational observers agree that no physical

quantity can grow exponentially forever. This is true, for example, of population, the production of energy and other raw materials, and the generation of wastes. But is there anything about the 1970s—as opposed, say, to the 1920s or 1870s— that should make this the decade in which limits to growth become apparent? It should not be surprising that, when limits do appear, they will appear suddenly. Such behavior is typical of exponential growth. If twenty doublings are possible before a limit is reached in an exponentially growing process (characterized by a fixed doubling time if the growth rate is constant), then the system will be less than half "loaded" for the first nineteen doublings—or for 95% of the elapsed time between initiation of growth and exceeding the limit. Clearly, a long history of exponential growth does not imply a long future.

But where does mankind stand in its allotment of doublings? Are we notably closer to a limit now than we were 50 years ago? We are certainly moving faster. The number of people added to the world population each year in the 1970s has been about twice what it was in the 1920s. And according to one of the better indices of aggregate environmental disruption, total energy consumption, the annual increase in man's impact on the environment (in absolute magnitude, not percentage) is ten times larger now than then (33, 36). We have seen, moreover, that man is already a global ecological force, as measured against the yardstick of natural processes. While the human population grows at a rate that would double our numbers in 35 years, ecological impact is growing much faster. The 1970 M.I.T.-sponsored Study of Critical Environmental Problems estimated that civilization's demands upon the biological environment are increasing at about 5% per year, corresponding to a doubling time of 14 years (3). Continuation of this rate would imply a fourfold increase in demands on the environment between 1972 and the year 2000. It is difficult to view such a prospect with complacency.

Momentum, time lags, and irreversibility. The nature of exponential growth is such that limits can be approached with surprising suddenness. The likelihood of overshooting a limit is made even larger by the momentum of human population growth, by the time delays between cause and effect in many environmental systems, and by the fact that some kinds of damage are irreversible by the time they are visible.

The great momentum of human population growth has its origins in deep-seated attitudes toward reproduction and in the age composition of the world's population—37% is under 15 years of age. This means there are far more young people who will soon be reproducing—adding to the population—than there are old people who will soon be dying—subtracting from it. Thus, even if the momentum in attitudes could miraculously be overcome overnight, so that every pair of parents in the world henceforth had only the number of children needed to replace themselves, the imbalance between young and old would cause population to grow for 50 to 70 years more before leveling off. The growth *rate* would be falling during this period, but population would still climb 30% or more during the transition to stability. Under extraordinarily optimistic assumptions about when replacement fertility might *really* become the worldwide norm, one concludes that world population will not stabilize below 8 billion people (*37*).

The momentum of population growth manifests itself as a delay between the time when the need to stabilize population is perceived and the time when stabilization is actually accomplished. Forces that are perhaps even more firmly entrenched than those affecting population lend momentum to growth in per capita consumption of materials. These forces create time lags similar to that of population growth in the inevitable transition to stabilized levels of consumption and technological reform. Time delays between the initiation of environmental insults and the appearance of the symptoms compound the predicament because they postpone recognition of the need for any corrective action at all.

Such environmental time delays come about in a variety of ways.

Some substances persist in dangerous form long after they have been introduced into the environment (mercury, lead, DDT and its relatives, and certain radioactive materials are obvious examples). They may be entering food webs from soil, water, and marine sediments for years after being deposited there. The process of concentration from level to level in the food web takes more time. Increases in exposure to radiation may lead to increases in certain kinds of cancer only after decades and to genetic defects that first appear in later generations. The consequences of having simplified an environmental system by inadvertently wiping out predators or by planting large areas to a single high-yield grain may not show up until just the right pest or plant disease comes along a few years later.

Unfortunately, time lags of these sorts usually mean that, when the symptoms finally appear, corrective action is ineffective or impossible. Species that have been eradicated cannot be restored. The radioactive debris of atmospheric bomb tests cannot be reconcentrated and isolated from the environment, nor can radiation exposure be undone. Soil that has been washed or blown away can be replaced by natural processes only on a time scale of centuries. If all use of persistent pesticides were stopped tomorrow, the concentrations of these substances in fish and fish-eating birds might continue to increase for some years to come.

Vigorous action needed

The momentum of growth, the time delays between causes and effects, and the irreversibility of many kinds of damage all increase the chances that mankind may temporarily exceed the carrying capacity of the biological environment. Scientific knowledge is not yet adequate to the task of defining that carrying capacity unambiguously, nor can anyone say with assurance how the consequences of overshooting the carrying capacity will manifest themselves. Agricultural failures on a large scale, dramatic loss of fisheries productivity, and epidemic disease initiated by altered environmental conditions are among the possibilities. The evi-

dence presented here concerning the present scale of man's ecological disruption and its rate of increase suggests that such possibilities exist within a time frame measured in decades, rather than centuries.

All of this is not to suggest that the situation is hopeless. The point is rather that the potential for grave damage is real and that prompt and vigorous action to avert or minimize the damage is necessary. Such action should include measures to slow the growth of the global population to zero as rapidly as possible. Success in this endeavor is a necessary but not a sufficient condition for achieving a prosperous yet environmentally sustainable civilization. It will also be necessary to develop and implement programs to alleviate political tensions, render nuclear war impossible, divert flows of resources and energy from wasteful uses in rich countries to necessity-oriented uses in poor ones, reduce the environmental impact and increase the human benefits resulting from each pound of material and gallon of fuel, devise new energy sources, and, ultimately, stabilize civilization's annual throughput of materials and energy.

There are, in short, no easy single-faceted solutions, and no component of the problem can be safely ignored. There is a temptation to "go slow" on population limitation because this component is politically sensitive and operationally difficult, but the temptation must be resisted. The other approaches pose problems too, and the accomplishments of these approaches will be gradual at best. Ecological disaster will be difficult enough to avoid even if population limitation succeeds; if population growth proceeds unabated, the gains of improved technology and stabilized per capita consumption will be erased, and averting disaster will be impossible.

References

1. See, e.g., National Research Council/ National Academy of Sciences. 1969. *Resources and Man.* San Francisco: W. H. Freeman and Co. Paul R. Ehrlich and John P. Holdren. 1969. Population and panaceas—a technological perspective. *BioScience* 12:1065–71.

2. Institute of Ecology. 1972. *Man in the Living Environment.* Madison: University of Wisconsin Press.

3. Report of the Study of Critical Environmental Problems (SCEP). 1970. *Man's Impact on the Global Environment: Assessment and Recommendations for Action.* Cambridge: M.I.T. Press.

4. Jacques M. May. 1972. Influence of environmental transformation in changing the map of disease. In *The Careless Technology: Ecology and International Development,* M. Taghi Farvar and John P. Milton, eds. Garden City, N.Y.: The Natural History Press.

5. Eugene P. Odum. 1971. *Fundamentals of Ecology.* 3rd ed. Philadelphia: Saunders, p. 46.

6. E. O. Wilson and W. A. Bossert. 1971. *A Primer of Population Biology.* Stamford, Conn: Sinauer Associates; and Brookhaven National Laboratory. 1969. Diversity and stability in ecological systems. *Brookhaven Symposia in Biology,* N. 22, BNL 50175 C–56. Upton, N.Y.: Brookhaven National Laboratory.

7. P. S. Martin and T. E. Wright, Jr., eds. 1957. *Pleistocene Extinctions: The Search for a Cause.* New Haven: Yale University Press.

8. Thorkild Jacobsen and Robert M. Adams. 1958. Salt and silt in ancient Mesopotamian agriculture. *Science* 128:1251–58.

9. M. Kassas. 1970. Desertification versus potential for recovery in circum-Saharan territories. In *Arid Lands in Transition.* Washington, D.C.: American Association for Advancement of Science. B. R. Seshachar. 1971. Problems of environment in India. In *International Environmental Science.* Proceedings of a joint colloquium before the Committee on Commerce, U.S. Senate, and the Committee on Science and Astronautics, House of Representatives, 92nd Congress. Washington, D.C.: U.S. Government Printing Office.

10. Carl O. Sauer. 1956. The agency of man on earth. In *Man's Role in Changing the Face of the Earth,* William L. Thomas, Jr., ed. Chicago: University of Chicago Press, p. 60.

11. Jeremy A. Sabloff. 1971. The collapse of classic Maya civilization. In *Patient Earth,* John Harte and Robert Socolow, eds. New York: Holt, Rinehart and Winston, p. 16.

12. Georg Borgstrom. 1969. *Too Many.* N.Y.: Macmillan.

13. Albert Ravenholt. 1974. Man-land-productivity microdynamics in rural Bali. In *Population: Perspective, 1973,* Harrison Brown, John Holdren, Alan Sweezy, and Barbara West, eds. San Francisco: Freeman-Cooper.

14. Albert Ravenholt. 1971. The Philippines. In *Population: Perspective, 1971,* Harrison Brown and Alan Sweezy, eds. San Francisco: Freeman-Cooper, pp. 247–66.

15. Mary McNeil. 1972. Lateritic soils in distinct tropical environments: Southern Sudan and Brazil. In *The Careless Technology,* op cit., pp. 591–608.

16. O. H. Frankel et al. 1969. Genetic dangers in the Green Revolution. *Ceres* 2(5): 35–37 (Sept.-Oct.); and O. H. Frankel and E. Bennett, eds. 1970. *Genetic Resources in Plants—Their Exploration and Conservation.* Philadelphia: F. A. Davis Co.

17. See, e.g., R. W. Risebrough, R. J. Huggott, J. J. Griffin, and E. D. Goldberg. 1968. Pesticides: Transatlantic movements in the northeast trades. *Science* 159:1233–36. G. M. Woodwell, P. P. Craig, and H. A. Johnson. 1971. DDT in the biosphere: Where does it go? *Science* 174:1101–07.

18. D. R. Keeney and W. R. Gardner. 1970. The dynamics of nitrogen transformations in the soil. In *Global Effects of Environmental Pollution,* S. F. Singer, ed. New York: Springer Verlag, pp. 96–103.

19. G. M. Woodwell. 1970. Effects of pollution on the structure and physiology of ecosystems. *Science* 168:429–33.

20. Teodoro Boza Barducci. 1972. Ecological consequences of pesticides used for the control of cotton insects in Canete Valley, Peru. In *The Careless Technology,* op. cit., pp. 423–38.

21. John H. Ryther. 1969. Photosynthesis and fish production in the sea. *Science* 166:72–76.

22. FAO. 1972. *State of Food and Agriculture 1972.* Rome: Food and Agriculture Organization.

23. Roger Revelle, Edward Wenk, Bostwick Ketchum, and Edward R. Corino. 1971. Ocean pollution by petroleum hydrocarbons. In *Man's Impact on Terrestrial and Oceanic Ecosystems,* William H. Matthews, Frederick E. Smith, and Edward D. Goldberg, eds. Cambridge: M.I.T. Press, p. 297.

24. W. W. Kellogg, R. D. Cadle, E. R. Allen, A. L. Lazrus, and E. A. Martell. 1972. The sulfur cycle. *Science* 175:587.

25. Gene E. Likens, F. Herbert Bormann, and Noye M. Johnson. 1972. Acid rain. *Environment* 14(2):33.

26. Report of the Study of Man's Impact on Climate. 1971. *Inadvertent Climate Modification.* Cambridge: M.I.T. Press, pp. 188–92.

27. George M. Woodwell. 1970. The energy cycle of the biosphere. *Scientific American* 223(3):64–74.

28. John P. Holdren. 1971. Global thermal pollution. In *Global Ecology,* J. P. Holdren and P. R. Ehrlich, eds. New York: Harcourt Brace Jovanovich.

29. William D. Sellers. 1965. *Physical Climatology.* Chicago: University of Chicago Press. M. King Hubbert. 1971. Energy resources. In *Environment,* William Murdoch, ed. Stamford, Conn.: Sinauer Associates.

30. Sherwood B. Idso. 1971. Potential effects of global temperature change on agriculture. In *Man's Impact on Terrestrial and Oceanic Ecosystems,* op. cit., p. 184.

31. Barry Commoner. 1972. The environmental cost of economic growth. In *Population Resources and the Environment,* Vol. 3 of the Research Reports of the Commission on Population Growth and the American Future. Washington, D.C.: U.S. Government Printing Office, p. 339.

32. Paul R. Ehrlich and John P. Holdren. 1972. One-dimensional ecology. *Science and Public Affairs: Bull. Atomic Sci.* 28(5):16–27.

33. United Nations Statistical Office. 1972. *Statistical Yearbook, 1971.* N.Y.: United Nations Publishing Service.

34. United Nations Statistical Office. 1954. *Statistical Yearbook, 1953.* N.Y.: United Nations Publishing Service.

35. American Chemical Society. 1969. *Cleaning Our Environment: The Chemical Basis for Action.* Washington, D.C.: American Chemical Society. U.S. Congress, Joint Committee on Atomic Energy. 1967. *Hearings on Radiation Exposure of Uranium Miners,* Parts 1 and 2. Washington, D.C.: U.S. Government Printing Office. E. P. Lichtenstein, K. R. Schulz, T. W. Fuhremann, and T. T. Liang. 1969. Biological interaction between plasticizers and insecticides. *J. Econ. Entom.* 62(4):761–65.

36. Joel Darmstadter et al. 1971. *Energy in the World Economy.* Baltimore: Johns Hopkins Press.

37. Nathan Keyfitz. 1971. On the momentum of population growth. *Demography* 8(1):71–80.

James R. Echols

Population vs. the Environment: A Crisis of Too Many People

Views

Without drastic population control measures, high fertility in the less developed countries will overtake food production by the twenty-first century

The rationale for a solution to the population explosion now taking place in the less developed countries (LDCs) of the world has been based on the hope that the theory of demographic transition would be as applicable to these countries as it was to the countries of Western Europe and North America in the nineteenth century. The historical process of demographic transition starts with high birth and high death rates; the death rate declines first, followed by a decrease in the birth rate, leaving both a low birth rate and a low death rate and thus a relatively stable population. By the end of the first quarter of the twentieth century, the transition from high birth and death rates was virtually complete in the now-developed countries, and these nations currently have relatively balanced populations with low birth and death rates.

James R. Echols has until recently served as President of the Population Reference Bureau and is now a member of its Board of Trustees. Previously he was Population Communication Advisor in the Office of Population of the Agency for International Development and the Office of International Health of the Department of Health, Education and Welfare. A retired foreign service officer, Dr. Echols worked in Latin America, Asia, and other parts of the world in the cultural and informational fields. His most recent publications include People and Population *(East-West Center), a basic textbook on demography and resources, and* Fertility and Ideal Family Size *(Airlie Foundation).*
Dr. Echols is a Consultant to the East-West Communication Institute in Honolulu. He recently returned from Dacca where he directed a World Bank/East-West Center training program in population communication for Government Population Planning Officers in Bangladesh. Address: 3114 Wisconsin Ave. NW, Washington, DC 20016.

Demographers had hoped that by the mid-twentieth century a comparable process would be discernible in the LDCs. Yet, although death rates tumbled following World War II, birth rates remained high, and as of 1976, except for a very few developing countries, there is little indication that the transition is taking place. Some optimistic demographers and family planners maintain that it is too early for the fertility-reduction stage of the transition and that it will come with time. I do not share this optimism. The momentum of population growth in most of these countries is too strong to stop; thus, instead of completing the transition—through which the high birth rates will decrease to near the level of already low death rates—it is my opinion that the LDCs will have a "recession" to higher death rates. These death rates will balance high (though decreasing) birth rates at some middle point short of the moderate population stability of low birth and death rates that the developed countries have achieved.

This is a tragic conclusion, for it means that we will not solve the population problem by a rational, humane limitation of births but through an irrational "natural selection" during which millions of people in the LDCs will die. In this article I attempt to trace back to the roots of this problem, examine the situation in the "explosion" countries as it stands today, and review some of the analyses and possible alternatives put forward by food, family planning, and demographic experts. With these facts before us, we can make some conjectures regarding the future of this small planet, on which, as of 1976,

the population is projected to double every 36 years.

Population growth

Natural disasters such as earthquake, fire and flood, hunger and malnutrition, lack of water and other natural resources have dogged humanity throughout its history. Man-made disasters such as war, political and economic depression, unemployment and underemployment, and destruction of the environment have also hindered man's struggle toward the goal of a better life. But for many people on earth, there now *is* a better and longer life. The terrible scourges of plague, smallpox, and cholera are for the most part over. The death rate, which through all of known history had been over 45 deaths per year per 1,000 people in the population, is now below 15, and of the more than 30 people who now live instead of die, many live more comfortable lives and have at least some of the advantages that the industrial, medical, sanitation, and agricultural revolutions of the past 200 years have brought about.

It is difficult to realize, therefore, that out of these positive developments has emerged one of man's grimmest dilemmas, for at a growth rate of 20 people per 1,000 per year, 80 million people are added to the world's population each year. The populations of Europe and North America increased at almost this rate during the eighteenth and nineteenth centuries, and in many developing countries today the natural increase continues at these or even higher rates. In Europe and North America, however, after the population increase had continued

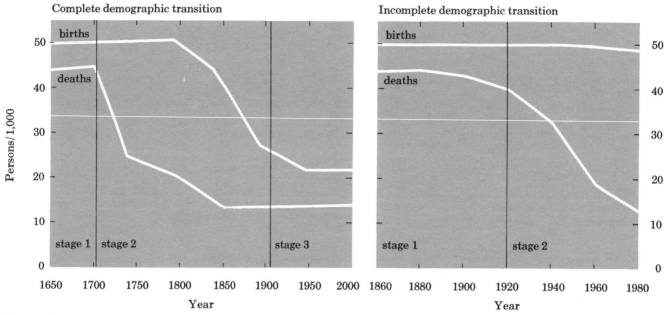

Figure 1. The complete demographic transition, *on the left,* shows birth and death rates for a typical developed country from 1650 to 2000 (after Echols 1974, p. 106). *On the right,* rates for a typical developing country are plotted for 1860 to 1980.

for a century or so as a result of the lowered death rate, the birth rate, too, began to fall, and by the twentieth century was down to about 20 per 1,000. With the death rate by this time reduced to about 10 per 1,000, the rate of natural increase was about 1 percent per year (see Fig. 1).

While the demographic transition was going on in Europe, high mortality continued unabated in most of the rest of the world until well into the twentieth century, when modern advances began to reach Asia, the Middle East, Latin America, and parts of Africa. Thus, as the transition was being completed in Europe and North America, it appeared to begin in other areas of the world: the death rate began to fall and, in a fraction of the time it took to reach this point in Europe and North America, was well below 20 per 1,000 per year in most of Asia and Latin America and below 25 in most of Africa by the 1950s (Fig. 1).

As of 1976, however, there is little sign of lower birth rates in most LDCs. A few countries—among them Taiwan, Korea, and Sri Lanka, in Asia, and Argentina, Chile, Uruguay, and some of the Caribbean Islands, in Latin America—have brought their birth rates down to 30 or below. The People's Republic of China, with one of the world's largest populations (over

800,000,000), claims to have a birth rate of 27 per 1,000 per year. India, with over 600,000,000 people, has a birth rate of 40 per 1,000 per year, Indonesia, 43. Most of the other LDCs are in the upper 30s and 40s, while some African nations such as Tanzania, Mali, Togo, Rwanda, Zambia, and Niger are in excess of 50 per 1,000 per year. Thus, the annual growth rate for South Asia and Africa is about 2.6% per year and for most of Latin America, almost 3% per year (Population Reference Bureau 1975a).

The 1976 total world population is over 4 billion. The annual rate of population growth is about 19.7 per 1,000 per year; the birth rate is 31.5 per 1,000 per year and the death rate is 12.8. These world averages are made up of widely varying rates, with the low rates of the countries that have already passed through the demographic transition partially offsetting the high rates of the LDCs. North America, with a birth rate of about 17 and a death rate of about 10, has an annual growth rate of less than 1% per year. The same is true of most of Europe. In fact, in the last few years, owing primarily to the easy availability of birth control measures, including abortion, a number of countries in Eastern Europe have reached replacement (approximately two children per family), and some are near zero population growth (ZPG).

Once replacement is achieved, maintaining a stable population should become a relatively easy matter. Although there is little experience in this area, such things as adjustments in the availability of family planning advice and contraceptive materials, restriction or relaxation of regulations concerning abortion, easing or tightening tax exemptions based on the number of children, and other social and economic regulators could be used to maintain a population at a size that its citizens desire in order to maintain the quality of life to which they aspire. It appears increasingly doubtful, however, that the developing nations, whose populations are now expanding at more than 3% per year, can pass through the demographic transition to achieve replacement, much less ZPG. If they cannot control fertility and thus pass through the transition, then there is only one way to stop rapid population growth: increased mortality. These nations would find themselves once again with high mortality and high fertility until a new balance was achieved.

It is difficult, however, to envision a world in which the developed nations with stable populations and high standards of living can peacefully exist side-by-side with the underdeveloped nations suffering under high death rates and low standards of living. The rising dissatisfaction of the semideveloped nations is already evident in the United Nations, in the nationalization of foreign companies, and in terrorist activities around the world. With growing population pressures in LDCs it would be foolish to assume that developed nations could be immune from the resultant problems. There is no doubt that some balance will be achieved. The question is whether it can come from a reduction in fertility or whether it must come about through the agonizing process of increased mortality.

Population vs. resources

The basic problem of the developing world for the future will be how to produce enough food for a large and rapidly growing population; the problem of the developed world will be how to control its use of the world's limited natural resources. Both problems relate to the struggle of the LDCs to raise their standard of living, particularly in view of the fact that lower fertility has traditionally accompanied development. These problems also relate to the increasing competition for resources at a time when populations in the LDCs are growing at a rate that makes it difficult even to maintain their present per capita share of resources, much less to improve the lot of their citizens.

Gross National Product (GNP) has frequently been used to compare the relative economic strength of countries even though exchange rates, currencies, and economic conditions vary greatly and many people, particularly in developing countries, live outside the money economy. Per capita GNP is also a useful national indicator, although it tells nothing about how national income is distributed among the people of a country.

Table 1 presents the per capita GNP for each geographic area of the world. Between 1960 and 1972 the annual worldwide growth rate of per capita GNP was 2.7%. For developed countries (29 countries of North America and Europe, Oceania, Israel, and Japan), the annual per capita growth rate was 3.9%. For developing nations the annual per capita growth rate was 1.1%. Recent exceptions to this, of course,

Table 1. Per capita Gross National Product (GNP) for major areas of the world

Area	Per capita GNP (U.S. $)
Africa	240
Asia	270
Latin America	650
USSR	1,400
Europe	2,380
Oceania	2,480
North America (Canada and U.S.)	5,480
World average	940

SOURCE: Population Reference Bureau 1975a

are the oil-producing nations, where per capita GNP has shot up over $10,000. For the rest of Asia, however, the per capita GNP remains at a precarious level. Latin America is somewhat better off; Africa, the poorest geographic area, is afflicted with the highest fertility and mortality.

Food is of course the most vital issue in the struggle between population and resources, and during the past 30 years world food production has more or less kept pace with population growth. By the mid-1960s, however, there was increasing food scarcity, and in 1967 a World Food Panel estimated that the increase in food production in developing countries was only half the rate of population increase. At about that time wheat-breeding studies in Mexico and rice production experiments in the Philippines created new varieties that tripled production, and the Green Revolution began. By 1973, however, population growth once again began to overtake food production: bad weather resulted in poor crops in Asia, Africa, and the Soviet Union; and another food crisis was in the offing.

Although the decline in total world cereal production was only about 3% during the 1972–73 crop year, population in the LDCs grew more than 3%. In addition, there was increasing reliance on grains for cattle feed. These factors more than doubled the shortfall by the spring of 1974, and, by the end of the year, the coarse-grain crop was 4% less than it was in 1973. Carry-over stocks into 1975 were thus not only

less than the year before but were almost half the size of the grain stocks at the beginning of 1971–72 (FAO 1975). However, the world's 1975–76 total wheat and coarse-grain harvest is now projected to be 3.3% higher than that of 1974–75, though much of this is due to the substantial increases in the United States over last year's abnormally low production. In addition, the world rice crop for 1975–76 appears to be good and is therefore expected to increase the 1976 stocks over those of last year (USDA 1975). In the last two years in developing nations the oil crisis has greatly exacerbated the fertilizer shortage, the manufacture of which consumes large quantities of natural gas and naphtha. Thus, in 1976–77 higher costs of energy, greater demand for fertilizer, and more food consumption, plus heavy grain importation by the Soviet Union, presage grain shortages for the very countries that need more grain.

Inequitable distribution of resources has increased during the past 25 to 30 years, even though the world food supply has kept pace with population growth. Between 1953 and 1971 the world food supply grew by 2.9%, which, when balanced with a population growth of 2.6%, yielded a per capita increase of 0.3%. Of the developing areas, Latin America fared best with an annual per capita gain of 0.9%. Asia, however, increased by only 0.2%, and Africa declined by 1.1% per year. In Asia the increase was small in spite of increases in cultivated land of up to 20%, a doubling of irrigated land, and a 30-fold increase in the use of fertilizers (Revelle 1974, pp. 119–21).

What appear to be the possibilities that food production will keep up with population growth and that a more equitable distribution of resources can be achieved in the next 25 to 50 years? More can be done in the cultivation of potentially arable land in LDCs, especially in Africa and Latin America, where the areas that can be put into agricultural production could be increased by 200 to 400%. Throughout the world there is about 80% more land that can be profitably cultivated (Revelle 1974, pp. 126–27). At the present population growth rate of 2% per year, this new agricultural land would allow for food production for another 40 years. In addition, cultivation can be intensified, using mass production techniques, in some LDCs. Unfortunately, much of the agricultural land in LDCs is in small parcels, and land reform, though good in many ways, has aggravated this situation. Thus, it will be necessary, through cooperatives or other forms of social engineering, to consolidate these fields to accommodate modern equipment.

My observation of many of these countries over the past 25 years and my recent work in Mexico and Bangladesh lead me to believe that many landowners may guard their small holdings literally to the death. We know very little about the changes that have been carried out in China in this connection, but we do know that they have been accompanied by an almost complete communization of private property and abolition of individual liberty. Many LDCs are moving in this direction already, adding complicated social and political variables to the question of food and population.

Researchers continue to seek new food sources from the ocean and to develop new strains of existing foods. In addition, medical and public health specialists are continuing in their attempts to reduce undernourishment due to infections that prevail in the developing countries, where estimates suggest that up to 80% of some populations are infested by parasites that consume a large percentage of ingested food.

All the efforts to increase the food supply are tied to total national production. Thus, if the GNP can increase faster than the population, there will be some hope for a more adequate food supply. However, the massive programs in support of economic development in LDCs are slowing down as the developed nations themselves begin to face shortages of resources and goods, unemployment, and other economic and social problems. This is particularly true of the United States, which, since World War II, has borne the heaviest burden of assistance to LDCs and has been the strongest proponent of applying a "can do" philosophy to world prob-

lems. Although many of us strongly believed that we could and should shoulder this burden, feeling that it would be possible to foster the development of a prosperous and peaceful world community, recent events have given us pause for re-evaluation. Thus, while I do not totally despair of the possibility of creating a functioning balance of economic and military power in the world, I do feel that it will be longer and harder coming than we had envisioned in the postwar period. And rapid population growth will become the major deterrent to achieving this balance.

The depletion of many basic natural resources, the increasing competition for capital, the lack of skilled labor in the LDCs, and the crushing burden of doubling population every 20 to 25 years will cause strains with which many LDCs will be unable to cope. I am afraid that it is unlikely that development and modernization can occur in time to offset mass starvation and political upheaval and destruction in many of these countries.

Controls of growth

Population size is regulated by three variables: fertility, mortality, and migration. Thus, population growth can be controlled only by lowering fertility, by increasing mortality, or through migration. Migration has been one of the great safety valves of history as people have moved around the globe in search of a better life. Migrations have taken two major forms: international migration, such as the vast movement from Europe to America from the seventeenth through the nineteenth centuries, and internal migration, exemplified by the tremendous movement of rural people to the cities.

International migration has continued into the twentieth century and includes the migrations following independence in India, Indonesia, and Bangladesh, the movement of Mexicans and other Latin Americans into the United States, the emigration of workers from Southern Europe into Switzerland and Germany and even Australia, and migrations resulting from wars in China, Korea, and Indochina. Although national limitations are be-

coming more restrictive, international migration may be expected to continue as excess population growth in the LDCs creates increasing pressures, with the effect of creating greater tensions between the developed nations to which migrants will be attracted and the LDCs from which the most sophisticated and well-educated will continue to escape.

Even more significant demographically than international migrations have been internal migrations. In 1800 less than 3% of the population of the world lived in cities. By the 1970s the percentage had increased to 74% in North America, 70% in Oceania, 62% in Europe, 57% in the Soviet Union, 57% in Latin America, 33% in East Asia, 18% in South Asia, and 20% in Africa (AID 1973).

While on the one hand these increases have put great pressures on the educational, social, and health services of the cities, urban populations have tended to exhibit decreasing fertility. Thus, urbanization, along with industrialization and development in general, contributes to the modernization process which is primarily responsible for the completion of the demographic transition and which is probably the most significant factor in fertility reduction in rapidly developing countries such as Taiwan and Korea. Other LDCs are not so fortunate, however, and it is extremely doubtful whether the modernization process can continue in the face of increasing population growth. In a recently completed study of rural-to-urban migrants in Mexico, I found that although fertility is much lower in large capitals such as Mexico City, it did not decline significantly among rural migrants to the small urban area I studied. A similar pattern also appears true of small cities in other LDCs, and there is growing evidence that the fertility of migrants to large urban areas may even increase for a time before it decreases.

Another significant finding in my Mexico study was that, in addition to high fertility in the rural areas (an average of six children per family) and almost as high fertility in the small city (an average of over five children per family), the *inclination* of the Mexican women I surveyed was for continuing the large-family tradition. Women of all groups (urban, rural, migrants, non-migrants, Indian, and non-Indian) began their married years desiring an average of at least four children. This ideal rose to five to seven children as the wives reached the middle years of their marriages and to an average of nine children by the end of their fertile years. Since the vast majority of the populations of LDCs lives in rural areas and small cities, such a finding raises a crucial question concerning the effect of urbanization on a country's fertility.

I would suggest that the whole spectrum of urbanization, industrialization, food production, and development in general, when viewed in the context of rapidly rising population, poses the important question: Can fertility be reduced before it places such strains on the economy that development will fail to keep pace with population demands? If it cannot, then the very bases upon which the demographic transition depends will be eliminated and thus the transition will never be completed.

Mortality increases have also been among the great population controls. The epidemics of Europe in the centuries just prior to the Industrial Revolution are close enough in time to be part of recent history. This process, in one form or another, has balanced high fertility and has been the primary cause of the slow growth rate of the human race. Mortality, in fact, was a major theme of Thomas Malthus, who as early as 1798 warned of the food-population imbalance with the illustration that while food could increase only arithmetically, population, when unchecked, increased geometrically. Factors limiting population growth, Malthus felt, were of two types: preventive checks such as abstinence and delayed marriage (he was against birth control) and positive checks such as "insufficient food, disease, epidemics, war, infanticide, plague, and famine."

The economic and social systems of the world almost 200 years after Malthus are drastically different. Mortality is a fraction of what it was in the late eighteenth century, and there have even been short periods such as the early years of the Green Revolution when food did increase at more than an arithmetic rate. Neo-Malthusians, however, feel that it will not be possible to continue increasing food production at higher rates than present population growth rates or to decrease fertility in time to stop runaway population growth. Thus, they feel there remains only one other "solution"—rising mortality. More optimistic demographers have supported the thesis that fertility control is possible, and, therefore, great efforts are underway in many parts of the world not only to make contraceptives widely available but to encourage smaller families through motivational and educational programs.

Given low mortality and increasing limits to migration, the only rational way to control population growth is through reduction in fertility. Remarkably, the demographic transition in Europe and North America was carried out without the benefit of modern birth control methods or family planning programs. For this and other reasons, in fact, many demographers feel that government and private family planning programs have little impact on fertility reduction. To date, however, such family planning programs are the principal strategy for reducing fertility in most LDCs. Over half the countries of the world—which include two-thirds of the world's population—have some form of family planning program. Sixty-one of these are government directed or officially sanctioned. On the other hand, 38 countries, including Burma, Saudi Arabia, Argentina, Brazil, Upper Volta, and the Cameroons, have neutral or negative attitudes toward family planning (Population Reference Bureau 1975b).

Figure 2 reveals an interesting relationship between contraceptive use and world birth rates (Berelson 1974). As may be seen, the developed nations lead the list of countries with low birth rates and high contraceptive use, while the least developed ones are generally those in which fertility is extremely high and the practice of contraception very low. But, while contraceptive use is closely correlated with birth rates, so is development. Thus, the question may be raised: Is it development that brings on the practice of contraception, or is it family planning programs?

One hopes the answer is "both." In Korea and Taiwan, each with excellent family planning programs and a high level of development, fertility has decreased in 20 years from over 40 births per 1,000 per year to 24 in Taiwan and 28.7 in Korea. In Japan, which had a high birth rate and its own baby boom following World War II, fertility decreased to approximately that of developed Western nations by 1960, primarily through abortion, which, although assisted by government and private management, was done mainly without the benefit of family planning programs. In 1975 Japan's birth rate was 19.2 per 1,000 per year. Therefore, it is possible to say that, as in the developed countries of Europe and America a half century earlier, *development* in Japan, and not a family planning program per se, created the social and economic pressures on the Japanese family that facilitated rapid fertility reduction.

Population control programs

For 15 years the term *population control* has been avoided because of its connotations of the use of force in the sensitive area of family planning and sexual relations; instead, the term *beyond family planning* has been used. A number of developing nations are studying the feasibility of tax incentives, housing benefits, employment bonuses, and other controls which, unlike the pro-natalist benefits of the United States and other countries in the past, penalize parents with large families rather than subsidize them. A few, such as Singapore, are actually using negative pressures such as taxes as well as incentives to limit family size to two children.

Beyond family planning will undoubtedly mean *population control* as nations face food and employment shortages, GNP deficits, and increasing public costs with decreasing public revenues. India, Pakistan, and Bangladesh, convinced that rapid fertility reduction is essential and yet reluctant to use sterner measures, have fought val-

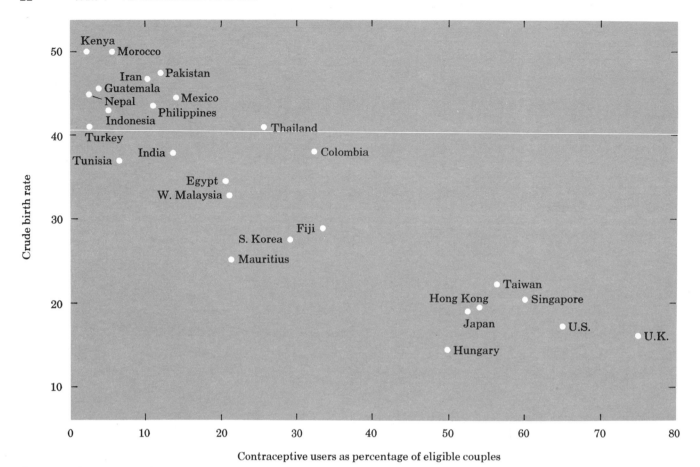

Figure 2. The use of fertility-control measures correlates closely with birth rates for many countries, despite such cultural variations as age at marriage or the proportion of the population married. A contraceptive user rate of 5% or less means a birth rate of 50 per 1,000 persons; a user rate of 30% means a birth rate around 30; a user rate of 60% or more means a birth rate of approximately 15. Percentages for Indonesia, Tunisia, and India are based on data from the public sector only. (From Berelson 1974, with permission of The Population Council.)

iantly under the voluntarism/family planning banner but are now moving toward "control." Argentina and a few other nations at the 1974 Bucharest Conference, however, felt that voluntarism and internal and international migration will be sufficient to maintain a sound growth level. Some feel that population expansion is beneficial to their national development and are strongly opposed to population control, and some are even against family planning, which many consider a plot to keep LDCs in a subservient position.

Argentina, with a growth rate of 1.3% per year, may go through a period of policy-stimulated fertility increase. Brazil, with a growth rate of 2.8, but with over 80% of its terrain underpopulated, may also be able to cope with population increases for some time. Unfortunately, however, most of the rest of Latin America lacks both the time and the available land resources to permit unchecked population

growth without dire consequences. Can Mexico support 100 million people in 15 years, as over against the present 59 million? Mexican national planners, as indicated by the adoption of a family planning policy in 1973, have decided that they cannot. Yet family planning in Mexico is just beginning, *beyond family planning* is years away, and *population control* is anathema.

Certainly many couples in Mexico and other less developed countries are opposed to any kind of control over their fertility. It is worth emphasizing that the ideal family size of the Mexican women I surveyed averaged over five children per family. Similarly high ideal or desired family size has been found in studies of other LDCs, which indicates that smaller families are not in the offing in such areas unless attitudes are changed or limits to childbirth established. The problem this poses for national planners is that voluntary family planning for the average couple will result in a national aver-

age of at least five children per couple. If the national goal is to reduce fertility to replacement, the country must indeed go beyond family planning—either by persuasion through information and education programs or incentive systems, or by a rigidly enforced population control program.

Bangladesh is the first large nation to attempt a stated policy of population control, and in April and May of 1975 I worked with the government of Bangladesh, the World Bank, and the East-West Center to help establish the communication aspects of the program. Six population planning officers, appointed to the Ministries of Agriculture, Labor and Social Welfare, Rural Development, Education, and Information, will conduct the information, education, and motivation programs in their ministries while working closely with the Ministry of Health and Population Control and the Planning Commission. This population control program is planned to reach far beyond the family planning programs that have been in operation in Bangladesh and East Pakistan in the past.

The effort is led by the new president of the country, who in recent months has assumed the chairmanship of the National Population Council, composed of the heads of all ministries, which coordinates the health, family planning, and population control programs. The major concentration, other than contraceptive programs, will be in information, education, and motivation. Mothers' clubs are being established; cooperatives, agricultural extension centers, labor unions, and all other organizations in the country are setting up family planning centers or training programs; schools are increasing the time spent on population education; and media programs in family planning and population awareness are being vastly increased. In addition, community incentive programs, legalization of abortion, and other legal and social measures aimed at reducing fertility are being studied. As is now the case in India, some leaders are recommending strong punitive measures, such as compulsory sterilization, fines, and even jail sentences, for families that have more than two children.

The government of Bangladesh, in its most recent figures, reports a crude birth rate of 47 per 1,000 per year and a crude death rate of 17, with a growth rate of 3% per year and a life expectancy of 48 years. More recent United Nations figures, however, show a crude birth rate of 49.5 and a death rate of 28.1, with a growth rate of 1.7 and a life expectancy of 36 years. These figures are five-year averages that include the period of the war of independence from Pakistan (March–December 1971), during which there was also heavy emigration to India, and the floods and famines of 1969 and 1974. Whichever figures are correct, they demonstrate the immensity of the problem, especially when combined with a per capita GNP of about $70 per year and a population density of 1,380 people per square mile, a density that would mean a population of over 5 billion Americans.

There is no need to look further to find the neo-Malthusian prediction: it is already happening in Bangladesh. If, indeed, life expectancy is 36 years and, in spite of that, the fertility is such that the population will double in 41 years (or 23 years if the Bangladesh growth rate of 3% per year is used), it is no wonder that many Bengalis are filled with despair. And thus it is even more to the credit of the handful of population control pioneers with whom I worked in 1975: they know the dimensions of the problem, they are aghast, and yet they are going to try to control it.

The future

At the current 1.9% yearly growth rate, the world's population would double every 36 years; at this rate, population projections "go off the top of the page" as the present world population of approximately 4 billion doubles to 8 billion by 2012, 16 billion by 2048, and 32 billion by 2084. Projections, however, vary with changes in fertility and mortality and thus do not forecast the future population in any way other than an immediate mirroring of the recent past. Population projections for the United States in the 1930s, for example, which were based on low fertility resulting from the depression, forecast a 1970 population of only about 170 million, whereas forecasts made during the postwar baby boom estimated a population higher than the actual 1976 figure.

Demographic projections for the world must therefore be weighed in terms of economic, social, and political variables, many of which are almost impossible to predict. Food experts have forecast shortages and resultant deaths but have produced no mortality projections. Family planners have estimated contraceptive acceptance rates and have made guesses as to when the two-child family might be realized in certain nations. A few demographers have projected world population based on their estimates of falling fertility.

Freedman and Berelson (1974) have worked out a growth *rate* projection based on the past and present growth history of the human race, which was, for most of the past, less than 0.1% per year until it rose to the current growth rate of almost 2% per year within the last few hundred years. They pose three alternatives for the future, the first assuming that fertility can be brought down to replacement by the year 2000, the second that replacement can be reached by 2020, and the third that replacement will be a reality by 2040. They then conclude from these projections that (1) the present growth rate of 2%, except for the immediate future, has risen as high as it ever will and (2) even the most pessimistic of their three alternatives (i.e. replacement by the year 2040) will find the world with a growth rate of about 0.1%, or ZPG, in less than 300 years. These conclusions are based only on fertility reduction; Freedman and Berelson do not speculate as to how much mortality may rise or how much the world population will increase. I would concur with their guesses on fertility reduction, as well as with their projection that the growth rate will not increase, but I would also guess that mortality will rise. As we saw in the case of Bangladesh, the growth rate of 1.7% per year, rather than 3%, is based on a mortality of 28.1 per 1,000 instead of only 17 per 1,000 per year. Thus, in this instance, there is no cause to rejoice in the lower growth rate.

The formidable and significant work of Thomas Frejka (1973) presents several valuable population projections but no predictions. Frejka describes "alternative paths to equilibrium" and concludes that cessation of world population growth during the 1980s is impossible. According to Frejka, even to arrive at an average of two children per family by the year 2000 would require a fertility decline at the rate experienced by Taiwan in the 1950s and 1960s, which was one of the most rapid in the world in recent history. He feels that to reach a leveling off of the total world population of approximately 6.5 billion by the middle of the twenty-first century would require a fertility decline almost double that of Taiwan. He further concludes that "profound changes in several fundamental facets of economic and social life, including fertility behavior, are essential in order to avoid a collapse of the world system" (p. 200). I have found no evidence that such fundamental changes will occur in the near future.

Although Frejka states that "there may be a period ahead of us in which some countries or regions of the world populations will experience increased mortality rates," he does not feel that this will have a great impact on world population. These predictions are based on calculations that all national and regional disasters since 1850 have delayed population growth only about 10 years. In other words, without these disasters, world population might have reached 3.5 billion by 1960 instead of by 1970 (p. 163).

It appears to me, however, that "disasters" resulting from the crisis of population vs. resources may well create situations more severe than those encountered since 1850. For between 1975 and 2000 the population of Africa is projected to increase from 401 million to 813 million, Asia from 2.255 billion to 3.636 billion, Latin America from 324 million to 620 million, and even Europe from 473 to 540 million (Population Reference Bureau 1975a).

Many countries can handle this increase. But whether Bangladesh (73.7 million to 144.3 million by 2000), Mexico (59.2 million to 132.2 million), or India (613.2 million to 1.059 billion) can meet the challenge of more than double the amount of food, let alone resources and public services, is a serious question. And whether they can double the food and other supplies *again* in another 20 to 25 years is an even more serious question.

Little has been done to quantify these questions, since it is almost impossible to estimate mortality increase resulting from food shortages or to estimate how many people can live on a given food supply. Revelle (1974) estimates that, technically, a world population of 40 to 50 billion people could be fed. He agrees, nevertheless, with other food and demographic experts that this is not desirable or even feasible at a standard of life other than mere subsistence.

Mesarovic and Pestel (1974) have projected the effect that a food deficit in South Asia would have in terms of the death of children, esti-

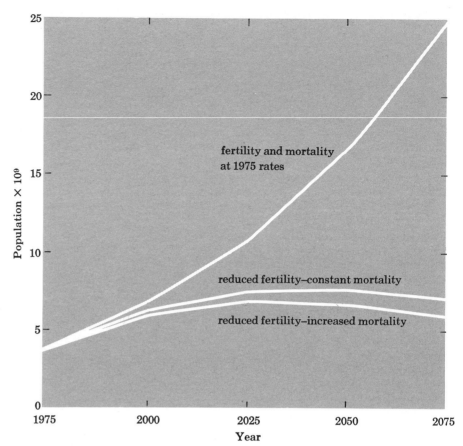

Figure 3. In the first projection, calculated at 1975 rates (total fertility rate, TFR = 4.5; life expectancy = 55 years), the world population would theoretically reach 24 billion by 2075, although in actuality such a large population is highly unlikely. The second projection shows a reduction in TFR to 2.2 by 2025 and the mortality rate remaining the same. In the third projection, TFR is again decreased to 2.2 in 50 years, when it stabilizes; mortality, however, gradually increases to a life expectancy of 45 in 2025 and then decreases to 63 years by 2075. (Projections courtesy of R. W. Gardner.)

mating as many as 45 million deaths per year in the face of a severe protein deficit. They point out, however, that this is not a forecast but rather an indication of the population vs. food problem that would develop in one area of the world if a balance is not achieved.

Three projections

Because birth and death rates do not easily lend themselves to detailed projection procedures, age-specific fertility rates and the total fertility rate (total number of children who would be born to 1,000 women during their child-bearing years—ages 15 through 49—given a certain schedule of age-specific fertility) are used for fertility projections, and life tables (life expectancy at birth) are used for mortality. The world total fertility rate (TFR) in 1975 was 4.5; life expectancy at birth was 55 years. These rates constitute the standard population projection—the first projection (see

Fig. 3). It is merely a view of the future should things continue as they are now; it is not considered a forecast of what might happen.

Next let us make a second projection, similar to that of Freedman and Berelson and others based on falling fertility and constant mortality. In this projection world fertility would slowly decrease from its 1975 level to allow approximate replacement (2.2 per 1,000) by 2025, stabilizing at that level. Mortality would remain constant at 1975 rates—i.e. life expectancy of 55 years.

The third projection combines the falling fertility estimates in the second projection with rising mortality, such as that suggested by a number of food experts and projected for child mortality in South Asia by Mesarovic and Pestel. Demographers have shied away from making mortality projections, and I am aware that we are treading on thin ice in attempting to do so. However, I am deeply concerned that we are faced with this terrible prospect and that we should begin to attempt to estimate its extent and, if possible, its impact.

I have presumed to suggest a rising mortality projection, not only because the prognosis of food experts coincides with my own observations but also because available demographic data seem to support this. In Africa, mortality is already high (19.8 per 1,000 per year, with a life expectancy at birth of 45). South Asia, especially Bangladesh, India, and Pakistan, also have high mortality, which may well increase to more than 30 per 1,000, with a life expectancy of 40. (Bangladesh, if we use the figures given earlier, may well have a death rate of 28.1 and a life expectancy of 36.) Mortality in other less developed countries, including Indonesia, Thailand, and the Philippines, could begin to increase in less than 20 years; mortality might increase in Latin America more slowly but, with doubling populations every 26 years, would not be far behind.

The extent of decreasing fertility and rising mortality will depend on economic developments such as availability of new sources of power and agricultural improvements, social and cultural factors related to the development and acceptance of contraceptives, and political changes that may well have a role in the future even surpassing economics in their effect on population. Political influence may be especially pronounced if authoritarian regimes with strong anti-natalist policies, such as the People's Republic of China, become the model for the future political development of the LDCs. Projections of rising mortality will also depend upon the type of demographic balance that is achieved and how soon such balance may occur.

With the above caveats in mind, I would project the following as my own population model for the next 100 years: fertility decreases to approximate replacement in 50 years, while mortality gradually increases from a life expectancy of 55 in 1975 to 45 in 2025. At this point fertility stabilizes and remains at a total fertility rate of 2.2 per 1,000 for the

next 50 years, while mortality slowly decreases, bringing life expectancy up to age 63, closer to that of today's developed nations, by 2075.

From the first projection we note that, at the 1975 rates, world population would increase to over 24 billion by 2075; most food experts agree that this is a near-impossibility and that at some point between now and 2075 the death rate would have to increase. Furthermore, we must view all projections based on present growth rates as mere extrapolations of the present into the future without benefit of the many economic, social, ecological, or political indicators that can be applied.

The reduced fertility–constant mortality path, given fertility reduction at even greater than 1975 rates and mortality stable at 1975 rates, would almost double world population in the first 75 years, then reduce it to about 7 billion by 2075; this *could* come to pass, but the chances of reducing fertility to replacement in 50 years while maintaining the current low mortality rates appear to me to be a near-impossibility.

The reduced fertility–increased mortality projection is an unpleasant prospect from the point of view of increased deaths during the next 50 years, but, with rising life expectancy between 2025 and 2075 and a very optimistic fertility projection throughout the period, this projection indicates a world population of only about 6 billion by 2075. This prognosis negates the completion of the demographic transition in its conventional form. However, after a period of rising mortality, it does forecast ultimate stability at low birth and death rates. It is a projection that does not take into consideration a disaster such as nuclear war, which would devastate the Northern Hemisphere. In fact, it is a forecast of terrible suffering for the less developed Southern Hemisphere, though the developed countries themselves may well suffer some of this higher mortality.

The third projection also assumes that the developed nations will continue to contribute heavily to fertility reduction in the LDCs through economic assistance and that the

LDCs will establish effective population control programs. Although such control programs may not be easy to establish today, one doubling of the population in the already overpopulated nations should make their necessity evident. Those already at work in family planning and population control could well be the pioneers for what will become a massive effort in another 20 years.

How successful fertility control will be and how great the mortality increase will be will depend on the degree of cooperation manifested by developed countries, the flexibility of the nations in need, and the efficiency of world organizations. There is no doubt in my mind that a balance will be achieved and that mankind will survive, although in 2075 when demographers plot the curve indicating demographic history for the past 100 years, it will probably be far different from the clumsy projections of 1976.

References

Agency for International Development. 1973. *Population Program Assistance.* Washington, D.C.: Office of Population, AID, pp. 133–38.

Berelson, Bernard. 1974. World population: Status report 1974. *Reports in Population/Family Planning* 15:34. N.Y.: The Population Council.

Echols, James R. 1974. *People and Population.* Honolulu: East-West Communication Institute.

Food and Agriculture Organization. May 1975. *Monthly Bulletin of Agriculture and Economic Statistics,* United Nations (FAO), p. 16.

Freedman, Ronald, and Bernard Berelson. 1974. Introduction to *The Human Population.* San Francisco: W. H. Freeman.

Frejka, Thomas. 1973. *The Future of Population Growth.* New York: John Wiley.

Gardner, Robert W. East-West Population Institute, Honolulu.

Mesarovic, Mihajlo, and Eduard Pestel. 1974. *Mankind at the Turning Point.* New York: E. P. Dutton.

Population Reference Bureau. 1975a. *The World Population Data Sheet.* Washington, D.C.: Population Reference Bureau.

Population Reference Bureau. 1975b. *Population Policies around the World.* Washington, D.C.: Population Reference Bureau, p. 21.

Revelle, Roger. 1974. Food and population. In *The Human Population.* San Francisco: W. H. Freeman.

U.S. Department of Agriculture. 3 Nov. 1975. *Foreign Agriculture.* Washington, D.C., p. 8.

David W. Ehrenfeld

The Conservation of Non-Resources

Conservation cannot rely solely on economic and ecological justifications. There is a more reliable criterion of the value of species and communities

Conservation is usually identified with the preservation of natural resources, and this was certainly the meaning intended by the person who probably coined the word, Gifford Pinchot. Resources can be defined very narrowly as reserves of commodities that have an appreciable money value to man, either directly or indirectly. Since the time that Pinchot first used the word, it has been seriously overworked. A steadily increasing percentage of "conservationists" has been preoccupied with preservation of natural features—species, communities, and ecosystems—that are not conventional resources.

An example of such a non-resource is an endangered amphibian species, the Houston toad, *Bufo houstonensis* (*1*). This animal (Fig. 1) has no demonstrated or conjectural resource value to man, other races of toad will replace it, and its passing is not expected to make an impression on the *Umwelt* of the city of Houston or its

David W. Ehrenfeld received his B.A. in history from Harvard College, his M.D. from Harvard Medical School, and his Ph.D. in zoology and biochemistry from the University of Florida. Dr. Ehrenfeld has taught at Florida and at Barnard College, Columbia University, and is now Professor of Biology at Cook College, Rutgers University, and a member of the Rutgers graduate training programs in ecology and zoology. His research is on the behavior, physiology, and conservation of sea turtles. He is an associate editor of the journal* Human Ecology *and the author of two books on conservation ecology, the most recent being* Conserving Life on Earth *(NY: Oxford Univ. Press, 1972). The author thanks Ian Baldwin, William Goldfarb, Harold Hayes, James Raimes, and, especially, Joan Ehrenfeld for their criticism and suggestions. Parts of this paper were presented in April 1976 at the annual meeting of the Association of American Geographers in New York. Address: Cook College, Rutgers University, P.O. Box 231, New Brunswick, NJ 08903.*

suburbs. Yet someone thought enough of the Houston toad to give it a page in the International Union for the Conservation of Nature's lists of endangered animals and plants (*2*), and its safety has been advanced as a reason for preventing oil drilling in a Houston public park (*3*).

The Houston toad has not claimed the undivided attention of conservationists, or they might by now have discovered some hitherto unsuspected value inherent in it; and this is precisely the problem. Species and communities that lack an economic value or demonstrated potential value as natural resources are not easily protected in societies that have a strongly exploitative relationship with nature. Many communities, probably the majority of plant and animal species, and some domesticated strains of crop plants fall in this category, at or near the non-resource end of a utility continuum. Those in favor of their preservation are often motivated by a deeply conservative distrust of irreversible change and/or a socially atypical attitude of respect for the components and structure of the natural world. These attitudes are not acceptable as a basis for conservation in Western-type societies, except in those few cases where preservation costs are minimal and there are no competing uses for the space now occupied by the non-resource. Consequently, defenders of non-resources generally have attempted to secure protection for their "useless" species or environments by means of a change of designation: a "value" is discovered, and the non-resource metamorphoses into a resource.

Perhaps the first to recognize this process was Aldo Leopold (*4*), who wrote in "The Land Ethic" that "one basic weakness in a conservation

system based wholly on economic motives is that most members of the land community have no economic value.... When one of these non-economic categories is threatened, and if we happen to love it, we invent subterfuges to give it economic importance."

Economic value of non-resources

The values attributed to non-resources are diverse and sometimes rather contrived, hence the difficulty of trying to condense them into a list. In my efforts I have relied, in part, on the thoughtful analyses provided by several members of the Nature Conservancy (*5*). All values listed below can be assigned a monetary value and thus become commensurable with ordinary goods and services—although in some cases it would require a good deal of ingenuity to do this. All are anthropocentric values.

1. Recreational and esthetic values. This is one of the most popular ways of assigning value to non-resources, because although frequently quite legitimate, it is also easily fudged. Consequently, it plays an important part in cost-benefit analyses and impact statements, filling in the slack according to need. The category includes items that involve little interaction between man and environment: scenic views can be given a cash value. Less remote interactions are hiking, camping, sport hunting, and the like. Organizations such as the Sierra Club stress many of these qualities, in part because their membership values them highly. It is no coincidence, for example, that among the Australian mammals, the large, showy, beautiful, diurnal ones, those that might be seen on safari, are zealously protected by conservation-

Figure 1. In perhaps the only photograph of a live Houston toad, *Bufo houstonensis,* this male toad was calling at Barking Dog Pond, Bastrop County, Texas, 1966. The quintessential non-resource, this drab and ordinary-looking species of bufonid has no economic value of any kind. Photograph by M. J. Littlejohn, University of Melbourne, Parkville, Australia; courtesy of Dr. Lauren E. Brown, Illinois State University, Normal, Illinois.

ists and are mostly doing well, while the small, inconspicuous, nocturnal marsupials include a distressingly large number of seriously endangered or recently exterminated species (6).

Some of the most determined attempts to place this recreational and esthetic category on a firm resource footing have been made by those who claim that the opportunity to enjoy nature, at least on occasion, is a prerequisite for sound mental and physical health. Several groups of long-term mental patients have supposedly benefited more from camping trips than from other treatments, and physiologically desirable effects have been claimed for the color green and for environments that lack the monotony of man-organized space (7).

2. *Undiscovered or undeveloped values.* In 1975 it was reported that the oil of the jojoba bean, *Simmondsia californica,* is very similar to oil of the threatened sperm whale in the stability of its responses to high temperatures and pressures. Overnight, this desert shrub of the American Southwest was converted from the status of a minor to a major resource (8). It can safely be assumed

that many other species of hitherto obscure plants and animals have great potential value as bona fide resources once this potential is discovered or developed. Plants are probably the most numerous members of this category: in addition to their possibilities as future food sources, they can also supply structural materials, fiber, and chemicals for industry and medicine (9).

Animals have potential resource uses that parallel those of plants, but this potential is being developed at an even slower rate. The potential for domestication and large-scale production of the vicuña, the source of one of the finest animal fibers in the world, was only recognized after its commercial extinction in the wild had become imminent.

Some species are potential resources indirectly, by virtue of their ecological associations. Galston (10) has described one such case involving the water fern, *Azolla pinnata,* which has long been cultivated in paddies along with rice by peasants in northern Vietnam. This inedible and seemingly useless plant harbors colonies of nitrogen-fixing blue-green algae in pockets on its leaves. Not surpris-

ingly, villages that have been privy to the secrets of fern cultivation have tended to produce exceptional quantities of rice.

Species whose resource possibilities are unknown cannot, of course, be singled out for protection, but most or all communities are likely to contain such species. Thus the undeveloped resource argument has been used to support the growing movement to save "representative," self-maintaining ecosystems in all parts of the world. Such ecosystems range from the stony and comparatively arid hills of Galilee, which still shelter the wild ancestors of wheat, oats, and barley, to the tropical forests of the world, whose timber, food, and forest product resources remain largely unknown even as they are destroyed (11).

3. *Ecosystem stabilization values.* This item is at the heart of the complex controversy that has arisen over the ecological theory of conservation. In its general form, Commoner (12) has stated it clearly:

The amount of stress which an ecosystem can absorb before it is driven to collapse is also a result of its various interconnections and their relative speeds of response. The more complex the ecosystem, the more successfully it can resist a stress.... Like a net, in which each knot is connected to others by several strands, such a fabric can resist collapse better than a simple, unbranched circle of threads—which if cut anywhere breaks down as a whole. Environmental pollution is often a sign that ecological links have been cut and that the ecosystem has been artificially simplified.

A more general, less controversial formulation of this "diversity-stability" concept is discussed separately under item 9.

One fairly specific (and less troublesome) derivation of the diversity-stability hypothesis concerns monocultures in agriculture and forestry. It has long been known that the intensive monoculture that characterizes modern farms and planted forests generates greater ease and reduced costs of cultivation and harvesting, and increased crop yields; but this is at the expense of higher risk of epidemic disease and vulnerability to insect and other pest attack (13). Here a reduction of species diversity results in much closer spacing of similar crop plants, which in turn facilitates the spread of both pests and disease organisms. It also eliminates plant species that constitute shelter for natural enemies of the specialized plant pests. Monocultures also create problems in ranching and fish farming, often because of incomplete use of available food resources by the single species involved.

4. *Examples of survival.* Communities and, to a lesser extent, species can have a value as examples or models of long-term survival. Humke et al. (5) observed that "most natural systems have been working in essentially their present form for many thousands of years. On the other hand, greatly modified, man-dominated systems have not worked very reliably in the past and, in significant respects, do not do so at present." The economic value here is indirect, consisting of problems averted (money saved) by virtue of good initial design of man-dominated systems or repair of faulty ones, based on features abstracted from natural systems. This viewpoint is becoming increasingly popular as disillusionment with the results of traditional planning grows. Thus it may make sense to look to successful natural communities for clues concerning the organization of traits leading to persistence or survival. Wright (14) has stated this non-resource value in its strongest form in the final sentence of an interesting article on landscape development: "The survival of man may depend on what can be learned from the study of extensive natural ecosystems."

5. *Environmental baseline and monitoring values.* The fluctuation of animal or plant population sizes, the status of their organs or by-products, or even the mere presence or absence of a given species or group of species in a particular environment can be used to define normal or baseline environmental conditions and to determine the degree to which communities have been affected by extraordinary outside influences such as pollution or man-made habitat alteration. Biological functions such as species diversity (in the full sense of the term, which includes both richness and equitability measurements) are the best possible indicators of the meaningful effects of pollution, just as behavior is the best single indicator of the health of the nervous and musculoskeletal systems. Species diversity is a final common path, a re-

sultant of all forces that impinge on ecosystems. It should also be noted that the traditional economic value of a species is of no significance in determining its usefulness as an environmental indicator—an important point if we are concerned with the metamorphosis of non-resources into resources.

With the exception of the biological monitoring of water pollution, this branch of conservation ecology is still in its infancy. In the case of water pollution, much of the pioneering work on algal and invertebrate communities has been done by Ruth Patrick and her associates (15). Lichens are sensitive indicators of air pollution, especially that caused by dust and sulfur dioxide (16). The common lilac, *Syringa vulgaris*, develops a disease called leaf roll necrosis in response to elevated levels of ozone and sulfur dioxide. The honey of honeybees can be used to monitor environmental heavy metal pollution (17). Organ analyses of snakes have been recommended as a way of following organochlorine pesticide and PCB residues in terrestrial environments (18). The presence of kinked or bent tails in tadpoles may be an indicator of both pesticides and local climatic change (19).

6. *Scientific research values.* Many creatures that are otherwise economically negligible have some unique or special characteristic that makes them extremely valuable to research scientists. Because of their relationship to man, orangutans, chimpanzees, and even the lower prosimians fall in this category. Squids and the sea hare, *Aplysia*, have nervous system properties that make them immensely valuable to neuroscientists. The identical quadruplet births of armadillos and the hormonal responses of the clawed toad, *Xenopus*, make them objects of special study to embryologists and endocrinologists, respectively. The odd life cycle of slime molds has endeared these fungi to biologists studying the chemistry of cell-cell interactions.

7. *Teaching values.* The teaching value of an intact ecosystem may be quantified by noting the economic value of displaced land-use alternatives. For example, a university administration may preserve a teaching forest if the competing use is as an

extra parking lot for maintenance equipment, but it may not be so inclined toward conservation if the land is wanted for university housing.

In one case, in 1971, a U.S. Federal District Judge ordered the New York State National Guard to remove a landfill from the edge of the Hudson River and restore the brackish marsh that had occupied the site previously. One of the reasons he cited, although not the most important one, was the marsh's prior use by local high school biology classes (20).

8. *Habitat reconstruction values.* If we wish to restore or rebuild an ecosystem in what was once its habitat, we need a living, unharmed ecosystem of that type to serve as both a working model and a source of living components. This is tacitly assumed by tropical forest ecologists, for example, who realize that clear-cutting of very large areas of tropical moist forests is likely to be incompatible with maintaining a sustained yield of the full diversity of tropical hardwoods. In some north temperate forests, strip-cutting, with intervening strips of forest left intact for reseeding and animal habitat, is now gaining favor in commercial timber operations. Actual cases of totally rebuilt ecosystems are still rare: the best example may be the salt marsh reconstructions by Garbisch and his co-workers (21). If certain future endangered ecosystems are recognized as useful to man, then any remnant patches of these ecosystems will assume a special resource value.

9. *Conservative value: Avoidance of irreversible change.* This is a general restatement of a basic fear underlying every other item on this list; sooner or later it turns up in all discussions about saving non-resources. It expresses the conservative belief that man-made, irreversible change in the natural order—the loss of an evolved gene pool or community—may carry a hidden and unknowable risk of serious damage to humans and their civilizations. Preserve the full range of natural diversity because we do not know the aspects of that diversity upon which our long-term survival depends. This was Aldo Leopold's basic argument (4): "A system of conservation based solely on economic self-interest is hopelessly lopsided. It tends to ignore, and thus eventually to eliminate, many ele-

ments in the land community that lack commercial value, but that are (as far as we know) essential to its healthy functioning."

Without in any way impugning the truth of this statement, two serious oversights or omissions might be pointed out in Leopold's argument. First, Leopold provides no real justification for preserving those animals, plants, and habitats that are almost certainly not essential to the "healthy functioning" of any large ecosystem. This is not a trivial category, and includes, in part, the great many species and even communities that have always been extremely rare or that have always had very restricted distributions. Second, although Leopold rejected "economic self-interest" as a sole motive for conservation, he evidently did not realize that preserving the "healthy functioning" of land communities is also an economic self-interest argument, albeit one that manifests its resource benefits indirectly and over the long term.

Exaggerations and distortions

In surveying the preceding list of reasons for valuing and hence preserving non-resources, the most striking feature is its practical political weakness. Regardless of the truth of these explanations of value, they are not as convincing as those that are backed by a promise of short-term economic gain. In a capitalist society, any private individual or corporation that treats non-resources as if they were resources is likely to go bankrupt. In a socialist society, the result will be nonfulfillment of growth quotas. People do not seem ready to assign resource values on the basis of long-term considerations or mere statistical probabilities of danger. As Matthews has pointed out (22), even "human health, especially in areas outside of cancer (for example, [sickness] from asbestos) and massive deaths (for example, from nuclear reactor accidents), is often given a second priority to the economic criteria [of GNP, employment, and the standard of living]."

If we examine the "conservative value" of non-resources discussed above, the difficulty immediately becomes plain. The economic value in this case is a remote and nebulous one: it is protection from the un-

known dangers of irreversible change. An added problem is that if a danger materializes, it may be too late to reverse policy or it may be impossible to prove a connection with the initial loss of the non-resource. Even in those cases where loss of a non-resource seems likely to initiate long-term undesirable change, the argument may be too complex and technical to be widely persuasive among non-scientists or it may be contrary to popular belief. An excellent example has been provided by Owen (13) and by Ormerod (29) who have claimed that the tsetse fly, dread vector of African trypanosomiasis, may be essential to the well-being of large parts of sub-Saharan Africa.

In summary, the usual reasons that are advanced to persuade people to accept non-resources as resources are not very likely to convince them, regardless of their truth. When everything is called a resource, the word loses all meaning—at least in our value system.

One consequence of the failure to persuade is that conservationists are provoked into exaggerating and distorting the alleged values of non-resources. The most vexing and embarrassing example for conservationists concerns the diversity-stability issue. It is important to make clear at the outset that the necessity of maintaining diversity is not questioned. As one critical ecologist put it (23), "From a practical standpoint, the diversity-stability hypothesis is not really necessary; even if the hypothesis is completely false it remains logically possible—and, on the best available evidence, very likely—that the disruption of the patterns of evolved interaction in natural communities will have untoward, and occasionally catastrophic consequences."

The first comprehensive statement of the diversity-stability hypothesis was made by Margalef (24). In a classic paper he claimed that the successional drive toward a "climax" community ("mature" ecosystem in his terminology), which is characteristic of all natural ecosystems, is one of several strong pieces of evidence that the late stages of succession are more "stable" than earlier ones. These late ecosystems were also thought to be more diverse, and using information theory Margalef claimed to have

demonstrated that the higher information content and greater number of interactions is responsible for the increased stability. This was widely interpreted to mean that mature ecosystems were better able to buffer their environments, were more resistant to man-made perturbations (such as chemical pollution), than were earlier and simpler stages. From this were derived analogies such as the one quoted above from Commoner, in which the strength of a late successional community was compared with that of a net. There is much intuitive support for this hypothesis. As Goodman has said (23), there is a "basic appeal of its underlying metaphor. It is the sort of thing that people like, and want, to believe."

Even as Margalef was refining his hypothesis, four lines of investigation and evidence were combining to undermine part of it. First, the results of many separate studies of terrestrial and aquatic ecosystems showed that diversity does not always increase with succession, particularly in the final phases. Second, investigations of plant associations by Whittaker and his colleagues (25) tended to show that the interdependence and interactions of the species found in mature communities had been exaggerated—at least if one looked at a single trophic level. Third, the mathematical analysis of May (26) failed to confirm the intuitively attractive notion stated by Commoner that the greater the number of interactions, or links, the greater the stability of the system. May's models worked the other way: the more elements (species and species interrelationships) there were, the greater the fluctuation of the populations in the system when a simulated external perturbation was applied. In theory, the most complex systems were therefore at the greatest risk of collapse. Fourth, the direct evidence of conservationists and ecologists was against the hypothesis: the diverse, mature communities were almost always the first to fall apart under heavy, man-imposed stress and were always the most difficult to protect (at least in the case of terrestrial systems). Indeed, Margalef's own description of early colonizing species (Hutchinson's "fugitive species") indicated that these immature community residents were usually resilient, opportunistic, genotypically and phenotypically plastic, and behaviorally adaptable, and had high reproductive rates. They are the vermin, weeds, and common game species, among others, and very few of them are exclusive residents of climax communities (27).

As May and others had perceived, the diversity-stability hypothesis, in the restricted sense described here, was a case of inverted cause and effect. The most diverse communities were those that had occupied the most stable environments for the longest period of time: they were dependent on stability—not the reverse.

The most comprehensive and lucid review of the diversity-stability controversy has been written by Goodman (23). Although Goodman may place too much emphasis on population fluctuation and not enough on persistence as a measure of stability (28), it does not alter the moral of the story for conservationists. In our eagerness to demonstrate a present "value" for the magnificent, mature, and most diverse ecosystems of the world—the tropical rain and cloud forests, the coral reefs, the temperate zone deserts, etc.—we stressed the role they were playing in immediate stabilization of their environments (including their own component populations). This was a partial distortion that not only caused less attention to be paid to the real, long-term values of these ecosystems but also helped to obscure, for a while, their extreme fragility in the face of human "progress."

Many different kinds of stability are indeed dependent on biological diversity. This is especially evident today in those places, often tropical, where soils are prone to erosion, nutrient loss, or laterite crust formation, and where desertification can occur (29); but none of these effects, however deadly and durable, is ever likely to be as easy to explain to laymen as the "stable net" hypothesis.

A much less complex example of an exaggeration or distortion that has resulted from the impulse to find values for non-resources concerns African game ranching. In the 1950s and 1960s it was first pointed out that harvesting the wild animals of the bush and savanna might produce at least as much meat per acre as cattle raising, without the reduction in carrying capacity that traditionally

has been associated with cattle in Africa (30). This suggestion cannot be faulted in ecological theory, which recognizes that the phenomenon of niche specialization enables the dozens of species of native, large herbivores to utilize the primary productivity much more efficiently and completely than cattle alone.

The pitfalls in this straightforward plan have only recently made themselves felt. Apart from serious cultural problems, the major drawback is ecological. The early game ranching theory and the subsequent cropping programs of Parker tacitly assume that the animals to be cropped will replace themselves, or, to put it another way, that the populations of edible, wild herbivores will be able to adapt to a heavy, annual loss to market hunters. This is no doubt true of some of the r-selected species, but not all are likely to be r-selected. Hippopotamus and elephant supposedly have been cropped successfully in several places; nevertheless, the population dynamics and management ecology of nearly all species are still largely unknown (31), and exploitation, illegal and legal, is proceeding with little more than speculation about the long-term consequences. The issue here is the danger of assuming, with an air of infallibility, that one knows what the ecological effects of cropping will be. This point has been made repeatedly by Hugh Lamprey and others most knowledgeable about east African ecology, and is beautifully illustrated in an anecdote told by John Owen, the noted former park director at Serengeti (32). Owen was describing the controversy over the return of elephants, 2000 strong, to Serengeti and the alleged damage they were doing to the park ecosystem:

When I would come down from Arusha the wardens would take me around and show me the trampled acacias. Next day the scientists [from the Serengeti Research Institute] would take me out and show me the new acacia shoots blooming in another part of the park. Acacia seeds are carried and fertilized by elephant dung.

At this time, much of the trouble is with poachers, and there is admittedly the remote possibility that supervised game ranches and cropping schemes on a large scale will have the effect of making poaching (for cash sale) uneconomical. But there is also

the possibility that game ranching and cropping will affect species diversity and ecosystem stability as much as poaching or even, in some cases, cattle raising. In our haste to preserve zebra, wildebeest, dik dik, and springbok by endowing them with a tangible economic value, we may have exaggerated one type of resource potential (they have many others) and in the process endangered them further.

One of the lessons of the examples cited above is that conservationists should not assume that ecological theory will always support their cases, especially when these cases concern specific, immediate objectives and when the scope of the debate has been artificially restricted by a short-term, cost-benefit type of approach.

Another example of a situation where ecological theories, if viewed in a restricted context, do not support conservation practices was described by Janzen (33):

One possible remedy [for the year-round persistence of agricultural pests and diseases in the tropics] is unpleasant for the conservationist. The agricultural potential of many parts of the seasonally dry tropics might well be improved by systematic destruction of the riparian and other vegetation that is often left for livestock shade, erosion control, and conservation. It might be well to replace the spreading banyan tree with a shed. . . . Some studies even suggest that "overgrazed" pastures may have a higher overall yield than more carefully managed sites, . . . especially if the real costs of management are charged against the system.

What is important here is that Janzen has demonstrated that it is quite possible for ecological theory to endow non-resources with a negative value, to make them out to be economic liabilities. In this particular case, long-term ecological considerations (such as the ultimate costs of erosion, nutrient dumping, and factors related to all the other items on the list given above) would probably militate against the short-term ecological considerations described by Janzen. But the practical net result of any conservationist's attempt to demonstrate a resource value for natural riparian and other vegetation in the seasonally dry tropics, based on ecological theory, would be to expose the conservation position to unnecessary attack.

The point being made here is easy to misinterpret. At the risk of seeming obvious, I must make clear that the purpose of this paper is a restricted one; it is to identify the honest and durable reasons for saving non-resources. This does not mean that I reject resource arguments when they are valid. The Amazonian rain forest, the green turtle, and many other forms of life contribute heavily to the maintenance of human well-being. The prospect of their loss is frightening to anyone with ecological knowledge, and it is not my aim to make it appear less so. But this is only one of the rationales for conservation, and it should not be applied carelessly, if for no other reason than the likelihood of undermining its own effectiveness.

Additional risks

Even when it is quite legitimate to find economic values for quondam non-resources, it may be risky, from a conservation viewpoint, to do so. Gosselink et al. (34) have conducted an elegant and painstaking investigation of the value of tidal marshes along the coast of the southeastern United States which can serve as an illustration of these risks.

The purpose of the project was to establish a definite monetary value for tidal marsh based on tangible resource properties. Esthetic values were therefore not considered. The properties studied included the function of tidal marshes in removing pollutants from coastal waters (tertiary sewage treatment), sport and food fish production, potential for commercial aquaculture, and an assortment of other less quantifiable functions. The income-capitalized value of intact marsh, computed on the basis of its energy flow, amounted to $82,940 per acre. Although the validity of the energy/money conversion might conceivably be challenged, it is unlikely that more laborious methods of estimating value, if they were sufficiently inclusive, would change the results significantly. Salt marshes are valuable.

Is calling attention to this value the best way to conserve salt marshes? If a given marsh were worth less if put to competing use than in its intact condition, the answer might be yes, provided that the marsh were publicly owned. But discovering value can be dangerous. First, any competing use with a higher value, no matter how slight the differential, would be entitled to priority in the use of the marsh site. Because most competing uses are for all intents and purposes irreversible, future change in relative usage values subsequent to the alteration of the marsh would have no effect, even if a marsh usage later were able to claim higher value and priority. We do not generally tear down luxury, high-rise apartments.

Second, values change. If, for example, a new process is discovered and tertiary treatment of sewage becomes suddenly less expensive (or if the sewage acquires value as a raw material), then that component of the marsh value will decline proportionally.

Third, the implication of the study is that both the valuable and diseconomic qualities of the salt marsh are all known and identified. Conversely, this means that those qualities of the salt marsh that have not been assigned a conventional value are not very important. This is a dangerous implication.

Fourth, Clark (35) has shown that quick profits from immediate exploitation, even to the point of extinction, often are economically superior to long-term, sustained yield gains of the sort generated by intact marsh, provided that the profits and the discount rate are each sufficiently high.

Given these four objections, the hazards of even legitimate reassignment of non-resources as resources become quite plain, as do the hazards of overemphasizing the cost-benefit approach in conserving more traditional resources.

Formal priority rankings

Another consequence of assigning resource value to non-resources deserves separate consideration: when real values are computed, it becomes possible to rank endangered ecosystems, or even species, for the purposes of assigning conservation priority. Because dollar values of the sort worked out for tidal marshes are generally not available, other ranking methods have been devised. These are meant to be applied in a mechanical, objective fashion.

Ranking systems based in large part on vegetation type have been devised for use in Wisconsin by Tans (36) and in Texas by Gehlbach (37). Properties that are scored and totaled in Gehlbach's system include "climax condition," "educational suitability," "species significance" (presence of rare, relict, peripheral, endemic, or endangered species), "community representation" (number and type of communities included), and "human impact" (current and potential), in order of increasing importance. Gehlbach evidently believes that the numerical scores generated by this system can be used, without additional human input, to determine conservation policy. He states that "it is suggested that if offered for donation [to the State of Texas], an area be accepted only when its natural area score exceeds the average scores of the same or similar community-type(s) in the natural area reserve system." Other ranking systems for both species and, more commonly, natural areas either exist in the literature or could be developed along the lines of the methods described above.

There are two fundamental problems with ranking systems that militate against their uncritical or mechanical use. First, there is the problem of incomplete knowledge. It is impossible to survey all the properties of any natural area (or species), and the dangers of overlooking value (positive or negative) are very great. Community descriptions, especially short ones, are largely artificial abstractions; they are designed to facilitate talking about vegetation, not deciding what to do with it. It is presumptuous to assume that any formal system of ranking can serve as a substitute for personal acquaintance with the land or informed human intuition about its meaning or value in the world of today or 100 years from now.

Second, formal ranking sets natural area against natural area in an unacceptable and totally unnecessary way. The need to conserve a particular community or species must be judged independently of the need to conserve anything else. Limited resources may force us to make choices against our wills, but ranking systems encourage and rationalize the making of choices. Ranking systems can be useful to conservationists as an adjunct to decision making, but the more formal and generalized they become, the more damage they are likely to cause.

There is only one account in Western culture of a conservation effort greater than that now taking place; it concerned endangered species. Not a single species was excluded on the basis of low priority, and by all accounts not a single species was lost. ("Of clean beasts, and of beasts that are not clean, and of fowls, and of everything that creepeth upon the earth, There went in two and two unto Noah into the ark, the male and the female, as God had commanded Noah" *Genesis* 7:8,9.) It is an excellent precedent.

Non-economic values

When one is confronted with a "double bind" that resists attempts at solution, the only rational approach short of surrender is to alter both one's viewing perspective and the general statement of the problem until the double bind disappears (*38*). The attempt to preserve non-resources by finding economic value for them generates a double bind. Much of the value discovered for non-resources is indirect in the sense that it consists of avoiding costly problems that might otherwise appear if the non-resources were lost. On the one hand, if the non-resource is destroyed and no ecological disasters ensue, then the conservation argument loses all capacity to inspire credence. On the other hand, if disaster does follow extinction of a supposed non-resource, then it will usually be too late to do anything about it, and it may well prove impossible to prove a causal relationship between the initial loss of the non-resource and the subsequent disaster. Indeed, no one may even think of the connection.

A way to avoid the non-resource double bind is simply to identify the *non*-economic values inherent in all natural communities and species and to weight them at least equally with resource values. The first of these universal qualities might be described as the "natural art value." It has been best articulated by Carr (*39*):

It would be cause for world fury if the Egyptians should quarry the pyramids, or the French should loose urchins to throw stones in the Louvre. It would be the same if the Americans dammed the Valley of the Colorado. A reverence for original landscape is one of the humanities. It was the first humanity. Reckoned in terms of human nerves and juices, there is no difference in the value of a work of art and a work of nature. There is this difference, though. . . . Any art might somehow, some day be replaced—the full symphony of the savanna landscape never.

This viewpoint is not common but is apparently gaining in popularity. In an article on Brazil's endangered lion tamarins or marmosets, three species of colorful, tiny primates of the Atlantic rain forests, Coimbra-Filho et al. advanced the notion of natural art in a frank and thoughtful statement remarkably similar to the preceding quotation (*40*):

In purely economic terms, it really doesn't matter if three Brazilian monkeys vanish into extinction. Although they can be (and previously were) used as laboratory animals in biomedical research, other far more abundant species from other parts of South America serve equally well or better in laboratories. Lion tamarins can be effectively exhibited in zoos, but it is doubtful that the majority of zoo-goers would miss them. No, it seems that the main reason for trying to save them and other animals like them is that the disappearance of any species represents a great esthetic loss for the entire world. It can perhaps be compared to the destruction of a great work of art by a famous painter or sculptor, except that, unlike a man-made work of art, the evolution of a single species is a process that takes many millions of years and can never again be duplicated.

It should be noted that this natural art, unlike man-made art, has no economic worth, either directly or indirectly. No one can buy or sell it for its artistic quality, it does not always stimulate tourism, nor does ignoring it cause, for that reason, any loss of goods or services. It is distinct from the recreational and esthetic resource value described earlier and may apply to communities and species that no tourist would detour a single mile to see or to qualities that are never revealed to casual inspection.

Free as it is of some of the problems associated with resource arguments, the natural art rationale for conservation is nevertheless, in its own way, a bit contrived, and a little bit confusing. Do all ecological associations have equal artistic value? Most critics would say that El Greco was a greater painter than Stubbs, but is the African savanna artistically more valuable than the New Jersey Pine Barrens?

Even if we concede that the art rationale for conservation does not foster the kind of comparisons that are the essence of traditional art criticism, there is still something wrong: the natural art concept is still rooted in the same homocentric, humanistic world view that is responsible for bringing the natural world, including us, to its present condition. If the natural world is to be conserved because it is artistically stimulating to man, there is still a condescension and superiority implied in the attitude of man, the kindly parent, toward nature, the beautiful problem-child. This attitude is not in accord with humility-inspiring discoveries of community ecology or with the sort of ecological world view, emphasizing the connectedness and immense complexity of the man-nature relationships, that now characterizes a large bloc of conservationist thought (*41*). Nor is it in accord with the growing bloc of essentially religious sentiment that approaches the same position of equality in the man-nature relationship from a nonscientific direction.

The exponents of natural art have done conservation a great service, being the first to point out the unsatisfactory nature of some of the economic reasons advanced to support conservation. But something else is needed. Elton (*42*) has indicated another non-resource value, the ultimate reason for conservation and the only one that cannot be compromised:

The first [reason for conservation], which is not usually put first, is really religious. There are some millions of people in the world who think that animals have a right to exist and be left alone, or at any rate that they should not be persecuted or made extinct as species. Some people will believe this even when it is quite dangerous to themselves.

This non-economic value of communities and species is the simplest of all to state: they should be conserved because they exist and have existed for a long time. Long-standing existence in nature is deemed to carry with it the unimpeachable right to continued existence. Existence is the only criterion of value, and diminution of the number of existing things is the best measure of decrease of value. This is, as mentioned, an ancient way of evaluating "conservability," and by rights ought to be named the "Noah Principle" after the person who was one of the first to put it into practice.

Currently, the idea of rights conferred by other-than-human existence is becoming increasingly popular (and is meeting with increased resistance). I shall give only two examples. In a book entitled *Should Trees Have Standing?* Stone has presented the case for existence of legal rights of forests, rivers, etc. apart from the vested interests of people associated with these natural entities. Describing the earth as "one organism, of which Mankind is a functional part," Stone extends Leopold's land ethic in a formal way, justifying such unusual lawsuits as *Byram River, et al. v. Village of Port Chester, New York, et al.* If a corporation can have legal rights, responsibilities, and access, through its representatives, to the courts ("standing"), argues Stone, why not rivers? The merits and deficiencies of this notion are not important here, but its emergence at this time is a significant event (43).

The ultimate example, however, of the Noah Principle in operation has been provided by Dixon in a short but profound article on the case for the guarded conservation of *Variola*, the smallpox virus, as an endangered species (44):

If we experience twinges of guilt about the impending extinction of large creatures, why should we feel differently about small ones? Conservationists lavish just as much time and energy on butterflies as they do on elephants. Why discount the microbes?

Dixon, in other parts of the article, makes a strong case for preserving smallpox as a resource (not for biological warfare, though), but his non-resource, "existence" value argument is clearly stated:

Some of us who might happily bid farewell to a virulent virus or bacterium may well have qualms about eradicating forever a "higher" animal—whether rat or bird or flea—that passes on such microbes to man. . . . Where, moving up the size and nastiness scale (smallpox virus, typhoid fever bacilli, malarial parasites, schistosomiasis worms, locusts, rats . . .), does conservation become important? There is, in fact, no logical line that can be drawn.

It is not the purpose of this paper to discredit the economic and selfish uses of nature or to recommend the abandonment of the resource rationale for conservation. Selfishness in the sense of environmental exploitation, within bounds, is necessary for the survival of any species, ourselves included. Furthermore, should we rely exclusively on non-resource motivations for conservation, we would find, given the present state of world opinion and material aspirations, that there would soon be nothing left to conserve. But we have been much too careless in our use of resource arguments—distorting and exaggerating them for short-term purposes and allowing them to confuse and dominate our long-term thinking. Resource and non-resource reasons for conservation must always be presented together, and conservationists should make clear that the non-resource reasons are ultimately more significant in every case. If resource arguments seem legitimately strong there is no reason to ignore them, although they must be used with caution because of their potential to weaken the conservation position at unpredictable times and in unpredictable ways. Conversely, when a community or species has no known economic worth, there is no need either to trump up weak resource values for it or to abandon the effort to conserve it. Its non-resource value is enough to justify (but not necessarily to assure) its protection.

A number of years ago, Elton (42) proposed that there were three different reasons for the conservation of natural diversity: "because it is a right relation between man and living things, because it gives opportunities for richer experience, and because it tends to promote ecological stability—ecological resistance to invaders and to explosions in native populations." He stated that these reasons could be harmonized and that together they might generate a "wise principle of co-existence between man and nature." Since these words were written, we have ignored this harmony of conservation rationales, shrugging off the first, or religious, reason as embarrassing or ineffective and relying on inadequate but "hard scientific" proofs of value.

Allen (45), for example, in summing up his resource-type arguments for preserving diversity, has said that the

economic climate is now such that "only the most severely practical arguments will prevail. Faint-hearted ecologists who fear that their favourite species *are* damned-well useless will just have to risk it. No doubt there is some redundancy in the system, but there are strong theoretical grounds for believing that most of the species on this planet are here for a better reason than that they are poor galactic map-readers."

What Allen is saying is that everything—including nearly all species—is interconnected and nearly everything has its own part to play in maintaining the natural order: consequently, nearly all species are significant, have resource value. Remove a species, even a seemingly trivial one from a resource standpoint, and we are more than likely to feel the consequences somehow, somewhere, someday (46). But have there been permanent and significant effects of the extinction, in the wild, of John Bartram's great discovery, the beautiful tree *Franklinia alatamaha*? Or a thousand species of tiny beetles that we never knew existed before or after their extermination? Can we even be certain that our eastern forests suffer the loss of their passenger pigeons and chestnuts in some tangible way that affects their vitality or permanence?

As a faint-hearted ecologist, I am not so certain that Allen's "strong theoretical grounds" can protect the Houston toad, the cloud forests, and a vast host of other living things that deserve a chance to play out their evolution unhindered by us. Nor am I willing to "risk it" on behalf of other creatures and communities that will suffer the immediate consequences if the risk fails. There is no genuine responsibility (or feedback) when the consequences of risk-taking are not borne by those who make the decisions.

If non-resource arguments are ever to carry their deserved weight, cultural attitudes will have to be changed. Morally backed missionary movements, such as the humane societies, are doing quite well these days, but I have no illusions about the chance of bringing about an ethical change in our Faustian culture without the prompting of some general catastrophe. What sort of change in world view would favor the conservation of non-resources? Nothing less than a rejection of the heroic, Western ethic with its implicit denial of man's biological roots and evolved structure.

Not all problems have acceptable solutions; I feel no constraint to predict one here. On the one hand, conservationists are unlikely to succeed in a general way using only the resource approach; and they will often hurt their own cause. On the other hand, an Eltonian combination of resource and non-resource arguments may also fail, and if it succeeds, as Mumford has implied, it will probably be because of forces that the conservationists neither expected nor controlled (47). But in this event we will at least be ready to take advantage of favorable circumstances—and will have had, whatever the outcome, the small, private satisfaction of having been honest for a while.

References

1. I thank Walt Frey for first calling this notable non-resource to my attention.
2. R. E. Honegger. 1970. *Red Data Book III: Amphibia & Reptilia.* Morges, Switzerland: IUCN.
3. R. Sayre. 1976. Audubon action. *Audubon* 78:138–39.
4. A. Leopold. 1966. *A Sand County Almanac,* pp. 225–26. NY: Oxford Univ. Press.
5. G. A. Lieberman. 1975. The preservation of ecological diversity: A necessity or a luxury? *Naturalist* 26:24–31. J. W. Humke et al. 1975. Final report. The preservation of natural diversity: A survey and recommendations. Prepared for U.S. Dept. of Interior by the Nature Conservancy. Contract No. CX0001-5-0110.
6. R. Strahan. 1975. Status and husbandry of Australian monotremes and marsupials. In *Breeding Endangered Species in Captivity,* ed. R. D. Martin, pp. 171–82. NY: Academic Press.
7. H. H. Iltis, O. L. Loucks, and P. Andrews. 1970. Criteria for an optimum human environment. *Bull. Atomic Sci.* 26:2–6.
8. National Academy of Sciences. 1975. *Underexploited Tropical Plants with Promising Economic Value,* pp. 105–10. Washington, DC: National Research Council, Commission on International Relations.
9. S. Altschul. 1973. *Drugs and Foods from Little-Known Plants.* Cambridge: Harvard Univ. Press.
10. A. Galston. 1975. The water fern–rice connection. *Natural History* 84:10–11.
11. O. H. Frankel. 1970. Genetic conservation in perspective.In *Genetic Resources in Plants—Their Exploration and Conservation,* ed. O. H. Frankel and E. Bennett, pp. 469–89. Philadelphia: Davis.
12. B. Commoner. 1972. *The Closing Circle,* p. 38. NY: Knopf.
13. C. Yarwood. 1970. Man-made plant diseases. *Science* 168:218–20; D. Owen. 1973.

Man in Tropical Africa. NY: Oxford Univ. Press.
14. H. E. Wright, Jr. 1974. Landscape development, forest fires, and wilderness management. *Science* 186:487–95.
15. R. Patrick. 1972. Aquatic communities as indices of pollution. In *Indicators of Environmental Quality,* ed. W. A. Thomas, pp. 93–100. NY: Plenum/Rosetta.
16. C. S. Brandt. 1972. Plants as indicators of air quality. In Thomas, ibid., pp. 101–7.
17. *New York Times,* 24 Sept. 1975, p. 41.
18. B. Bauerle, D. L. Spencer, and W. Wheeler. 1975. The use of snakes as a pollution indicator species. *Copeia* 1975:366–68.
19. J. Hillaby. 1975. Deformed froglets and walking catfish. *New Scientist* 67:32–33. The pH of rain may also be a factor: see F. H. Pough. 1976. Acid precipitation and embryonic mortality of spotted salamanders, *Ambystoma maculatum. Science* 192:68–70.
20. D. W. Ehrenfeld. 1972. *Conserving Life on Earth,* pp. 243–50. NY: Oxford Univ. Press.
21. E. W. Garbisch, P. B. Woller, W. J. Bostian, and R. J. McCallum. 1975. Biotic techniques for shoreline stabilization. In *Estuarine Research II,* ed. L. E. Cronin, pp. 405–26. NY: Academic Press.
22. W. H. Matthews. 1975. Objective and subjective judgements in environmental impact analysis. *Environmental Conservation* 2:121–31.
23. D. Goodman. 1975. The theory of diversity-stability relationships in ecology. *Quart. Rev. Biol.* 50:237–66.
24. R. Margalef. 1963. On certain unifying principles in ecology. *Am. Nat.* 97:357–74.
25. R. H. Whittaker. 1960. Vegetation of the Siskiyou Mountains, Oregon and California. *Ecol. Monogr.* 30:279–338; 1965. Dominance and diversity in land plant communities. *Science* 147:250–60; 1967. Gradient analysis of vegetation. *Biol. Rev.* 42:207–64. An excellent historical summary of the arguments of Gleason, Whittaker, and similarly minded plant ecologists against the organic ecosystem concepts of Clements, Margalef, E. Odum, and others is found in P. Colinvaux. 1973. *Introduction to Ecology,* esp. ch. 40. NY: Wiley.
26. R. M. May. 1973. *Stability and Complexity in Model Ecosystems.* Princeton Univ. Press.
27. A. S. Leopold. 1966. Adaptability of animals to habitat change. In *Future Environments of North America,* ed. F. F. Darling and J. P. Milton, pp. 66–75. Garden City, NY: Natural History Press.
28. L. B. Slobodkin. 1964. The strategy of evolution. *Am. Sci.* 52:342–57.
29. A. H. Westing. 1971. Ecological effects of military defoliation on the forests of South Vietnam. *BioScience* 21:893–98; J. Otterman. 1974. Baring high-albedo soils by overgrazing: A hypothesized desertification mechanism. *Science* 186:531–33; W. E. Ormerod. 1976. Ecological effect of control of African trypanosomiasis. *Science* 191:815–21.
30. L. M. Talbot et al. 1965. The meat production potential of wild animals in Africa. *Commonwealth Agricultural Bureaux*

Technical Publications 16; R. F. Dasmann. 1964. *African Game Ranching.* Oxford: Pergamon.
31. E. O. A. Asibey. 1974. Wildlife as a source of protein in Africa south of the Sahara. *Biol. Cons.* 6:32–39.
32. H. T. P. Hayes. In press. *The Last Place on Earth.* NY: Stein & Day.
33. D. Janzen. 1973. Tropical agroecosystems. *Science* 182:1212–19.
34. J. G. Gosselink, E. P. Odum, and R. M. Pope. 1974. The value of the tidal marsh. Baton Rouge: Louisiana State Univ. Center for Wetland Resources, LSU-SG-74-03.
35. C. W. Clark. 1973. The economics of overexploitation. *Science* 181:630–34; Profit maximization and the extinction of animal species. *Jour. Pol. Economy* 81:950–61.
36. W. Tans. 1974. Priority ranking of biotic natural areas. *Michigan Botanist* 13:31–39.
37. F. R. Gehlbach. 1975. Investigation, evaluation, and priority ranking of natural areas. *Biol. Cons.* 8:79–88.
38. G. Bateson. 1972. *Steps to an Ecology of Mind.* NY: Ballantine.
39. A. Carr. 1964. *Ulendo: Travels of a Naturalist in and out of Africa.* NY: Knopf.
40. A. F. Coimbra-Filho, A. Magnanini, and R. A. Mittermeier. 1975. Vanishing gold: Last chance for Brazil's lion tamarins. *Animal Kingdom,* Dec., pp. 20–26.
41. For an example of this viewpoint, see the critical comments concerning the life-support systems that have been proposed for orbiting space colonies, especially remarks by J. Todd. 1976. *Coevolution Quarterly,* Spring, pp. 20–21, 54–65.
42. C. S. Elton. 1958. *The Ecology of Invasions by Animals and Plants,* pp. 143–45. London: Methuen.
43. C. D. Stone. 1974. *Should Trees Have Standing?* Los Altos, CA: Wm. Kaufmann, Inc. It is my impression that Stone's argument is unlikely to make any significant headway in the courts unless the national value systems that ultimately mold judicial practice undergo a fundamental change.
44. B. Dixon. 1976. Smallpox—Imminent extinction, and an unresolved dilemma. *New Scientist* 69:430–32; but see also P. Razzell. 1976. Smallpox extinction—A note of caution. *New Scientist* 71:35.
45. R. Allen. 1974. Does diversity grow cabbages? *New Scientist* 63:528–29.
46. The scientific origins of this idea are contained in the nineteenth century writings of Babbage and Marsh: C. Babbage. 1838. *The Ninth Bridgewater Treatise,* 2nd ed., ch. 9. London: John Murray. Repr. 1967. London: Cass; G. P. Marsh. 1865. *Man and Nature; or, Physical Geography as Modified by Human Action,* pp. 548–49. NY: Scribner's.
47. L. Mumford. 1956. Prospect. In *Man's Role in Changing the Face of the Earth,* ed. W. L. Thomas, Jr., pp. 1142–43. Chicago Univ. Press.

PART 2 *Global and Local Pollution*

Hinrich L. Bohn
Robert C. Cauthorn

Pollution: The Problem of Misplaced Waste

Inefficiency of resource use and misplacement of spent resources are the physical causes of the pollution phenomenon

Pollution is said to be the unavoidable result of a high material standard of living, of economic, agricultural, and industrial growth, and of the rapid increase in the population. Its abatement is decried as inadequate, expensive, hopeless, and sometimes even unnecessary. The topic is rarely discussed as a general phenomenon except as an inevitable evil of affluent societies, and lack of understanding has contributed to the fear and resignation expressed by many in recent years. Yet pollution can be discussed objectively; economists have done so by describing its results and costs (*1*), but pollution itself is undefined.

We propose to define chemical and physical pollution as matter in a harmful oxidation state or place, or energy in a harmful place. Pollution is a maldistribution of matter and energy among and within the earth's three great media: air, water, and soil. For example, oxygen and carbon as diatomic oxygen and carbon dioxide are useful to organisms, but ozone and carbon monoxide are toxic. Nitrogen and phosphate compounds in soils are beneficial to plants, but in lakes and streams they can be indirectly deleterious to fish. Sulfur compounds are plant nutrients in soils, but are pollutants in the atmosphere. Dust in the atmosphere can be productive

soil. Hot water dumped into a stream can cause thermal pollution but might increase plant growth if applied to soils.

This definition of pollution may be too broad—floods, forest fires, and lightning bolts in this sense are pollution problems—but it may be preferable to one that is too narrow. Also, the definition assumes that the concentration limit beyond which a substance becomes a pollutant is known. Anything in excessive amounts can be a pollutant. In this discussion we shall disregard the enormous problem of defining pollution thresholds (*2*).

Our contention is that pollution is the direct result of inefficiency—waste—in the use of our material and energy resources and of the misplacement of those resources after use. While pollution is not the necessary result of high living standards, urbanization, industrialization, agriculture, or population growth, they have accentuated the maldistribution of matter and energy in our environment. The antithesis of pollution is recycling because it maintains resources in desirable states and reduces the pollution inherent in developing new resources.

The public's attention is understandably drawn to those pollution problems which most directly and immediately threaten life and beauty. Pollution of air and water is the most obvious; pesticide residues, solid wastes, thermal pollution, food contamination, and others are secondary in degree though not in kind. The urgent importance of all these issues is not in doubt, but the discussion seems to have nurtured the implicit assumption that the atmosphere, hydrosphere, and lithosphere are in equal states of distress. The extent of pollution in these media will be compared below.

The atmosphere, hydrosphere, and, especially, the soil are all capable of cleaning up their own pollu-

Hinrich L. Bohn, associate professor of agricultural chemistry in the Department of Soils, Water, and Engineering of the University of Arizona, is interested in waste utilization and the absorption and conversion reactions of pollutants with soils. He received B.S. and M.S. degrees from the University of California and a Ph.D. from Cornell University. He was a research chemist for the Tennessee Valley Authority.
Robert C. Cauthorn, associate professor of economics at the University of Arizona, is primarily concerned with interdisciplinary studies of urban and regional systems. He received his B.S. from Georgia Tech. and Ph.D. from Tulane University. He was a faculty member of the Center for Appalachian Studies of West Virginia University and a private consultant before coming to Arizona.
Addresses: Dr. Bohn, Department of Soils, Water, and Engineering; Dr. Cauthorn, Department of Economics, University of Arizona, Tucson, AZ 85721.

tion; the self-abatement process is basically the same in all three media, but the time required for each to return to an unpolluted state is determined by the interaction of its physical, chemical, and biological properties. These properties, and consequently the capability of pollution abatement, vary greatly among water, air, and soil.

Abatement potential

The abatement potential of pollution in air, water, or soil can be taken as the reciprocal of the time during which substances or energy remain in undesirable chemical or physical states. The duration of the undesirable physical state of particles suspended in air and water depends on the interactions of particle density, flow velocity, turbulence, and other complications of sedimentation phenomena. Such physical pollution *in* soil corresponds to compaction of soil particles by foot and vehicular traffic and to the dispersion, or breakdown, of soil aggregates in "alkali" soil and soil recently flooded by sea water. Physical pollution *by* soil is another name for wind and water erosion.

The elimination of chemical pollution in air, water, or soil is related to the reaction rates, primarily the oxidation rates, of the pollutants. The highest oxidation states of carbon, sulfur, and phosphorus compounds that are stable in air usually have the lowest pollution potential. For example, carbon dioxide is harmless compared to carbon monoxide; sulfate is harmless compared to hydrogen sulfide and sulfur dioxide; phosphate has a lower pollution potential than have elemental phosphorus and the lower phosphorus oxides (3). Elemental phosphorus and its lower oxides are toxic in themselves as well as being sources of phosphate.

Unfortunately, this generalization does not hold as well for nitrogen compounds. Virtually all the soluble species of lower nitrogen oxidation states, except diatomic nitrogen, are somewhat toxic or can lead to water pollution by encouraging algal growth. The highest oxidation state, nitrate, is perhaps the least toxic, but gastrointestinal organisms reduce nitrate to the much more toxic form, nitrite, which interferes with oxygen transfer by hemoglobin. This leads to "blue baby" symptoms and also affects some susceptible human adults, ruminants, and horses.

With the exception of some photochemical reactions in the atmosphere, almost all the reactions of a pollutant reduce its subsequent reactivity and hence its pollutant potential. These reactions are generally functions of the interaction of the pollutant con-

centration, temperature, amounts of water and oxygen available, degree of catalytic activity, surface area, and microbial activity. Catalytic agents, surface area, and microbial activity might be lumped together as "catalysis." The decrease of a pollutant's concentration with time, t, is a function of

$$-\frac{\Delta(\text{pollutant})}{\Delta t} = f(\text{pollutant concentration,}$$

$$T, H_2O, O_2, \text{catalysis})$$

where f also includes a reaction rate parameter of the particular pollutant, T is the temperature, and H_2O and O_2 are moisture and aeration functions. These variables are not strictly independent. Microbial activity, for example, is dependent upon temperature, oxygen content, water content, and available nutrients. This equation is slanted toward oxidation reactions; other pollutant reactions such as adsorption, precipitation, and flocculation of heavy metal ions, for example, are less dependent upon oxygen concentration and microbial activity and more dependent upon pH. For biologically catalyzed reactions, 37°C may be the optimum temperature. Higher temperatures rapidly decrease biological reaction rates unless the organisms are thermophilic.

To quantify the foregoing equation is tempting, but the complexity of nature rules out an early solution. Nevertheless, the equation has direct implications for pollution control. For example, pollutant concentrations in air and water are manipulated by dilution with unpolluted water and increasing the height of smoke stacks in order to reduce the local intensity of pollution. Dilution increases the area polluted and, by reducing the pollutant concentration, reduces the rate of abatement. Dilution, therefore, is hardly a progressive step in pollution control. Likewise, dumping garbage into the depths of the sea, where oxygen is rapidly depleted, is a poor way to oxidize the organic matter.

The ability of air, water, and soil to counteract pollution can be compared in the light of the equation. Note that all of the factors listed are important: the absence of even one seriously reduces the rate of pollution abatement.

The atmosphere

The earth's atmosphere is a highly elastic fluid medium containing, most importantly for this discussion, oxygen, water, and finely divided organic and solid matter. The atmospheric phenomena most pertinent to dispersal or diminution of waste are air movement, temperature, temperature distributions, water content, particulate matter, light intensity, and the volume and frequency of moisture precipitation. Landforms such as mountains, valleys, and bodies of water are also frequently alluded to as factors in air pollution, but they affect pollution indirectly by influencing movement, temperature, water content, and other factors. In addition, air movement and temperature, to name only two, are closely interrelated.

Given multiple interdependencies among the variables, as in the equation, even slight changes in a single atmospheric variable can produce astonishingly large changes in the system as a whole. Dispersal by the atmosphere is therefore unreliable and uncontrollable. But more significantly, the atmosphere is not an effective pollutant reactant medium, or sink. Even oxidation reactions, despite the high oxygen concentration, are slow owing to the lack of microorganisms and adsorptive surfaces, which provide catalysis, and to the possible absence of moisture. The common air pollutant sulfur dioxide, for example, oxidizes in air to form sulfur trioxide and, ultimately, stable sulfuric acid and sulfates. In humid air containing iron and manganese-rich dusts, sulfur dioxide is oxidized at a rate of perhaps one percent per minute. In dry dust-free air, however, the oxidation rate for sulfur dioxide may fall to as low as one percent per hour—one-sixtieth the catalyzed rate.

Some oxidation of pollutant material is accomplished in air by direct photochemical reactions. This phenomenon is not nearly productive enough, however, to compensate for the low rates of chemical oxidation in the atmosphere. Also, photolysis generates some products such as ozone and peroxyacetylnitrates, which are more toxic than the original pollutants.

The hydrosphere

Throughout much of the world, water, like air, appears to be superabundant and to possess an almost limitless capacity to absorb wastes. We have learned to our dismay, however, that this appearance is far removed from reality; waste in water may be out of sight but it cannot be safely put out of mind.

The hydrosphere oxidizes wastes under the same rules that apply to air, but in water the temperature and lack of oxygen and catalysis often limit the reaction rate. In still water, carbon compounds can accumulate at even a few cm depth because of the slow diffusion of oxygen. Water takes up oxygen at its air interface, but oxygen's solubility in water is

low, and its diffusion rate in water is $1/10,000$ that in air. The initial oxidation of substances in water can quickly deplete the concentration of dissolved oxygen and prevent further oxidation. As a comparison of air and water as oxidation media, sulfite (the aqueous state of SO_2) persists for hours even in flowing streams where oxygen exchange is rapid. The oxidation of sulfur dioxide to sulfuric acid is hardly faster in water than in air. In addition, because the pH-buffering capacity of natural water is almost nil, the acidity of the sulfuric acid is toxic.

In shallow water, organic matter deposits form swamps and marshes that support a rich plant and animal life and ultimately convert to relatively stable organic matter such as humus and peat. Oxygen production by algal photosynthesis and oxygen and carbon dioxide transfer between water and air are sufficient to supply oxygen for aquatic animal life. At depths of a few meters, however, the more limited oxygen diffusion reduces oxidation and causes greater accumulation of more reactive organic matter. Deep waters, such as Lake Erie, the Hudson River, and ocean dumping sites, have too little oxygen to absorb the wastes they receive and thus serve mainly as pollutant reservoirs rather than disposal sites. Organic life is limited to anaerobic and marginally aerobic species that can utilize low oxygen concentrations.

Over all, the hydrosphere has only a limited capacity to oxidize pollutants. Most of the earth's water is in the ocean depths and contains insufficient oxygen to allow pollutant oxidation. Even those portions of the hydrosphere—swamps, shallow lakes, and streams—which could conceivably oxidize large amounts of wastes are sometimes so misused that their capacity is actually declining. This is due not only to excessively high pollution rates but also to other changes, the effects of which are less well recognized: surface films of chemical wastes hinder gas exchange with the air and curtail microbial activity; lake and river "development" reduces oxidation capacity through deepening, thus increasing flow rates, eliminating water vegetation, and reducing turbulence.

The soil

At the outset, soil pollution may be placed in sharp contrast to that of the other two media. Some soils have been contaminated by arsenic, heavy metals, and hydrocarbons; mining and lumbering have caused soil disruption and erosion; thoughtless and short-sighted cultivation and irrigation have caused considerable damage through erosion and salt accumulation. The degree of soil pollution, however, is minute compared to air and water pollution and to the total pollution abatement capacity of the earth's soils.

The soil does not suffer from the lack of moisture and catalysis affecting the atmosphere or from limiting oxygen and surface area, as in the hydrosphere. Unlike air, the relative humidity of the soil atmosphere almost always exceeds 98%. Unlike water, soil porosity permits rapid oxygen diffusion; soil is 40–50% pore space which is occupied by air and water. About half this space is filled with water when a wet soil drains freely; the remaining 20–25% of the soil's bulk volume is air that has ready access to the atmosphere.

In addition to abundant water and oxygen, the soil has a large area of reactive surface and an enormous and vigorous microbial population. Each gram of soil has a surface area of ten or more square meters and contains, as a very low estimate, one million microorganisms. This is equivalent to 1,000 square miles of surface and 10^{15} microorganisms per acre-foot of soil. The microbial population increases by many factors of ten under conditions favorable to its growth, such as the addition of organic wastes.

The soil has an acid-buffering capacity that neutralizes the acids from, for example, the oxidation of sulfide in mining wastes and from the absorption and oxidation of sulfur dioxide from the atmosphere. The short-term capacity ranges from a ton or so, expressed in terms of sulfuric acid, per acre-foot in humid regions to several hundred tons per acre-foot in arid regions (4, 5, 6, 7). The long-term capacity is even greater. Using again the example of sulfur dioxide, once in contact with the soil it is absorbed from air and oxidized to sulfate within seconds (7). In comparison, sulfur dioxide oxidation requires hours in water and air. The sulfuric acid produced by the oxidation is neutralized by the soil's bases at the site of soil absorption, whereas in the air and water the sulfuric acid is carried on to pollute further.

The primary interest in the ability of soil, water, and air to counter pollution is in their capacity to remove organic wastes. In tropical regions, the natural rate of organic matter decomposition in soils is as much as 8 tons per acre annually, with slower rates prevailing in colder and drier climates (8). These rates, however, are only the natural rates of organic matter oxidation and are limited by the rates of organic matter added to the soil; the potential rates are much greater. For example, 14 tons of manure per acre have been added annually for over a century to the cultivated soils of the Broadbalk plots of the Rothamsted Experiment Station in England. The soil organic matter content has been constant for more than 70 years and is less than the organic matter content of the adjacent virgin soils (9). Since the organic matter production there is perhaps 5 tons per acre, the soil's continuous capacity to remove completely organic matter is more than 3 to 4 times its capacity to produce it. Should the addition rate exceed the oxidation rate, the more reactive, noxious components are acted upon first, and the remainder accumulates as nontoxic soil organic matter, humus. In an infertile California soil, each increment of dried sewage sludge, added at rates up to 80 tons per acre, gave an increased plant yield (10). Even at the high rate, no toxicity was found.

Nitrogen and phosphate pollutants are also removed by interaction with soils, phosphate compounds being strongly adsorbed by all but the sandiest soils. Movement of phosphate in aqueous solutions more than a few centimeters through soils is unusual. Large amounts of nitrogen compounds are removed by soils from sewage and solid organic wastes. The mechanisms are not fully understood but include plant and microbial absorption of nitrogen and denitrification (conversion to N_2 and some N_2O) of a significant fraction of the nitrogen in organic matter (11).

In the central United States, the pollution abatement capacity of the soil is estimated to require only 4 acres per thousand people for *all* solid and liquid wastes, both municipal and industrial (12). Very conservative estimates place the land requirement at 100 acres per thousand population (13).

These soils need not be taken from their present uses when used also for waste disposal. Wildlife sanctuaries, watersheds, groundwater-recharging basins, green belts, fire breaks, and possibly all agricultural pursuits except truck crops and animal feedlots are compatible with waste disposal (13, 14, 15). The products of waste absorption and transformation remain localized in the soil so that they can be continually monitored. With judicious management, soils could be used continuously for waste disposal. Today, after filling is completed, urban landfills are being used extensively for parks and industrial and home sites. The time required for settling, as all the organic matter oxidizes, often determines the use to which the land is put. Long before the oxidation is complete, however, these areas could be reused as landfills; the noxious properties of the wastes disappear before the waste totally oxidizes. Urban and agricultural wastes are mostly soil-derived substances that are pollutants in air and water but are the chemical elements which are in short supply in soils. The soil not only "covers up" wastes—in itself an important function—but also transforms pollutants and returns them to the food chain.

At the risk of making the soil appear to be the pollution panacea, we must add that the soil can even minimize the hazards of thermal pollution. Using hot water for heating soils is already under study and holds promise of increasing plant growth, lengthening the growing season, and increasing yields. The heat is lost mostly by evaporation of water from the soil as well as by convection and radiation. Heating the soil will cause some ecological change, but compared to thermal pollution of water, the change is local and can be much more easily measured, controlled, and modified. Up to a soil temperature of 37°C (98°F), the change would probably be beneficial to the growth of plants and soil microorganisms. Temperatures higher than 37°C sharply curtail the growth of many organisms.

Our handling of wastes has been unimaginative and expensive. We have been wrong in considering wastes useless, rather than as matter and energy in a less useful form and place. Man's role has been to shift matter and energy from the lithosphere to the hydrosphere and atmosphere. His insistence upon removing wastes in the shortest possible time has also played a part in this mismanagement: the fluid media rapidly flush away waste material but do not eliminate it, thereby making one man's pollution another man's problem. Those pollutants which in water and air give rise to serious and costly problems are disposed of quickly in the soil and converted into plant nutrients with little or no intervention by man. Eutrophication of the soil rather than water enhances the production of food and the type of environment which we cherish. In summary, compared to air and water, the soil has a vastly greater potential for waste disposal and transformation. It has been absorbing and recycling nature's wastes for some three and one-half billion years on earth without impairment of its functions, and it still has the capacity to absorb far more material than it can produce or that is added to it.

References

1. Solow, Robert M. 1971. The economist's approach to pollution and its control. *Science* 173:498–502.

2. Stokinger, H. E. 1971. Sanity in research and evaluation of environmental health. *Science* 174:662–65.

3. Bohn, H. L., G. V. Johnson, and J. H. Cliff. 1970. Detoxification of white phosphorus in soil. *Journal of Agricultural and Food Chemistry* 18:1172–73.

4. Faller, N., and K. Herwig. 1969/70. Untersuchungen über die SO₂-oxydation im verschiedenen Böden. *Geoderma* 3:45–54.

5. Seim, E. C. 1970. Sulfur dioxide adsorption by soil. Unpublished Ph.D. dissertation, University of Minnesota.

6. Abeles, F. B., L. E. Craker, L. E. Forrence, and G. R. Leather. 1971. Fate of air pollutants: removal of ethylene, sulfur dioxide, and nitrogen dioxide by soil. *Science* 173:914–16.

7. Bohn, H. L., and G. Slawson, Jr. 1972. SO₂ absorption capacities of calcareous soils. Unpublished ms.

8. Bolin, Bert. 1970. The carbon cycle. *Scientific American* 223(3):124–32.

9. Russell, Sir E. John. 1912. *Soil Conditions and Plant Growth* (9th edition, E. Walter Russell, ed.) N.Y.: John Wiley and Sons, 1961.

10. Vlamis, J., and D. E. Williams. 1971. Utilization of municipal organic wastes as agricultural fertilizers. *California Agriculture* 25(7):7–10.

11. Schmehl, William. Colorado State University, Fort Collins. Personal communication.

12. *Chemical and Engineering News.* March 23, 1970, p. 44.

13. Sheaffer, John R. Reviving the Great Lakes. *Saturday Review,* Nov. 7, 1970, pp. 62–65.

14. Kardos, L. T. 1967. Waste water renovation by the land—a living filter. In *Agriculture and the Quality of our Environment,* N. C. Brady, ed. Washington, D.C.: Amer. Assoc. Advancement Sci. Publ. 85, pp. 241–250.

15. Wilson, C. W., and F. E. Beckett, eds. 1970. *Municipal Sewage Effluent for Irrigation.* Symposium published by the Louisiana Tech Alumni Foundation, 169 pp.

"You win a little and you lose a little. Yesterday the air didn't look as good, but it smelled better."

Morris A. Wessel
Anthony Dominski

Our Children's Daily Lead

Lead poisoning is a continuing, underestimated, and preventable danger

Lead is one of the most dangerous and insidious metallic poisons known to man. All forms of lead are potentially toxic, but lead poisoning most commonly occurs after the inhalation of lead fumes or finely divided lead dusts. Lead poisoning also follows the ingestion of food or drink contaminated with lead. The risk of poisoning increases with decrease in particle size or increase in the rate of solution of the lead compound encountered. Lead is a cumulative poison in every sense of the word.

Marshall Clinton (1950)

Lead poisoning is a preventable disease, yet each year 200 children die of this condition; 12,000 to 16,000 are treated and survive, but at least one quarter of these suffer permanent injury to the nervous system. Recent studies suggest that children with moderate increase in body burden of lead, although clinically asymptomatic, experience serious interference with important body processes. If one includes this asymptomatic group, at least 400,000 children in the United States suffer annually from deleterious effects of lead (Novick, unpubl. 1971).

Morris Wessel is Clinical Professor of Pediatrics at the Yale University School of Medicine and practices in New Haven. Dr. Wessel, who received his M.D. from Yale, is consulting pediatrician to the Celentano Pre-School Handicapped Program of the New Haven Board of Education and to the Clifford Beers Child Guidance Clinic. He is also a member of the Advisory Commission on Lead Poisoning of the City of New Haven.
Anthony Dominski, Associate Adjunct Professor of Ecology at Pratt Institute School of Architecture, is an ecologist who does interdisciplinary work with architects and planners. He received his Ph.D. in ecology from the Yale School of Forestry and Environmental Studies. His specialty is the development of ecological criteria for town planning and zoning. Address for Dr. Wessel: 878 Howard Ave., New Haven, CT 06519.

The etiology of the disease is clear. Lead poisoning occurs when a human being absorbs, through the air he breathes or the food or other material he ingests, substantially more lead than his body can excrete. This highly toxic substance flows from the gastrointestinal and respiratory tracts into the blood stream and accumulates in body tissues, particularly the kidneys, bones, and nervous system. The fetus, infant, and child are particularly vulnerable. Once absorbed, lead remains in the body for months or years.

Symptomatic lead poisoning is the culmination of a continuum of biological effects that accompany an increasing body lead burden. An early detectable adverse effect is interference with the production of hemoglobin; another early sign is interference with kidney function. Lead also has serious effects on the nervous system. Mild neurologic disability occurs with moderate elevations, while severe, acute encephalopathy is the end result of higher accumulation of lead in the body.

The toxic effect of lead has been known since ancient times. Nicander, a Greek poet and physician living before the Christian Era, recognized the disease and the cause. Gilfillan (1965) suggests that chronic lead poisoning among the Romans in the first and second centuries B.C. was introduced through water collected from troughs and cisterns lined with lead and through wine, grape syrup, and preserved fruits prepared in lead-lined earthenware containers. One of the factors in the decline of the Roman Empire, Gilfillan believes, may have been a decrease in reproductive capacity due to the toxic effects of lead, particularly after 150

B.C. when rules forbidding wives and mistresses to drink wine were relaxed.

George Baker, physician to the British Royal Household in the eighteenth century, recognized that a widespread epidemic of colic was due to lead contamination from the apparatus used in making cider (Major 1932). Condemned by clergy, farmers, mill owners, and professionals, he nevertheless convinced the cider producers to stop using lead pipes, and the disease disappeared. His recommendation to remove the lead pipes was suggested by correspondence with Benjamin Franklin, who had mentioned that complaints of "dry gripes" from imbibers of rum stored in lead-lined containers had resulted in prohibition of the use of lead in equipment for making alcoholic beverages in New England.

Benjamin Franklin was well aware of the toxic effects of lead, and his scientific mind led him to accumulate considerable knowledge about lead poisoning. He noted that various trades were more prone than others to this condition, recognizing that his own craft—printing—was one of the greatest culprits because of its use of lead type. Franklin had himself noted obscure pain in his hands after heating type in front of the fire, and wondered whether this discomfort might be due to the toxicity of lead (McCord 1953).

Gene V. Ball (1971), a professor of medicine at the University of Alabama, has suggested that an epidemic of gout among the British gentry in the eighteenth and nineteenth centuries resulted from drinking prodigious amounts of wine contaminated with lead. Ball also observed in

1968 that 37 of 43 patients in Appalachia with gout also suffered from chronic lead poisoning. Most of the patients lived in rural areas and produced their own "moonshine" alcohol in discarded automobile radiators and other lead-lined containers, in which contamination of the beverages was inevitable. Ball concluded that his Appalachian patients and the British gentry had the same disease—saturnine gout, secondary to the effect of chronic lead intoxication on the kidneys (see Ball 1969). The damaged tubules cause retention of uric acid, which many clinicians believe is responsible for gout.

The realization early in this century that vast numbers of American factory workers were suffering from symptomatic lead poisoning was due to the single-handed efforts of Alice Hamilton. This dedicated and determined physician, born into a patrician family that placed high priority on duty to mankind, was the first American doctor to study industrial hazards and to insist that employers bore the responsibility for the health of workers. She began her crusade in 1910, literally marching from factory to factory, sharing her observations with management officials and plant owners with such vigorous determination that they did indeed begin to improve working conditions (Grant 1967).

Hamilton's astute observations on the effects of chronic lead intoxication in her 1925 classic, *Industrial Poisons in the United States,* indicate the wide spectrum of symptomatology associated with this condition. She included anemia (secondary to interference with red blood cell function), loss of appetite, abdominal colic, constipation, abnormalities in renal excretion, jaundice due to liver damage, localized palsy (as demonstrated in the "wrist drop" frequently observed among factory workers and painters exposed to high lead concentrations), irritability, drowsiness, stupor, and coma. She also noted the high frequency of abortions and stillbirths and the increased morbidity and mortality among infants born in families where the adults were exposed to lead. She ascribed this to the damaging effect of lead on both male and female germ cells, as well as to the direct effect of the lead that crossed the placenta and continually bathed the fetus during gestation.

Hamilton's firm conviction that airborne lead was of great importance in the etiology of chronic lead poisoning has received too little attention. Only in the past decade, after 20 years of focusing on the ingestion of paint chips as the primary source of lead poisoning, has the importance of airborne lead begun to receive appropriate recognition by health officials, clinicians, and legislators. Since 1923, when tetraethyl lead was introduced as a gasoline additive, the amount of lead disseminated into the atmosphere has steadily increased. Present estimates are that approximately one kilogram per person is released into the atmosphere annually in the United States (Commoner 1971). Clair Patterson, a geochemist, emphasized in 1965 that industrialization and modern technological development have resulted in increasing contamination of the ecosystem. He challenged the belief that lead levels of "25 micrograms per 100 cc of blood," though "typical," are safe or harmless. His concerns were well founded and were voiced at the same time by other ecologists and clinicians.

The clinical disease

The nonspecificity of the symptoms makes it difficult to diagnose lead poisoning, particularly in its early phases in childhood when complaints such as stomachache, weakness, irritability, and fatigue may be blamed on teething, viral infections, birth of a sibling, or other stresses. When marked elevation of the body lead burden persists, headache, loss of appetite, pallor, drowsiness, irritability, vomiting, cramps, clumsiness, convulsions, or stupor occur. When enough lead accumulates in the body, softening of cerebral tissues and massive accumulation of fluid in the brain can bring death from acute encephalopathy.

A concentration of 80 or more μg of lead per 100 cc of blood is always associated with demonstrable metabolic toxicity, and the development of acute and fatal lead intoxication and encephalitis is a distinct likelihood. A lead concentration of 60 or more $\mu g/100$ cc of blood, regardless of whether overt symptoms are present, demands immediate chelating treatment to eliminate the lead from the body. A physician cannot wait for "further symptoms" to appear, for by

the time a child shows signs of clinical illness, permanent damage may have taken place. The Center for Disease Control of the Department of Health, Education and Welfare (1975) advises physicians that inner-city children between the ages of one and five should be considered high-risk candidates for undue lead absorption (the first phase of lead poisoning), particularly if they live in an old house or close to a busy highway, or have the habit of pica (mouthing unusual items such as dirt and paint chips). It recommends annual testing of blood lead levels in order to identify children in the early stage of the disease, before clinical symptoms are observable.

Two recent statements from the Center for Disease Control indicate official recognition of the magnitude of the lead-poisoning epidemic among American children. The revised 1975 statement suggests that $30 \mu g/100$ cc of blood be considered the level at which the child is in potential danger of developing clinical lead poisoning (a revision of the U.S. Surgeon General's 1970 recommendation that 40 $\mu g/100$ cc of blood be the cut-off point) and that the elevation of the free erythrocyte protoporphyrin (a by-product of lead-induced interference with enzyme systems involved in the production of hemoglobin) be considered of diagnostic importance (Piomelli et al. 1973).

A large body of evidence demonstrates that relatively low lead concentrations interfere with many enzyme processes vital to human body functions, particularly in childhood. How much inhibition can be tolerated without harm to the individual is uncertain, but the possibility of serious damage as a result of interference with many enzymatic functions cannot be dismissed.

Neurologic symptoms of lead poisoning have been recognized since antiquity. Histologic changes in peripheral nerves and brain tissue, localized weakness and paralysis, as well as clinical encephalitis accompanied by the destruction of brain tissue are common signs of severe lead intoxication. The subtle neurologic effects of chronic low-grade poisoning concern many clinicians, educators, psychologists, and public health workers, particularly because of a possible relationship to the 10% or more children suffering from learning disabilities—pupils who have difficulty progressing educationally at a rate commensurate with their level of intelligence.

Numerous studies suggest that a current or past history of moderate elevations of blood lead (40–70 μg/100 cc) is an important factor in producing significant impairment in cognitive, verbal, perceptual, and fine motor skills when compared to a control group with levels of below 30 μg/100 cc (Perino and Erphart 1974; Landrigan et al. 1975). Another approach, which uses the lead concentration in discarded deciduous teeth as an indicator of past exposure, reveals that children with the highest lead concentrations in their teeth have deficits in cognitive, perceptual, and behavioral performance when compared with a control group with lowest lead concentrations in deciduous teeth (de la Burde and Choate 1975). These data suggest that blood lead concentrations previously considered "normal" may in fact significantly impair brain function.

Experimental data

There are numerous reports of experiments on the deleterious effects of minimal and moderate concentrations of lead, but in this article we can present only a few studies that indicate the methods and results of interest to clinicians and public health officials. (The interested reader is referred to the summary volume by Waldron and Stofen, 1964, which reviews more than 1,000 papers.)

Hernberg and Nikkanen (1970) studied the effects of lead in vitro in concentrations of 5 to 30 μg/100 cc of blood. They noted inhibition of erythrocyte delta-aminolevulinic acid dehydrogenase at even the lowest lead level; the extent of interference with this enzyme, which is vital for hemoglobin synthesis, increased proportionally to the lead concentration. These investigators believe that there is no lead level at which there is a complete absence of inhibitory effect. Their conclusions are substantiated by in vitro and in vivo studies reviewed in detail by Chisholm and his co-workers (1975). Although "reserve enzyme capacity" appears to compensate at low lead levels for this detrimental effect, significant inhibition definitely occurs

at concentrations above 30 μg/100 cc of blood, particularly in women of child-bearing age, fetuses, infants, and young children. Recent in vitro studies by Hernberg and his colleagues (1970) demonstrate the deleterious effects of low lead levels on red blood cells, including alterations of mechanical fragility and osmotic resistance, increased glucose consumption, and loss of potassium.

Darrow and Schroeder (unpubl. 1973) compared the sensitivity of the mouse fetus to noxious stimuli with the sensitivity of the mature animal. Mice who were exposed to lead *in utero* by feeding the mother water contaminated with lead (in a concentration of 25 ppm, an amount which results in no measurable signs of toxicity in the mother or other adult mice) were found to have elevated DNA and protein in the brain, suggesting a proliferation of fewer brain cells comparable to that reported in lead encephalopathy and produced in experimental encephalopathy in animals.

Silbergeld and Goldberg (1974) have found that infant mice who ingested lead with their mother's milk or their drinking water demonstrated hyperactivity levels twice as high as the level of the control group. The hyperactivity in the mice with elevated lead concentrations decreased markedly with the administration of methylphenidate (Ritalin) and amphetamines (Dexedrine), and increased with the administration of phenobarbital. This pharmacologic response is comparable to that observed in children diagnosed as suffering from "minimal brain dysfunction." The authors advance the possibility that the hyperactivity of both the mice and the children may be a result of chronic low level lead intoxication in infancy. Carson and his co-workers (1974) reported in a similar study that the visual discrimination of young sheep is reduced if their mother was subjected to lead levels of 34 μg/100 cc of blood during gestation. The authors suggest that evaluations of children with visual motor deficits consider the possibility of lead toxicity.

An elevated body lead burden also decreases the resistance of experimental animals to infections and to effects of bacterial endotoxins. Selye and his colleagues (1966) reported

that a single injection of lead acetate at a dose which normally produces no other detectable disturbance causes a rat to become 100,000 times more sensitive to an intravenous administration of *E. coli* endotoxins. Hemphill and his co-workers (1971) found that daily injections of lead acetate reduced the ability of mice to survive a *Salmonella typhimurium* infection. This decreased resistance is believed to result when lead binds with the antibodies or interferes with the phagocytic activity of white blood cells, and, as Hemphill goes on to point out, we must consider the possibility that exposure to lead may similarly decrease the immune responses of humans and other animals.

We need to consider carefully a child's daily permissible lead intake, for when an excess of this toxic substance is absorbed, which cannot be eliminated, cumulative poisoning results. A special HEW Committee concluded in 1970 that a child's intake of lead from all sources must not exceed 300 μg a day (King 1971). This ceiling, however, assumed a fairly low rate of lead absorption of 10%, whereas studies by Alexander and his colleagues (1973) have shown that the absorption rate in the gastrointestinal tract of infants and children is actually closer to 50%. Barltrop (1973), Darrow and Schroeder (unpubl. 1973), and Mahaffey (1977) indicate that the rate of absorption of inhaled and ingested lead in infants and children is higher than that assumed by the HEW Committee. They suggest that a lower intake of lead is necessary to prevent undue absorption, stating that 150 μg per day ought to be the maximum. If a child's level of lead concentration exceeds 30 μg/100 cc of blood, the concentration is likely soon to become even higher because of the cumulative effects of continual exposure. Sachs (quoted in Lin-Fu 1972) studied children in Chicago who had concentrations in the "moderate" range (40 μg/100 cc of blood): a few months later 40% of the children were observed to have significantly higher levels.

Ingestion and inhalation of lead

The oral route is an important pathway by which lead enters the body, particularly in infants and young children, who handle every item within reach and transfer many toys and other objects to the mouth. The habit of pica, often present in children with lead intoxication, is only an intensification and prolongation of this normal infant behavior. Unfortunately, the habit appears frequently in inner-city children who live in old houses with layers of peeling lead paint within easy reach or in areas where lead fallout is excessive.

The Lead Poisoning Prevention Act passed by Congress in 1971 limited the acceptable lead concentration in residential paint to 1%; in 1977 this legislation was amended to reduce the acceptable level to 0.06%. Nevertheless, we must still contend with interior woodwork, painted plaster, and wallpapers in houses built prior to 1940: a tiny flake of paint from these sources may contain as much as 100 mg of lead, and ingesting only a few provides 30 times the daily permissible intake.

Another important source of ingested lead is the dust falling from walls covered with lead paint. Hardy (1971) reports that dirt near a barn in rural Massachusetts contained a lead concentration of 2,000 ppm, while dirt only 7 meters away had a concentration of less than one-tenth as much. Sayre and his co-workers (1974) measured the lead content of indoor household surfaces in Rochester and found that the dust in old houses contained four times as much lead as did the dust in new houses.

Many common household items often contain surprising quantities of lead. Brightly colored magazine pages may have as much as 2,800 ppm, and daily ingestion of a 22-cm^2 piece of a page can result in an intake of 280 μg from this source alone. Printed food wrappers (lead concentrations of 8–10,000 ppm) and handles of kitchen utensils (0–97,000 ppm) are often sources of lead for the toddler who sits on the floor putting one item after another into his mouth (Hankin 1972; Hankin et al. 1973, 1974, 1976). Acid foods and beverages can dissolve the lead in improperly glazed earthenware pottery and have been responsible for fatal and nonfatal cases of human lead poisoning (Klein et al. 1970).

Significant amounts of lead are absorbed into the body with the air we breathe. Patterson (1965) has suggested that the average body burden of lead among children and adults in the United States is 100 times greater than the "natural burden" and that the existing rates of lead absorption are 30 times the levels in preindustrial society. He warned that the lead concentration in the atmosphere would become increasingly dangerous to human health unless steps were taken to eliminate factory and automotive emissions of the metal. Analysis of ice layers in the interior of Greenland reveals that there is 400 times more lead in layers deposited in 1965 than in layers dating back to 800 B.C. It is interesting that the ice deposited in 1750 (the beginning of the Industrial Revolution) has a lead concentration 25 times the natural level; during the second half of the eighteenth century this concentration tripled, and from 1945 to 1965 it tripled again. Thus even on an island far removed from industrial society the lead concentration on the ground is increased by lead discharged into the atmosphere elsewhere in the world (NAS 1972).

Although factories contribute to lead in the air, studies by the Bureau of Air Pollution of the U.S. Environmental Protection Agency (EPA) indicate that of the 165,880 metric tonnes of lead released into the air in the United States in 1968, 162,900 tonnes, or 98%, was emitted through the exhaust pipes of automotive engines. Not only do automobiles release more lead into the atmosphere than any other source, but because most of the particles discharged from combustion engines are microscopic they are readily absorbed into the body through the respiratory and gastrointestinal system (NAS 1972).

Epidemiological studies of children and adults living in urban areas reveal that the amount of lead in the body is directly proportional to the amount of lead in the air. Federal health officials reported that between 10 and 50% of urban children carry a chronic body lead burden in excess of 40 μg/100 cc of blood—the level designated safe by the Surgeon General's 1970 recommendation (EPA 1973). With the newly established "safe level" of 30 μg/100 cc, the estimated percentage of children with a serious risk of lead poisoning is far higher. The closer one lives to factories emitting lead or to heavily traveled highways, the higher the total body burden of lead. A recent study (Osborne et al. 1976) reported that a pregnant woman living in an old house near a street with a daily traffic flow of more than 10,000 cars had a lead concentration of 37 μg/100 cc of blood and that the concentration in the umbilical cord at birth was 44 μg/100 cc—which suggests that infants of families living near highways can suffer from increased lead concentration from the moment of conception. (See also Darrow and Schroeder, unpubl. 1973; Cohen et al. 1973; Needleman 1973; Chow 1973.)

The EPA, recognizing that the inhalation and ingestion of lead from fallout is a source of chronic lead poisoning, issued a statement in 1972 that "human blood levels begin to rise appreciably with exposure to airborne lead concentrations in excess of two micrograms per cubic meter of air." The California Air Resources Board established 1.5 μg/m^3 as the top level of acceptability, and the World Health Organization set the acceptable level at 2 μg/m^3 (Chow 1973). Despite these recommendations, millions of children are constantly exposed to concentrations of lead far above the established safety levels. In 1970, the daily average concentration of atmospheric lead on 45th Street in New York City was found to be 7.5 μg/m^3, with higher levels of 9.3 μg/m^3 at peak traffic flow. In Los Angeles the average lead concentration in air samples obtained near the freeway was found to be 3.6 μg/m^3, with levels at peak hours as high as 71.3 μg/m^3 (NAS 1972).

Clinical studies indicate that in adults an increased air lead concentration of 1 μm/m^3 results in an increased blood lead concentration of 1.2 μg/100 cc. In children, however, the same increase in ambient air concentration increases the level in the blood to 3.2 μg/100 cc. The careful "before and after" studies by Angle and McIntyre (in press), following the passage of a local Clean Air Act in Omaha, Nebraska, produced important results. Their data reveal a marked decrease in the lead concentration in air and dust-fall in the five-year period following the institution of limits on factory emissions. This reduction was accompanied by a parallel decrease in blood lead concentrations in a group of 10- to 13-year-old children—from an average of 25 μg/100 cc to 16 μg/100 cc.

Reducing the risks

The forces in our society that prevent elimination of lead poisoning are complex. The EPA, in line with its responsibility to reduce the incidence of this disease, issued in 1973 a set of regulations intended to decrease over a period of years the permissible amount of lead in gasoline; however, automobile manufacturers and gasoline producers challenged in the courts the EPA's right to carry out this plan. Although the U.S. Supreme Court upheld the authority of the EPA to regulate lead in gasoline, progress in decreasing the levels of atmospheric lead is disappointingly slow, and most of the gasoline used in the United States still contains large amounts of lead.

Lead poisoning is only one of the instances of society's failure to protect human beings. Evidence of multiple, hidden effects of slow poisoning challenges current concepts of "safe limits" of toxic substances in the environment. Apparently, these limits are set and environmental regulations are administered in the belief that subclinical poisoning is not serious. This approach fails to take into account the fact that there can be great harm to vast numbers of children and adults long before obvious clinical symptoms appear. The only way to avoid disastrous consequences is to revise our technological practices to fit the biological needs of human beings by drastically limiting the production and release of toxic substances. As René Dubos stated almost ten years ago, "The problem [of lead poisoning] is so well defined, so neatly packaged, with both causes and cures known, that if we don't eliminate this social crime, our society deserves all the disasters that have been forecast for it" (Oberle 1969).

References

Alexander, F. A., H. Delves, and B. Clayton. 1973. The uptake and excretion by children of lead and other contaminants. In *Proceedings of International Symposium on Environmental Health Aspects of Lead* (Oct. 1972). Amsterdam, Luxembourg: Commission of European Communities.

Angle, C., and M. McIntyre. In press. Environmental controls and the decline of blood lead. *Pediatrics.*

Ball, G. 1969. Pathogenesis of hyperuremia in saturnine gout. *New Eng. J. of Med.* 280: 1199–1202.

Ball, G. 1971. Two epidemics of gout. *Bull. Hist. Med.* 45:401–08.

Barltrop, D. 1973. Source and significance of environmental lead for children. In *Proceedings of International Symposium on Environmental Health Aspects of Lead* (Oct. 1972). Amsterdam, Luxembourg: Commission of European Communities.

Carson, T., G. VanGelder, G. Karas, and W. Buck. 1974. Development of behavioral tests for the assessment of neurologic effects of lead in sheep. *Environ. Health Perspectives,* Experimental Issue No. 7:233–37.

Center for Disease Control. 1975. Increased lead absorption and lead poisoning in young children. *J. Pediatrics* 87:824–30.

Chisholm, J., M. Barrett, and E. Mellito. 1975. Dose effective and dose responsibilities in relationships for lead in children. *J. Pediatrics* 87:1152–60.

Chow, T. J. 1973. Our daily lead. *Chemistry in Britain* 9:258–63.

Clinton, M. 1950. The intoxications. In *Principles of Internal Medicine,* ed. T. Harrison, p. 751. Blakiston.

Cohen, C., G. Bowers, and M. Lepow. 1973. Epidemiology of lead poisoning: A comparison between urban and rural children. *J.A.M.A.* 226:1430–33.

Commoner, B. 1971. *The Closing Circle,* p. 74. Knopf.

Darrow, D., and H. Schroeder. Childhood exposure to environmental lead. Presented 29 Aug. 1973, American Chemical Society.

de la Burde, B., and M. S. Choate. 1975. Early asymptomatic lead exposure and development at school age. *J. Pediatrics* 87:638–41.

EPA. 1973. *EPA's Position on the Health Implications of Airborne Lead.* Washington, DC: U.S. Environmental Protection Agency.

Gilfillan, S. C. 1965. Lead poisoning and the fall of Rome. *J. Occup. Med.* 7:53–60.

Grant, M. 1967. *Alice Hamilton.* Abelard Schuman.

Hamilton, A. 1925. *Industrial Poisons in the United States.* Macmillan.

Hankin, L. 1972. Lead poisoning: A disease of our time. *J. Milk and Food Technology* 35:86–97.

———, G. Heichel, and D. Botsford. 1973. Lead poisoning from colored printing inks. *Clin. Pediatrics* 12:664–68.

———, G. Heichel, and D. Botsford. 1974. Lead on wrappers of specialty foods. *Clin. Pediatrics* 13:1064–65.

———, G. Heichel, and D. Botsford. 1976. Lead on painted handles of kitchen utensils. *Clin. Pediatrics* 15:635–36.

Hardy, H. 1971. Lead as an environmental poison. *Clin. Pharmacol. Therapy* 12: 982–87.

Hemphill, F., M. Kaeberle, and W. B. Buck. 1971. Lead suppression of mouse resistance to *Salmonella typhimurium. Science* 172: 1031–32.

Hernberg, S., and J. Nikkanen. 1970. Enzyme inhibition by lead under normal urban conditions. *Lancet* 1:63–64.

Hernberg, S., J. Nikkanen, G. Mellin, and H. Lilius. 1970. Delta-aminolevulinic acid dehydrase as a measure of lead exposure. *Arch. Environ. Health* 21:140–45.

King, B. 1971. Maximum daily intake of lead without excessive body lead burden in children. *Am. J. Diseases in Children* 122: 337–40.

Klein, M., R. Namer, E. Harper, and R. Corbin. 1970. Earthware containers as a source of fatal lead poisoning. Case study and public health considerations. *New Eng. J. Med.* 283:669–71.

Landrigan, P. J., R. W. Baloh, W. F. Barthol, R. H. Whitworth, N. W. Staehling, and B. F. Rosenbloom. 1975. Neuropsychological dysfunction in children with chronic low-lead level lead absorption. *Lancet* 1:708–12.

Lin-Fu, J. 1972. Undue absorption of lead among children: A new look at an old problem. *New Eng. J. Med.* 286:702–10.

McCord, C. D. 1953. Lead poisoning in early America: Benjamin Franklin and lead poisoning. *Indus. Med. Surg.* 72:393–99.

Mahaffey, K. R. 1977. Relation between quantities of lead ingested and health effects of lead in humans. *Pediatrics* 59:448–54.

Major, R. 1932. *Classic Descriptions of Disease,* pp. 347–50. Charles Thomas.

NAS Committee on Biologic Effects of Atmospheric Pollutants. 1972. *Lead: Airborne Lead in Perspective.*

Needleman, H. 1973. Lead poisoning in children: Neurologic implications of widespread subclinical intoxication. *Seminars in Psychiatry* 5:27–53.

Novick, R. E. Remarks at Lead Poisoning Symposium, May 1971, Lankenau Hospital, Philadelphia.

Oberle, M. W. 1969. Lead poisoning: A preventable childhood disease of the slums. *Science* 165:991–92.

Osborne, R., J. Raye, G. Bowers, and M. Lepow. 1976. The influence of environmental factors on maternal and neonatal blood lead levels. *Conn. Med.* 40:452–55.

Patterson, C. C. 1965. Contaminated and natural lead environments of man. *Arch. Environ. Health* 11:344–60.

Perino, J., and C. Erphart. 1974. The relation of subclinical lead level to cognitive and sensorimotor impairment in black preschoolers. *J. Learning Disabilities* 7:26–30.

Piomelli, S., B. Davidow, V. Gunell, P. Young, and G. Guy. 1973. The free erythrocyte protoporphyrins test: A screening micromethod for lead poisoning. *Pediatrics* 51: 254–59.

Sayre, J., E. Charney, J. Vostal, and I. Pless. 1974. House and hand dust as a potential source of childhood lead exposure. *Am. J. Diseases of Children* 127:167–72.

Selye, H., B. Tuchweber, and L. Bertok. 1966. Effect of lead acetate on the susceptibility of rats to bacterial endotoxins. *J. Bact.* 91: 884–90.

Silbergeld, E., and A. Goldberg. 1974. Hyperactivity: A lead induced behavioral disorder. *Environ. Health Perspectives,* Experimental Issue No. 7:227–32.

Waldron, H., and B. Stofen. 1964. *Subclinical Lead Poisoning.* Academic Press.

Bernard L. Cohen

Impacts of the Nuclear Energy Industry on Human Health and Safety

Evaluation of the hazards of various stages of power production, coupled with analysis of existing data on radiation effects, permits experts to predict the magnitude of the risk involved in an all-nuclear energy economy

Although many people believe that the effects of radiation on human health are poorly understood, at least the upper limits of these effects are well known from incidents in which people have received large doses of radiation. The data have been analyzed in reports by two prestigious groups of radiation biomedical experts—the National Academy of Sciences–National Research Council Committee on Biological Effects of Ionizing Radiation (BEIR) (*1*) and the United Nations Scientific Committee on Effects of Atomic Radiation (UNSCEAR) (*2*). In addition, there is continuing surveillance of the information by the International Commission on Radiological Protection (ICRP) and the National Council on Radiation Protection and Measurements (NCRP), groups mainly concerned with setting standards for maximum permissible exposure. Their conclusions will be used here to estimate the effects on human health of radioactivity released into the environment by various aspects of the nuclear energy industry.

The principal health effects of radiation are acute radiation sickness, cancer, and genetic defects. Acute radiation sickness, which can be fatal

Dr. Cohen, an experimental nuclear physicist, is a professor of physics and Director of the Nuclear Physics Laboratory at the University of Pittsburgh. For the past five years he has been active in research on environmental impacts of nuclear power, especially regarding plutonium and waste problems. He is a past Chairman of the American Physical Society Division of Nuclear Physics, and a member of the National Council of American Association of Physics Teachers, the Health Physics Society, and the American Nuclear Society. Address: Department of Physics and Astronomy, University of Pittsburgh, Pittsburgh, PA 15260.

in a matter of days, results from exposures in excess of 100 rem (1 *r*oentgen-*e*quivalent-*m*an = energy deposit per unit mass of tissue, in units of 100 erg/gram, times relative biological effectiveness). Gamma-ray exposures of about 500 rem (as it enters the body) without medical treatment and of 700–1,400 rem with various levels of treatment (*3*) have a 50% probability of causing death. If death does not result, the patient recovers after several weeks. There have been seven fatalities (none since 1961) from acute radiation sickness in the United States—all of them workers on nuclear projects where something went wrong.

Cancer induction by radiation is a much broader threat, and there is a rather substantial body of data on human victims. The largest single source is the Japanese atomic bomb survivors. About 24,000 people were exposed to an average of about 130 rem, and more than a hundred excess cancer deaths have resulted. Almost 15,000 people in the United Kingdom who were treated with heavy X-ray doses for ankylosing spondylitis, an arthritis of the spine, received an average whole-body exposure of almost 400 rem, which resulted in more than a hundred excess deaths. Among 4,000 uranium miners who received average doses to the lung approaching 5,000 rem from radon inhalation, deaths have also exceeded that toll. Several situations have caused about 50 excess cancer deaths, including those involving 775 American women employed in painting radium numerals on watch dials between 1915 and 1935, almost 1,000 German victims of ankylosing spondylitis treated with Ra^{224}, and fluorspar and metal miners exposed to radon gas. Several other situations which led to ten or so

excess deaths have also been studied.

In digesting these data, it is usually assumed that the cancer risk is proportional to the total exposure in rem. This "linear–no threshold" hypothesis involves a very large extrapolation; it assumes, for example, that the probability of cancer induction by 1 millirem (mrem), which is typical of most exposures of interest, is 10^{-5} times the probability of induction by 100 rem, which is the region for which most data are available. For a number of reasons, however, this assumption seems more likely to overestimate than to underestimate the effects of low dosage. That there are mechanisms in the body for repairing radiation damage is well established (*4*): chromosomes broken by radiation have been observed under a microscope to reunite, and 1,000-rem doses that are lethal to mice in a single exposure have little effect when distributed over several weeks. Rapidly multiplying cells are more susceptible to radiation injury than normal cells because there is less time for repair between cell divisions—this is the basis for cancer radiation therapy. In addition, cancer induction by radiation is known to be a multi-event process: if cancer were caused by a single hit on a single cell, the risk would be proportional to the number of cells, and a given exposure would be much less effective on small animals like mice. Good evidence exists that the latent period before cancers develop (15 years for large exposures) increases with decreased exposure, and for small exposures it may well exceed life expectancy. For these reasons, all four of the monitoring groups mentioned above have acknowledged that the linear–no threshold hypothesis is highly conservative, and although they all accept it as a basis for setting exposure standards, only the BEIR Committee condones using it for estimating risks; UNSCEAR pointedly refuses to do so, and NCRP has been highly critical of it.

The linear–no threshold hypothesis greatly simplifies calculations, making total effects proportional to the population dose in "man-rem," the sum of the exposures in rem to all those exposed. I shall use it here with the understanding that it yields upper limits for radiation effects. In particular, I shall use the BEIR estimate of 180×10^{-6} cancer deaths per man-rem (5), which means that for every rem of radiation a person receives to his whole body, his probability of ultimately dying of cancer is increased by 1.8 parts in ten thousand above the normal probability (16.8% for the average American). On this basis, one rem of whole-body radiation reduces life expectancy by a little more than one day (6). For perspective, it may be noted that the life expectancy reduction from smoking a single cigarette is equivalent to that of 5 mrem.

If radioactive material enters the body, exposures to individual organs are more of a problem than whole-body exposure, and the BEIR Report gives the risks separately. For example, the number of cancer deaths per million man-rem exposure to bone is 6; to thyroid, 6; to lungs, 39; and to the gastrointestinal tract, 30. Studies of the survivors of the Japanese atomic bombings show no evidence that the incidence of diseases other than cancer is affected by radiation (7).

Genetic defects, which normally occur in about 3% of all live births (2), number about 100,000 per year in the U.S.; they are generally caused by spontaneous mutations in the sex cells. Because there is no evidence from human data for genetic defects in offspring from radiation received by parents, all estimates of such damage are based on animal data. Averaging the BEIR and UNSCEAR estimates gives 150×10^{-6} eventual genetic defects per man-rem exposure of the entire population (5). The defects range from color blindness or an extra finger or toe (usually removed by simple surgery shortly after birth) to serious deformities that make life very difficult, and include diseases

which develop much later in life. Studies of the Japanese survivors of the atomic bombings (8) have yielded no evidence for excessive genetic defects among offspring—a result which virtually ensures that the above estimate is not too small—and a recent reassessment indicates that it may be an order of magnitude too large (9).

Routine emissions from nuclear installations

A light water reactor consists of long, thin rods of UO_2 (fuel pins), enriched to about 3% in U^{235}, submerged in water. In the proper geometry, this arrangement permits a chain reaction in which a neutron striking a U^{235} nucleus induces a fission reaction, which releases neutrons, some of which induce other fission reactions. Each fission reaction releases energy (about 200 MeV), which is rapidly converted to heat, warming the surrounding water. The reactor therefore serves as a gigantic water heater; as water is pumped through at a rate of thousands of gallons per second, it is heated to 600°F. The hot water may then be converted to steam either in the reactor (boiling water reactor, BWR) or in an external heat exchanger (pressurized water reactor, PWR); the steam then drives a turbine which turns a generator to produce electric power.

The fuel is in the form of UO_2 ceramic pellets about 1.5 cm long by 1 cm in diameter. About 200 of these pellets are lined up end to end inside a zirconium alloy tube (cladding), which is then sealed by welding. The reactor fuel consists of about 40,000 of these fuel pins, or a total of about 8 million pellets.

When a U^{235} nucleus is struck by a neutron and undergoes fission, the two pieces into which it splits are ordinarily radioactive—this is the principal source of radioactivity in the nuclear energy industry. The pieces fly apart with considerable energy (about 80% of the 200-MeV energy release is in their kinetic energy), but they are stopped after traveling only about 0.02 mm, so nearly all the radioactivity remains very close to the original uranium nucleus inside the ceramic fuel pellet. The same is true for the second most important source of radioactivity, the neutrons captured by the uranium to make still

heavier radioactive nuclei—neptunium, plutonium, americium, and curium—called actinides.

Although nearly all the radioactive nuclei remain sealed inside the ceramic pellets, a few of the fission products have a degree of mobility, and some small fraction of them eventually diffuse out of the pellets but remain contained inside the cladding. During the operation of the reactor, about one or two per thousand of the fuel pins develop tiny leaks in the cladding, releasing the radioactive material that has diffused out of the pellets into the water. Chemical cleanup facilities remove the radioactive material from the water, but they do not remove the gaseous fission products, which include krypton and xenon isotopes and iodine. The iodine is so volatile that, in spite of elaborate equipment for trapping it out, a fraction of one percent of it comes off with the gases. These gases, including also small fractions of one percent of a few other volatile fission products, are held for some time within the power plant to allow the short half-life activities to decay away. Eventually they are released into the environment. This is one way in which the public is exposed to radiation by routine operation of a nuclear plant.

Nuclear Regulatory Commission regulations require that no member of the public, including those living closest to the plant, receive a radiation dose from these emissions larger than 5 mrem/yr to the whole body, or 15 mrem/yr to the thyroid. It is estimated that if all the electric power now used in the U.S. (approximately 400 million kilowatts) were produced by light water reactors, the average American would receive an average annual exposure from the Kr and Xe of about 0.05 mrem/yr (10). The iodine released yields exposures to human thyroids of the same order of magnitude (11), mostly due to the concentration in cow's milk of material settling on grass; but this does considerably less harm because it is less effective in inducing cancer.

Another source of routine emissions of radioactivity is tritium (H^3). In about one fission reaction out of 500, the uranium nucleus splits into three parts (ternary fission) rather than two, and in about 5% of these cases (once in 10,000 fissions) one of the three pieces is H^3. Other sources of H^3 in reactors are neutron reactions in boron and H^2. The difficulty with H^3 is that it mixes with the ordinary hydrogen in the water and cannot be separated from it; thus, when water is released from the plant, it passes some H^3 into a nearby river, lake, or ocean. NRC regulations require that no member of the public be exposed to more than 5 mrem/yr of whole-body radiation from this water, and that value is calculated on the assumption that a person derives all his drinking water and fish from the plant discharge canal and swims in it for an hour a day. It is estimated that, if all our power were nuclear, the average American would receive less than 0.01 mrem/yr from this source (12).

When the fuel in a reactor has been burned up as much as possible consistent with proper operation, it must be removed from the reactor and replaced with fresh fuel (typically one-third of the fuel is replaced in one such operation per year). The spent fuel is stored for about six months in the power plant to allow short half-life radioactivity to decay away, and it is then shipped to a fuel reprocessing plant. There the fuel pins are cut into pieces of manageable size and dissolved in acid, and the solution is chemically processed to remove the uranium, which is useful for making fresh fuel, and the plutonium, which may be used for making future fuels. Everything else is classified as "waste"—including all the fission products that contain the vast majority of the radioactivity, the uranium and plutonium that escaped removal in the chemical processing (typically 0.5% with current technology), and the other actinides produced. The eventual disposal of this waste is an important topic which will be discussed below.

When the fuel pins are dissolved, the gases once again present a problem. Since xenon has no long half-life isotopes, no radioactive Xe is present, but Kr^{85} has a ten-year half-life, and in current technology all of it is released to the atmosphere from a tall stack. The tritium is released as water vapor in the same way. It is estimated that if all our present electric power were nuclear, the average American would be exposed to 0.02 mrem/yr from the Kr^{85} and 0.15 mrem/yr from the tritium (13). In addition, people

Table 1. Annual cancer (plus acute radiation sickness) deaths due to radiation from aspects of a U.S. nuclear energy industry generating 400 million KW of electricity*

Source	Deaths/yr
Routine emissions	8.7
Reactor accidents	10.0 (600)†
Transportation accidents	0.01
Waste disposal	0.4
Plutonium (routine release)	0.1
Total	20.00 (600)†

* Does not include effects of long half-life radioactivities, sabotage, or terrorism.
† Numbers in parentheses represent worst claim by critics of the nuclear energy industry.

in other countries would be exposed to 0.02 mrem/yr from Kr^{85} produced in the U.S. Active and advanced development programs are in progress for greatly reducing the emissions of Kr^{85}, but reducing the tritium emissions is a much more difficult problem.

When these exposures are added to the 0.05 mrem/yr from the power plants, we see that the exposure to the average American from routine emissions if all our power were nuclear would be about 0.23 mrem/yr. If we compare this average exposure with other radiation we experience (14), we find that it is less than 1/500 of our exposure from natural radiation (U.S. average = 130 mrem/yr) and about 1/300 of our exposure from medical and dental X rays. Natural radiation varies widely, from an average of 250 mrem/yr in Colorado and Wyoming to 100 mrem/yr in Texas and Louisiana. In parts of India and Brazil, where average exposures are 1,500 mrem/yr from monazite sands rich in thorium and uranium, studies of the population have revealed no unusual effects. Even within a single city exposures may vary considerably: the radiation level is 10 mrem/yr higher (15) in Manhattan (built on granite) than in Brooklyn (built on sand). Building materials such as brick and stone also contain significant quantities of radioactive material. Living in a typical brick or stone house (rather than a wooden one) adds about 30 mrem/yr exposure and in eight months causes more exposure than a lifetime of all-nuclear power. The 0.23 mrem/yr from routine

emissions if all our power were nuclear is substantially exceeded by even such minor sources of radiation as (14) luminous-dial watches (1 mrem/yr) and airplane flights (0.7 mrem/hr at 30,000 feet), and is comparable to the average child's dosage from watching television (0.3 mrem/yr from X rays).

The consequences of 0.23 mrem/yr of whole-body radiation to the average American may be readily calculated using the risk estimates given in the previous section: 8.3 additional cancer deaths per year and 7.0 additional genetic defects. Uranium and its daughters are released from various other elements of the nuclear fuel cycle besides the power plant and fuel reprocessing facilities, but because these involve alpha-particle emitters, which do their damage to a few specific organs following inhalation, the effects cannot be expressed in terms of whole-body radiation. The numbers of deaths caused by these agents if all our power were nuclear are (16): uranium ore mills, 0.16/yr; conversion facilities, 0.09/yr; enrichment facilities, 0.01/yr; fuel fabrication plants, 0.03/yr; transportation, 0.08/yr. Adding these effects to the 8.3 deaths per year from power plants and fuel reprocessing gives a grand total of 8.7 deaths per year (17). This is the first entry in Table 1.

The preceding estimates are based on steady production of 400 million kilowatts for a period long enough to bring the effects of Kr^{85} and H^3 into equilibrium with their decay, which would be a few decades. However, no such equilibrium can be achieved with long half-life radionuclides like C^{14} (5,600 yr) and Rn^{222}, which is a granddaughter of Th^{230} (8×10^4 yr), and their effects would grow linearly with time. At present and for the near future, because they contribute to population exposure in a very minor way, control of their emissions is not considered to be an urgent matter and is receiving little attention. However, unless the linear–no threshold theory of biological effects of radiation is abandoned, action on these matters cannot be long delayed.

The issue of C^{14} was first raised in mid-1974. C^{14} is produced by neutron reactions on the rare oxygen isotope O^{17} and on N^{14} impurities in the fuel and coolant. If all our power were from light water reactors, about 4,000 curies per year would be released from these plants, and an additional 8,000 Ci/yr would be discharged from fuel reprocessing plants with current technology (18). The discharge will presumably mix with the carbon in the biosphere, and if its effects are integrated to infinity with populations remaining constant, on the linear–no threshold theory it would eventually cause 20 cancer deaths in the U.S. plus a proportionate number in the rest of the world. However, it seems likely that equipment now being developed to freeze out the Kr^{85} in reprocessing plants will simultaneously remove the C^{14}, thus eliminating two-thirds of the effects.

When uranium is separated from the mined ore in the ore processing mill, the residue containing radium and its precursor Th^{230} is accumulated in large piles, typically 1 km^2 in area × 5 m deep. The radon gas emitted from the tailings piles resulting from one year of all-nuclear power (2.5 piles of the above dimensions) is estimated (19) to cause 0.8 lung cancers per year in U.S. (my estimate, ref. 20, is an order of magnitude smaller)—but this situation will continue for tens of thousands of years if it is not remedied. Mill tailings have caused local problems, for example, in Grand Junction, Colorado, where they were used for building construction (21) and in Salt Lake City, where there is a large pile within the city limits. As a result, the problem has been under intense investigation, and plans are being made to remove or cover the piles (22). For example, a half-inch of asphalt protected by a few feet of earth cover stabilized by rock would reduce the emissions by a factor of 500 and would cost about $3.5 million per year if all U.S. power were nuclear (23)—only 0.01% of the value of the electricity. For perspective it might be pointed out that if nothing were done about the piles, the tailings from one year of all-nuclear power would increase the natural radon background by only one part in 6,000 and would contribute less radon than is currently being released by phosphate mining. The whole problem would, of course, be grossly reduced with breeder reactors and one might question the validity of equating health effects tens of thousands of years in the future with those of the present day (23).

It is difficult to deal with emissions of C^{14} and Rn^{222} in Table 1. If nothing is done about them and their entire potential cost in human lives is eventually realized, they would be dominant contributors in that table, but if they are properly handled, they will be of minor importance. The NRC policy (24) requiring emission control devices in power plants where the cost is less than $1,000 per man-rem exposure avoided, which corresponds to $6 million per life saved, leads us to expect the latter. Since these problems are so recently discovered, are doing little harm as yet (radon emissions from mill tailings begin only after the mill is closed and the pile dries out), and are being actively worked on, it does not now seem reasonable to include them in Table 1.

Power plant accidents

In the routine operation of the nuclear industry, nearly all the radioactivity produced in reactors ends up as waste at the fuel reprocessing plant, which, as we shall see, is not difficult to dispose of safely. However, the danger exists that, due to some sort of accident in the reactor, an appreciable fraction of this radioactivity will be released into the environment at the power plant. If this should happen, the potential for damage is very great.

Because essentially all the radioactivity produced is sealed inside the UO_2 ceramic fuel pellets, the only way for it to be released is for these pellets to be melted. Thus any reactor accident of large consequences must involve a "melt-down." Since the melting temperature of UO_2 is over 5,000°F, whereas normal operating temperatures are near and below 1,000°F, a melt-down cannot result from small abnormalities. One possible cause of a melt-down might seem to be a large reactivity excursion produced by withdrawing control rods too far and too fast. Several mitigating effects would follow, however: initially, the power level would escalate rapidly, but as a result the reactor would heat up. As the temperature increases, U^{238} captures more neutrons in the "resonance region" (due to Doppler broadening of resonances) leaving fewer neutrons to be slowed down to thermal energies where they induce fission in U^{235}; moreover, as the temperature increases, water becomes a poorer moderator (in a BWR more water boils into steam, which is essentially an elimination of the moderator). Hence, these reactors have a large "negative temperature coefficient of reactivity" which works powerfully against large reactivity excursions. In addition, the emergency insertion of control rods (called "scram") is such a simple operation that it would rarely fail. Because it depends only on gravity (PWR) or on stored fluid pressure (BWR), it does not require electric power.

These safety features are challenged rather frequently. About once a year on average, a generator is suddenly taken off-line because of some abnormal electrical occurrence, and when this happens, the turbine which drives it can no longer accept steam. The resulting back pressure causes the steam bubbles to collapse in a BWR, thereby suddenly increasing the reactivity, which greatly increases the reactor power. If the emergency control rods should fail to insert, the pressure would build up dangerously. This accident is called ATWS (anticipated transient without scram), and in many reactors the scram system is the only defense against this once-a-year challenge. A backup "poison-insertion system" which would inject boron solution (a strong neutron absorber) would be another defense, but there has been strong resistance to this because, if it were to activate unnecessarily, it would keep the reactor shut down for many hours.

Safety experts agree that the most likely cause of a reactor fuel melt-down is not a reactivity excursion but a loss of coolant accident (LOCA) resulting from a large leak in the cooling water system. The water temperature in these reactors is about 600°F (high temperatures produce high efficiencies), and to prevent or control boiling, the pressure must be very high, about 1,000 psi in the BWR and 2,200 psi in the PWR. If there were a rupture in the high-pressure system, the water would flash into steam and escape at a tremendous rate (this is called a "blow-down"), leaving the reactor core without coolant. Loss of the water moderator would immediately shut down the chain reaction, but it would not, of course, halt the radioactivity decay process.

The power generated by the radio-activity in the fuel pellets immediately after the chain reaction stops is very substantial—about 6% of the full power level of the reactor—and it is easily enough to eventually melt the fuel. In the PWR, if the fuel were left without coolant for 45 seconds (possibly even for 30 seconds), the temperature would get so high that bringing in water might do more harm than good; at high temperatures water reacts chemically with the zirconium fuel cladding in an exothermal reaction which would raise the temperature still more. Thus, if cooling is not restored within about 45 seconds, the reactor may be doomed to melt-down (in a BWR, this critical time is about 3 to 5 minutes), releasing the radioactive material. Complete melt-down of the fuel would take about 30 minutes, and after an hour or so the molten fuel would melt through the reactor vessel. An appreciable fraction of the radioactivity would at this point come spewing out in the form of a radioactive dust or gas.

A great deal of engineering effort has been expended to minimize the probability of a LOCA, to reduce the chance that a LOCA would lead to a melt-down, and to mitigate the consequences of a melt-down if it should occur. Quality standards on materials and fabrication methods match or exceed those in any other industry, and rarely is expense an issue in this regard. A very elaborate program of inspections is maintained during the fabrication stage, including X-raying of all welds, magnetic particle inspections, and a very elaborate series of ultrasonic tests aimed at detecting imperfections that might lead to failures of materials. Once the reactor comes into operation, periodic shutdowns are scheduled for extensive ultrasonic and visual inspections. (It was in these visual inspections that the hairline pipe cracks in a few BWRs were discovered in early 1975).

Since large leaks develop from small leaks, the next line of defense is in systems for detecting small leaks if they should occur. Since the water is at high temperature and under high pressure, any leak would release steam, which would increase the humidity. Two types of systems, based on different physical principles, are used to detect increases in humidity around the high-pressure system. Because radioactivity in the water would emerge with the steam, two particularly sensitive types of systems capable of detecting increases of airborne radioactivity are also used.

If, in spite of these precautions, a LOCA should occur, the next line of defense is the emergency core cooling system (ECCS), an elaborate arrangement for injecting water back into the system to reflood the reactor core (because all pipes enter the reactor vessel above the core, reflooding is possible unless the rupture is in the lower part of the reactor vessel itself; the latter is of very thick, high-quality steel, and its rupture is orders of magnitude less probable than breaks in piping or external components). The ECCS is a highly redundant system, and simple failures of pumps or valves would not prevent its operation. All estimates indicate that it is about 99% certain of delivering water in the event of a LOCA.

Nevertheless, there has been extensive controversy over whether the ECCS will prevent a melt-down in the event of a large LOCA. By the time the water from the ECCS fills the reactor vessel up to the bottom of the fuel pins, the latter are quite hot, and the water flashes into steam. The steam exerts a back pressure which retards flooding to a rate not much more than one inch per second, and there is a period during which the heat transfer is principally by water droplets entrained in steam. This type of heat transfer is not well understood, and there is considerable uncertainty about cooling by the water-steam mixture during the initial blow-down. In order to assess these problems, engineers conducted experiments with full-length electrically heated fuel-pin mock-ups and developed empirical "theories" to explain their observations. They then used these empirical theories in computer codes to calculate the operation of the ECCS. This procedure is highly inaccurate, and the engineering approach to such a situation is to apply a factor of safety.

In 1971, the Union of Concerned Scientists (UCS) headed by Henry Kendall studied these matters and declared that they did not consider the factor of safety adequate. In the controversy that followed, the AEC organized hearings that lasted more than a year to consider the question, and several AEC safety experts came forward to support Kendall's contention. As a result of the hearings, the AEC increased the factor of safety and some reactors were forced to reduce their power levels until fuel pins with smaller diameters could be installed. The AEC safety experts who had supported Kendall said (according to an AEC statement) that they were now satisfied that the precautions are adequate, but Kendall is still far from convinced. Very elaborate tests to develop further understanding of the problems are scheduled for 1977, using a reactor especially constructed and instrumented for the purpose.

If a LOCA should occur and the ECCS should fail to perform its function, there would be a melt-down. In order to mitigate the consequences, the entire system is enclosed in a "containment," constructed of very thick, heavily reinforced concrete lined with steel plate (the most common type is tested to withstand an internal pressure of 5 atmospheres). The containment is strong enough to repel a wide variety of external threats, including missiles that a tornado might hurl at it (automobiles, trees, etc.) and conventional explosives and bombs. The function of the containment in a melt-down accident is to contain the radioactive dust for a time. Inside it are systems for pumping the air through filters to remove the dust and sprays for removing iodine. Because the walls are relatively cool, many of the radioactive materials would plate out on them. Thus if the containment holds for at least a few hours, most of the airborne radioactivity would be removed and the consequences of the accident to the public would not be serious.

The situation could be much more serious if the containment should fail shortly after the molten fuel melts through the reactor vessel. This could happen immediately as a result of a very violent (but highly improbable) explosion as the molten fuel drops into water, or relatively early as a result of high steam pressure if the water sprays designed to condense the steam inside the containment should fail to function. In such situations, the airborne radioactive dust would be released into the environment, and the consequences would then depend on weather conditions. Ordinarily the radioactivity would be widely dispersed and cause little obvious damage (25), but if there were a strong temperature inversion the radioactive cloud would be concentrated close to the ground—anyone it passed would be exposed externally and would inhale radioactive dust. There could be thousands of fatalities.

Among the many surveys of the probabilities and consequences of reactor accidents, the most elaborate is the recent study financed by the AEC and directed by Norman Rasmussen of MIT. This project involved 60 man-years of effort and cost $4 million; its results were published in draft form in August 1974, and, after extensive criticism and revision, in final form in November 1975 as the multivolume document WASH-1400. If one is willing to accept the Rasmussen study, answers are immediately available to a wide variety of questions. For example, there would be a melt-down about once in 20,000 reactor-years; if all our power were nuclear (400 reactors), we might expect an accident every 50 years on an average. The average annual consequences (1/50 the average consequence per melt-down) would be 0.2 deaths from acute radiation sickness plus 10 eventual cancer deaths (see Table 1), and $6 million in damages, mostly in cleanup and evacuation costs. The frequency of accidents of varying severity (as indicated by the number of fatalities) is shown in Table 2.

The consequences of the worst possible accident are estimated to be 3,500 fatalities from acute radiation sickness plus 45,000 later cancer deaths. An accident of this magnitude is predicted to occur about once in a million years in the U.S. if all our power were nuclear. This catastrophe would do little property damage, but other accidents, especially those accompanied by widespread heavy rainstorms, would cause few fatalities but would contaminate large areas and require extensive evacuation and clean-up. In the worst accident of this type, expected once in a million years, these would cost $14 billion.

Although it is often said that the worst nuclear accident would be much more terrible than any other accident connected with man's pro-

Table 2. Severity distribution of accidents

Number of fatalities	Frequency⁻¹ (average years between accidents)		
	Nuclear	Other man-caused*	Natural disasters
>100	100	1.5	2
>1,000	300	25	8
>10,000	10,000	500	50

* Includes dam failures, airplane crashes in crowded areas, fires, explosions, releases of poison gas, etc.

duction of energy, this is by no means correct. There are hydroelectric dams whose failure could cause over 200,000 fatalities, and such failures are estimated to be much more probable than a very bad nuclear accident (26). Gas explosions, especially those connected with the transport of liquified natural gas, have been envisioned which could cause 100,000 fatalities. Moreover, unlike these situations, the great majority of the fatalities from the nuclear catastrophe would be essentially unnoticed, arising from a slight increase in cancer occurrence many years later.

The critics of nuclear power have not accepted the Rasmussen report. Perhaps their most concrete objection has been to the emergency core cooling system, as discussed above; if they are correct on this matter, the probability of a melt-down would be increased threefold to one in 6,000 reactor-years. They have also objected to the general approach of the Rasmussen group to predicting the probability of a melt-down ("fault-tree analysis"). While they have never offered a numerical estimate of this probability, they would be hard put to justify a number larger than one in 2,000 reactor-years, 10 times the WASH-1400 estimate. Naval reactors, which have all the same problems and potential dangers, have already operated 2,000 reactor-years without a melt-down, and civilian reactors of this type have operated 250 reactor-years without a significant LOCA (there can be no doubt that the ECCS would prevent a melt-down in the great majority of LOCAs, which would be relatively small and slow in developing).

On the other basic element, the consequences of a melt-down, WASH-1400 is open to criticism in that it did not use the linear–no threshold dose-effect relationship recommended by the BEIR Report (1) but

introduced a dose-reduction factor recommended by its prestigious advisory panel on health effects. This reduces its cancer estimates by a factor of two. The critics also object to the assumptions about evacuation and claim that WASH-1400 underestimates the consequences of accidents by about a factor of six (27). Combining this with the factor of 10 disagreement on probability of accidents, the critics could claim that WASH-1400 underestimates the average number of fatalities from reactor accidents by a factor of 60, giving an annual average of 600 fatalities per year from all-nuclear power. This number is shown in parentheses in Table 1.

Transportation accidents

When spent fuel is shipped from the power plant to the fuel reprocessing plant, there is a possibility of an accident in transit which would release radioactivity to the environment. Several features differentiate such releases from those in power plant accidents. First, only a very small fraction of the fuel in a reactor is involved in any one shipment. Second, the fuel is stored in the plant for about six months before shipment to allow the short half-life radioactivity to decay away; this reduces the potential danger by two orders of magnitude. Third, and most important, the highest temperatures that would ordinarily be encountered in a transport accident are those of a gasoline or organic solvent fire—about 1,500°F, far below the 5,000°F temperature to melt the UO_2 ceramic fuel pellets. Thus, since nearly all the radioactivity remains trapped in the pellets, the major danger is that the cladding tubes will be ruptured, releasing the small fraction of the radioactivity that had migrated out of the pellets to become trapped inside the tubes. This radioactivity is principally Kr^{85}, which is destined to be released from the fuel reprocessing plant under more controlled conditions. In addition, it is sometimes assumed that, in some unspecified way, a very small fraction of the solid fission products are released (*28, 29*).

In order to minimize the danger of such releases, spent fuel is shipped in casks costing about $2 million each, designed and prototype-tested to withstand, without release of radioactivity, a 30-mph crash into a solid and unyielding obstacle, envelopment in a gasoline fire for 30 minutes, submersion in water for 8 hours, and a puncture test. It seems reasonable to expect a high degree of protection against accident damage from such an elaborate effort.

The same precautions are also taken with the waste glass to be shipped from the fuel reprocessing plant to a burial site. Moreover, by the time the glass is shipped, radioactivity has decayed by another factor of six, and the glass is enclosed in a thick stainless steel container which is far stronger than the fuel pin cladding. Thus the risk in waste glass transport is considerably less than in spent fuel transport.

Studies of the problem, including estimates of releases and their consequences from all types of waste transport accidents, indicate that if all U.S. power were nuclear there would be an average of less than one fatality per century due to radioactivity releases in these accidents (*30*). There would, of course, be orders of magnitude more fatalities from the traffic aspects of these accidents, but coal-fired power requires a hundred times more transport and hence would cause a hundred times as many transport accident fatalities.

Radioactive waste disposal

At present the high-level wastes that accumulate in fuel reprocessing plants are kept in solution and stored in large tanks. There is currently 600,000 gallons of this waste from nuclear power plants, and more than 100 times that much from government operations, principally the production of plutonium for weapons. The plans for waste from civilian power are very different. NRC regulations require that it be converted to a suitable solid form (as yet unspecified) within five years and delivered

to a government repository within ten years. The first deliveries may be expected in the late 1980s (the little waste that has already been generated is exempted from this schedule by a "grandfather" clause). Plans for the repository are not yet final, but the waste will be buried in some suitably chosen geological formation about 600 m underground. Probably it will be in the form of glass cylinders 0.3 m diameter $\times$ 3 m long (0.2 m^3 volume); a typical power plant would produce about 10 of these per year.

I have evaluated the hazard from these buried wastes previously in both a summary (*31*) and a detailed (*32*) paper, and so I review the situation only very briefly here. The principal danger once the material is buried is that it might be contacted by groundwater, be leached into solution, move through aquifers with the water, and, eventually reaching the surface, contaminate food and drinking water. The ingestion hazard from the waste generated in one year if all our present electric power were from light water reactors is shown in Table 3.

The material must be isolated from our environment for a few hundred years; before worrying about longer times one should consider some of the other chemical and biological poisons in the earth and those produced by man. For example, a lethal dose of arsenic (As_2O_3) is 3 grams, and we import ten times as much of it into our country each year as we would produce radioactive waste if all our power were nuclear. This arsenic is not buried deep underground; in fact much of it is scattered on the surface as herbicides in regions where food is grown.

The requirement that radioactive waste be isolated for hundreds of years seems alarming to some because few things in our environment last that long. Deep underground, however, the time constants for change are in the range 10^7–10^8 years. The following factors provide additional

protection against release during the few-hundred-year critical period: (1) The material will be buried in a geological formation that has been free of groundwater for tens of millions of years and in which geologists are quite certain there will be no water for some time into the future. (2) If water should get into the formation, the rock constituting it would have to be leached or dissolved away before water could reach the waste. Even if the rock were salt, dissolution would typically require thousands of years. (3) Once the water reached the waste glass, the latter would be leached at a rate of only about 1% per century. (4) Groundwater flows through aquifers rather slowly, requiring typically 1,000 years to reach surface waters from a depth of 600 m. (5) Most of the radioactive materials would be held up by ion exchange processes, traveling 100 to 10,000 times slower than water.

A quantitative evaluation of the hazard from the waste throughout its existence may be obtained using a model in which the waste is buried at random locations throughout the U.S. but always at a depth of 600 meters. It is assumed that an atom of buried waste is no more likely to reach the surface and get into a person than is an atom of radium in the rock or soil above it. The probability for an atom of radium is easily estimated because we know the amount of radium in the top 600 meters of the U.S. and the amount of radium in people (from measurements on corpses). For radium the probability is 4×10^{-13} per year. When this probability is applied to the waste, the number of fatalities expected annually from one year's waste may then be calculated as a function of time and integrated over time to yield the ultimate consequences. If the integration is extended over a million years, the result is 0.4 eventual fatalities from the waste generated by one year of all-nuclear power (see Table 1).

By comparison, burning up the uranium to produce this waste would

Table 3. Ingestion hazard from waste generated in one year if all U.S. electric power were from light water reactors

| | \multicolumn{8}{c|}{Years after reprocessing} |
	0	*100*	*200*	*300*	*500*	*1,000*	*10*^{6}	*10*^{8}
Grams ingested for 50% cancer risk	0.025	0.25	2.5	25	150	400	4,000	25,000

save about 50 fatalities due to radon emissions. Thus, on any long time scale, nuclear power must be viewed as a method for *cleansing* the earth of radioactivity. It should be noted that this estimate is based on no surveillance, since there is no surveillance of the radium with which it is compared in the model. Also, the model is a conservative one: random burial offers less security than careful choice of a burial site based on geological information, and the average radium in the top 600 m includes material near the surface where most erosion takes place and where it is thus more likely to be accessible for ingestion than material buried 600 m below.

Estimates were made of the fatalities that would result from releases as airborne particulates and as gamma-ray emissions from the surface of the ground, and from releases by natural cataclysms and human intrusion, but all of these predicted fewer fatalities than the groundwater-ingestion pathway considered above.

Hazards from plutonium toxicity

One of the radioactive materials produced in reactors—plutonium—is too valuable to be buried with the waste, since it can be used as a fuel in future reactors. However, plutonium has received a great deal of bad publicity because of its toxicity and its potential as a material for nuclear bombs. I have considered the problems arising from plutonium toxicity extensively in another paper (*33*) and will treat them only very briefly here. Claims of great harm resulting from plutonium toxicity are commonly based on the assumption that all the plutonium under consideration will find its way into human lungs and acceptance of the "hot particle" theory of alpha-particle carcinogenesis, in which it is assumed that concentration of alpha-particle emitters in a relatively few particles causes a few cells of the victim to be exposed to much more than the average amount of radiation and consequently to a greatly increased risk of cancer. The "hot-particle" theory has now been studied and rejected by many prestigious official groups, including the NCRP, the NRC, the AEC, the British Medical Research Council, a committee of the National Academy of Sciences, and the United Kingdom Radiological Protection Board. In addition, the ICRP and the U.S. Environmental Protection Agency have inferentially rejected it by not changing their standards on allowable exposure to plutonium. No prestigious or official group has accepted the "hot particle" theory.

If the usual procedures accepted by these groups are used and if normal meteorological dispersion is assumed, dispersal of reactor-plutonium (6 times more radioactive than Pu^{239}) in a large city would typically result in about 25 eventual cancers per pound dispersed. Seventy percent of these would result from exposure to the cloud of dust generated by the initial dispersal, and nearly all the rest from resuspension of the ust by winds within the first few months after it first settles on the ground. Less than 3% of the effects are due to exposures during the tens of thousands of years during which the plutonium remains in the soil.

Radium is about 40 times per curie more dangerous than plutonium as a component of soil, and there is as much radium in every 18 cm of depth of the earth's crust as there would be plutonium in the whole world if all the world's electric power were derived from fast breeder reactors. About 10,000 pounds of plutonium has been dispersed in bomb tests, whereas it is expected that about 0.01 pounds per year would be released from an all-fast-breeder nuclear power industry. About 0.1 fatalities per year (Table 1) are expected as a consequence of these releases.

Theft of plutonium

Widespread concern has been expressed that plutonium may be stolen from the nuclear energy industry by terrorists for fabrication of nuclear bombs. While this threat cannot be quantified for use in Table 1, it cannot be ignored in assessing the environmental impacts of nuclear power.

The principal protection against this threat is to prevent plutonium from becoming available to prospective terrorists. The method for keeping track of it since the 1940s has been to weigh all plutonium entering and leaving a facility, but errors in weighing leave substantial room for undetectable losses. It is not impossible that enough plutonium has already been diverted to make many bombs. On the other hand, there is no evidence that plutonium has ever been stolen in quantities as large as one gram.

The AEC has long conducted programs for improving security, but in 1973, T. B. Taylor, a former bomb designer, became disenchanted with the slow progress in these programs and "blew the story open" in a remarkable series of articles in the *New Yorker* magazine and a book (*34*) in which he gave information on how to make nuclear bombs. As a result of the publicity he received, plutonium safeguard procedures were greatly tightened and new regulations are constantly being added.

Clearly, the issue of terrorism should have been considered in the 1950s, before the nuclear industry began. It seems almost irresponsible to raise the problem after so much money and effort has been expended on the industry and we need its product so badly. Nevertheless, the threat of terrorism has continued to escalate in importance, and it is now one of the principal points of contention in the nuclear power controversy.

A number of factors should be considered in evaluating the risk of terrorism. First, stealing plutonium would be very difficult and dangerous under present safeguards. Taylor has estimated (*35*) that a group of thieves would have much less than a 50% chance of escaping with their lives. Fabrication of a bomb from stolen plutonium would also be very difficult, expensive, time-consuming, and dangerous. Estimates vary considerably, but a rough median of the opinions of experts indicates that it would require three people highly skilled in different technical areas a few months and perhaps $50,000 worth of equipment to develop a bomb with a 70% chance of doing extensive damage, and that the people involved would have a 30% chance of being killed in the effort.

Terrorist bombs would be "block-busters," not "city-destroyers." Taylor's principal scenario (*34*) is that an explosion of this sort could blow up the World Trade Center in New York, killing the 50,000 people that building can contain. Of course, there are many much easier ways to kill as many people (e.g. introducing a poison gas into the ventilation system of the World Trade Center).

Terrorists have always had many options for killing thousands of people, but they have almost never killed more than a few dozen. And, of course, plutonium and highly enriched uranium that would be much more suitable for the making of bombs could be obtained from sources which have no connection with nuclear electric power.

Safeguards in the U.S. are constantly being improved, and even what Taylor considers to be a very adequate system would add only 1% to the cost of nuclear power. On the other hand, safeguards are generally less stringent in foreign countries than in the U.S., and only if we maintain our involvement with nuclear power can we influence international regulations.

Some statistically comparable risks

Table 1 reveals that estimates based on acceptance of WASH-1400 predict that an all-nuclear energy economy would result in about 20 deaths per year; critics of nuclear energy claim that the number is about 600. I shall now attempt to put these estimates in perspective. Since cancer is delayed by 15 to 45 years after exposure, the average loss of life expectancy per victim is 20 years. The loss of life expectancy for the average American from these 20 deaths per year is then $(20 \times 20$ man-years lost$/2 \times 10^8$ man-years lived$) = 2 \times 10^{-6}$ of a lifetime = 1.2 hours.

Some of us subject ourselves to many other risks that reduce our life expectancy, such as smoking cigarettes. One pack per day (3.6×10^5 cigarettes) reduces life expectancy by about 8 years (36) which, assuming linearity, corresponds to 12 minutes loss of life expectancy per cigarette smoked; thus the risk of nuclear power is equivalent to that of smoking 6 cigarettes in one's lifetime, or one every 10 years.

Statistics show that life expectancy in large cities is 5 years less than in rural areas (37). This phenomenon may be explained in part by differences in racial makeup, but it is believed to be largely due to the strains of city life. If linearity is assumed, the risk of nuclear power (1.2 hr loss of life expectancy) is equal to the risk of spending 16 hours of one's life in a city.

Traveling in an automobile subjects us to a death risk of 2×10^{-8} per mile, or if 35 years of life are lost in an average traffic fatality, loss of life expectancy is 7×10^{-7} years per mile traveled. The risk of nuclear power is then equal to that of riding in automobiles an extra 3 miles per year.

Riding in a small rather than a large car doubles one's risk (38) of fatal injury, so the 1.2 hours loss of life expectancy from all nuclear power is equivalent to the risk of riding the same amount as at present, but 3 miles per year of it in a small rather than a large car.

Another risk some of us take is being overweight. If we assume loss of life expectancy to be linear with overweight, the 1.2 hour loss from all-nuclear power is equivalent to the risk of being 0.02 ounces overweight (39). However, Pauling (40) has shown that the data are better fit by a quadratic dependence, and if this is accepted the risk of all-nuclear power is equivalent to that of being 0.3 pounds overweight.

All these estimates are based on the government agency projection of 20 deaths per year. If we instead accept the critics' estimate of 30 times as many deaths, the risk of nuclear power is equivalent to the risks of smoking 3 cigarettes per year, spending 20 days of one's life in a city (one day every three years), riding in automobiles an extra hundred miles per year, riding in automobiles the same amount as at present but 100 miles of it per year (1%) in a small rather than a large car, or being 0.6 ounces overweight on the linear hypothesis or 1.6 pounds overweight on the quadratic hypothesis.

Additional perspective may be gained by comparing the effects of an industry deriving electric power from coal by present technology. The most important environmental impact of coal-fired power is air pollution, which, it is estimated, would cause about 10,000 deaths per year (41), at least an order of magnitude more than even the critics estimate would be caused by nuclear power. In addition, this air pollution would cause (41) about 25 million cases per year of chronic respiratory disease, 200 million person-days of aggravated heart-lung disease symptoms, and about $5 billion worth of property damage; there are no comparable

problems from nuclear power. Mining of coal to produce this power would cause about 750 deaths (42) per year among coal miners, more than 10 times the toll from uranium-mining for nuclear power, and the uranium figure would be reduced about 50-fold with breeder reactors. Transporting coal would cause about 500 deaths per year (43), two orders of magnitude more than would be caused by transportation for the nuclear industry.

It is important to point out that the numbers in Table 1 (and the perspective I have put them in) are based on annual averages. As the critics are constantly reminding us, if their estimates are correct, there might be an accident every ten years with several thousand deaths and every 50 years with tens of thousands of deaths. It is not difficult to make this prospect seem extremely dismal. On the other hand we should not envision these accidents as producing stacks of dead bodies; the great majority of fatalities predicted are from cancer that would occur 15 to 45 years later. In nearly all cases, the affected individuals would have only about a 0.5% increased chance of getting cancer. The average American's risk of cancer death is now 16.8%; typically it would be increased to 17.3%. For comparison, the average risk varies from 18.4% in New England to 14.7% in the Southeast, but these variations are rarely noticed.

If an area were affected by a nuclear accident and authorities revealed that, as a result, the average citizen's probability of eventually dying of cancer was increased from 16.8 to 17.3%, it would hardly start a panic. We have had some experience with a similar but much more serious situation: when reports first reached the public of the risk in cigarette-smoking, tens of millions of Americans were suddenly informed that they had accrued a 10% increased probability of cancer death, 20 times larger than the effects from a nuclear accident. Even that story did not stay in the headlines long, and it brought very little counteraction.

Critics often raise the point that the risks of nuclear power are not shared equally by all who benefit but are disproportionately great for people who live close to a nuclear power plant. This, of course, is true for all technology, but let us put it in perspective. The risk is 10^{-6} per year if we accept the WASH-1400 accident estimates, or equal to the risk of riding in an automobile an extra 50 miles per year or 250 yards per day.

Thus if moving away from a nuclear power plant increases one's commuting distance by more than 125 yards (half a block), it is safer to live next to the power plant. If one prefers the estimates we attribute to the critics (20 times larger), it does not pay to move away if doing so increases commuting distances by more than 1.5 miles per day. Even with the critics' estimates, living next to a nuclear power plant reduces life expectancy by only 0.03 years, which makes it 150 times safer than living in a city.

References

1. Committee on Biological Effects of Ionizing Radiation (BEIR). 1972. The effects on populations of exposure to low levels of ionizing radiation. National Academy of Sciences—National Research Council.

2. United Nations Scientific Committee on Effects of Atomic Radiation (UNSCEAR). 1972. Ionizing radiation: Levels and effects. NY: United Nations.

3. U.S. Nuclear Regulatory Commission. 1976. WASH-1400, Reactor safety study. Appendix VI.

4. NCRP. 1975. Review of the current state of radiation protection.

5. B. L. Cohen. 1976. Conclusions of the BEIR and UNSCEAR reports on radiation effects per man-rem. Health Phys. 30:351.

6. One rem gives 180×10^{-6} probability of cancer death which, on an average, causes 20 years loss of life; thus it reduces life expectancy by $3,600 \times 10^{-6}$ years, which is 1.3 days. Smoking one pack of cigarettes per day (about 4×10^5 cigarettes) reduces life expectancy by about 7.5 years (calculated from Surgeon-General's Report on effects of cigarette smoking, 1962) or 2,700 days. Assuming linearity, one cigarette then reduces life expectancy by 7×10^{-3} days. This is equal to the effect of $(7 \times 10^{-3}/1.3)$ rem, or about 5 mrem of radiation.

7. Data from Atomic Bomb Casualty Commission are tabulated in B. L. Cohen, 1974, Nuclear Science and Society (NY: Doubleday), p. 64.

8. J. V. Neel, H. Kato, and W. J. Shull. 1974. Mortality of children of atomic bomb survivors and controls. Genetics 76:311.

9. H. B. Newcombe. Mutation and the amount of human ill health. Paper presented at Int. Congress of Radiation Research, Seattle, 1974.

10. Environmental Protection Agency. 1973. Report EPA 520/9-73-003, pt. C, pp. 135, 137. The cheapest noble gas hold-up systems that are capable of limiting site boundary doses to the required 5 mrem/year are no system at all for a PWR with a population dose of 89 man-rem per year for twin reactors and charcoal adsorption for BWR with an annual population dose of 27 man-rem. Averaging these yields 58 man-rem/yr, or, for the 200 required sites exposing 2×10^8 people, 0.058 mrem/yr to the average person. Actually, most PWR plants use physical hold-up for more than 60 days, reducing their population dose by a factor of ten.

11. Ibid., pt. C, pp. 141, 142; the cheapest iodine control systems that reduce site boundary doses to below the required 15 mrem/yr give annual population doses to the thyroid of about 7 man-rem for elemental iodine and 13 man-rem for organic iodine; the average exposure is thus of the order of 10 man-rem $\times$ 200 sites/2×10^8 people, or about 0.01 mrem/yr to the thyroid.

12. Ibid., pt. C, p. 130.

13. Ibid., pt. D, p. 10. Kr^{85} from a plant capable of reprocessing 5 metric tons per day would yield an average dose commitment in the U.S. of 520 man-rem/yr. Because such a plant would service about 50 reactors, about 8 plants would be needed, yielding a total of 4,200 man-rem. Dividing this by a population of 2×10^8 gives an average dose of 0.02 mrem/yr. For tritium, the result is larger, in the ratio of 3,700/520. The Kr^{85} exposure is worldwide, but the tritium exposure is largely limited to the U.S.

14. Environmental Protection Agency. Estimates of ionizing radiation doses in the United States, 1960–2000. Report ORP/CSD 72-1.

15. M. Eisenbud. 1970. Standards of radiation protection and their implications for the public health. In Nuclear Power and the Public, ed. H. Forman. U. Minnesota Press.

16. EPA Report 520/9-73-003, pt. B, pp. 39, 88, 109, 128, 146.

17. Several other estimates deviate widely in the detailed contributions of noble gases and tritium, but the overall result is always close to this. See International Atomic Energy Agency (Vienna), Nuclear power and the environment, quoting EPA estimates for 1971; EPA, 1974, Environmental radiation dose commitment: An application to the nuclear power industry, EPA-520/4-73-002; and ref. 14 above.

18. R. O. Pohl. 1976. Nuclear energy: Health impact of carbon-14. Preprint from Physics Dept., Cornell University.

19. W. H. Ellett (EPA), pers. comm., 2 July 1975.

20. The meteorology in refs. 16 and 19 is not given in sufficient detail to be followed, but according to ref. 16 (and other sources) a standard pile 1 km² in area emits 500 pCi/m²-sec, and 2.5 such piles per year would be accumulated if all our power were nuclear, whereas the 7×10^6 km² of soil in the U.S. emits an average of about 1 pCi/m²-sec. Thus, natural radon exceeds the annual increase from tailings piles by a factor of $7 \times 10^6/2.5 \times 500$ = 6,000. Ref. 19 estimates 4,000 deaths per year from natural radon in the U.S.—which at first seems reasonably consistent with their estimate of effects from tailings piles. However, we give here two alternative calculations of deaths from natural radon which circumvent the rather uncertain meteorology. Ref. 2 gives 0.15 rem/yr as an average exposure to the tracheo-bronchial tree which, multiplied by 39×10^{-6} cancer deaths per man-rem from ref. 1 and the 2×10^8 population, gives 1,200 deaths per year. As another approach, one "working level" (WL) is 150×10^3 pCi/m³ and BEIR gives 0.5 rem to lung per WL-"month" where one working "month" is 170 hours or 0.02 years; these combine to give $5,000/150 \times 10^3 \times .02$ = 1.6 mrem/yr per pCi/m³. (This is 2.5 times smaller than the value used in ref. 16, but more significant than this discrepancy is the fact that the BEIR value was used in assessing lung cancer incidence in miners, which was instrumental in determining the value 39×10^{-6} lung cancers per man-rem.) From ref. 2, the average Rn^{222} level in the U.S. is about 120 pCi/m³ which (when multiplied by the above 1.6) gives an average dose of 190 mrem/yr to the lung. Multiplying this by 39×10^{-6} cancers/man-rem and 2×10^8 population gives 1,500 deaths per year from natural radon, in agreement with our above estimate of 1,200. Since radon from tailings piles is 6,000 times smaller, these would give 0.20–0.25 deaths per year from the latter. However, the latter radon originates in sparsely populated regions and must travel about 1,500 miles to reach populous regions; since, during this travel more than half of the Rn^{222} (3.6-day half-life) would decay away, the average toll would be no more than 0.1 death per year from each year of all-nuclear power.

21. EPA Office of Radiation Programs. 1974. Summary report on Phase I: Study of inactive uranium mill sites and tailings piles. Phase II, which involves remedial action, began in 1975.

22. M. B. Sears et al. 1975. Oak Ridge National Laboratory Report ORNL-TM-4903, vol. 1. Correlation of radioactive waste treatment costs and the environmental impact of waste effluents in the nuclear fuel cycle.

23. B. L. Cohen. 1976. Environmental impacts of nuclear power due to radon emissions. Bull. Atomic Scientists, Feb. 1961, p. 61.

24. Federal Register 40:19441, 5/15/75.

25. USAEC. 1957. WASH-740: Theoretical consequences of major accidents in large nuclear power plants. Washington, DC.

26. P. Ayyaswamy, B. Hauss, T. Hseih, A. Moscati, T. E. Hicks, and D. Okrent. 1974. Estimates of the risks associated with dam failure. UCLA Report ENG-7423.

27. H. Kendall. Testimony before Udall Committee on Energy and the Environment, 28 April–2 May 1975. Factors are corrected to those in the final version of WASH-1400.

28. USAEC. 1972. WASH-1238: Environmental survey of transportation of radioactive materials to and from nuclear power plants. See also L. B. Shappert et al., 1973, Nuclear Safety 14:597.

29. M. Ross has proposed that a rather large fraction of the Cs^{137} might be released in an accident (Proc. Int. Symp. on Packaging and Transportation of Radioactive Materials, Miami Beach, 1974, USAEC doc. CONF-740901, p. 830). However, recent studies by G. Parker and L. B. Shappert (pers. comm., letter to U.S. Energy Research and Development Agency, and testimony before Atomic Safety Licensing Board, docket numbers STN50-483, STN50-486) indicate that Ross's estimates were far too large. Far smaller amounts were found to migrate out of the fuel pellets and the Cs was found to be in nonvolatile forms.

30. U.S. NRC document NUREG-0034. The transportation of radioactive material by air and other modes, March 1976. Other studies giving much lower results are C. V. Hodge and A. A. Jarrett, 1974, EPA Report NSS-8191.1, Transportation accident risks in the nuclear power industry, 1975–2020; and USAEC, 1975, WASH-1535: Environmental impact statement for the liquid metal fast breeder reactor, sec. 4.5.

31. B. L. Cohen. 1976. Environmental hazards in radioactive waste disposal. Physics Today Jan. 1976, p. 9.

32. B. L. Cohen. In press. High-level radioactive waste from light water reactors. Rev. Mod. Phys.

33. B. L. Cohen. In press. Hazards from plutonium toxicity. Health Phys.

34. J. McPhee. 1974. The Curve of Binding Energy. NY: Farrar, Strauss, and Giroux.

35. T. B. Taylor, at Hearings of Joint Committee on Atomic Energy, June 1975.

36. U.S. Surgeon-General. 1962. Report on cigarette smoking.

37. E. Teller and A. L. Latter. 1958. Our Nuclear Future. NY: Criterion Books. p. 124.

38. Insurance Institute for Highway Safety, vol. 10, no. 12 (9 July 1975), gives 24.6 fatalities per 100,000 vehicle years registered for small cars and 11.3 for large cars. A similar conclusion is obtained from National Safety Council, Accident Facts-1965 (Chicago).

39. Being overweight by 25% (about 40 lb for the average adult male) reduces life expectancy by about 5 years (L. I. Dublin and H. Marks, 1952, Mortality among Insured Overweights in Recent Years, NY: Metropolitan Life Insurance Co.). Since 1.2 hours is 1.4×10^{-4} years, a linear hypothesis gives the risk to be that of $8 \text{ lb/yr} \times 1.4 \times 10^{-4} \text{ yr} = 1.2 \times 10^{-3} \text{ lb} = 0.02 \text{ oz}$.

40. L. Pauling. 1958. Proc. Nat. Acad. Sci. 44:619.

41. U.S. Senate Committee on Public Works, 1975, "Air quality and stationary source emission control, gives values for an urban plant (p. 631) and a remote plant (p. 626); we use the average of these and multiply by 400 for the number of plants. A larger number of deaths is estimated by R. Wilson, paper presented at Energy Symposium, Boulder, CO, June 1974.

42. B. L. Cohen. 1974. Nuclear Science and Society. NY: Doubleday-Anchor. pp. 139, 140.

43. L. Sagan. 1974. Nature 250:109.

PART 3 *Changing the Air*

John T. Middleton

Views

Planning against Air Pollution

The Acting Commissioner of the Air Pollution Control Office discusses the major sources of air pollution and methods used for its measurement and control

Our environment is changing—we are changing it—and serious questions are being raised as to whether man can adapt to some of these changes. Our air for example is heavily burdened with dirt and chemicals. It constricts our throats and makes us sick; it kills some of us ahead of our time. It besmirches our great cities and destroys some of the material goods and pleasures for which we began enduring the pollution in the first place.

We could solve this problem instantly by stopping our cars, closing our industries, and giving up many of the things that we believe are worthwhile. In time the air would purge itself of most of its impurities and we could live primitively and pastorally in a dull, uncomfortable Walden. But most of us would prefer something else. And so, as a matter of national policy, government at several levels is working within its financial and professional capabilities to limit pollution.

The motor vehicle

The automobile is at present the source of almost half of all air pollution in this

An international authority in the broad field of air pollution, Dr. John T. Middleton was first recognized for his early detection of photochemical air pollution as an adverse economic factor to California agriculture in the mid-1940s. After a career on the plant pathology faculty of the University of California (Riverside and Los Angeles), during which he also was for ten years director of the University of California Statewide Air Pollution Research Center, he was appointed on January 1, 1967, to be director of the newly created National Center for Air Pollution Control, under the Department of Health, Education and Welfare, and has headed the national air pollution control program ever since. He is now Acting Commissioner of the Air Pollution Control Office in the Environmental Protection Agency. Dr. Middleton is a member of numerous professional associations and has served on many government boards. Address: Environmental Protection Agency, Air Pollution Control Office, 5600 Fishers Lane, Rockville, MD 20852.

country. It accounts for more than half the hydrocarbons, nearly half the nitrogen oxides, and two-thirds of the carbon monoxide that are released into the air of the United States each year. It is also the chief source of lead in the atmosphere. The hydrocarbons are a vast family of chemicals, most of which are directly harmful only in high concentrations as gases. However, some hydrocarbons are toxic in themselves, and others participate in a series of reactions with the oxides of nitrogen that takes place in the presence of sunlight. This leads to the formation of new, highly troublesome and toxic products called "oxidants," which cause eye irritation, allergenic responses, reduced work performance, depressed mitochondrial activity, altered functioning of several biological systems, and destructive effects on vegetation, polymers, cellulose, and dyes.

Even quite low levels of oxidant pollution, on the order of 200 to 590 $\mu g/m^3$ (0.05 to 0.30 ppm), have been shown to cause eye irritations and to impair the performance of young athletes. Eight-hour exposure to carbon monoxide concentrations that are common in cities has been shown to produce temporary impairment of mental performance.

We have little information on the effects on man's health of exposure to the levels of nitrogen oxides commonly found in urban air. However, a study made in Chattanooga, Tennessee, has tentatively linked low levels of these oxides to children's susceptibility to respiratory illness.

We do not know the significance of urban smog in geophysical changes caused by pollution on a global scale. But photochemical smog is known to

affect city climates, and it appears to be responsible for widespread chronic and acute damage to vegetation hundreds of miles from urban centers, so the possibility of secondary long-term effects must be considered.

Finally, there is lead. Emissions of lead into the nation's air are now about 200,000 tons per year. Ten years ago the total was about 130,000 tons. Symptoms of lead poisoning in humans have been reported at blood levels as low as 60 micrograms of lead per 100 grams of blood. It has been shown that persons who are frequently exposed to lead, such as traffic policemen, have more of it in their blood than other persons; and the normal blood levels of persons who are not unusually exposed now range from 10 to 30 micrograms of lead per 100 grams of blood. This is not much of a safety factor in view of the increase in emissions that expose more and more of us to the hazard. Recognizing this fact and the need to provide a new motor vehicle emission-reduction technology, the petroleum industry has shown that the lead can be removed.

The Environmental Protection Agency (EPA) has been requiring progressively more stringent pollution controls on automobiles. First it required the elimination of hydrocarbon emissions from the crankcase and partial control of exhaust hydrocarbons in new models for 1968. Then it tightened the exhaust and carbon monoxide standards for 1970 cars. The 1971 models also had to meet the first standards limiting the evaporative loss of hydrocarbons from the engine and fuel system. The cars of 1972 will have to meet new standards for evaporative hydrocarbons and will be tested under far more exacting conditions than any that have been used heretofore, to achieve a 69 percent reduction in carbon monoxide and an 80 percent reduction in hydrocarbons. The first limit on emissions of oxides of nitrogen will go into effect in 1973.

The 1970 Clean Air Amendments provide for the testing of production-line models of automobiles, as well as the prototypes that were tested under the 1967 Clean Air Act. The Amendments also provide for the reduction of 1975-model carbon monoxide and hydrocarbon emissions to a level that is 90 percent lower than was allowed on 1970 prototypes, and for the reduction of 1976-model emissions of nitrogen oxides to a level that is 90 percent below those that were reported in 1971-model cars. Reductions of this order, however, may not by themselves be adequate to achieve healthful air quality levels in the most congested urban areas; other steps and further emission reductions may be necessary.

To stimulate inquiry and uncover possible new approaches to the problem, the EPA began a Federal Clean Car Incentive program. It is hoped that this program will attract the talent and energy of a large number of inventive people and forward-looking companies, and lead to the production by the late 1970s of a pollution-free passenger car. Such a car should equal the convenience and performance of the present-day automobile and allow the matching of fuels to vehicles for better air pollution control. And all of this is an add-on—not a substitute for mass transit.

Industrial pollution

Let us turn to the effort to reduce emissions from stationary sources—mainly industrial plants. Since the Clean Air Act of 1967, we have been drawing geographical boundaries around air quality control regions for those places where air pollution is a particularly serious problem. We have so far designated 101 such regions and will increase that number as the states request that additional areas be designated as set out in the Clean Air Amendments of 1970.

We have published criteria reports to tell what science has thus far been able to reveal of the insidious as well as the obvious effects of air pollution on man and his environment. So far, these reports cover the five most important classes of pollutant—sulfur dioxide,

particulate matter, carbon monoxide, hydrocarbons, and photochemical oxidant. With each of these reports, we have published also a summary of methods for controlling these pollutants.

It has been up to the States with federal help to devise, adopt, and implement regional air quality standards that would safeguard the public health. But under the time schedule set forth in the Clean Air Act, only 26 States submitted standards, and only 17 regional implementation plans designed to achieve those standards have been submitted.

Now the Clean Air Act has been amended to provide for faster action. By February 1st, we will issue proposed national air quality standards on the pollutants that I have already mentioned, plus another—oxides of nitrogen—for which the criteria and technology reports also will be issued at the same time.

These standards will be based on the criteria documents, which represent the best evidence presently attainable on the effects of air pollution. To protect the public health, there will be nationwide primary air quality standards which will define how clean the air must be in order to be healthful to breathe. To safeguard the public welfare, there will be nationwide secondary air quality standards, which will say how clean the air must be in order to protect us against the known or anticipated effects of air pollution on property, materials, climate, economic values, and personal comfort.

It is significant, I think, that these standards will be set entirely on the basis of the need to protect public health and welfare, and the need to attain them will either force the use of available technology or create new pressure for the discovery and demonstration of new methods to control air pollution; we will set the goals and it will be up to scientists, technicians, and planners to find ways to meet them.

Under the 1970 amendments, the states will continue to have primary responsibility for devising regulatory and enforcement procedures to achieve the necessary improvements in air quality. This is work that must begin at once; it must reflect the kind of social and political decisions that are

inherent in reforms of this magnitude. Public participation in this process is encouraged by law. As a result, what the *Wall Street Journal* has called a "breathers' lobby" has developed to press for cleaner air across the country.

The new law also provides for the establishment in 1971 of federal performance standards for new stationary sources of air pollution, reflecting the use of the best system of emission reduction that has been adequately demonstrated, and for the establishment of federal emission limitations for hazardous pollutants that may cause or contribute to an increase in mortality or an increase in serious irreversible or incapacitating illness. New sources, let me make clear, are those that are built after the date of any proposed standards, or modified in such a way as to emit any pollutant not previously emitted or cause an increase in present pollutants.

The states may also be empowered to administer these provisions if their clean-air officials have authority to review plans and specifications of new industrial facilities, to prohibit the construction of those that fail to meet the national standards, and in the case of hazardous pollutants, to provide adequate and speedy enforcement procedures to safeguard public health.

So far, progress in the control of pollution from stationary sources is furthest advanced in the control of sulfur oxides and particulate matter. The sulfur oxide problem is particularly urgent because the pollutant is so hazardous, so common, and so closely linked to vital industries. More than half of all sulfur oxide emissions in this country come from electric generating plants. Nationally, approximately 37,000,000 tons of sulfur oxides will be discharged into our atmosphere this year. Unless adequate control measures are taken, our most optimistic forecasts indicate that these emissions will increase over 60 percent by 1980 and almost fourfold by the year 2000.

National energy policy

The issue of control hinges, in the short term, on the development of a wise energy policy for the nation, a policy which will reflect our concern with social and environmental objectives as well as promote economic progress. The creation of such a policy should be a matter of pressing concern

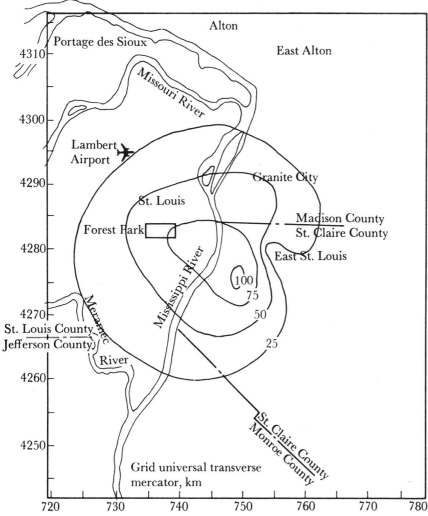

Figure 1. Observed sulfur oxide concentrations (annual arithmetic mean, $\mu g/m^3$) in 1967 in East St. Louis–Granite City, Illinois, and St. Louis, Missouri.

to the scientist both as scientist and citizen. To reduce the air pollution from oxides of sulfur, particulates, and oxides of nitrogen by using other energy-producing techniques will not solve the overall environmental problem if new types of air pollution problems are generated, and if no solution is found for thermal pollution. In the case of nuclear generating plants, it is assumed that environmental problems will be resolved so that we will be able to use as much atomic power as we now expect. The use of solar cells and fuel cells to generate electricity could, by the 1980s, be increasingly important factors in solving the nation's total energy problem with a minimum of environmental pollution.

Attention is already being given to attempting to define the possible implications of various fuel policy options. The Federal Power Commission, the Atomic Energy Commission, the Office of Science and Technology, and the Office of Energy Preparedness will certainly influence any final decisions, as will the Department of Interior, the industries affected, and the public. Certainly the voices of the Council on Environmental Quality and the EPA will also be heard.

I cannot attempt to predict what will finally emerge when these various viewpoints have been weighed. But I can mention some of the considerations of the EPA.

It is becoming more evident all the time that the United States lacks adequate reserves of gas and oil to supply indefinitely our growing demand for energy. Coal is the only readily available domestic fossil fuel with reserves that are large enough to fill such needs for generations to come; but most of the coal in the country contains large quantities of sulfur, which are changed into sulfur oxides by the combustion process. We may have to take steps to get our reserves of low-sulfur coal and oil developed preferentially. If we adopt a goal of obtaining within ten years adequate supplies of low-sulfur gas from coal, we can perhaps take a less restrictive view toward problems of depleting reserves of natural gas.

We may have to consider providing incentives for importing more liquefied natural gas and developing more liquid natural gas storage facilities. Environmental problems and increasing costs of fuel make importation of liquefied natural gas seem to be probable future steps.

The EPA's present approach within its own purview is to couple state regulation of emissions with the development of technology in order to provide alternate solutions to reconcile our energy demands with the demand for a clean environment. We have to look for new technology in order to assure that air quality standards will be attainable in a reasonable time.

While a national energy policy is being developed and applied, we should be developing, testing, and providing techniques to remove sulfur from fuels and the products of combustion. Inquisitive and talented men and women are needed to develop more efficient combustion techniques by the end of the decade and to determine whether or not our limited oil supplies are to be used for chemical production or for heat. What do we do with our abundant coal supplies—gasify them? Is it better resource management to produce sulfur as a reclamation product of combustion or to mine it?

Sulfur oxides

Unless scientists and others apply themselves to answering these questions, we shall continue to make ourselves sick with sulfur dioxide. A study in Rotterdam showed a positive association between total mortality and exposure for a few days to 24-hour average concentrations of 0.19 ppm of sulfur dioxide; there was an indication that the association held true even at lower levels. These levels are often exceeded in many cities in the United States. A major British study found an association between air pollution and deaths from bronchitis and lung cancer in an area where the yearly average level of sulfur dioxide was 0.04 ppm;

this level is quite common now in our cities.

Solid or liquid particulate matter in the air can carry sulfur dioxide deep into the lungs, causing injuries much more severe than are encountered in laboratory experiments using sulfur dioxide alone. The health hazards of air polluted with sulfur dioxide and particulates have been demonstrated in a number of air pollution disasters; for example in Donora, Pennsylvania, in New York City, and in London.

In the atmosphere sulfur dioxide reacts rather quickly with other materials to form sulfuric acid and salts of sulfuric acid. From the geophysical point of view, the EPA is studying the formation and persistence of sulfate aerosol; from the biological point of view, we are looking at the accumulation in soil and surface waters of sulfuric and sulfurous acids and their salts following rain and fallout. There is some evidence that over some seas and tropical land areas the condensation nuclei are largely ammonium sulfate; and the sulfate aerosol is estimated to persist for days in the troposphere and for hundreds of days in the stratosphere.

On a local scale, the sulfur family of pollutants corrodes metals, disintegrates paints, causes fibers to weaken and fade, discolors building materials and makes them deteriorate. Agricultural production drops as plant growth and yield are suppressed. And sulfur oxides contribute to the reduction of visibility that often accompanies air pollution.

Particulate pollution

By itself, undifferentiated particulate pollution—from particles under 500 microns in diameter—can injure surfaces within the respiratory system and affect climate, visibility, building materials, textile fibers, and vegetation. Specific substances that may become suspended in the air as particulate matter of course require individual assessment. One of the most common, and the only one I shall deal with here, is lead. Not only are human-body burdens of lead rising near points of peril; the total environment is accumulating lead. Particles of lead from air pollution—most of them originating in the automobile, which spews out 90 percent of its lead particles at sizes smaller than two-tenths of a micron—have been found in the snow

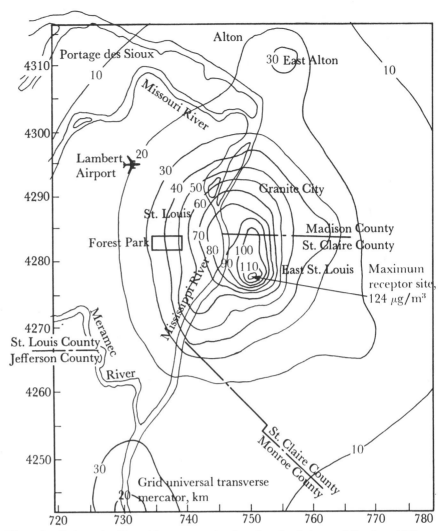

Figure 2.   Estimated sulfur oxide concentrations based on simulation modeling from 1967 emissions data.

of polar ice caps. In these layerings of one winter's snow upon the next it is possible to discern the annual increase in the earth's airborne lead pollution.

As we approach the danger point for human beings, are we approaching the danger points for other forms of life? I do not know, but I do believe that lead, once it is in the environment, is an ominous and persistent threat, narrowing our margins of life-safety.

Weather as a factor

Weather is a vital factor in the pollution problem that is of particular interest to the scientist. On the one hand, we may be raising the earth's temperature with carbon dioxide that blocks the long-wave radiation of heat away from our planet; on the other hand, we may be cooling our earth by blocking solar energy with a great shield of particulate pollution. And not only do pollutants affect the weather in various

other ways—as by nucleating clouds and producing acidic rainfall—but there are reciprocal effects. Weather conditions, as I have said, affect the transformation of automotive emissions into photochemical smog; and they can clamp the smog tightly upon the communities where it is produced.

Ordinarily, thermal and mechanical turbulence mix and dilute pollutants in the atmosphere; and the wind, if it is strong enough, can scatter them. Ultimately, natural processes can remove man-made pollutants from the atmosphere. Some, in time, escape into space. Rain and snow eventually wash out the rest—whether in solid, liquid, or gaseous form—and deposit them in the earth's soil and water. But when the surface air is cooler than a layer of air above it, and mixing cannot occur, the atmosphere is said to be stable—the condition is known as an inversion—and pollutants accumulate in the limited air space. At one time

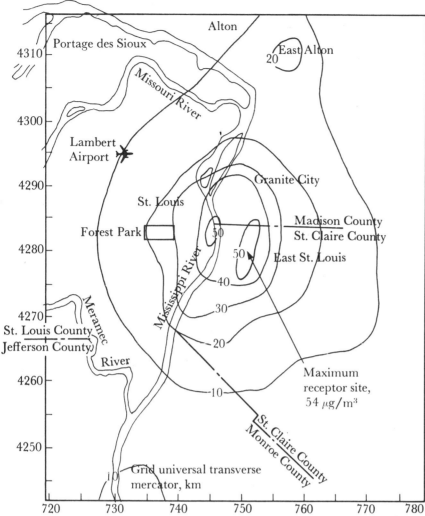

Figure 3. One emissions strategy, tested through simulation modeling, reduces estimated SOx pollution by 30 percent.

this was believed to be a problem only in Los Angeles—but times have changed.

Antipollution strategies

The design of strategies to reduce hazards to health from air pollution hinges on an ability to predict phenomena of this nature precisely enough and well enough in advance so that positive emergency actions may be taken and the availability assured of adequate technologies to control the sources of pollution.

Some of us remember the dismal, dark, black, coal smoke days of the 1930s. Some progressive urban areas have traded those old black days for new whiskey-brown days of photochemical smog.

Let us use St. Louis as a case study. Wind currents from East St. Louis on some days transport the Illinois con-

tribution to air pollution and add it to the Missouri problem. On other days, of course, Missouri gives it back. In the St. Louis air quality control region, the airborne burden of sulfur oxides will have to be reduced by 81 percent in the next few years in order to meet Missouri air quality standards. The present burden of particulate matter there will have to be reduced 61 percent. The improvements called for in Los Angeles under the California standards are 64 percent for sulfur oxide and 54 percent for particulates. For Cleveland they are 70 percent each. These are not measurements of the efficiency of control devices; these are the reductions needed in ambient pollution in order to meet the state standard of air quality.

Simulation modeling

The task of relating such goals to the design of emission controls to achieve the goals is a function of simulation

modeling involving sophisticated use of computers and plotting techniques. Only through the use of a simulation model can air pollution control be advanced from the haphazard to the systematic.

Let us say that the state or local control agency has measured a number of different concentrations of sulfur dioxide in St. Louis (Fig. 1). (Such measurements have already been made in a number of air quality control regions across the country.) The control officer needs to know how stringently to limit this or that source or group of sources in order to achieve healthful air at the point where pollution is worst.

Air pollution concentrations in our simulation model are a function of rates of emission, rates of pollutant decay, the height at which the pollutant is released into the air, its temperature at emergence, the topography of the community, and weather conditions. The related variables provide a basis for drawing on a map of the community isopleths of concentration from a source or group of sources. The simulation model (Fig. 2) will fill in the gaps left by local control agency measurements.

Most local sampling networks are not sufficiently extensive to identify all heavily contaminated areas or to indicate in any detail the differences in levels of pollution. The estimates provided by the model supplement the observed data and furnish much of this detail. This added information is subject to confirmation by comparison with the data gathered directly from the air sampling network. We see that there is a high degree of correlation between Figures 1 and 2. Also, the simulation indicates the need for additional sampling to the north of present sites; in this way it can be used as a basis for appropriate expansion and rearrangement of the air sampling network.

Further, the simulation provides the control officer with a ready tool for theoretical testing of various limits that might be selected for different sources or categories of sources. These limits—called emission standards—would be put into effect through legally enforceable control regulations.

By using various emission standards in the model, reductions in pollution levels ranging from around 30 to 80 percent can be achieved (Figs. 3, 4, 5). Some cities might not need to achieve as great reductions as other cities and might select different emission strategies. What is important is that intelligent choices be available.

Somewhat different approaches are used to set up simulation models for individual plants or factories—"point sources"—and area sources, such as a residential neighborhood having many minor sources of air pollution, or a congested highway; but the modeling procedure generally is similar. Also the model has limitations: it is more accurate over large areas than over areas the size of, say, a city block; and it is more accurate over the long term than the short. It is possible, however, to use the model to estimate short-term and neighborhood concentrations, if geometric standard deviations are used carefully.

The possibilities for the use of a tool such as the simulation model are not restricted to the control agency, nor are they restricted to the United States alone. The North Atlantic Treaty Organization—an agency set up primarily for the common defense—is attempting to use its technical resources to assist the Committee on Challenges to Modern Society to develop emission-reduction strategies for Frankfort, in Germany, and Ankara, in Turkey. NATO is using simulation modeling to achieve this goal, which is related to one of its lesser known but highly significant purposes: social and economic improvement in member countries.

Wherever the simulation model is used, it not only lends itself to the solution of immediate problems offering a variety of choices to correct conditions that exist today, but also provides insight into the problems that may exist in the future, when the community will have been further changed by growing urbanization and industrialization.

In the long term, strategies for emission reduction will have to take account of the changes projected in air quality due to changes in population trends, transportation, marketing, manufacturing, employment, energy requirements, solid-waste disposal needs, and the like—questions that have to do with the proper design of communities. Some communities

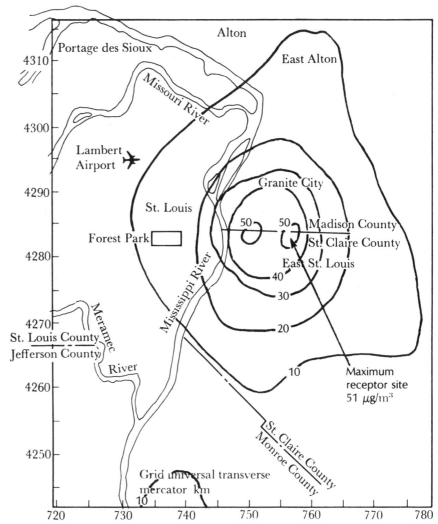

Figure 4. Simulation modeling reveals that another strategy would achieve a slightly greater reduction.

doubtless will discover that some neighborhoods—and some regions—simply cannot tolerate any more of certain kinds of industry, even after the best available technology is applied to that industry's pollution problems. Such situations may not be too far in the future for some urban areas.

It is also quite possible that simulation modeling may indicate the need for changes in highway planning or traffic patterns in order to reduce the hazard to the health of residents of some particular neighborhood. Given a continuation of present automobile marketing trends, such considerations will become of greater urgency to city planners and elected officials; in fact, there are some neighborhoods in this country where such problems are already causing concern.

These will not be easy decisions for the responsible authorities. One can imagine the consternation of shopkeepers if traffic past their shopping center had

to be rerouted during certain peak hours in order to avoid dangerously high levels of carbon monoxide or lead pollution in nearby suburbs. A high level of statesmanship, matching our concern for the public health, will be required of local officials.

Chicago plan for "emission rights"

One plan, under study in Chicago, would use the zoning ordinance as a device to control legally the effective emission density associated with each parcel of land in the region. This would limit the use of land to the extent necessary to achieve the regional air quality standards. The owner of a given parcel of land would own certain specific "emission rights" that are attached to the land until it is rezoned. Unused emission rights associated with one parcel of land might be sold to the owner of a neighboring parcel if he needed them.

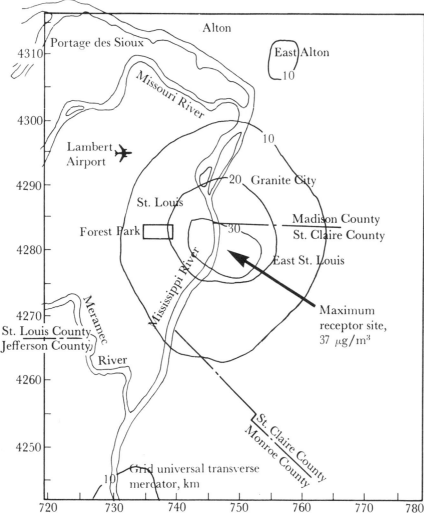

Figure 5.   A third strategy would achieve an 80 percent reduction; officials may choose among the various strategies to achieve the result they desire.

The Chicago approach could be modified as required for emission controls based on global as well as regional (or zoning) perspectives. The global concern would reflect the general need to reduce pollution in order to limit the long-term buildup in the atmosphere. The regional perspective relates to the need to limit shorter term dosages as measured at ground-level receptor points. Global considerations, for example, might require all plants to reduce particulate emissions by 80 percent, regardless of stack height and location. The regional rule, however, might require more stringent levels of control for plants situated in specific neighborhoods.

Whatever is finally decided upon, the Chicago approach is at least interesting and reflects the broad-scale rethinking of pollution-control efforts and an awareness of the relationship between land use and pollution. President Nixon accented this relation-

ship in his first Environmental Report to the Congress last August: "The uses to which our generation puts the land can either expand or severely limit the choices our children will have. ... Society as a whole has a legitimate interest in proper land use." The President's message was the first clear-cut national policy statement in our history on the prospect of land-use reform as a tool to achieve a more livable environment. The 1970 Clean Air Amendments insist on the use of that tool whenever it is needed to meet the national standards.

The broader role of the scientist

The scientist too has a new and vital role to play. In the past he was relied upon to enlarge the range of options that were available to the policymaker, but now those two functions are coming together. The needs of the time summon those who have special

knowledge to use their influence when policy decisions are being made, so that the decisions will be more likely to be correct.

It is a difficult task that we are thrusting upon the scientist, but it will be even more difficult to evade. That disinterested impartiality so necessary for scientific inquiry may no longer, in these times, be cited to excuse the scholar from participation in the decisions of the nation. Such aloofness has nearly always been distrusted in the past, and in a social sense this disapproval is very healthy because it is based on deep instincts for the welfare of the nation as a whole.

Scientists must prepare themselves to meet this new responsibility and apply their special knowledge to the general welfare. The old and rigid disciplines of academic life are in need of crosspollination. This is the time of the specially trained generalist, the man of many parts.

Our young people, many of them, see this. They are resisting the inflexible categorization of the outmoded university system. Help me become, they say, not a chemical engineer but a citizen engineer; not a chemist or physicist or biologist but a specially trained and highly aware citizen with responsibilities and tasks that cut across the old professional boundaries. The United States in the last half of the twentieth century desperately needs the participation and services of such universal men, for we are in a pretty pickle and our principles as well as our people are in danger. Only with the devoted effort, the courage, and the counsel of skilled and responsible scientists and technicians can America discover the options and select the best among them in order that our tomorrows may be as bright as our yesterdays seem to have been.

The Congress, in the National Environmental Policy Act of 1969, summoned each one of us to the task of preserving what we have left and repairing what we have lost. Our land and air and water, and the animal and plant life that sustains our human lives, are in our own hands. We as scientists have some of the knowledge of how to protect them and the responsibility for educating and training the new generations who will join the quest for a livable environment.

Paul F. Fennelly

The Origin and Influence of Airborne Particulates

Both man-made and natural processes contribute to the concentration of particulate matter in the atmosphere; the effects of this aerosol on human health, environment, and climate are just beginning to be understood

When we think about the air around us, we usually think of gases: oxygen, nitrogen, argon, carbon dioxide, water vapor. Yet the air also contains a variety of microscopic particles which, despite their exceedingly small size and low concentration, can exert a significant influence on atmospheric behavior and on human health and property.

Microscopic particles in the air, commonly called particulates, are not a new phenomenon. The haze characteristic of rural areas like the Smokey Mountains of North Carolina or the Blue Ridge Mountains of Virginia, for instance, is caused by airborne particulates. The particulates form after certain vapors emitted from the trees absorb sunlight and undergo a series of photochemical reactions in the atmosphere. The haze or coloration, caused by the manner in which the particles scatter sunlight, is part of the natu-

Paul F. Fennelly is a staff scientist with the GCA/Technology Division, an environmental consulting and research firm. His current activities deal mainly with assessing the environmental impact of new energy systems and investigating the role of particulates in urban atmospheres. Dr. Fennelly received his Ph.D. in physical chemistry from Brandeis University in 1972. As a postdoctoral fellow at the Center for Research in Experimental Space Science at York University in Toronto, he was involved in a research program investigating the reactions of ions and radicals with atmospheric gases. He later joined AeroChem Research Laboratories in Princeton, N.J., where he participated in the development of techniques for monitoring atmospheric pollutants. This paper is based on a project supported by the Environmental Protection Agency; however, it should not be taken to represent the official agency view of any of the problems discussed. Address: GCA/Technology Division, Burlington Rd., Bedford, MA 01730.

ral cycle, and no adverse effects are usually attributed to it.

A more recent phenomenon is the appearance over the last twenty-five years or so of intense hazes in our cities and industrial areas—the so-called urban smog (Fig. 1). The adverse effects of smog are common knowledge: dirt, grime, reduced visibility, and, in many cases, increases in morbidity and mortality rates. The accumulation of these adverse effects eventually triggered the passage of air pollution control legislation which set limits on the concentrations of various species in the air.

One of the targets of this legislation was to control the amount of particulate matter in the air. A standard of 75 micrograms per cubic meter was established as an acceptable upper limit for the annual average of total suspended particulates in the atmosphere in any given region (roughly 75 parts per billion by weight of dry air). For any given 24-hour period, a concentration of 260 μg/m^3 was established as a maximum tolerable limit.

To achieve these standards, limits were set on the amount of solid material that could be discharged from various industrial smokestacks or automobile exhausts. Standards were also established for emissions of the gases SO_2, NO_2, O_3, CO, and hydrocarbons, which can cause adverse effects by themselves but are also of interest here because they contribute to the formation of particulates in the atmosphere.

In many urban areas, the air quality standards for suspended particulate matter are not being met, and there are those who think that the proce-

dures for attaining these standards may be inadequate. On the other hand, some scientists are questioning whether the established standards are a realistic goal. There is some evidence that natural and uncontrollable sources of particulate matter in many cases contribute to the atmospheric loading in quantities which make the present standards unattainable. The situation is further complicated by the possibility of long-range transport of airborne particulates. A mounting body of data indicates that particulate matter or gases leading to the formation of particulate matter which are injected into the atmosphere in one location can be deposited at locations up to several hundred miles away. The implication is obvious: in regions where deposition or fallout occurs, the enforcement of strict pollution control procedures on a local basis will have little impact on air quality. The debate over standards for airborne particulate matter will probably intensify in the next few years.

Particulates are minute solid particles or liquid droplets ranging in size from 0.005 to about 500 microns. (A human hair, by comparison, is about 100 microns thick.) The size limits are rather arbitrary but are meant to indicate that the particles can be as small as a cluster of several molecules or as large as a visible dust kernel. The physical and chemical properties of particulate matter are extremely varied.

Very fine particulates behave almost like a gas or vapor: they are subject to Brownian motion, follow fluid streamlines, and are capable of coagulation and condensation. Larger particulates have more of

Figure 1. Airborne particulates are a prime constituent of urban smog. The photograph shows an atmospheric inversion over Hartford, Connecticut, viewed from the Talcott Mountain Science Center in Avon, about 6 miles west of the city. Automobile and industrial emissions have become trapped beneath the overlying warmer air, and the murky layer containing high concentrations of sulfates, nitrates, and hydrocarbons persists until a new front restores atmospheric mixing. The plume of steam, issuing from an East Hartford industrial plant, was energetic enough to pierce the inversion but dissipated in 3–4 minutes. The horizon, barely visible as a faint gray band above the darker gray of the inversion, is about 18 miles away. The photograph was taken at about 8 a.m. on a cold winter day; by noon, the city was no longer visible through the smog. (Photo courtesy of G. C. Atamian, Talcott Mountain Science Center, Avon, CT.)

the characteristics of solid matter: they are strongly influenced by gravity and seldom coalesce or condense. The chemical behavior of particulates is determined either by the composition of the particles themselves or by the gases adsorbed by the surfaces of the particles. In some cases, the combination of particle and adsorbed gas produces a synergistic chemical effect more powerful than that of the individual components.

Particulates are usually characterized as primary or secondary. Primary particulates—usually 1 to 20 μm in size—are those injected directly into the atmosphere by chemical or physical processes. Secondary particulates are produced as a result of chemical reactions that take place in the atmosphere. They are relatively smaller and can be generally classified chemically as sulfates, nitrates, and hydrocarbons. Not surprisingly, the heaviest concentrations of airborne particulates are usually located along the coastlines and in the heavily industrialized mid-central states. However, as shown in Figure 2, air quality standards are exceeded fairly uniformly across the nation, even in rural areas—despite a general national decline in the total suspended particulate levels during the period 1970–73, when the legal controls were first put into effect. The evidence of violations even in nonindustrial rural areas is being used in many quarters to argue for a reinvestigation of the standards.

Primary particulates

Primary particulates, produced directly by the physical or chemical processes peculiar to a specified emitter, come from extremely varied sources, ranging from those in the industrial sector, such as gravel crushers and blast furnaces, to those in nature, such as forest fires and ocean spray. The chemical compositions, of course, vary with the type of source.

Particle size can be expressed either in terms of the physical or geometric diameter or in terms of an equivalent diameter pertaining to an optical, electrical, or aerodynamic property of the particle. The technique used to measure individual particles often determines which category of size is reported. For example, sieves, which are effective only in sizing particles larger than about 5 μm, measure the geometric or physical diameter. Impactors, usually effective in sizing particles in the range 0.1–5.0 μm, determine the aerodynamic diameter—a measure related to the density of the

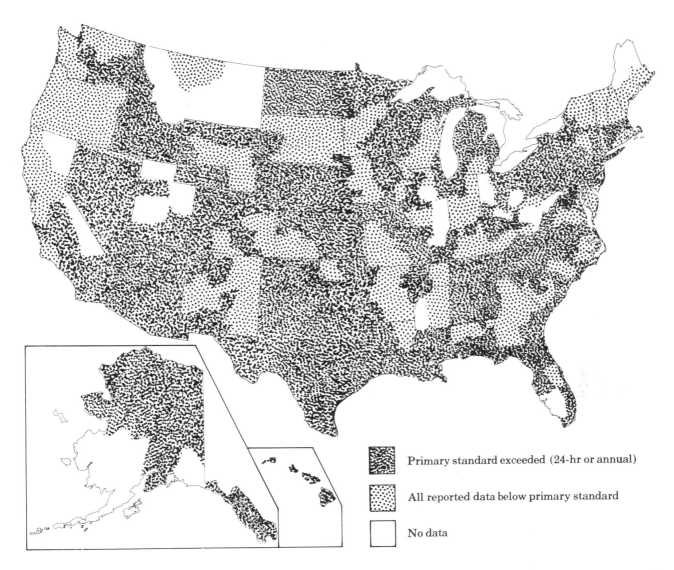

Figure 2. Although the legal controls on air pollution instituted nationwide in the period 1970–73 brought about a general decline in the level of suspended particulates, the map, based on measurements taken in 1973, shows that air quality standards continue to be exceeded in urban and rural areas alike throughout the U.S. Frequently, violations of the standards result from the presence of particulates formed by uncontrollable natural processes such as windblown dust. (Adapted from ref. *61*.)

particle and its behavior in a flowing air stream. In an impactor, the airstream containing the particulates is passed through a series of orifices and collection plates which are separated by successively smaller distances. Particles are selectively deposited on the collection plate on the basis of their inertia in the gas stream. Particles on the order of 0.1 μm can be monitored with light-scattering techniques that determine the size peculiar to the optical properties of the particle.

In compiling data on particulates, the use of standard sizing and sampling methods is very important. At present, we lack standardized techniques, and, as a result, much of the available data on particulate size is

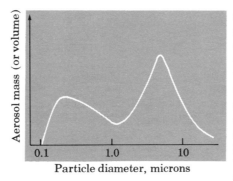

Figure 3. Recent experiments indicate that atmospheric particulates show a bimodal size distribution (represented schematically in the graph) which reflects their different formation mechanisms. Larger, primary particulates are formed by a variety of physical and chemical means; they include soil dust and solid industrial emissions released directly into the air. The smaller, secondary particulates are the product of chemical reactions taking place in the atmosphere.

difficult to assess. Until a few years ago, data compiled by traditional aerosol sizing techniques indicated that atmospheric aerosols had a unimodal size distribution. Recent data acquired with more sensitive aerosol sizing instrumentation indicate a bimodal size distribution, as shown schematically in Figure 3. Since different techniques were used it was unclear whether the observed distribution was an atmospheric effect or an instrumental artifact. The validity of the conflicting results was recently debated (*1, 2, 3, 4*), and the consensus was that smog does have a bimodal size distribution with respect to particle volume and mass and that the older sizing techniques were inadequate to detect it.

Figure 4. A wide variety of types and sizes of primary particulates are found in the aerosols of both urban and rural areas. The sizes of the species represented here are based on the geometric diameter of equivalent spheres, measured in microns. (Adapted from ref. *62*.)

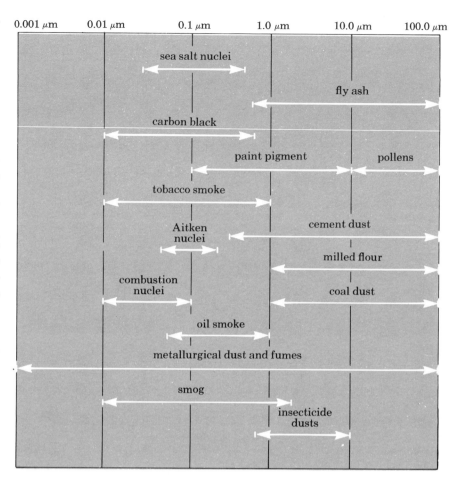

Other evidence supports this finding, indicating that most particles larger than 2.0 µm are primary particulates and most of those smaller than 1.0 µm are secondary particulates. Distinctions of this sort can have significant implications for particulate control technology. For example, the cost of removing particulates from gas streams increases drastically as the size of the particles to be removed decreases. If indeed most of the particles in the atmosphere that are smaller than 1.0 µm are secondary particulates, then the development of a technology for removing ultrafine particles from stack gases may be a waste of time and money. The effort might better be devoted to controlling the gaseous precursors of secondary particulates. Which suspected culprits air pollution control technology should try to control (and to what degree) remains a question. But until standard sizing and sampling methods can be established, it is imperative that more comparisons of data acquired with different sizing techniques be conducted.

The size ranges of some common particles are summarized in Figure 4, and Table 1 offers data on the relative contributions of various sources to the particulate loading of the atmosphere. The data in Table 1 involve gross averages and are probably reliable only to within an order of magnitude. For the most part any data based on particulate mass loading must be cautiously assessed because there is no direct correlation between the mass of particulates in the air and their effect on air quality in general. Natural dust, although it constitutes almost half the total mass of particulate matter injected into the atmosphere, has a relatively small impact. Because dust particles are generally larger than 10 µm and are fairly dense, they quickly settle out of the atmosphere as a result of gravity-induced sedimentation.

Dustfall is a nuisance, but it is usu-

Table 1. Significant sources of man-made particulate pollution in the United States

Source	Emissions (millions of tons/yr)	Total
Natural dusts		63
Forest fires[a]		56.3
Wildfire	37	
Controlled fire		
Slash burning	6	
Accumulated litter	11	
Agricultural burning	2.4	
Transportation		1.2
Motor vehicles		
Gasoline	0.420	
Diesel	0.260	
Aircraft	0.030	
Railroads	0.220	
Water transport	0.150	
Nonhighway use		
Agriculture	0.079	
Commercial	0.012	
Construction	0.003	
Other	0.026	
Incineration		0.931
Municipal incineration	0.098	
On-site incineration	0.185	
Wigwam burners (excluding forest products disposal)	0.035	
Open dump	0.613	
Other minor sources		1.284
Rubber from tires	0.300	
Cigarette smoke	0.230	
Aerosols from spray cans	0.390	
Ocean salt spray	0.340	
Total		122.715

SOURCE: Ref. *6*.
[a] More recent estimates indicate that the emission rates for forest fires are as much as a factor of 5 lower than those listed here.

ally a local condition, although some instances of long-range transport of dust have been reported. High concentrations of airborne particulates observed in the Caribbean have been correlated with severe dust storms in the Sahara (5). Long-range transport of soil dust, however, is usually limited to areas with special meteorological conditions, such as the prevailing trade winds of the Caribbean. The long-range transport of secondary particulates or very fine combustion nuclei, however, may be more common.

Transportation systems contribute only about 1% of the total mass of particulate matter, yet their impact is far more severe than that of natural dust, because most particles produced by motor vehicles are very small. Approximately 60–80% of the particulate mass in automobile exhaust is composed of particles having aerodynamic diameters smaller than 2.0 μm (7). The distribution of these smaller particles depends on atmospheric turbulence and wind conditions, and they can be transported over long distances. There is evidence that fine particulates produced in urban areas can be transported to rural areas several hundred miles away; in fact, lead particles presumably stemming from emissions in North America have been detected in Greenland's glacial ice. Further, these smaller particles are generally more hazardous to human health than their larger counterparts, both because they are more effectively embedded in the human lung and because they are typically emitted at ground level in places where population density is high.

Particles ranging from 10 to 100 μm in diameter tend to have characteristics in common with local soil conditions or effluents from local industries. In maritime areas, airborne sea salt is in this size range. Industries using grinding systems, such as grain elevators, feed mills, cement factories, and ore smelters also produce particles of this size. Friedlander (9) has recently discussed techniques for estimating the percentage contributions of various sources to the total atmospheric aerosol, using certain elements as tracers for specific pollution sources. The main requirement for a tracer element is that it not be present in large amounts in the emissions from other sources (e.g. Pb, Br for automobiles, Ca for cement, V for fuel oil). These techniques have been used with fair success in studies of California aerosols.

It is very difficult to create particles smaller than a few microns in diameter by pulverizing or grinding larger particles. The limiting factor is the large amount of energy required to provide the additional surface energy that accompanies an increase in the number of smaller particles. Thus small primary particulates (i.e. those smaller than a few microns) are produced almost exclusively in high-energy systems such as combustion engines and metal-processing furnaces.

Combustion produces particulates having very diverse chemical compositions as well as a wide range of particle sizes (0.01–10 μm). Particles are created in a combustion system in a number of ways: (1) mechanical processes may reduce either fuel or ash to particles on the order of several microns in diameter; (2) partial combustion of fossil fuels may lead to the formation of soot, with particle sizes from 0.01–1.0 μm; (3) if the fuel itself is an aerosol, a very fine ash may escape during combustion, resulting in particles on the order of 0.1–1.0 μm; (4) fuel material can vaporize and subsequently condense to form particles ranging in size from 0.1–1.0 μm; and (5) the available high energy can ionize some species and, through electrostatic interactions with other gases, the ions can generate particles of very small size, ranging from unstable clusters of a few molecules to condensation nuclei on the order of 0.01 μm.

A comprehensive summary of the chemical composition and size distribution of particles from potential sources of primary particulates has not yet been compiled. Resolution of particle sizes smaller than several microns is not included in most of the available data because early control strategies were based primarily on mass loading and ignored the potential hazards of lightweight fine particles. The extent of these hazards has only recently gained attention (10).

Another crucial lack in much of the existing data base that has just begun to be investigated is the chemical composition of particulate matter as a function of size. Recent studies (11, 12) of the chemical composition of fly ash as a function of particle size have found that toxic elements such as lead, manganese, cadmium, thallium, chromium, arsenic, nickel, and sulfur increase markedly in concentration with decreasing particle size. The mechanism controlling this selective concentration is not yet under-

Table 2. Global emission of all particulates

	Millions of tons/yr	Total
Man-made		296
Particles	92	
Gas-particle conversion		
SO_2	147	
NO_x	30	
Photochemical (hydrocarbons)	27	
Natural		2,312
Soil dust	200	
Gas-particle conversion		
H_2S	204	
NO_x	432	
NH_3	269	
Photochemical (terpenes, etc.[a])	200	
Volcanic dust	4	
Forest fires	3	
Sea salt	1,000	
Total		2,608

SOURCE: Ref. 19.

[a] Considerably higher estimates have been made for the natural production of aerosol by photochemical polymerization of terpene vapors, but the amount of experimental data available is inadequate to permit certainty.

stood, nor is it yet clear that this is a general phenomenon, since these studies were performed on stack gases from only a few power plants. Information about chemical concentrations could have important environmental consequences, for smaller particles have longer atmospheric residence times and are very effectively deposited in human lungs. Similar studies should be extended to other sources of primary particulates.

Secondary particulates

Secondary particulates, the products of chemical reactions occurring in the atmosphere, can initiate in the gas phase or as a result of reactions between gases and already existing particles. They are a major source of the ubiquitous Aitken nuclei, or solid condensation centers, that are essential for most of the condensation processes that take place in the atmosphere. They are also a prime component of urban smog.

Secondary particulates range in size from molecular clusters having diameters on the order of 0.005 μm to particles with diameters as large as several microns. Field studies of several urban aerosols (13, 14, 15) have shown that the highest concentrations of secondary particulates are usually in the range 0.01–1.0 μm. The data also indicate that within this range are two rather distinct groups, one having mean diameters less than 0.05 μm and the other having diameters from 0.05–1.0 μm. The smaller particles result directly from photochemical reactions, and the larger particles in turn are produced by the coagulation or condensation of the photochemically generated particles. The concentration of particles in both groups varies directly with intensity of sunlight and concentration of ozone.

The principal factors governing distribution by size are the respective rates of particulate formation and removal. The smallest particles, which are created constantly during the daylight hours, have lifetimes on the order of several minutes before they coagulate with larger particles (0.01–0.1 μm), which then persist up to about 12 hours before they eventually coagulate or con-

dense to form even larger particles. The overall life cycle of secondary particulates is difficult to determine; estimates range from one week to 40 days (18). In the end, the particles are either washed out of the atmosphere by rain, or they coagulate with larger primary particles that eventually settle out of the atmosphere.

The main ingredients in the formation of secondary particulates are sunlight (and to some extent cosmic rays and terrestrial radiation) and chemicals such as sulfur dioxide, ammonia, nitric oxide, water, and hydrocarbons, which enter the atmosphere from both natural and man-made sources (see Table 2). Robinson and Robbins (19) estimate that about 8% of the total global aerosol is composed of anthropogenic secondary particulates, from sources such as combustion systems, vehicle emissions, and industrial processes, and about 56% is composed of secondary particulates from natural sources, including the oceans, volcanoes and geysers, and the vapor from trees, plants, and decaying organic matter.

Mechanisms of formation

Found in both urban and rural areas, secondary particulates are in general composed of three types of chemical compounds: sulfates, hydrocarbons, and nitrates.

Sulfates. Sulfates are ubiquitous. A large fraction of the background global aerosol is ammonium sulfate $(NH_4)_2SO_4$ (20). Sulfuric acid (H_2SO_4), which along with sulfate salts such as $PbSO_4$ is found in most urban aerosols, results from the reaction of SO_3 and water. The sulfate salts, in turn, derive from the reactions of compounds such as ammonia or metallic oxides with sulfuric acid droplets. These reactions are exceedingly fast; Cadle and Robbins (21) estimate that, in the case of ammonia and sulfuric acid, reaction occurs at every collision between an acid droplet and a gas molecule. Because of the speed of the reactions, the key step in sulfate formation is the oxidation of SO_2 to form the SO_3 needed to produce sulfuric acid.

There are four basic mechanisms for the oxidation reaction that

creates SO_3: reaction with oxygen atoms, direct photochemical oxidation, catalytic oxidation, and free radical reactions. The relative importance of each mechanism in the overall atmospheric sulfur cycle is still a matter of heated debate.

SO_3 is produced by combining SO_2 with oxygen atoms in the three-body reaction

$$SO_2 + O + M \rightarrow SO_3 + M$$

where M is an inert gas such as nitrogen or argon. Recent estimates of the rate of this reaction range from 0.02 to 1.2% per hour (22), which is consistent with the observed rates of disappearance of SO_2 in clean air (about 0.1 to 0.6% per hour) (23, 24, 25).

In the lower atmosphere, the primary source of oxygen atoms for the reaction is probably NO_2, which photodissociates with practically unit efficiency when irradiated with light in the region 300–360 nanometers (26). Sunlight in this wavelength region is able to penetrate the lower atmosphere. Recent studies by Bricard et al. (27) have confirmed that NO_2 in concentrations as low as 0.5 parts per million significantly increases the oxidation of SO_2 in air when the gas mixtures are irradiated with light at wavelengths longer than 300 nanometers.

The validity of this mechanism is still in question. We do not know whether sufficient concentrations of oxygen atoms are available for reaction in the troposphere. Light capable of dissociating O_2, a potentially vast source of oxygen atoms, usually does not reach the troposphere, and the minute quantities of oxygen atoms that may be produced there can react quickly with abundant gases such as N_2 and CO; hence they should be essentially unavailable for reaction with SO_2. Other potential sources such as NO_2 may not be large enough to provide significant concentrations of oxygen atoms. At higher altitudes, however, this mechanism is almost certainly important. In the boundary between the stratosphere and the troposphere, for example, there is a significant sulfate aerosol (28), which probably results from reactions initiated by photodissociated oxygen atoms diffusing from the stratosphere.

The basic mechanism for photochemical oxidation has been postulated by a number of workers, among the first of whom were Dainton and Ivin (29):

$$SO_2 + light \rightarrow SO_2^*$$

$$SO_2^* + O_2 + M \rightarrow SO_4 + M$$

$$SO_4 + SO_2 \rightarrow 2SO_3$$

$$SO_4 + O_2 \rightarrow SO_3 + O_3$$

The principal reactive excited state of SO_2 is believed to be the long-lived triplet state (30), which is formed predominantly by intersystem crossing from the singlet state produced by absorption of light in the wavelength region 240–320 nanometers. Some triplet SO_2 results from direct absorption of sunlight (at 340–400 nanometers), but this process occurs infrequently and is probably unimportant in atmospheric photochemistry.

Experiments by Gerhart and Johnstone (31) support the validity of this mechanism, but Bricard et al. (27) suggest that the results could be explained equally well by the presence of impurities in the gas samples. There are important potential flaws in the theory: Cadle (32) has pointed out that, although reactions like the second one listed above are exceptionally fast, the quantum yields for the production of electronically excited SO_2 may be too small to be of importance to atmospheric chemistry. Further, rate coefficients for the third and fourth reactions listed above have yet to be measured and may be very slow. In fact, the species SO_4 has never been conclusively observed.

In the catalytic oxidation mechanism, SO_2 is oxidized either in aqueous droplets in the reactions

$$SO_2 + H_2O \rightarrow H_2SO_3$$

$$2H_2SO_3 + O_2 \rightarrow 2H_2SO_4$$

or on the surface of metal oxide particles such as PbO, Fe_2O_3, CaO, and Al_2O_3 (22). Iron oxide is known to be particularly effective as a catalyst both in the solid phase and in solution (22, 23), in some cases en-

hancing oxidation rates by several orders of magnitude. The catalytic effect is strong enough to produce significant oxidation of SO_2 even in the dark, demonstrating a potential mechanism for significant aerosol production at night.

A major uncertainty in these catalytic mechanisms results from our ignorance about what happens at a microscopic scale on the surface of a particle. In addition, a question remains as to whether laboratory studies have adequately duplicated atmospheric conditions.

Atmospheric sulfate formation is also enhanced by the presence of free radicals, which are often formed in mixtures of hydrocarbons and ozone or other oxidants. Ordinarily, the reaction of ozone with SO_2 takes place slowly, but in the presence of hydrocarbons it is considerably accelerated (34). Laboratory simulations of urban smog reactions have shown that SO_2 can also be oxidized rapidly in mixtures of NO_x and hydrocarbons. For certain mixtures (e.g. SO_2, 50 parts per billion; NO, 30 ppb; and cis-pentane, 100 ppb), SO_2 oxidation rates as high as 10% per hour have been reported (35). Evidence indicates that the aerosol resulting from olefin/NO_x/SO_2 mixtures is predominantly H_2SO_4 droplets for hydrocarbons with less than 5 carbon atoms; for larger hydrocarbons, carbonaceous matter also appears in the aerosol (36).

The hydrocarbon/NO_x/SO_2 mixtures can be described as synergistic systems—no two of the components react effectively, but the presence of all three provides a powerful oxidizing system. These mixtures are suspected to be major sources of sulfate particulates, but they are still the least well understood of all the oxidation mechanisms. Undoubtedly they involve the formation of intermediate, highly reactive free radical species, but which ones is still unclear. Recently, Davis and his coworkers (37, 38) have pointed to hydroxyl radicals as significant atmospheric oxidizing agents. With respect to SO_2, the proposed oxidation reaction is

$$OH + SO_2 + M \rightarrow HSO_3 + M$$

Once HSO_3 is formed, a series of re-

actions can take place with species such as O_2, NO, or hydrocarbons that ultimately results in the formation of H_2SO_4 or organic sulfates.

Of course, the relative importance of sulfate-forming mechanisms varies according to local conditions. In urban areas with relatively high concentrations of NO_2, oxidation by oxygen atoms or oxygen-containing free radicals could be important. In the plumes from large smokestacks with heavy particulate loadings and high relative humidity, heterogeneous catalytic oxidation probably predominates. In rural areas with relatively clean air, photochemical oxidation of SO_2 may be the primary mechanism of sulfate formation.

Hydrocarbons. The second major constituent of particulates is hydrocarbons, which react with oxidants (e.g. NO_2, O_3) in the atmosphere to produce peroxide radicals. Through a series of chain reactions, these radicals eventually form large organic molecules which condense to form droplets or solid particles. The mechanism is as follows:

$$NO_2 + light \longrightarrow NO + O$$

$$O + O_2 + M \longrightarrow O_3 + M$$

$$O_3 + olefins \longrightarrow RO\cdot + O_2$$

$$RO\cdot + olefins \longrightarrow R\text{–}R'O \text{ or } R\overset{\displaystyle O}{\underset{}{\diagdown\diagup}}R$$

$RO\cdot$ represents the hydrocarbon peroxide radicals which are readily formed by ozone attack at the carbon-carbon double bond position in olefinic hydrocarbons. Once formed, organic molecules represented by R–R'O are also susceptible to photochemical excitation and further reaction. Estimates indicate that about 5% of the organic vapor in photochemical smog reacts to form particulates.

Primary sources of hydrocarbons in urban areas are automobile exhaust, power-generating stations, and industrial effluents. In rural areas, a rich source is the vapor produced by various plants, which often contains a class of compounds known as terpenes. One very common terpene, α-pinene, is found in oils of more than 400 plants. Many terpenes are highly unsaturated, and in some cases they can even be oxidized in the dark by reaction with O_2. Rasmussen and Went (39) have estimated that the worldwide emission of organic vapor is 4.4×10^8 tons per year. As mentioned earlier, the particulates formed by oxidation of these organic vapors are often the cause of the haze observed in rural areas (40).

Nitrates. The key intermediary in nitrate formation is nitric acid (HNO_3) in either vapor or droplet form. Nitric acid can be produced in the atmosphere through the following series of reactions:

$$NO_2 + O_3 \rightarrow NO_3 + O_2$$

$$NO_2 + NO_3 \rightarrow N_2O_5$$

$$N_2O_5 + H_2O \rightarrow 2HNO_3$$

Nitric acid also results directly from reactions involving hydroxyl radicals:

$$NO_2 + OH + M \rightarrow HNO_3 + M$$

After the formation of nitric acid, nitrates are created by its reaction with gaseous or solid species. For example:

$$NH_3 + HNO_3 \rightarrow NH_4NO_3$$

Ammonia is also known to form NH_4NO_3 directly in reactions with ozone (41). The mechanism is not yet understood, but it presumably involves the formation of HNO_3 in some intermediate step.

One further mechanism for the formation of nitrate particles is the adsorption of nitric acid on the metal-bearing particulates often found in urban smog. The net result is compounds such as $Pb(NO_3)_2$. Nitrate particulates are also frequently found in coastal cities and are thought to result from reactions between gaseous species and particles from ocean spray:

$$NaCl + NHO_3 \rightarrow NaNO_3 + HCl$$

Deleterious effects of particulates

Some of the ill effects of particulate matter on human health are obvious and annoying, as anyone with an allergy or hay fever will confirm. At times, however, the effects of particulates in the air can be catastrophic. Usually the most serious threats to health result from a com-

Table 3. Estimated annual health costs of air pollution, reduction in incidences of particular diseases attainable by 50% reduction in air pollution, and the resulting estimated savings (1970)

Disease	Lost income and medical expenditures (millions)	Reduction in incidences	Savings (millions)
Respiratory	$4,887	25%	$1,222
Cardiovascular	4,680	10%	468
Cancer	2,600	15%	390
Lung cancer	132	25%	33
Total savings			~$2,080

SOURCE: Ref. *49.*

bination of heavy concentrations of particulate matter from industrial or man-made sources with weather conditions that prevent adequate atmospheric mixing.

Atmospheric inversion is the cause of most air pollution episodes. Normally, the temperature of the atmosphere decreases with increasing altitude, but during an atmospheric inversion, this situation is reversed, and the temperature of the air increases with increasing altitude. The warm air in the upper reaches of the atmosphere acts as a "lid" which prevents vertical mixing from below; hence, concentrations of pollutants can build up rapidly. Inversions can result from the mixing of warm and cold weather fronts, the interaction of sea and land breezes, or the radiation of heat from the land into the atmosphere.

It is estimated that 3,500 to 4,000 people died as a result of the severe fog of 5–9 December 1952 in London (42). The diseases for which mortality figures are quoted in the records of that incident are bronchitis, coronary diseases, myocardial degeneration, pneumonia, vascular lesions of the central nervous system, respiratory tuberculosis, and cancer of the lung. Other tragic air pollution episodes took place in the Meuse River Valley in Belgium in December 1930 (60 people died and 6,000 became seriously ill), in Donora, Pennsylvania, in 1948, and in London again in 1962.

The long-term effects of air pollution, and especially of airborne particulates, may be even more insidious. Specifying exactly which pollutants have the most significant effects on human health is difficult

and little definitive information is available; expanded research is needed. The length of time required for compiling accurate data has limited our assessments of these long-term effects, but some advances have been made. In many epidemiological studies, for example, particulates have been shown to have a significant effect. Growing evidence indicates a consistent relationship between exposure to particulates combined with SO_2 and impaired ventilatory function in children 5 to 13 years of age (43). In Japan, the incidence of diseases such as chronic bronchitis, bronchial asthma, and pulmonary edema has been linked to sulfuric acid mist and suspended dust particles (44). The U.S. National Academy of Sciences has said that exposure to particulate polycyclic organic matter can result in cancer of the skin and lungs, nonallergic contact dermatitis, hyperpigmentation of the skin, folliculitis, and acne (45). The effects of suspended sulfates on human health have also been examined by Shy and Finklea (46), who indicate that these particles contribute substantially to the aggravation of chronic respiratory disease.

Although it is not yet possible to isolate the actual disease-producing mechanisms or even to know which specific types of particulates are the main villains, there is a growing consensus that fine particulates (i.e. those smaller than several microns in diameter) are primary suspects. These species are especially troublesome because they are capable of bypassing the body's respiratory filters and penetrating deep into the lungs. More than 30% of the particles smaller than 1 μm that penetrate the pulmonary system remain there (47, 48). The ability of fine particulates to become embedded in the tissue is a function primarily of their geometry and is independent of their chemical composition. Once the particles have been deposited, however, their chemical nature is a prime determinant of their toxicity. As noted above, growing evidence suggests that poisonous elements, especially heavy metals such as lead, cadmium, vanadium, and nickel tend to be concentrated in these smallest particles, but even materials such as silicones, which for the most part are chemically inert, can cause acute physical irritation of sensitive lung tissue and lead to diseases such as silicosis. Particulates deposited in the lungs can also impair oxygen transfer, and, because they have fairly long lives in the atmosphere and are capable of adsorbing significant quantities of toxic gases such as SO_2 and HCl, they can produce severe synergistic effects if inhaled.

In an extensive review of the literature, Lave and Seskin (49) attempted the difficult task of estimating the cost of air pollution with respect to human health. They found significant correlations of illnesses such as respiratory disease, cardiovascular disease, and cancer with air pollution indices (e.g. dustfall, sulfation rate, concentration of suspended particulates, etc.). The correlations were so impressive that the authors point out that the only way to discredit the results would be to argue that the "real" cause of ill health was the presence of a third unknown agent which happens to correlate with levels of air pollution—an event that seems most unlikely. Their cost estimates (summarized in Table 3) are conservative and, of course, do not account for the inflation which has occurred since 1970. Perhaps a more relevant index of the cost of air pollution would be their estimate that a decrease of about 4.5% of all economic costs associated with morbidity and mortality could be achieved by a 50% reduction of air pollution in our major urban centers.

Curtailed visibility, a hazard to people traveling both by land and by air, is another way in which airborne particulates can endanger human safety. The effects of particulate matter on visibility have been

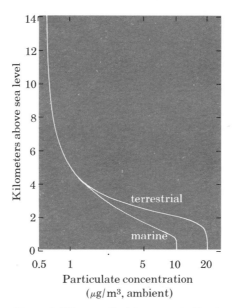

Figure 5. When particulate concentration is measured as a function of altitude, it is found that almost the total weight of particulate matter in the atmosphere is in the 2 kilometers nearest the ground. (Adapted from ref. 19.)

discussed thoroughly by several authors (50, 51). When particles scatter the light passing from the sun or some other source through the line of sight of the observer, visibility is impaired because the reduced light flux decreases the contrast between objects and their background. On the basis of a correlation of visibility with the atmospheric light-scattering coefficient and the concentration of airborne suspended particulates made by Charlson and coworkers (52), it is estimated that, in rural air where particulate concentrations are about 20 $\mu g/m^3$, visibility will be 50–60 km. In urban air where particulate concentrations are typically as high as 100 $\mu g/m^3$, visibility will be 8–10 km. The most significant reduction in visibility is generally attributed to particles in the size range 0.1–1.0 μm, which are especially effective light scatterers because their diameters are comparable to the wavelengths of light in the visible region. Small particles scatter light of shorter wavelengths (i.e. blue light) more effectively; hence, during pollution episodes, the sun often takes on a distinct red color. And, of course, the reddish hue of sunsets is also caused by the influence of atmospheric particulates.

Particulates are involved to some

extent in the transmission of odors. Sometimes they themselves are volatile, and sometimes they simply serve as a transport medium for volatile matter. Odors from restaurants, paint spraying, roofing and paving, incinerators, and open dump fires are known to be transmitted by particulates (53). If particulate matter is removed from diesel exhaust, the odor of the fumes is significantly reduced (54).

The visible effects of particulate air pollution on property are familiar to everyone: soot adsorbed on the surfaces of urban buildings is unsightly, but a hidden and more dangerous effect is the concomitant disintegration of the masonry by acids and tars adsorbed on the soot deposit. In addition, airborne particulates are capable of corroding metals and soiling and eroding metal coatings, painted surfaces, and textiles. The corrosiveness of particulates is due either to their own chemical activity or to their ability to adsorb reactive gases such as NO_2 and SO_2. The contribution of airborne particles to corrosion has been investigated by Preston and Sanyal (55). Soiling is also a problem; one study estimates that annual costs for personal property cleaning are $85 more per person in a pollution-prone city than in a clean city (56).

Particles in the atmosphere can affect the climate in several ways, but as yet the predominant effect of atmospheric particulate loading has not been determined. Field test data in both rural and urban areas indicate that concentrations of airborne particles vary widely. Mean or average concentrations must always be considered as general approximations of the atmospheric condition. Some idea of the vertical distribution of particulates can be gained from Figure 5, which indicates that almost the total weight of the aerosol is in the lowest 2 kilometers of the atmosphere. The interaction of the frictional drag of the earth's surface and the higher-level air flows occurs primarily in the first kilometer or two of the atmosphere. This region, which is called the planetary boundary layer, governs most of the transport and deposition of particulates (57) through the surface winds which predominate here.

Particles both absorb and scatter sunlight, thus reducing the amount of radiation reaching the surface of the earth and lowering surface temperatures. But particles can also absorb energy and reradiate it in the infrared spectrum, creating a "greenhouse effect" (in a greenhouse, sunlight transmitted by the glass is absorbed by the plants within; when some of the absorbed energy is reradiated in the infrared part of the spectrum, this radiation with longer wavelengths is not effectively transmitted by the glass, and the heat is trapped). Whether the presence of particulates results in a net heat loss or gain depends in a complicated way on the optical properties of the particles, the temperature structure of the atmosphere, and the degree of reflectivity, or albedo, of the surface below.

Computational models have been developed to assess the influence of the particulate greenhouse effect. In general, they indicate that the warming effects of particulates do not compensate for the surface cooling caused by attenuation of solar radiation (58). However, these averaged global models are not sufficiently sensitive to indicate significant modifications in local climate. For example, particulates originating in volcanic activity often alter local atmospheric temperature: the Mount Agung eruption in Indonesia in 1963 raised the temperature in the stratosphere by about 6 to 7°C (59). The effect of Agung was observed for about 15 degrees of latitude north and south of the source at stations around the world. Many cities generate what is sometimes called the "heat island" effect, wherein the air directly over the city is 3 to 4°C warmer than that in the surrounding countryside.

Particulates have also been implicated in altering weather patterns, but the evidence relating to this phenomenon is unclear. Both cloud formation and precipitation seem to be affected, and although both increases and decreases in their occurrence have been attributed to the injection of particulates into the atmosphere from either fires or industrial sources (60), increased particulate loadings have not so far been shown to have any systematic effect on precipitation patterns, at least in urban areas. Apparently the increase in condensation nuclei is offset by the chemical reactivity of the polluted air, which prevents the formation of ice particles.

There is evidence that particulate concentration reaches a maximum in the zone between 30 and 60° north latitude (19)—a finding that is consistent with the concentration of industrial sources in these latitudes—and that this concentration has led to a change in atmospheric electrical conductivity over the North Atlantic. Just how this might affect weather and climate patterns, however, is not well documented. The influence of particulates on both climate and weather is still poorly understood. Possibly their main impact is felt on a local, not a global, scale. Undoubtedly, our understanding of the climatic effect of airborne particulates will be subject to considerable revision as more information becomes available in the next several decades.

References

1. R. E. Lee, Jr. 1972. The size of suspended particulate matter in air. *Science* 178:567.

2. K. T. Whitby, R. B. Husar, and B. Y. H. Liu. 1972. The aerosol size distribution of Los Angeles smog. *J. Colloid Interface Science* 39:177.

3. K. T. Whitby, R. E. Charlson, W. E. Wilson, and R. K. Stevens. 1974. The size of suspended particle matter in air. *Science* 183:1098.

4. R. E. Lee, Jr. 1974. The size of suspended particle matter in air. *Science* 183:1099.

5. J. M. Prospero. 1968. Atmospheric dust studies on Barbados. *Bull. Amer. Meteorol. Soc.* 49:645.

6. Midwest Research Institute. 1971. *Particulate Pollutant System Study.* Vol. I: *Mass emissions.* Project No. 3326-C, Report Prepared for Air Pollution Control Office, Environmental Protection Agency.

7. P. K. Mueller, H. L. Helwig, A. E. Alcocer, W. K. Gong, and E. E. Jones. 1964. *Concentration of Fine Particles and Lead in Car Exhaust.* American Society for Testing and Materials, Special Technical Publication 352, pp. 60–73.

8. National Air Pollution Control Administration. 1969. *Air Quality Criteria for Particulate Matter,* Pub. AP-49, U.S. Dept. of Health, Education, and Welfare, Washington, D.C. pp. 23–27.

9. G. Gartrell, Jr., and S. K. Friedlander. 1975. Relating particulate pollution to sources. *Atmos. Environ.* 9:279. See also S. K. Friedlander. 1973. Chemical element balances and the identification of air pollution sources. *Environ. Sci. and Technol.* 7:235.

10. N. F. Surprenant. 1974. *R&D Program for Fine Suspended Particulates.* GCA Corp. Report, Environmental Protection Agency Contract 68-02-1316.

11. R. L. Davison, D. F. S. Natusch, J. R. Wallace, and C. A. Evans, Jr. 1974. Trace elements in fly ash. *Environ. Sci. Technol.* 8:1107.

12. R. E. Lee, Jr., and D. J. von Lehmden 1973. Trace metal pollution in the environment. *J. Air Pollution Control Assoc.* 23:853.

13. K. T. Whitby, R. B. Husar, and B. Y. H. Liu. 1971. The aerosol size distribution of Los Angeles smog. In *Aerosols and Atmospheric Chemistry,* ed. G. M. Hidy. N.Y.: Academic Press. pp. 237–64.

14. C. E. Junge. 1963. *Air Chemistry and Radioactivity.* N.Y.: Academic Press.

15. W. E. Clark and K. T. Whitby. 1967. Concentration and size distribution measurements of atmospheric aerosols and a test of the theory of self-preserving size distributions. *J. Atmos. Sci.* 24:677.

16. C. N. Davies. 1974. Particles in the atmosphere—natural and man-made. *Atmos. Environ.* 8:1069.

17. F. W. Went. 1966. On the nature of Aitken condensation nuclei. *Tellus* 18:549.

18. R. D. Cadle. 1973. Particulate matter in the lower stratosphere. In *Chemistry of the Lower Stratosphere,* ed. S. I. Rasool. N.Y.: Plenum Press.

19. E. Robinson and R. C. Robbins. 1971. *Emission Concentration and Fate of Particulate Atmospheric Pollutants.* Final Report, SRI Project SCC-8507. Menlo Park, Calif.: Stanford Research Institute.

20. G. Megaw. 1966. *Research Progress Report, Health Physics and Medical Division,* United Kingdom Atomic Energy Association.

21. R. D. Cadle and R. C. Robbins. 1961. Kinetics of atmospheric reactions involving aerosols. *Discussions of the Faraday Society* 30:155.

22. R. S. Berry and P. A. Lehman. 1971. Aerochemistry of air pollution. *Advances in Physical Chemistry* 22:47–84.

23. P. Urone, H. Lutsep, C. M. Noyes, and J. F. Parcher. 1968. Static studies of sulfur dioxide reactions in air. *Environ. Sci. and Technol.* 2:611.

24. N. A. Renzetti and G. J. Doyle. 1960. Photochemical aerosol formation in sulfur dioxide-hydrocarbon systems. *Int. J. Air Poll.* 2:327.

25. R. A. Cox and S. A. Penkett. 1970. Photo-oxidation of SO_2 in sunlight. *Atmos. Environ.* 4:425.

26. P. A. Leighton. 1961. *Photochemistry of Air Pollution.* N.Y.: Academic Press. p. 55.

27. J. Bricard, M. Cabane, G. Madelaine, and D. Viglia. 1971. Formation and properties of neutral ultrafine particles and small ions conditioned by gaseous impurities of the air. In *Aerosols and Atmospheric Chemistry,* ed. G. M. Hidy, N.Y.: Academic Press. p. 27.

28. R. D. Cadle, A. L. Lazrus, W. H. Pollack, and J. P. Sheldovsky. 1970. In *Proceedings of the Symposium on Tropical Meteorology,* ed. C. S. Ramage. Boston, Mass.: American Meteorological Society.

29. F. S. Dainton and K. J. Ivin. 1950. The photochemical formation of sulphinic acids from sulfur dioxide and hydrocarbons. *Transactions of the Faraday Society* 46:374–82.

30. H. W. Sidebottom, C. C. Badcock, G. G. Jackson, J. G. Calvert, G. W. Reinhart, and E. K. Damon. 1972. Photo-oxidation of sulfur dioxide. *Environ. Sci. and Technol.* 6:72.

31. E. R. Gerhart and H. F. Johnstone. 1955. Photo-oxidation of SO_2 in air. *Industrial and Engineering Chem.* 47:972.

32. R. D. Cadle. 1972. Formation and chemical reactions of atmospheric particles. In *Aerosols and Atmospheric Chemistry*, ed. G. M. Hidy. N.Y. Academic Press. p. 143.

33. H. F. Johnstone and D. R. Coughanower. 1958. Absorption of sulfur dioxide from air. *Industrial and Engineering Chem.* 50:1169.

34. W. E. Wilson, A. Levy, and D. Wimmer. 1972. A study of SO_2 in photochemical smog, II. The effect of SO_2 on formation of oxidant. *J. Air Pollution Control Assoc.* 22:311.

35. R. A. Cox and S. A. Penkett. 1971. Photo-oxidation of atmospheric SO_2. *Nature* 229:486.

36. P. J. Groblicki and G. J. Nebel. 1971. The photochemical formation of aerosols in urban atmospheres. In *Chemical Reactions in Urban Atmospheres*, ed. C. S. Tuesday. N.Y.: Elsevier. p. 241.

37. D. D. Davis, G. Smith, and G. Klauber. 1974. Trace gas analysis of power plant plumes via aircraft measurement: O_3, NO_x and SO_2 chemistry. *Science* 186: 733.

38. W. Payne, L. Stief, and D. D. Davis. 1973. A kinetic study of the reaction of HO_2 with SO_2 and NO. *J. Amer. Chem. Soc.* 95:7614.

39. R. A. Rasmussen and R. W. Went. 1965. Volatile organic material of plant origin in the atmosphere. *Proc. U.S. National Academy of Sciences* 53:215.

40. F. W. Went. 1960. Blue hazes in the atmosphere. *Nature* 187(4738):641.

41. K. J. Olszyna, R. G. de Pina, M. Luria, and J. Heicklen. 1974. Kinetics of particle growth, IV. NH_4NO_3 from the NH_3-O_3 reaction revisited. *J. Aerosol Sci.* 5: 421.

42. A. J. Lindsey. 1971. Air pollution and health. *Chemistry and Industry* (London) 14:378.

43. C. M. Shy, V. Hasselblad, R. M. Burton, C. J. Nelson, and A. A. Cohen. 1972. *Results of Studies in Cincinnati, Chattanooga, and New York.* American Medical Association Conference, Chicago, Ill.

44. Pollution Damages to Human Health and Countermeasures. n.d. In *Quality of the Environment in Japan.* Japan Environmental Agency. pp. 105–30.

45. Committee on Biologic Effects of Atmospheric Pollutants, National Academy of Sciences. 1972. *Particulate Polycyclic Organic Matter.* Environmental Protection Agency Contract CPA 70-42.

46. C. M. Shy and J. F. Finklea. 1973. Air pollution affects community health. *Environ. Sci. and Technol.* 7:204.

47. National Air Pollution Control Board. 1969. *Air Quality Criteria for Particulate Matter.* U.S. Dept. of Health, Education, and Welfare. Pub. No. AP-49. Washington, D.C.

48. Task Group on Lung Dynamics. 1966. Deposition and retention models for internal dosimetry of the human respiratory tract. *Health Physics* 12:173.

49. L. B. Lave and E. P. Seskin. 1970. Air pollution and human health. *Science* 169:723.

50. E. Robinson. 1969. Effects of air pollution on visibility. In *Air Pollution*, ed. A. C. Stern. N.Y.: Academic Press.

51. W. E. K. Middleton. 1952. *Vision Through the Atmosphere.* Toronto: Univ. of Toronto Press.

52. R. J. Charlson. 1968. Atmospheric aerosol research at the University of Washington. *J. Air Pollution Control Assoc.* 18:652.

53. National Air Pollution Control Board. 1969. *Air Quality Criteria for Particulate Matter.* U.S. Dept. of Health, Education, and Welfare. Pub. No. AP-49. p. 107.

54. R. H. Linnel and W. E. Scott. 1962. Diesel composition and odor studies. *J. Air Pollution Control Assoc.* 12:510.

55. R. Preston and B. Sanyal. 1956. Atmospheric corrosion by nuclei. *J. Appl. Chem.* 6:28.

56. I. Michelson and B. Tourin. 1966. *Comparative Method for Studying Costs of Air Pollution.* Public Health Report 81(6):505.

57. J. H. Seinfeld. 1975. *Air Pollution: Physical and Chemical Fundamentals.* N.Y.: McGraw-Hill. p. 10.

58. *Inadvertent Climate Modification.* 1971. Report of Man's Impact on Climate (SMIC). Cambridge, Mass.: MIT Press. p. 22.

59. *Man's Impact on the Global Environment—Assessment and Recommendations for Action.* 1970. Report of the Study of Critical Environmental Problems. Cambridge, Mass.: MIT Press. p. 104.

60. G. M. Hidy, W. Green, and A. Alkeyweeny. 1972. Inadvertent weather modification and Los Angeles smog. In *Aerosols and Atmospheric Chemistry*, ed. G. M. Hidy. N.Y.: Academic Press. p. 339.

61. *Monitoring and Air Quality Trends Report, 1973.* 1974. U.S. Environmental Protection Agency, Doc. No. EPA-450/1-74-007.

62. *CRC Handbook of Chemistry and Physics.* 1971. 51st ed. Cleveland: Chemical Rubber Company. p. F-199.

"It certainly becomes uncomfortable when the pollutants are up to 990,000 parts per million."

Owen B. Toon
James B. Pollack

Atmospheric Aerosols and Climate

Small particles in the Earth's atmosphere interact with visible and infrared light, altering the radiation balance and the climate

Small liquid and solid particles are ubiquitous in the atmosphere of Earth and the planets. With each breath an average terrestrial urban dweller may inhale 10^8 particles, or aerosols, composed of such diverse substances as sulfuric acid, sulfates of ammonia, nitrates, soil, and hundreds of organic compounds, some of which are carcinogenic. One out of four photons of visible light vertically traversing a typical urban atmosphere encounters an aerosol before reaching the ground, while a photon horizontally crossing a city may travel only about 10 km before intercepting a particle. During smoggy conditions, light is affected even more strongly by the particles. Pronounced optical effects due to aerosols are also noticeable outside the cities. Photochemically produced aerosols spread out over wide regions around cities; aerosols raised during desert dust storms are transported thousands of kilometers; and, after large volcanic eruptions, aerosols in the stratosphere can blanket the Earth (Fig. 1).

Atmospheric particles composed mainly of water are usually called cloud particles, despite their basic similarity to particles composed of other substances, which are classified

Owen B. Toon and James B. Pollack are research scientists at the National Aeronautics and Space Administration's Ames Research Center. Dr. Toon received his Ph.D. from Cornell University, and Dr. Pollack, from Harvard. Both scientists have an avid interest in studies of planetary atmospheres as well as in studies of aerosols and the Earth's climate. Dr. Pollack recently received the AIAA Space Sciences Award for his work on the effects of aerosols on climate. Address: Space Science Division, Ames Research Center, NASA, Moffett Field, CA 94035.

as aerosols. Clouds are affected by aerosols because every cloud drop in the sky forms around a particle. Aerosols can alter the optical properties of clouds by changing the cloud droplet composition, they can control precipitation by modifying the number and size of water drops, and they can alter cloud chemistry and lead to acid rainfall. Acid rainfall is a significant hazard to vegetation, to life in lakes and streams, and to exposed buildings and statues.

Other planets are even more influenced by aerosols than is Earth. On Mars, global dust storms dirty the atmosphere. Soil dust is the radiatively dominant material in the Martian atmosphere and is intimately tied to Martian climate change. On Venus, a dense photochemical smog, similar to the acid hazes of many terrestrial cities, blankets the entire planet and plays a significant role in Venusian meteorology. Aerosol clouds of various compositions also dominate the atmospheres of the outer planets Jupiter, Saturn, Titan, Uranus, and Neptune.

Aerosol studies for Earth and the planets are currently being carried out by a large number of scientists working in diverse fields. A particularly interesting controversy, which we will focus on in this paper, concerns the impact of terrestrial aerosols on the Earth's solar and infrared radiation budget and climate. Two questions are being debated: Do aerosols warm or cool the Earth? Is the effect climatologically significant?

The debate is caused partly by a lack of experimental data on the optical properties of aerosols and partly by our inability to predict accurately the

Earth's weather and climate. However, much of the confusion is due to an oversimplification of the problem that results from considering only one type of particle. Given a single type of aerosol, theorists who study the radiation budget agree reasonably well upon the magnitude of the climatic impact and on whether it should be warming or cooling. Unfortunately, real aerosols are temporally and spatially diverse. Therefore, since there is no single type of aerosol, theorists provide different solutions to the problem of the impact of aerosols on climate for different aerosols.

In this paper we will first define the optical properties that are important for characterizing the effect of aerosols on the radiation budget. Then we will discuss theoretical studies of the connection between the aerosol optical properties and the climate. After describing what is known about the optical properties of natural aerosols and their variability, we will review the available observational evidence linking aerosols and climate. Figure 2 presents a schematic summary of the climatically significant interactions between aerosols and light from the sun as well as between aerosols and infrared light from the Earth's surface and atmosphere.

Optical properties

The physical properties of aerosols, such as size, shape, refractive index, and concentration in the atmosphere, control the aerosol interaction with light according to a set of derived properties, which are known as optical properties. Three fundamental properties are the optical depth, a measure of the size and number of particles present in a given column of air; the single scattering albedo, the fraction of light intercepted and scattered by a single particle; and the asymmetry parameter, an integrated measure denoting the portion of light scattered forward in the direction of the original propagation and the portion scattered backward toward the light source. (For a detailed review see Hansen and Travis 1974.)

A light ray traversing an aerosol-laden column of air will be reduced by the effects of absorption and scattering as the exponent of the optical depth, τ, which is basically just the weighted product of the number of particles in a column of unit area and the cross-sectional area of a single particle. The weighting takes into account several optical phenomena. For example, a particle much smaller than the wavelength of light does not interact efficiently with light, so its full cross-sectional area is not counted. For visible light, a particle larger than about 0.1 μm contributes its entire cross-sectional area, or even a factor of 2 more than its area, to τ; particles of this size are very common in the atmosphere. Particles larger than about 1 μm interact most effectively with infrared radiation but are less common. The quantity τ varies in space and time from about 0.01 to 1.0 at visible wavelengths. Adequate space and time averages for τ are major observational unknowns, though τ is known for many local areas.

light, and when small quantities of these constituents are present, $\tilde{\omega}_0$ can be reduced to about 0.5. The worldwide and even the local prevalence of absorbing compounds is poorly known. Most aerosols strongly absorb infrared light, and thus $\tilde{\omega}_0$ is less than 0.1 in the infrared. The product $\tilde{\omega}_0\tau$ is the scattering optical depth: a light ray traversing an aerosol-laden column will be reduced due to scattering as the exponent of $\tilde{\omega}_0\tau$. The absorption optical depth is $(1 - \tilde{\omega}_0)\tau$.

Figure 1. The eruption of Krakatoa, in 1883, injected large quantities of volcanic gas and ash into the atmosphere. Some of the ash can be seen falling out of the volcanic plume in this lithographic reproduction of a photograph taken early in the eruption.

the asymmetry parameter, g, which varies from -1 to 1. If g were 1, all the light would be scattered into the hemisphere centered on the direction of the light beam's original propagation. If g were -1, all the light would be scattered backwards. For typical aerosols g is greater than zero. Due to the small particle size relative to infrared wavelengths, g is about 0.5 or less for most aerosols in the infrared. At visible wavelengths, g tends to be close to 0.7. Fortunately, g depends only weakly upon the particle size and composition, and thus the observational uncertainty about g is much less significant for climate than the uncertainty about $\tilde{\omega}_0$ and τ.

Aerosols are not uniformly distributed over the Earth, particularly in the lower atmosphere. At present, research into the effects of aerosols on climate is evolving from simple studies of global- and time-averaged problems toward more complicated regional, temporally varying problems. However, a basic understanding of the dependence of climate on the aerosol optical properties is most easily gained by reviewing global-average calculations (see Ramanathan and Coakley 1978 for modeling assumptions). In such calculations, atmospheric motions are generally ignored. The climate change, represented by a change in the global mean surface temperature, is found by balancing the solar energy absorbed by the gases and aerosols in the atmosphere and by the Earth's surface against the infrared energy radiated to space by the Earth's surface and atmosphere. The balance is required in order to conserve energy.

A fraction of the light intercepted by a particle is scattered and a fraction is absorbed. The fraction scattered by any single particle is called the single scattering albedo, $\tilde{\omega}_0$. Most atmospheric particles do not strongly absorb visible light, so $\tilde{\omega}_0$ for these particles is between 0.9 and 1.0. However, there are minor aerosol constituents such as soot that do absorb visible

The light scattered by aerosols is not scattered uniformly in all directions but has a complex angular distribution that can be a function of wavelength. Rainbows and diffraction coronas, most often seen in water clouds, are due to the wavelength dependence of the angular scattering distribution. A simple integrated measure of the angular scattering is

Climatic changes, such as droughts or

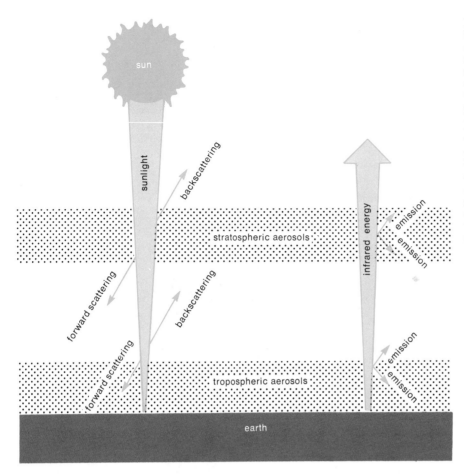

Figure 2. This schematic drawing shows the interactions between aerosols and sunlight, and aerosols and infrared light. Aerosols in the stratosphere, 20 km above the Earth's surface, absorb light from the sun and infrared light coming up from the lower atmosphere. Stratospheric aerosols have a warming effect on the surface by emitting infrared light toward the lower atmosphere, but this effect is offset by the aerosols' absorption of solar energy and backscattering of sunlight into space, which prevents it from reaching the surface. Whether the net effect of the stratospheric aerosols is to warm or cool the surface depends upon the size of the particles: since they are generally rather small, the effect is to cool the surface. Tropospheric aerosols, in the atmosphere just above the Earth's surface, cool it by backscattering sunlight, but they warm it by absorbing sunlight. Whether the net effect is warming or cooling depends upon the ratio of absorption to scattering, and this ratio depends upon the composition of the tropospheric aerosols, which is variable and poorly known.

a series of harsh winters, are usually restricted to small areas of the Earth. Often there will be compensating climatic changes from region to region: drought in one location may be nearly balanced by unusually high precipitation in another location. Periods of climatic extremes in numerous portions of the globe have been found to accompany small changes in global temperatures. We can calculate small changes in global temperature using global-average climate models, but not local temperature and precipitation changes—the quantities of real climatic importance. The local changes must simply be inferred from the global-average calculations on the basis of past climatic changes. Typical changes in the Earth's global mean surface temperature over the last thousand years, during which the climate has varied considerably, have been about 1°C, whereas the difference between the present and the ice-age mean temperatures is only about 5°C. Calculated global temperature changes of even several

tenths of a degree are therefore thought to be quite significant.

Many people have studied the relationship between surface temperature and aerosol loading. Figure 3 illustrates the dependence of the surface temperature upon the tropospheric aerosol optical properties τ and $\tilde{\omega}_0$, as calculated with a relatively sophisticated global-average radiative model (Hansen et al. 1979). The surface temperature scale is zeroed to a calculation using a "standard" aerosol distribution based upon an early analysis of the available observations (Toon and Pollack 1976). The standard model has a τ of 0.125 and a $\tilde{\omega}_0$ of 0.99 at a visible wavelength of 5500 Å, while the optical depth is 0.06 at an infrared wavelength of 10 μm. Most of the aerosols in the standard model are located close to the Earth's surface and are referred to as tropospheric aerosols.

The radiation budget of the Earth is dominated by water vapor and clouds, which raise the Earth's sur-

face temperature about 15°C above the temperature that the Earth would have without an atmosphere. Aerosols have a smaller but still significant effect. For example, Figure 3(*top left*) suggests that if there were no tropospheric aerosols, the Earth would be about 1.5°C warmer than it is. But if there were twice as many aerosols of the type found in the standard model, the Earth might be cooler than it is by 1.5°C. The reason for these differences is that the aerosols in the standard model do not absorb much solar radiation but they do scatter sunlight back into space, so less sunlight is available to warm the Earth's surface. As the aerosol concentrations increase, the surface would get progressively cooler. The aerosols are too small to interfere efficiently with infrared radiation.

The importance of the visible absorption is illustrated in Figure 3(*bottom left*). As $\tilde{\omega}_0$ decreases, the tropospheric aerosols absorb more solar energy and scatter less back to space, and their net cooling effect becomes less and less. Below $\tilde{\omega}_0$ of about 0.85, the critical albedo $\tilde{\omega}_c$, aerosols do not cool the Earth at all but absorb so much solar energy that they warm the Earth. (In this figure, the temperature scale is zeroed relative to the temperature calculated by using, as a "standard," aerosols that cool the Earth by about 1.5°C. If the temperature scale had been zeroed relative to the temperature calculated by assuming aerosols that neither warm nor cool the Earth, then the critical albedo would be at 0 of the temperature scale in Figure 3, *bottom left*).

The precise value of $\tilde{\omega}_c$ depends upon the model used. For example, several studies have shown that $\tilde{\omega}_c$ is much higher if the tropospheric aerosols are over very bright terrain such as a desert or a snow field rather than land, which has a typical albedo of 10%. This difference in $\tilde{\omega}_c$ occurs because the main climatic effect of the aerosol is to scatter sunlight back into space. However, if the ground already reflects most of the sunlight, the aerosols cannot much increase the total amount of sunlight reflected to space. Then the energy absorption by the aerosols may be greater than the scattering, causing a warming effect. The critical albedo also depends upon the asymmetry parameter, g, because if light is scattered forward, as most of it is, it still reaches the ground to warm the surface.

Figure 3(*bottom right*) illustrates the sensitivity of the surface temperature to the optical depth of aerosols at infrared wavelengths. Typical terrestrial aerosols have strong absorption bands near a wavelength of 10 μm. On the other hand, Earth's atmosphere is almost transparent near 10 μm, and consequently a large fraction of the infrared radiation escaping from the Earth to space is close to this wavelength. Aerosols prevent some of this radiation from escaping, which makes the Earth warmer through a "greenhouse" effect. As the infrared optical depth increases, the greenhouse effect warms the Earth more and more, thereby counteracting the cooling effect caused by the aerosols' scattering of solar radiation back to space. However, even in the extreme case when the infrared and visible optical depths are equal, the net effect of the tropospheric aerosols in the standard model would be to cool the Earth.

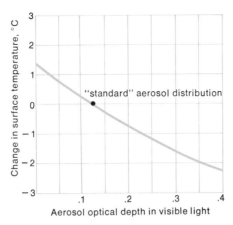

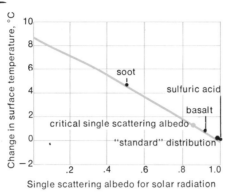

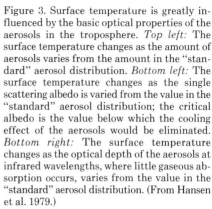

Figure 3. Surface temperature is greatly influenced by the basic optical properties of the aerosols in the troposphere. *Top left:* The surface temperature changes as the amount of aerosols varies from the amount in the "standard" aerosol distribution. *Bottom left:* The surface temperature changes as the single scattering albedo is varied from the value in the "standard" aerosol distribution; the critical albedo is the value below which the cooling effect of the aerosols would be eliminated. *Bottom right:* The surface temperature changes as the optical depth of the aerosols at infrared wavelengths, where little gaseous absorption occurs, varies from the value in the "standard" aerosol distribution. (From Hansen et al. 1979.)

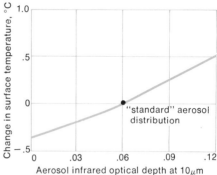

The ratio of infrared to visible opacity is controlled by the size distribution of the aerosols; the standard aerosol distribution assumes a relatively great abundance of large particles, so it is not likely that the standard distribution underestimates the infrared effect.

Most aerosols are near the Earth's surface, but an important layer of particles is found about 20 km above the surface, in the stratosphere. These aerosols normally have such a small τ that they are unimportant for climate. However, after large volcanic eruptions, their τ can be as large as that of the aerosols in the troposphere. The relation of climate to the optical properties of stratospheric aerosols is slightly different than for tropospheric aerosols, as has been demonstrated by several groups (Pollack et al. 1976a, b; Hansen et al. 1978).

Figure 4 shows that the relation between the optical depth and surface temperature for the stratospheric aerosols is quite close to that given in Figure 3 for tropospheric aerosols. However, for stratospheric aerosols,

the dependence of warming and cooling upon $\tilde{\omega}_0$ and upon the variation of τ with wavelength is different than for tropospheric aerosols. The stratosphere is not strongly coupled to the Earth's surface by atmospheric dynamics, and if the stratospheric aerosols absorb some incoming solar energy, the energy would not be conducted to the surface. Indeed, it is found both observationally and theoretically that the presence of stratospheric particles simultaneously causes the surface to cool and the stratosphere to warm. The aerosols warm the stratosphere by absorbing solar and infrared energy. The solar energy which the stratospheric aerosols absorb and backscatter does not reach the surface, causing cooling there. Hence, stratospheric aerosols cool the surface for all values of $\tilde{\omega}_0$.

The size of the stratospheric aerosols is an important factor in determining whether the climate warms or cools. Small particles, as shown in Figure 4, tend to cool the surface, whereas larger ones warm the surface. For stratospheric particles whose size is less than 0.1 μm, the ratio of the infrared τ to the visible τ is 0.1. For

0.25-μm-radius particles, however, the ratio is 0.5, and for 0.5-μm-radius particles the two optical depths are nearly equal. The reason infrared opacity is more important for stratospheric aerosols is that they are at high altitude and low temperature. The larger cold particles are very effective at blocking infrared radiation coming up from the atmosphere and surface below, thereby warming the surface. Because tropospheric aerosols lie below much of the atmosphere and are almost as warm as the ground,

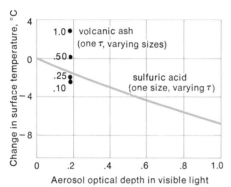

Figure 4. The surface temperature is influenced by the number of sulfuric acid particles in the stratosphere and by the size of volcanic dust particles. Large particles tend to warm the surface whereas small ones cool it; the sulfuric acid particles are usually smaller than 0.1 μm, and thus they have a cooling influence. (From Pollack et al. 1976a, b.)

they are not nearly as efficient at blocking the escape of the infrared energy.

Globally distributed stratospheric aerosols will always warm the stratosphere. However, the Earth's surface will cool if most of the aerosols are smaller than a critical size—near 0.5 μm, depending somewhat upon the aerosols' composition and the Earth's albedo. Hence τ and the size of the stratospheric aerosols are the most important parameters needed to estimate the effect of the aerosols on the climate. The major complicating factor is that, after a volcanic eruption, the aerosols evolve rapidly in size and composition as they spread out over the Earth. Although observational data are sparse, it seems that the size of the particles varies for several months: as the dust veil begins to form, the particles may be larger than the critical size.

As for the tropospheric aerosols, the Earth's surface will cool if globally distributed aerosols have a $\tilde{\omega}_0$ larger than the critical albedo (near 0.85), and the magnitude of the cooling will depend in a nearly linear manner upon τ. Hence, $\tilde{\omega}_0$ and τ are the principal variables that need to be known in order to relate tropospheric aerosols and climate. The major complication for the analysis is that aerosols are not uniformly distributed, either horizontally or vertically, throughout the troposphere, and therefore $\tilde{\omega}_0$ and τ vary widely with location. The value of the critical albedo also varies with location because it depends upon the ground albedo. In addition, once the aerosols affect the radiation budget in one area, the atmosphere responds with complex changes in the wind and clouds. Because aerosols are heterogeneous, climate theorists cannot provide a single answer to the question of whether tropospheric aerosols cool or warm the Earth: there is no single answer.

Variability of optical properties

The most important optical properties needed to determine the temperature at the Earth's surface are the stratospheric and tropospheric optical depths, the aerosol size distribution in the stratosphere, and the tropospheric aerosol single-scattering albedo at visible wavelengths. At present it is only possible to formulate a general outline of the range of these values (Toon and Pollack 1976).

The aerosols in the atmosphere form a complex mixture (Fig. 5), which can be separated into classes on the basis of the aerosols' elemental composition. Soil-derived aerosols, composed of minerals and organic debris of fairly large size (1–10 μm), comprise a large fraction (about 30%) of the global aerosol mass burden. Such aerosols spread far from the land of their origin, as evidenced by the great quantity of dust from the Sahara Desert that reaches the Caribbean (Carlson and Prospero 1972). Seaspray aerosols, composed mainly of sea salt and marine organics, are also fairly large (1–10 μm) but constitute only a modest fraction of the total aerosol mass (10–15%). Sea salt does not spread very far inland or to very high altitude because it is rapidly removed from the atmosphere by pre-

cipitation (Junge 1972). Sulfur compounds, mostly sulfuric acid and ammonium sulfate, constitute the largest fraction (about 50%) of the total tropospheric aerosol load and are found everywhere from the continents and the oceans to the poles. Sulfuric acid is the dominant aerosol in the stratosphere. Sulfates are primarily formed within the atmosphere by complex photochemical and solution reactions and are typically rather small (0.1 μm). Many other materials are also found in the atmosphere, including graphitic soot, forest-fire debris, nitrates, and numerous organic compounds. The optical properties of these various materials are quite different.

Experimental projects to determine $\tilde{\omega}_0$ have used one of three approaches: direct measurements of $\tilde{\omega}_0$ in the atmosphere (Herman et al. 1975; Weiss et al. 1978); laboratory measurements of the absorption by collections of atmospheric aerosols and calculation of $\tilde{\omega}_0$ (Lindberg 1975; Patterson et al. 1977); or laboratory measurements of the absorption by pure materials known to compose aerosols and calculation of $\tilde{\omega}_0$ (Palmer and Williams 1975; Toon et al. 1976; Twitty and Weinman 1971). The laboratory studies have shown that materials such as sulfates and sea salt are very transparent to visible light and have $\tilde{\omega}_0$ very close to unity. Most rock particles are only moderately absorbing and have $\tilde{\omega}_0$ above 0.9, although smaller values are occasionally found. The laboratory studies combined with observations of the most common aerosol materials suggest that $\tilde{\omega}_0$ is usually well above the critical value of 0.85, and thus we would expect that aerosols will generally cool the Earth. However, in certain regions wind-borne dark aerosols derived from soil over high-albedo surfaces might cause warming. In contrast, the direct studies of $\tilde{\omega}_0$ in the troposphere find that $\tilde{\omega}_0$ is normally at or well below the critical value, with a few exceptions.

Accurate direct measurements of $\tilde{\omega}_0$ are quite difficult to make, and the available values could be wrong. Also, measurements have not been performed in enough locations to obtain a "typical" value. Most of the lowest $\tilde{\omega}_0$ values have been found in urban regions, which comprise only a small fraction of the Earth's area. For these reasons, the available direct studies may be misleading when applied to the global problem. However, it is also quite possible that the laboratory studies have overlooked minor, highly absorbing materials such as iron oxides or soot. If 10 to 20% of the aerosols were composed of soot, the value of $\tilde{\omega}_0$ would be below the critical value even if the remaining bulk of the material were completely transparent. If the absorbing particles were much smaller than the typical aerosols, an even smaller mass fraction could be very significant (Bergstrom 1973). It has been found that a small amount of soot is responsible for the low values of $\tilde{\omega}_0$ in urban areas (Rosen et al. 1978).

Very little is known about the variability of $\tilde{\omega}_0$, and much of the debate about whether aerosol pollution will lead to a warming or cooling of the Earth depends upon which compounds are being added to the atmosphere. Those who believe anthropogenic aerosols are warming the climate point to the fact that $\tilde{\omega}_0$ is lowest in urban areas, suggesting that man is lowering $\tilde{\omega}_0$ globally by emitting soot and perhaps opaque hydrocarbons. One reason for restricting soot emissions from diesel engines is to prevent the lowering of $\tilde{\omega}_0$. Many of those who believe anthropogenic aerosols are cooling the Earth blame sulfate compounds, which are known to have a large $\tilde{\omega}_0$. Human activities now probably account for about half the sulfur compounds in the atmosphere (Bach 1976). Concern about sulfate aerosols is one reason for strict emission controls on sulfur dioxide. Another group points to the large quantity of soil debris that humans release to the atmosphere by agricultural activity. Most soil debris has $\tilde{\omega}_0$ above the critical value, and thus in most areas agricultural activity may have the effect of cooling the Earth.

Since aerosol optical depth is primarily a measure of the aerosol concentration, increased levels of pollution could be detected by monitoring τ. Although it is difficult to measure $\tilde{\omega}_0$, it is quite simple to measure τ. As the solar beam passes through the atmosphere, some sunlight is absorbed by aerosols and some is scattered and ends up as diffuse sky light. The optical depth is the natural logarithm of the ratio of the sunlight

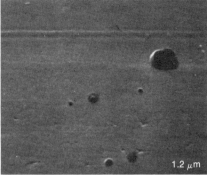
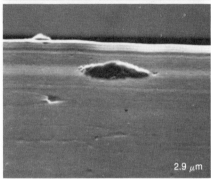
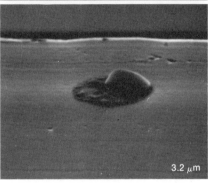

Figure 5. Stratospheric particles (*above*) are generally fluid sulfuric acid, though solid particles of diverse types are present, especially after large volcanic eruptions. These electron-microscope photographs show particles collected by N. Farlow using NASA's U2 aircraft flying near 20 km. (The number in each is the size of the largest particle.) *Below:* Tropospheric particles are extremely diverse, and their structure depends strongly upon when and where they are captured. This electron-microscope photograph shows particles obtained by D. Wood between 3 and 8 km altitude near Dallas, TX. The largest particles are about 5 μm in diameter, and x-ray diffraction studies indicate that they are soil particles; the small particles are probably sulfates.

reaching the ground in the direct solar beam to the sunlight impinging at the top of the atmosphere.

Observations of τ at visible wavelengths have been made since about 1900 at a few locations, but data from even a few places are useful for monitoring the stratospheric optical depth, because changes in the stratosphere occur on a nearly global scale. Figure 6 illustrates that changes in the stratospheric optical depth due to explosive volcanic eruptions have more than doubled the Earth's average aerosol optical depth for a year or two following each eruption. Explosive volcanic eruptions are episodic, and though many volcanoes erupted between 1870 and 1912, there has been only one large eruption since 1912. Indirect evidence (Lamb 1970) shows that there were large volcanic optical depths for the entire four centuries from 1500 to 1900, and studies of volcanic ash in polar cores reveal a 10-thousand-year period of explosive volcanic activity centered at the peak of the last ice age, twenty thousand years ago (Gow and Williamson 1971). NASA now has a satellite program designed to study the optical depths and the spread of aerosols after large volcanic eruptions.

The optical depth changes in the stratosphere following large volcanic eruptions are due partly to volcanic ash and partly to sulfuric acid particles. Unfortunately, we do not precisely know the ratio of these materials or their sizes. It is believed that ash particles larger than the critical size dominate the volcanic cloud initially but soon fall out of the atmosphere. Then sulfuric acid particles, formed from chemical reactions involving volcanic gas, dominate the period following the eruption (Toon and Pollack 1976). In order to test these ideas, NASA has an extensive aircraft sampling program in the stratosphere, and theoretical models of the aerosols have been constructed in an attempt to predict the aerosol sizes (Turco et al. 1979).

Considerable thought has been given to the possibility that human beings might alter the stratospheric aerosol optical depth by flying aircraft and rockets through the stratosphere or by adding sulfur gases to the stratosphere as industrial pollutants (Pollack et al. 1976b, c; Turco et al. 1980). At present, it does not appear that any of man's planned activities during the next several decades will cause a significant enhancement in the stratospheric optical depth, except possibly a small increase due to the release of carbonyl sulfide, an industrial pollutant (Turco et al. 1980).

The optical depths of tropospheric aerosols vary on shorter time and space scales than do those of stratospheric aerosols. A general trend areas, or agricultural areas, including parts of Japan, the eastern and southwestern United States, and the Soviet Union, we have evidence of large upward trends in optical depth during the past several decades (Yamamoto et al. 1971; Husar et al. 1979; Machta 1972; Trijonis 1979). Tropospheric aerosols come from local sources and are rapidly removed from the atmosphere. Hence the major changes are expected on regional but not global scales. At present, we have an incomplete picture of the regional regions and during droughts in semi-arid regions of the world. For example, the optical depth of the dust from the Sahara Desert often reaches 0.5 over the Atlantic and sometimes exceeds 2.0 (Carlson and Caverly 1977). Also, large variations in the dust over the Atlantic may be partially caused by drought in Africa (Prospero and Nees 1977). A well-known example of drought-caused dust was the Dust Bowl era of the 1930s, which affected the plains of the south-central United States. Although much dust is naturally released from the soil, human activities have greatly increased the amount supplied to the atmosphere by altering the natural vegetation that used to prevent soil from being eroded. No observations allow us to estimate exactly how much of an impact these soil particles have on the global average optical depth, but local anthropogenic enhancements are well known.

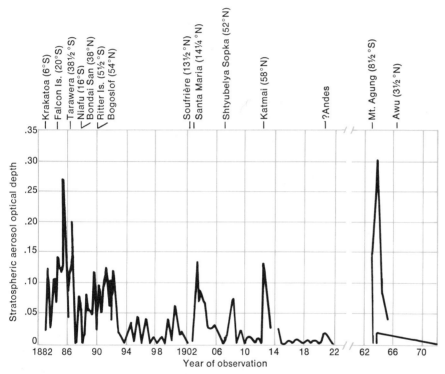

Figure 6. Observations of the change in stratospheric aerosol optical depth at visible wavelength over the past century show that large volcanic eruptions create optical depths for a year or two that are as large as those of tropospheric aerosols. The optical depths vary over the Earth. For example, the data after the 1963 eruption of Mt. Agung, which is south of the equator, show large optical depths in the Southern Hemisphere, and smaller ones in the Northern Hemisphere. (From Pollack et al. 1976a.)

Knowledge of the sulfate optical depth and its variability comes rather indirectly. Since sulfates seem to constitute about half the world's aerosol mass, they may supply half the global average aerosol optical depth. Indeed, since the optical depth is proportional to the surface area of the aerosols and the mass is proportional to their volume, a fixed mass of small sulfate particles has a much larger optical depth than the same mass of large rock or salt particles. Man's contribution to the sulfate supply is roughly half, or 25% of the total aerosol optical depth. Studies in New York City (Leaderer et al. 1978) suggest that sulfates are responsible for 50% of the light scattering there. Weiss and co-workers (1977) find that sulfates dominate the light scattering in the midwestern and southern United States, and Waggoner and co-workers (1976) reach a similar conclusion about light scattering in Scandinavia. Several pollution episodes of greatly enhanced sulfate levels and reduced visibility over extensive regions of the eastern United States have been mapped by large-scale monitoring networks (Hidy et al. 1978). Annual averages of aerosol optical depths are much higher in central Europe and the eastern United States than in surrounding regions (Flowers et al. 1969; Yamamoto et al. 1968); the difference seems to be due to sulfates most probably

shows much lower tropospheric optical depths at higher latitudes than at lower latitudes, and much lower optical depths over oceans than over continents (Toon and Pollack 1976). There is little evidence for large global-scale changes in the tropospheric optical depth. The optical depth has been monitored at remote mountaintop sites for several decades, and no long-term trends have yet been detected (Roosen et al. 1973; Ellis and Pueschel 1971). However, at many rural sites near cities, industrialized aerosol concentrations, but in several years we expect to have satellite-borne lasers that will be able to map tropospheric aerosol concentrations and greatly improve our knowledge.

Of the major aerosol constituents—sea salt, soil, and sulfates—large optical depth changes due to sea salt are the least likely, whereas changes due to soil particles are the most prevalent and best documented. Significant regional soil aerosol enhancements result from dust storms near desert produced by humans (Weiss et al. 1977). Trijonis (1979) has empirically linked anthropogenic sulfate emissions with increasing aerosol optical depth in the American Southwest.

Changes in climate

Regional and global changes in climate have yet to be explained satisfactorily. The radiative impact of stratospheric aerosols during the year or two following a volcanic eruption is probably the least controversial agent of climatic change, because the eruption serves as a time marker after which the Earth's climate can be carefully monitored for small changes until the volcanic debris has fallen from the sky. Large volcanic eruptions can provide a unique, well-defined check upon climate models. A major difficulty in testing climate models or in determining the cause of climate changes is that most agents, such as CO_2, tropospheric aerosols, or the sun's luminosity, vary rather slowly and thus their effects can be confused with each other and with natural fluctuations.

Benjamin Franklin first suggested that volcanoes might affect weather when he ascribed the harsh winter of 1784 to a "dry fog" whose origin he thought might have been a large volcanic eruption. Since Franklin's time, several people have studied the weather after an explosive eruption to see if they could discover an effect (Lamb 1970). A statistical correlation was found which suggested that an eruption cools the Earth by several tenths of a degree. Sometimes severe weather changes after a large eruption have caused much human suffering, as in 1816—the "year without a summer"—when frost and cold plagued New England and Western Europe (Hoyt 1958). Some of the suffering of 1816 still remains to haunt moviegoers, since the bad weather that year provided Mary Shelley the opportunity to write *Frankenstein*.

The only violent explosive volcanic eruption since 1912 was the eruption of Mt. Agung, in Indonesia, in 1963 (see Fig. 6), and thus most of our efforts to relate stratospheric aerosols and climate are based on very old data. The data from the Mt. Agung eruption indicate that the dust from that volcano was mainly restricted to

the tropical Southern Hemisphere. A 0.5°C cooling was observed in the tropics at the surface, whereas the stratosphere was observed to warm by several degrees. The empirically observed link between the atmosphere and the aerosols can be tested by calculating the climatic change that should have been caused by the observed aerosols. The calculation is based upon a sophisticated radiative-balance model (Fig. 7) including very simple dynamics (Hansen et al. 1978). Despite its basic simplicity, the

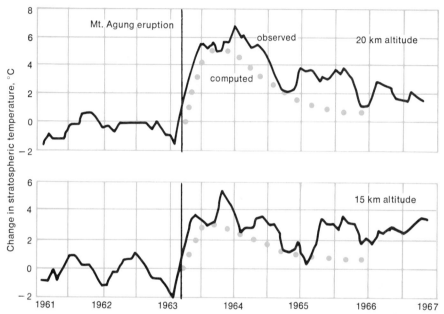

us added confidence that aerosols do affect climate and also helps to reassure us that we may one day actually be able to predict climate changes. Of course, climate models will require much further development and testing before we can use them with assurance.

Several studies based on observations of stratospheric volcanic optical depths (see Fig. 6) over the last century have suggested that some of the observed global mean temperature

Figure 7. After the Mt. Agung eruption, the stratospheric temperatures, measured at two altitudes, were found to increase due to the aerosols' absorption of solar and infrared radiation. The surface temperature in the tropics decreased because the aerosols reflected some sunlight back to space and absorbed some sunlight that would normally have reached the ground. The time evolution of the temperature

partly reflects the changing aerosol optical depths and partly the response time of the troposphere and the ocean. The calculation, which was based on observed aerosol optical depths, is a one-dimensional radiative model and not just an empirical fit. It is encouraging to find that a simple climate model correctly calculates the observed temperature change. (From Hansen et al. 1978.)

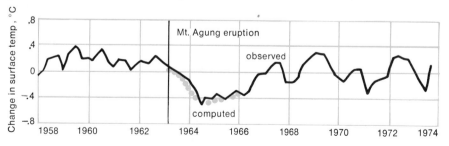

results of the calculation correspond quite well with the observed cooling at the surface (caused by the volcanic aerosols scattering sunlight back to space) and the observed warming in the stratosphere (caused by the aerosols absorbing infrared and solar radiation). This correspondence gives

changes were due to the changing level of volcanic activity (Robock 1978). Figure 8 presents the results of radiative-balance calculations of the Earth's global mean surface temperature in the Northern Hemisphere over the last century. Part of the change of temperature is due to the increasing levels of CO_2 in the atmosphere, and part is due to the decline in volcanic optical depth after 1912 (Pollack et al. 1976a, b). The calculations suggest that volcanic activity from 1880 to 1910 was more significant than CO_2 in causing the temperature difference between 1880 and 1940. Increasing carbon dioxide levels, which have had only a slight effect on the climate so far, will be much more significant in the future (Williams 1978).

Our knowledge of volcanic activity

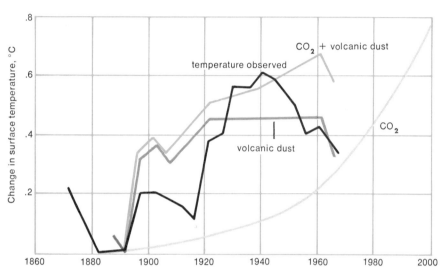

Figure 8. Radiative-balance calculations determine the temperature changes (recorded between 0° and 80° N) over the last century that may have been caused by the observed increase in CO_2, the observed decrease in dust from volcanic activity, and the combined changes from CO_2 plus volcanic dust. Comparison of the calculated and observed tem-

and climate before 1880 becomes increasingly poor the further back we go. The large volcanic optical depths between 1500 and 1900 suggested by Lamb (1970) may have played a causative role in the cool temperatures of that period, which has been called the "little ice age" (Pollack et al. 1976b). However, it is also possible that the climate was influenced by solar-luminosity fluctuations during those centuries (Eddy 1977; Pollack et al. 1979) or by surface albedo changes caused by deforestation and desertification (Sagan et al. 1980). Several scientists have suggested that volcanic eruptions are correlated with ice ages (Bray 1977), and it is true that there was a significant amount of volcanic activity during the coldest

phase of the last ice age, 20,000 years ago (Gow and Williamson 1971). However, we have no evidence of a significant burst of volcanic activity 100,000 years ago at the initiation of the last ice age, and the periodicity of ice ages strongly suggests that they are caused, at least in part, by variations in the Earth's orbit about the sun (Hays et al. 1976).

Perhaps the most famous theory connecting tropospheric aerosols and climate is R. Bryson's "human volcano" hypothesis (1972) that the

peratures suggests that the decline in volcanic activity made a major contribution to the observed climate warming in the Northern Hemisphere between 1880 and 1940. Estimates show that CO_2 warming may become significant during the next several decades. (Pollack et al. 1976b.)

0.3°C cooling which has been observed between 1940 and 1970 (see Fig. 8) is due to aerosols injected into the atmosphere by humans. Figure 3 suggests that if about 25% of the present aerosol optical depth were due to anthropogenic aerosols with a high value of $\tilde{\omega}_0$, they could be the cause of the observed cooling. But we do not even know if the globally averaged optical depth has changed by such a small amount as 25%, although the optical depths in many regions are known to have changed significantly since about 1940 (Yamamoto et al. 1971; Husar et al. 1979; Machta 1972; Trijonis 1979). The human contribution to tropospheric sulfates at present is probably great enough to have increased the optical depth by

25%, though the timing of the change is not known. Additional contributions to the optical depth could have been made by agricultural activities—one of Bryson's favorite ideas. Other possible causes of the temperature change since 1940 include surface albedo changes from alterations in human land use (Sagan et al. 1980) and natural, random climate fluctuations (Robock 1978).   .

The possible effects of tropospheric aerosols are more easily observed on a regional scale. Bryson (1972) has suggested that the dusty Rajputana Desert of India, site of the ancient Indus Valley civilization, is an example of an anthropogenic aerosol desert. He believes that overgrazing of arid lands by the domesticated animals of the Rajputana inhabitants allows the wind to blow large quantities of dust into the atmosphere; the dust increases the infrared radiation from the lower atmosphere, causing the air to cool and subside, which suppresses rainfall (rain normally falls only in ascending air parcels). Harshvardhan and Cess (1978) have reexamined this problem with a better radiative transfer scheme, and they find that the dust contributes negligibly to the infrared cooling of the air. As yet no one has considered the impact of the dust on the solar radiation, and whether the dust in the atmosphere over the Rajputana Desert is partly responsible for creating the desert remains to be determined by further study.

Another good candidate for empirical testing of the effects of aerosols on climate is Sahara dust over the Atlantic Ocean. The radiative properties of this dust have been characterized by Carlson and Caverly (1977), who suggested that the dust should lead to cooling at the surface and increased solar heating in the atmosphere above the ocean. The significance of these effects to the weather over the ocean has not yet been investigated.

Husar and co-workers (1979) have attempted to correlate for each season of the year observed increases in aerosol levels over the eastern United States with regional climate changes observed since 1948. Of the seasons and regions considered, they found that the aerosol levels increased most dramatically in the Smoky Mountain region during summertime. Simultaneously the same region also experienced the largest changes of any region in several climatological variables, including higher humidity and lower temperature, with noontime temperature decreasing by about 1°C.

One might imagine, because of the obvious importance of aerosols to visibility in urban areas, that the radiative effects of aerosols on the urban climate would be well known. But in addition to the large quantities of aerosols, cities also have large concentrations of gaseous absorbers, they release large quantities of heat into the environment, and their surface properties, such as ground-heat capacity and reflectivity, differ substantially from those of surrounding rural areas. Theoretical studies (Ackerman 1977) have shown that the radiative impact of aerosols on the urban climate is less important than the release of heat or the urban modification of surface properties. Although aerosols do greatly modify the surface radiation energy budget, these modifications seem to be partly offset by changes in other heat transfer processes, such as latent and sensible heat transfer by atmospheric motions.

The most significant radiative impact of the aerosols in urban areas seems to be that they warm the atmosphere and stabilize it against convection. Mixing processes that remove pollutants from urban areas are highly sensitive to the stability of the atmosphere. Urban dwellers quickly learn that temperature inversions, which cause the atmosphere to be stable, lead to high-pollution episodes. Although aerosols tend to promote such inversions, they are primarily caused by large-scale meteorological processes. Aerosols do seem to affect the climate of cities, but because other processes have a stronger influence, it is necessary to make detailed empirical studies that can ascertain the aerosol-climate relations.

The empirical and theoretical evidence for a cause-and-effect relationship between increased levels of stratospheric aerosols due to volcanic explosions and a cooling of the Earth's surface is the most secure of any relationship that has yet been explored by climatologists. However, much further experimental work needs to be done to determine more precisely the aerosol size distribution and the magnitude and types of climatic changes that occur after large eruptions. The climate shifts caused by large explosive volcanic eruptions can potentially be used to test climate models.

Although the empirical and theoretical evidence for a relationship between increased levels of tropospheric aerosols and climate change is tentative, it suggests that aerosols have affected the climate in many parts of the Earth. Several regions have high tropospheric aerosol levels, and further studies in these regions are needed. Adding nearly transparent materials to the lower atmosphere, such as sulfates and most soil particles, tends to cool the Earth's surface. Adding opaque materials to the atmosphere, such as soot, tends to warm the atmosphere. Since human activity is adding soot, sulfates, and soil to the lower atmosphere in different regions, some areas are probably being warmed and some are being cooled.

References

Ackerman, T. P. 1977. A model of the effect of aerosols on urban climates with particular application to the Los Angeles Basin. *J. Atmos. Sci.* 34:531–47.

Bach, W. 1976. Global air pollution and climatic change. *Rev. Geophys. Space Phys.* 14:492–73.

Bergstrom, R. W. 1973. Extinction and absorption coefficients of the atmospheric aerosol as a function of particle size. *Beit. Phys. Atmos.* 46:223–34.

Bray, J. R. 1977. Pleistocene volcanism and glacial initiation. *Science* 197:251–54.

Bryson, R. A. 1972. Climate modification by air pollution. *The Environmental Future*, ed. N. Polunin. London: MacMillan.

Carlson, T. N., and J. M. Prospero. 1972. The large-scale movement of Saharan air outbreaks over the northern equatorial Atlantic. *J. Appl. Meteor.* 11:283–97.

Carlson, T. N., and T. S. Caverly. 1977. Radiative characteristics of Sahara dust at solar wavelengths. *J. Geophys. Res.* 82:3141–52.

Eddy, J. A. 1977. Climate and the changing sun. *Climatic Change* 1:173–90.

Ellis, H. T., and R. F. Pueschel. 1971. Solar radiation: Absence of air pollution trends at Mauna Loa. *Science* 172:845–46.

Flowers, E. C., R. A. McCormick, and K. R. Kurfis. 1969. Atmospheric turbidity over the United States, 1961–1966. *J. Appl. Meteor.* 8:955–62.

Gow, A. J., and T. Williamson. 1971. Volcanic ash in the Antarctic ice sheet and its possible climatic implications. *Earth Plant. Sci. Lett.* 13:210–18.

Hansen, J. E., and L. D. Travis. 1974. Light scattering in planetary atmospheres. *Space Sci. Rev.* 16:527–610.

Hansen, J. W., W. C. Wang, and A. A. Lacis. 1978. Mount Agung eruption provides test of a global climate perturbation. *Science* 199:1065–68.

———. 1979. Climatic effects of atmospheric aerosols. *Proc. Conf. on Aerosols: Urban and Rural Characteristics, Source and Transport Studies.* New York Academy of Sciences, NY, Jan. 1979.

Harshvardhan and R. D. Cess. 1978. Effect of tropospheric aerosols upon atmospheric infrared cooling rates. *J. Quant. Spect. Rad. Trans.* 19:621–32.

Hays, J. D., K. Imbrie, and N. J. Shackleton. 1976. Variations in the Earth's orbit: Pacemaker of the ice ages. *Science* 194:1121–32.

Herman, B., R. S. Browning, and J. J. De Luisi. 1975. Determination of the effective imaginary term of the complex refractive index of atmospheric dust by remote sensing: The diffuse direct method. *J. Atmos. Sci.* 32:918–25.

Hidy, G. M., P. K. Mueller, and E. Y. Tong. 1978. Spatial and temporal distributions of airborne sulfate in parts of the United States. *Atmos. Environ.* 12:735–52.

Hoyt, J. B. 1958. The cold summer of 1816. *Assoc. Am. Geog.* 48:118–31.

Husar, R. B., D. B. Patterson, J. M. Holloway, W. E. Wilson, and T. G. Ellestad. 1979. Trends of Eastern U.S. haziness since 1948. *Proc. Fourth Symp. on Atmos. Turbulence, Diffusion and Air Pollution*, pp. 249–56. Reno, NV, Jan. 1979.

Junge, C. E. 1972. Our knowledge of the physico-chemistry of aerosols in the undisturbed marine environment. *J. Geophys. Res.* 77:5183–211.

Lamb, H. H. 1970. Volcanic dust in the atmosphere; with a chronology and assessment of its meteorological significance. *Phil. Trans. Roy. Soc. London* 266:425–533.

Leaderer, B., et al. 1978. Summary of the New York summer aerosol study. *J. Air Poll. Control Assoc.* 28:321–27.

Lindberg, J. 1975. The composition and optical absorption coefficient of atmospheric particular matter. *Quant. Elect.* 7:131–39.

Machta, L. 1972. Mauna Loa and global trends in air quality. *Bull. Amer. Meteor. Soc.* 53:402–20.

Mitchell, J. M., Jr. 1970. A preliminary assessment of atmospheric pollution as a cause of long-term changes of global temperature. In *The Changing Global Environment*, ed. S. F. Singer, pp. 149–75. Reidel.

Palmer, K. F., and D. Williams. 1975. Optical constants of sulfuric acid: Application to the clouds of Venus? *Appl. Opt.* 14:208–19.

Patterson, E., D. A. Gillette, and B. H. Stockton. 1977. Complex index of refraction between 320 and 700 nm for Sahara aerosols. *J. Geophys. Res.* 82:3153–60.

Pollack, J. B., W. J. Borucki, and O. B. Toon. 1979. Solar spectral variations: A drive for climatic changes? *Nature* 282:600–603.

Pollack, J. B., O. B. Toon, C. Sagan, A. Summers, B. Baldwin, and W. Van Camp. 1976a. Volcanic explosions and climatic change: A theoretical assessment. *J. Geophys. Res.* 81:1071–83.

———. 1976b. Stratospheric aerosols and climatic change. *Nature* 263:551–55.

Pollack, J. B., O. B. Toon, A. Summers, W. Van Camp, and B. Baldwin. 1976c. Estimates of the climatic impact of aerosols produced by space shuttles, SST's and other high-flying aircraft. *J. Appl. Meteor.* 15:247–58.

Prospero, J. M., and R. T. Nees. 1977. Dust concentration in the atmosphere of the equatorial north Atlantic: Possible relationship to the Sahelian drought. *Science* 196:1196–98.

Ramanathan, V., and J. A. Coakley, Jr. 1978. Climate modeling through radiative-convective models. *Rev. Geophys. Space Phys.* 16:465–89.

Robock, A. 1978. Internally and externally caused climate change. *J. Atmos. Sci.* 35:1111–22.

Roosen, R. G., R. J. Angionne, and C. H. Klemcke. 1973. Worldwide variations in atmospheric transmission observations. *Bull. Am. Meteor. Soc.* 54:307–16.

Rosen, H., A. D. A. Hansen, L. Gundel, and T. Novakov. 1978. Identification of the optically absorbing component in urban aerosols. *Appl. Opt.* 17:3859–61.

Sagan, C., O. B. Toon, and J. B. Pollack. 1980. Human impact on climate: Of significance since the invention of fire? *Science* 206:1323–62.

Toon, O. B., and J. B. Pollack. 1976. A global average model of atmospheric aerosols for radiative transfer calculations. *J. Appl. Meteor.* 15:225–46.

Toon, O. B., J. B. Pollack, and B. N. Khare. 1976. The optical constants of several atmospheric aerosol species: Ammonium sulfate, aluminum oxide and sodium chloride. *J. Geophys. Res.* 81:5733–48.

Trijonis, J. 1979. Visibility in the southwest: An exploration of the historical data base. *Atmos. Environ.* 13:833–43.

Turco, R. P., P. Hamill, O. B. Toon, R. C. Whitten, and C. S. Kiang. 1979. A one-dimensional model describing aerosol formation and evolution in the stratosphere, I: Physical processes and mathematical analogs. *J. Atmos. Sci.* 36:699–717.

Turco, R. P., R. C. Whitten, O. B. Toon, J. B. Pollack, and P. Hamill. 1980. Carbonyl sulfide, stratospheric aerosols, and terrestrial climate. *Nature* 283:283–86.

Twitty, J. T., and J. A. Weinman. 1971. Radiative properties of carbonaceous aerosols. *J. Appl. Meteor.* 10:725–31.

Waggoner, A. P., A. J. Vanderpol, R. J. Charlson, S. Larser, L. Granat and C. Tragardh. 1976. Sulfate-light scattering ratio as an index of the role of sulphur in tropospheric optics. *Nature* 261:120–22.

Weiss, R. E., A. P. Waggoner, R. J. Charlson, and N. C. Ahlquist. 1977. Sulfate aerosol: Its geographic extent in the midwestern and southern United States. *Science* 195:979–81.

Weiss, R. E., A. P. Waggoner, D. L. Thorsell, J. S. Hall, L. A. Riley, and R. J. Charlson. 1978. Studies of the optical, physical, and chemical properties of high-absorbing aerosols. In *Proc. Conf. on Carbonaceous Particles in the Atmosphere*, pp. 257–62. U.C. Berkeley, March 1978. Lawrence Berkeley publication 9037 (available from NTIS).

Williams, J. 1978. *Carbon Dioxide, Climate and Society.* Pergamon Press.

Yamamoto, G., M. Tanaka, and K. Arao. 1968. Hemispherical distribution of turbidity coefficient as estimated from direct solar radiation measurements. *J. Meteor. Soc. Japan* 46:287–300.

Yamamoto, G., M. Tanaka, and K. Arao. 1971. Secular variation of atmospheric turbidity over Japan. *J. Meteorol. Soc. Japan* 49:859–65.

C. F. Baes, Jr., H. E.
Goeller, J. S. Olson, and
R. M. Rotty

Carbon Dioxide and Climate: The Uncontrolled Experiment

Possibly severe consequences of growing CO_2 releases from fossil fuels require a much better understanding of the carbon cycle, climate change, and the resulting impacts

According to Revelle and Suess (1957), "Human beings are now carrying out a large-scale geophysical experiment of a kind that could not have happened in the past nor be repeated in the future. Within a few centuries we are returning to the atmosphere and oceans the concentrated organic carbon stored in the sedimentary rocks over hundreds of millions of years. This experiment, if adequately documented, may yield a far-reaching insight into the processes determining weather and climate." Thus well said is the need to *observe* vigilantly the consequences of man's consumption of fossil fuels—coal, oil, and natural gas—and the concomitant return of vast amounts of carbon to the atmosphere in the form of carbon dioxide.

Left unstated, however, is perhaps

C. F. Baes, H. E. Goeller, and J. S. Olson are, respectively, members of the Chemistry Division, the Program Planning and Analysis Office, and the Environmental Sciences Division of Oak Ridge National Laboratory. R. M. Rotty is a member of the Institute for Energy Analysis, Oak Ridge Associated Universities. The paper is an adaption of a report entitled "The Global Carbon Dioxide Problem" (U.S. Energy Research and Development Report ORNL-5194). The research was sponsored by the Energy Research and Development Administration under contract with Union Carbide Corporation. During the course of this review, the authors have benefited greatly from discussions with a number of individuals; they wish especially to thank W. Broecker, of the Lamont-Doherty Geological Observatory; V. Ramanathen, of the National Center for Atmospheric Research; L. Machta, Director of the Air Resources Laboratories, NOAA; J. M. Mitchell, of the Environmental Data Service, NOAA; S. Manabe, of the Geophysical Fluid Dynamics Laboratory, NOAA; and G. Marland, Oak Ridge Associated Universities. Address: Oak Ridge National Laboratory, or, for R. M. Rotty, Oak Ridge Associated Universities, Oak Ridge, TN 37830.

the greater need to *anticipate* the consequences of this process well enough in advance to keep them within acceptable limits. The urgency stems from the uncontrolled manner in which the "experiment" is being conducted. The release of fossil carbon as CO_2 has been increasing at an exponential rate since the beginning of the industrial revolution about 100 years ago (Fig. 1). As a result the concentration of CO_2 in the atmosphere, which thus far has grown only about 12%, may double in the next 60 years or so. The effects may well become visible suddenly and, because of the great momentum developed by the machinery that produces man's energy, could grow out of control before remedial actions become effective.

The principal effect of an increased concentration of CO_2 in the atmosphere should be a warming (Schneider 1975). While CO_2 is transparent to the incoming solar radiation, it absorbs a portion of the infrared radiation returned to space by the Earth. This "greenhouse effect" has given the words themselves a rather specialized meaning. The amount of warming produced by a given increase is, as we shall see, still quite uncertain, involving as it does all the complexities of the world climate. Yet the impacts of increased atomspheric CO_2 on man's environment could be large indeed, rendering this a problem in impact assessment of unprecedented scope and difficulty.

This matter has been considered extensively in the current literature by climatologists (e.g. Mitchell 1972, 1975; Schneider 1975), geochemists (e.g. Broecker 1975; Keeling, in press), and biologists (e.g. Reiners et al.

1973), but not often in all its important aspects. In the present article we shall attempt to consider these and especially the important uncertainties that presently limit the reliability of impact assessment. Effective remedial actions, if and when they become necessary, quite obviously cannot be expected unless and until their need can be foretold with a reliability that will match the considerable costs of their implementation.

The growth of atmospheric CO_2

Since the beginning of accurate and regular measurements in 1958, the concentration of CO_2 in the atmosphere has shown an accelerating increase upon which is superimposed annual fluctuations from photosynthesis and other seasonal effects (Fig. 2). The current average value is about 330 ppm, compared to estimated preindustrial values between 290 and 300 ppm (Callendar 1958). The measurements in Figure 2 were taken at Mauna Loa Observatory (3,400 m elevation) in Hawaii and were corrected for any temporary disturbances from local sources. Measurements at Point Barrow, Alaska, from aircraft over Sweden, and at the South Pole all show quite clearly the same secular increase (Machta et al. 1976).

The excess of the annual average concentration over the preindustrial value has grown about 4% per year (lower curve in Fig. 3). Over the same period the cumulative amount of CO_2 produced by the burning of fossil carbon (upper curve in Fig. 3) has been about twice as great as the atmospheric increase and has shown a similar rate of growth. (Except for brief interruptions during the two world wars and the great depression, the increase in the rate of release of fossil carbon has been 4.3% per year.) This suggests that, on the average, about half of the fossil carbon flux has been balanced by all the other fluxes in the carbon cycle, the excess carbon being stored in the oceans and the terrestrial biomass.

The correlation of the two curves in Figure 3 is the strongest evidence to date that the fossil carbon flux is primarily responsible for the secular increase in atmospheric CO_2. While perhaps it is not conclusive evidence, it certainly gives ample reason for concern. Will the fraction of released fossil carbon that, in effect, remains airborne increase, remain the same, or decrease? How accurately can we predict the future course of the CO_2 concentration in the atmosphere? Answers to these questions require a knowledge of the future rate of consumption of fossil fuel and of the response of the carbon cycle.

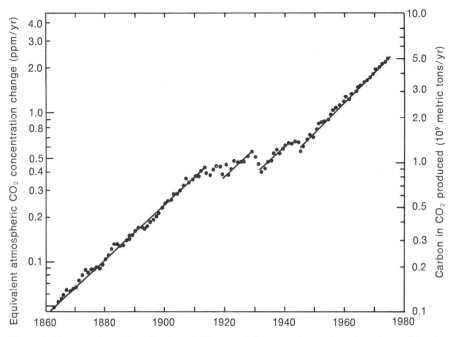

Figure 1. The annual world production of CO_2 from fossil fuels (plus a small amount from cement manufacture) is plotted since the beginning of the industrial revolution. Except for brief interruptions during the two world wars and the great depression, the release of fossil carbon has increased at a rate of 4.3% per year. (1860–1949 data from Keeling 1973a; later data from Rotty 1976.)

The carbon cycle

At the current concentration of 330 ppm of CO_2, the atmosphere contains about 700 Gt (1 Gigaton = 10^9 metric tons) of carbon (Fig. 4). This is substantially less than the carbon stored in living and dead biomass on land (about 1,800 Gt), somewhat more than that stored mostly as inorganic carbon in the well-mixed surface waters of the ocean, and much smaller than that stored in the deep oceans (about 32,000 Gt). The fluxes of carbon between the land and the atmosphere from photosynthesis (gross primary production, see Table 1) in one direction and respiration, decay, and fires in the other are estimated to be about 113 Gt/yr, and between the oceans and atmosphere, about 90 Gt/yr. Thus substantial portions of the carbon in the atmosphere, in the surface waters of the oceans, and on land are circulated each year in the carbon cycle. Quite obviously the relatively small amount in the atmosphere can be appreciably influenced by any changes in the major fluxes and pools of the cycle.

Most of the land biomass is present as relatively slowly exchanging material: humus and recent peat (about 1,000 Gt) and larger, long-lived stems and roots of vegetation (about 600 Gt). Only a relatively small fraction (about 160 Gt) is present as rapidly ex-

changing material: small stems and roots, litter, etc. These pools of slowly and rapidly exchanging carbon are allocated to groups of ecosystems in Table 1 and Figure 5. Also shown in Table 1 are the fluxes corresponding to gross photosynthesis (GPP) and, after subtraction of green plant respiration (R_g), the net production (NPP). Included as well are our estimates of the fluxes from fires (F) and from heterotrophic respiration (R_h) of animals and decomposers. (Heterotrophs are organisms that do not fix CO_2.)

It is clear from Table 1 and Figure 5 that man can have a significant influence on the fluxes between the land and the atmosphere. If, for example, he could cause the living biomass (about 600 Gt) to increase at a rate of 1% per year, this would more than counterbalance the current annual production of CO_2 from fossil fuel (5 Gt/yr). Since woods have more carbon per hectare, this could be accomplished by conversion of more land to woods. However, the maximum increase in biomass that could be realized would be small compared to the total mass of fossil carbon (perhaps 7,300 Gt) that man might ultimately consume.

Actually it is more likely that the biomass is being reduced by the ac-

tivities of man, particularly in the southern woods (south of 30° N latitude) where the traditional cycle of slash-and-burn agriculture may be shortened because of the pressures of growing population to the point where insufficient time is allowed for forest regrowth and soil replenishment during the fallow part of the cycle. As a result, a net conversion of woods to nonwoods may be taking place there. It is quite possible that the conversion rate is as much as 1% a year. Because of the lower concentration of carbon in nonwoods (Fig. 5) this could amount to a net flux of more than 1 Gt/yr of CO_2 to the atmosphere.

Another effect to be considered is the enhanced rate of photosynthetic production that might be caused by the increasing concentration of CO_2 in the atmosphere. Controlled studies of plant growth show that there is such an effect when other nutrients are not limiting (Allen et al. 1971); however, its importance in the carbon cycle is presently unclear. The common practice in modeling has been to assume that the fractional increase in the rate of photosynthesis is equal to the fractional increase in CO_2 times a factor β, which is less than unity as a result of deficiencies in other nutrients or water. Keeling's (in press) models seem most consistent with β

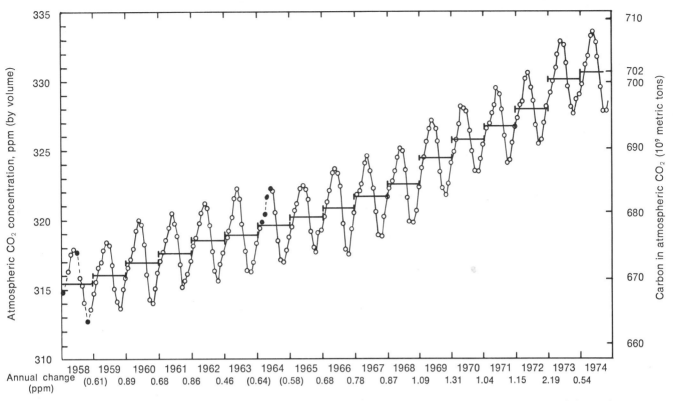

Figure 2. Monthly average values of the concentration of CO_2 in the atmosphere at Mauna Loa Observatory, Hawaii, are plotted since the beginning of accurate and regular measurements in 1958. A few of the annual changes are enclosed in parentheses because they include interpolated points, shown as dots. Variations in photosynthesis and other seasonal effects produce the annual cycle. Mean annual concentrations are well above the preindustrial level (290–300 ppm), and the secular increase is quite apparent. (1958–1971 data from Keeling et al. 1976; later data by pers. comm. from Keeling.)

= 0.27, while Oeschger et al. (1975) found values of β from 0 to 0.4 consistent with their model. This range corresponds to a 0 to 2.7 Gt/yr increase in the biomass carbon resulting from the 12% increase in atmospheric CO_2 that has occurred over the last 100 years.

The principal forms of carbon in the ocean are inorganic; i.e. "carbonic acid" (dissolved CO_2 plus H_2CO_3), bicarbonate ion (HCO_3^-) and carbonate ion ($CO_3^=$), amounting to about 1%, 89%, and 10%, respectively, of a total concentration of about 0.002 moles/liter and a total amount of about 39,000 Gt of carbon. The next most abundant dispersed form is dead organic matter, highly variable in concentration, averaging roughly 10^{-4} moles of carbon per liter and totaling about 1,650 Gt of carbon. It appears to exist in a continuum of particle sizes down to small organic molecules (Wangersky 1972). The living organic matter, principally plankton and confined largely to the surface region, is quite minor in amount (about 1 Gt of carbon, an estimate between those of Strickland [1965] and Whittaker [1975] or Bolin

[1970, 1974]). Another reactive form of carbon is the carbonate solids (mostly $CaCO_3$ formed by sea organisms), both suspended and in the surface layer of the bottom sediments. The top 10 cm or so of these deposits, amounting to 400 Gt of carbon (W. Broecker, pers. comm.), is mixed sufficiently by the foraging activities of bottom animals so that it may reasonably be included as a reactive part of the ocean reservoir.

Only the surface layer of the oceans, extending to a depth averaging about 70 m, is heated by the sun and agitated by the wind such that it is relatively well mixed. Beneath this is a stagnant region, the thermocline, stabilized by a decreasing temperature and an increasing density to a depth of about 1,000 m. Below this is the much larger region of the cold (<5°C) deep ocean, isolated from the surface waters by the thermocline. However, when the surface waters are sufficiently cold and/or saline the stabilizing density gradient weakens and the surface waters can sink (or mix) to various depths and spread horizontally. This produces a worldwide circulation that involves de-

scending surface waters mostly in polar regions and upwelling of deep water elsewhere.

The capacity of the surface waters alone to take up atmospheric CO_2 is determined largely by the reaction of CO_2 with carbonate ion to form bicarbonate ion

$$CO_2(g) + CO_3^= + H_2O \rightleftarrows 2HCO_3^-$$

As for the other reactions, the amount of neutral "carbonic acid" that can form is small, and the amount of CO_2 converted to HCO_3^- is limited by the constraint that the concentration of other ions must change to preserve the balance of ion charges.

To explore the consequences of this situation more fully, let us assume as an approximation that the above reaction is the only one occurring and that $CO_3^=$ and HCO_3^- are the only forms of carbon present in the ocean. The equilibrium condition for the reaction is

$$Q = \frac{[HCO_3^-]^2}{P_{CO_2}[CO_3^=]}$$

where Q is a constant at a given temperature. (Q is also affected slightly by small variations in the salinity of sea water.) Appropriate differentiation of this expression (with ion charge and material balances preserved) tells us that the ratio of fractional changes in the atmospheric pressure (P_{CO_2}) and the total dissolved carbon ($\Sigma C = [HCO_3^-] + [CO_3^=]$) is given solely by the ratio $R = [CO_3^=]/\Sigma C$.

$$\frac{d \ln P_{CO_2}}{d \ln \Sigma C} = \frac{1 + 3R}{R(1 - R)}$$

Since R is fairly small ($\sim$0.13), this ratio of fractional changes (called the buffer factor) is fairly large ($\sim$12.3). A more accurate calculation (described by Keeling 1973b), including contributions from other forms of carbon, gives a lower buffer factor, near 10. But the important point is that the capacity of the surface waters alone to take up CO_2 is quite limited, determined primarily by the small supply of $CO_3^=$ ion present. Since the surface waters contain an amount of carbon comparable to that in the atmosphere, less than a tenth of the current fossil carbon flux could be taken up by the surface waters alone, and this fraction should decrease as the carbonate ion is consumed.

Clearly if the oceans are a sink for a substantial part of the fossil carbon flux, this must be caused by the mixing that occurs between the surface waters and the deep waters. The distribution in the oceans of ^{14}C, which originates in the upper atmosphere from bombardment of ^{14}N by cosmic rays or from nuclear tests, indicates that the average residence time of water in the deep oceans is in the range of 500 to 2,000 years (Broecker and Li 1970; Oeschger et al. 1975). This is equivalent to circulation of only 2% to 8% of the surface water per year to the deep ocean. Hence simple box models, in which each region is assumed to be homogeneous, should not predict much capacity of the oceans to respond to the relatively rapid increases in atmospheric CO_2. Oeschger et al. (1975) point out, however, that if the mixing of surface water with deep water is assumed to occur by eddy diffusion, then the increase of CO_2 in the atmosphere can establish a concentration gradient of carbon to the deep oceans—a gradient that can store large amounts of CO_2, sustain a higher flux, and perhaps account for the entire amount that has left the atmosphere, equiv-

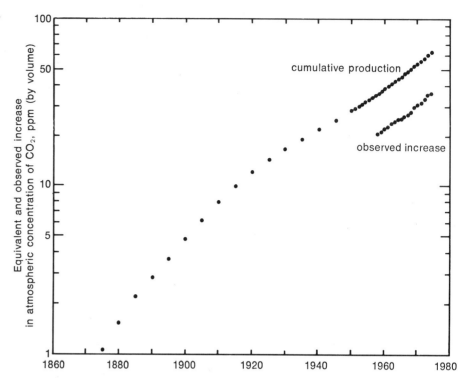

Figure 3. The cumulative production of CO_2 since 1860 (i.e. the summed changes from Fig. 1 expressed as the equivalent atmospheric concentration) is compared with the observed increase in the mean annual concentration (from Fig. 2) since that time. The similarity in the rates of increase (about 4% per year) provides strong evidence that these two quantities are related. About 50% of the fossil carbon flux apparently has been balanced, at least since 1958, by a flow of CO_2 to the oceans and/or the land biota. (The 1860 atmospheric concentration was assumed to be 295 ppm.)

alent to about 50% of the fossil carbon flux.

The ultimate capacity of the ocean system, including the $CaCO_3$, is far in excess of that required to deal with all the fossil carbon that mankind may wish to use. Indeed, as Sillén (1963) and Holland (1972) have pointed out, in the long run the concentration of CO_2 in the atmosphere should tend to remain near the present level by virtue of the reaction

$$CaCO_3(c) + CO_2(g) + H_2O$$
$$\rightleftarrows Ca^{2+} + 2HCO_3^-$$

and the equilibrium condition

$$Q = [Ca^{2+}][HCO_3^-]^2/P_{CO_2}$$

since the amounts of Ca^{2+} and HCO_3^- ion and $CaCO_3$ solid in all the oceans is far greater than the amount of fossil carbon. However, this natural control mechanism may be far too sluggish to cope with the high rate of fossil-fuel use.

Future levels of CO_2

The future growth of CO_2 in the atmosphere should depend primarily on the rate of fossil fuel consumption

and on the manner in which the carbon cycle responds to the resulting flux of CO_2. In view of the large uncertainties involved, we will consider here only high and low scenarios for fossil fuel use and ranges of response of the two largest fluxes of the carbon cycle, i.e. between the atmosphere and the oceans and between the atmosphere and the land.

Current estimates of recoverable fossil fuel suggest that about 5,600 Gt of carbon reside in forms other than oil shale (Averitt 1975; Hubbert 1974). The amount of carbon from shale containing more than 25 gallons of oil per short ton (104 liters per metric ton) is perhaps 1,700 Gt (Duncan and Swanson 1965), giving a total economic reserve of about 7,300 Gt of fossil carbon. If we were to assume, quite unrealistically, that the use of fossil fuel will continue to grow 4.3% each year until the supply is exhausted, then the Fossil Carbon Age would last 97 more years and the use rate at the very end would be over 300 Gt/yr, almost 64 times the current rate. The total CO_2 injected into the atmosphere in less than a century would be about twelve times the

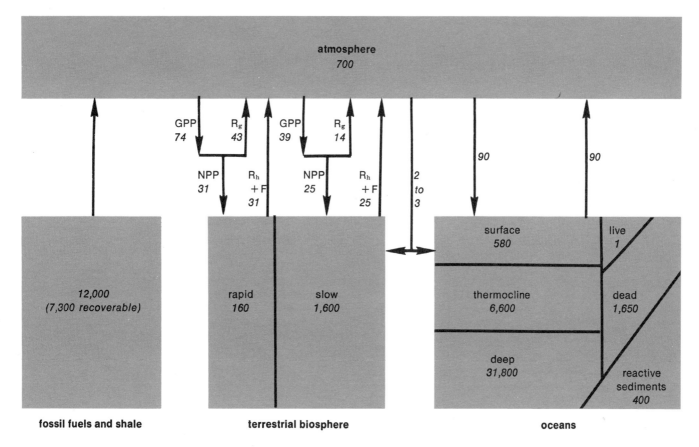

Figure 4. The major fluxes (in Gt/yr) and pool sizes (in Gt) of carbon are shown for the carbon cycle. Fluxes include gross primary production (GPP), green plant respiration (R_g), net primary production (NPP = GPP − R_g), respiration by heterotrophs (R_h), and fires (F).

preindustrial content of the atmosphere. Near the end the amount added every two years would equal the carbon content of the preindustrial atmosphere.

A much more reasonable assumption for the high-use scenario is that an initial growth rate of 4.3% per year will be reduced in proportion to the fraction of the ultimate supply of fossil fuel that has been used. This scenario (upper curve in Fig. 6) is equivalent to one of Keeling's (in press) projections. Since it predicts that more than half of all the fossil carbon will be released in less than 100 years, it still represents a strong perturbation of the carbon cycle.

For the low-use scenario let us assume that the growth rate will be only 2% per year until 2025, to be followed by a symmetrical decrease as renewable energy sources become more available and the use of fossil fuel is discouraged (lower curve in Fig. 6). The total fossil carbon released in this scenario is about one quarter that of the high scenario and about 1.5 times the carbon content of the preindustrial atmosphere.

But how will the carbon cycle respond to the flux of fossil carbon? If we make the assumption that it will continue to respond as in the recent past by taking up 50% in the oceans and/or the land biota, then we obtain the curves in Figure 7 for the growth of CO_2 in the atmosphere. This assumption may at first sight seem unduly pessimistic since the carbon cycle might well respond more strongly to prevent such large excursions above the "normal" atmosphere concentration of CO_2. Yet man's conversion of the forests to agricultural use as well as the decreasing capacity of the surface waters of the oceans to take up CO_2 could outweigh this tendency.

Without a more certain knowledge of how the other fluxes of the carbon cycle achieve the present net removal rate, perhaps the best that can be done is again to take two extreme cases and estimate the variations possible in the largest fluxes and the consequent effects on future levels of atmospheric CO_2. In the first case, population pressure forces the conversion of all arable land to food production in 100 years, thus con-

verting a substantial fraction of the standing crop of wood and a smaller fraction of the humus to CO_2. This could amount to as much as 200 Gt of extra carbon to the atmosphere, and over the next century the net flux would average 2 Gt/yr. In the second case, with decreasing growth of population, more efficient agriculture, increasing use of biomass as fuel (with planned regrowth), and less wasteful burning, a flux averaging 2 Gt/yr in the opposite direction might be achieved—especially if photosynthetic productivity increases with greater atmospheric CO_2 level.

On the basis of these two cases we assign a range of ±2 Gt/yr to plausible changes in the net flux between the land and the atmosphere averaged over the next 100 years. The resulting effect on the cumulative anthropogenic release of CO_2 and on future levels of CO_2 in the atmosphere (Fig. 7) is appreciable but fairly small compared to the possible variation from the fossil carbon flux.

The oceans are thought by many to be the sink that accounts for the largest part of the 50% equivalent of the anthropogenic flux that leaves the atmosphere. Because the capacity of the surface waters to take up CO_2 is so small, such an uptake would seem to require the supply of considerable additional capacity from the deep oceans. The net consumption by photosynthesis seems also to depend on the supply of certain limiting nutrients (e.g. phosphorous and silicon) from the deep oceans (Broecker 1974). Present knowledge of ocean circulation is insufficient to predict with any certainty how the oceans will behave as a sink for CO_2. We assume in Figure 7 that the uncertainty in net flux to the oceans will be equivalent to ±10% of the fossil carbon flux.

Climate change

A long history of natural climate change is revealed by the geologic record. In a recent review (ICAS 1974), fluctuations of the average surface temperature over the past one million years were represented approximately as the sum of sinusoidal variations with different periodicities (Table 2). The two longest periods may be caused by similar periodicities in the fluctuations of the shape of the Earth's orbit (Mitchell 1972). Attempts to correlate climate variation with other natural causes, such as sunspot cycles and related variations in the solar constant (Schneider and Mass 1975) seem less well founded.

We are presently in a very warm period, about 10,000 years since the end of the last glacial. In the last 100 years the global mean temperature rose about 0.6°K to 1940 and fell about 0.3°K in the following three decades (Mitchell 1961, 1972). The important point from the previous history of climate change is that natural fluctuations which occur rapidly enough (i.e. over a few generations) to produce easily recognized impacts on the affairs of man are likely to be of small amplitude. Over the next 100 years the mean global temperature may be expected to change no more than 0.5° to 1.0°K from natural causes. Broecker's (1975) analysis suggests that after 1980 there will be an onset of natural warming (if warming does not occur sooner because of increased atmospheric CO_2).

Any activity of man that can alter significantly the radiation balance of the Earth can affect the climate. In addition to the effect of increased

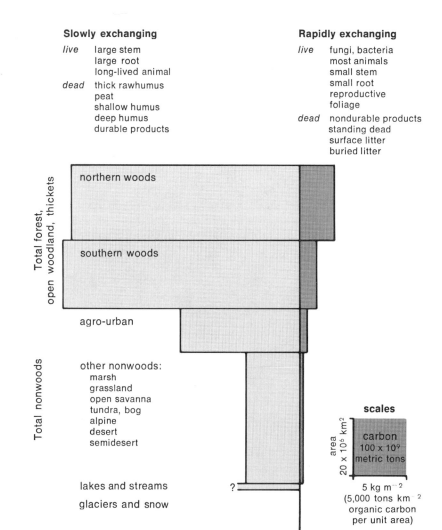

Figure 5. The quantities of carbon in the various terrestrial ecosystems are shown as concentration (vertical direction) vs. area (horizontal direction). The vertical line divides rapidly exchanging from slowly exchanging organic forms.

CO_2, there is the growing direct production of heat that results from man's use of energy, but this is presently an insignificant 0.01% of the solar flux and important only in areas of high energy utilization. There is the local effect of paved areas that alter the reflectivity (albedo) of the Earth's surface. A possibly important anthropogenic effect is that of airborne particulates which, it has often been suggested, might produce a cooling by backscattering solar radiation. But actually the magnitude of this effect, even whether it is one of cooling or warming, depends on many factors (Charlson and Pilat 1969). These include the altitude, size, concentration, and reflectivity or refractive index of the particles. Because of this the impact of anthropogenic particulates is quite uncertain. Those produced by the consumption of fossil fuels are relatively large, remain at low altitude, and are airborne but a short time. As a result, their effect on cli-

mate may remain a local one long after the effects of CO_2 become quite apparent.

The impact on climate to be expected from a particular stimulus has been deduced from models developed over the last several decades, from simple one-dimensional radiation-balance models of the Earth's atmosphere to quite complicated so-called general circulation models that include the circulation of the atmosphere in three dimensions. Such models indicate an increase in temperature with increased CO_2 and suggest that the temperature response is approximately logarithmic, i.e. each doubling in the concentration of CO_2 produces about the same increase in the average temperature of the troposphere. The more sophisticated models predict, moreover, that the temperature change is much greater at high latitudes. The amount of the average increase in temperature per doubling

Table 1. Terrestrial organic carbon pools and their fluxes[a]

Major global pool[b]	Turnover rate	Carbon inventory[c] (Gt)	Photosynthesis NPP[d]	Photosynthesis GPP/NPP	Photosynthesis GPP[d]	Respiration R_g[d]	Respiration R_h[e]	Fire[f] F[e]
Northern woods (N of lat. 30° N)	slow[c]	540	8			(3)	(7)	(1)
	rapid[c]	70	10			(6)	(9)	(1)
		610	18	1.5?	(27)	9	16	2
Nonwoods (world)	slow	540	8			(3)	(8)	(0)
	rapid	40	10			(15)	(8)	(2)
		580	18	2.0?	(36)	18	16	2
Southern woods (S of lat. 30° N)	slow	520	9			(8)	(7)	(2)
	rapid	50	11			(22)	(10)	(1)
		570	20	2.5?	(50)	30	17	3
Subtotals	slow	1,600	25			14	22	3
	rapid	160	31			43	27	4
		1,760	56		(113)	57	49	7

[a] Excluding incipient fossil fuel, buried humus, etc. (carbon with decay rate < 0.001 yr^{-1}). Estimates and geographic breakdown are slightly modified from Olson 1970; SCEP 1970, pp. 160–66; Reiners et al. 1973; Bazilevich 1974; and Lieth and Whittaker 1975.

[b] Woods (i.e. forest, open woodland, and woody swamp) is partitioned because it is such a large pool and because the seasonal contrast of photosynthesis and respiration on lands north of 30° N latitude is more striking than in south temperate, subtropical, and tropical zones.

[c] Rapidly exchanging pools (turnover averaging a few years) are estimated significantly higher than SCEP (1970, Table 2.A.2); slowly exchanging pools (many turnover times, averaging several decades) are only slightly higher than SCEP.

[d] The net primary production (NPP) estimate of SCEP is provisionally retained, but this and especially the allocation to pools and the indirect allowance for green plant respiration (R_g) and hence gross primary production (GPP) or photosynthesis are very tentative. Many literature estimates of photosynthesis are low because they deliberately or inadvertently omit the rapidly exchanging pools, overlook many processes of rapid turnover, or use old or conservative estimates of production.

[e] Heterotrophic respiration (R_h) of animals and decomposers (bacteria and fungi) recycles to atmospheric CO_2 that part of NPP which is not first burned (F), exported, or stored (e.g. in pools with decay rate < 0.001 yr^{-1} or mean residence time $> 1,000$ years). Such storage and export to oceans are assumed $< 1 \times 10^9$ tons/yr.

[f] The carbon fluxes from fires, which are very uncertain, were estimated assuming that in each woods pool a period averaging about 200 years elapsed between consuming fires in a given location.

of CO_2 (ΔT) given by the various models (Schneider 1975) are in the range 0.7 to 9.6°C. Schneider (1975) critically reviewed these and concluded that "a state-of-the-art, order-of-magnitude estimate" is in the range 1.5 to 3°K. He notes, however, that this estimate could prove to be high or low by severalfold as a result of "climate feedback mechanisms not properly accounted for in the state-of-the-art models."

Some mechanisms not adequately accounted for in present models include (1) *decreased snow and ice coverage*—a positive (amplifying) feedback since the resulting decrease in reflected radiation will produce further warming; (2) *changes in cloud cover and in the temperature of cloud tops*—thought to be the most important feedback mechanism not adequately treated; (3) *ocean coupling*—which cannot be fully accomplished without a better model of

ocean circulation, which itself is driven by the latitudinal temperature gradient; and (4) *land coupling*—which should include the effects of local changes in albedo and water balance as well as the direct effects of biota change on the levels of CO_2.

In addition to their differing magnitudes, these feedbacks have widely differing response times, from perhaps a few months for significant changes in average cloud cover to perhaps hundreds of years for significant changes in the extent of the polar ice caps. Since the sum of these feedback effects as a function of time is presently unknown, we will allow for their contribution to the relatively rapid climatic response by increasing Schneider's estimate of the range of the average ΔT to 1° to 5° per doubling of the CO_2 content of the atmosphere. This range of uncertainty in ΔT is combined with the uncertainties associated with the growth in

atmospheric CO_2 to produce the range of projections in Figure 7 of the increase in the average temperature over the next 100 years.

Temperature changes near the upper limits of these projections—for a high fossil-fuel use scenario and a ΔT near 5°C per doubling of atmospheric CO_2—would in less than 100 years exceed the amplitude of the glacial-interglacial cycle normally traversed in tens of thousands of years. A climatic change of such unprecedented rapidity can hardly be viewed as anything less than catastrophic. The changes projected near the lower extremes of Figure 7 are possibly acceptable, though even here the increases in global average temperature from anthropogenic causes may become larger than natural variations in the fairly near future.

Thus mankind confronts an increasingly familiar kind of dilemma: while the impending consequences of his activities are not so clearly unacceptable that emergency measures are called for, the probability that they might be so is great enough to demand strong action. Greatly increased efforts should be made to foresee more clearly the effects of anthropogenic CO_2.

Impact of climate change

Let us consider briefly some of the ways in which a general climate warming could affect man and his environment. These will obviously depend primarily upon the nature, the magnitude, and the rate of change of regional climates. Since at present such changes are even less predictable than the average warming, none of the effects can be estimated quantitatively and many may not even be foreseeable. We list here some that seem plausible.

At first thought a warmer climate might seem to be generally beneficial, with longer growing seasons that produce more food and milder winters that help save fuel. However, any rapid change in a regional climate is more likely to produce detrimental effects that far outweigh the beneficial ones. This follows simply because crops and other species have become tuned by experience and selection to match existing conditions. Most rapid changes will produce dislocations that reduce biological fitness and/or productivity before human or natural readjustments can become effective.

Dislocations from warming can take many forms. Rates of respiration and decay may increase faster than photosynthetic production. Microbial and insect pests from adjacent regions or endemic pests previously held in check may be favored. Since the average rate of evaporation should increase, a surface drying may occur in all climate zones but the wettest.

Year-to-year fluctuations in local weather is a fact of life in agriculture. Longer-term fluctuations have produced considerable economic dislocation and human suffering in developed countries and massive starvation in less developed regions. These larger, evidently natural, fluctuations are likely to produce ever more serious effects as the growing world population presses agriculture

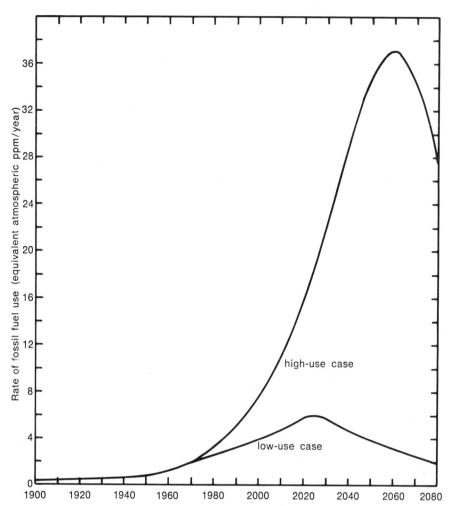

Figure 6. The two scenarios shown for the use of fossil fuels over the next 100 years are suggested as plausible limiting cases. With the high-use case, assuming an annual growth rate of 4.3% reduced in proportion to the fraction of the ultimate fossil fuel supply that has been used, more than half of all fossil fuel carbon will be released in less than a century. With the low-use case, assuming a 2% growth rate till 2025 followed by a symmetrical decrease, only about a fourth as much fossil carbon will be released as in the high-use case.

to its limits of productivity. Clearly, then, still larger unfavorable changes in some regional climates are likely to produce dire consequences indeed, and the more so if they appear suddenly and are not anticipated.

Perhaps the most often cited effect of a general warming is the rise in sea level that would accompany the melting of glacial ice. A complete melting could raise the level of the oceans over 50 m, and quite obviously even a partial melting could have profound effects on the shorelands of the world and all their associated

Table 2. Natural climate fluctuations represented as the sum of cyclic changes

Characteristic period (yrs)	Fluctuation in average temperature (°K)	Last temperature maximum (yrs ago)	Maximum rate of temperature change (°K/yr)
100,000	8.0	10,000	±0.00025
20,000	3.0	8,000	±0.00045
2,500	2.0	1,750	±0.0025
~200	0.5	75	±0.0075
~100	0.5	35	±0.015

SOURCE: ICAS 1974

values. The melting process, however, is quite complex and not yet understood well enough to predict the rate at which this could occur. Warmer air alone could produce only a slow melting (G. Marland, pers. comm.), but warm polar waters could induce a flow of ice from the continental shelves into the sea, possibly raising the sea level 5 m in 300 years (Hughes, cited by Gribbin 1976).

In contrast to a slowly rising sea level, inland lake levels and water supplies may be lowered more rapidly where climate is drier. For example, navigation, sewage, and water problems already experienced as a result of the low level of the Great Lakes in 1964 could become more costly in the future.

Diminished ocean circulation and weakened upwelling and nutrient replenishment around some fertile fisheries might add to the stress they already experience from overfishing. Other marine and freshwater food chains could become even more vulnerable because of impacts on nursery and feeding areas of the changing shores, rivers, and lakes.

These and other effects will have sociological and political repercussions that are difficult or impossible to predict and evaluate fully. Because costs and benefits of climatic change will fall very unevenly on different regions, groups perceiving themselves as unthreatened or even as beneficiaries of the change will question the validity or cost of steps that might be recognized elsewhere as desirable for correcting the situation. Groups quickly perceiving their own losses, and fearing more drastic changes yet to come, could look for scapegoats long before the several links from energy to atmospheric CO_2 to climate to ecological and social impact can be regarded as settled from a scientific standpoint. Many of these impacts will affect billions of people to a significant degree, and almost any summation of the possible social cost from excess CO_2 becomes far too great to languish in the realm of academic debate. The possibility that many may find some benefits in the total change in no way dismisses the imperative to estimate and balance the costs and benefits. Finally, there is also the serious ethical question of the commitment that we and our children may be making for scores of future generations to changes in the world environment that seem impossible to reverse for many centuries to come.

What is to be done?

As Revelle and Suess (1957) have said, "Man may learn much about the processes that determine weather and climate by observing carefully the course of the CO_2 experiment." But, of course, this in no way diminishes the present urgency. Man is not conducting a controlled experiment; he is using cheap, abundant fuel and will continue to do so until the impending consequences clearly become more costly than alternative sources of energy. Hence the most urgent thing to be done is to improve our ability to predict these consequences. The problem of how to do this seems to resolve itself into three parts.

1. *We must learn more about the carbon cycle.* In particular, we must learn to predict the fluxes of CO_2 between the atmosphere and the oceans and between the atmosphere and the land. This will require a greatly increased effort to monitor, study, and model the processes of the ocean and the land that control these fluxes.

For the ocean, the most important process is the circulation and mixing of surface water with the deep water. A greatly increased ocean monitoring effort seems to be called for, one that would provide information more comparable in detail to that of the atmosphere. It should include the continued study of the distribution of tracers such as ^{14}C and ^3H and the application of whatever other techniques that can give information on deep circulation and also on $CaCO_3$ reaction rates. In all ocean monitoring activities, the collection of data and the development of circulation models should be closely coupled.

For the land, the processes that most strongly influence the net flux of CO_2 to or from the atmosphere, aside from the burning of fossil fuel, are those of photosynthesis, respiration, decay, and the burning of biomass. Here a monitoring and modeling effort at least as extensive as that for the oceans may be needed. Of greatest importance is the effect of increased atmospheric CO_2 on photosynthetic production rates, the potential effects from increased land use for agriculture, and the turnover rates of live and dead organic matter. The overall objective should be to predict accurately the change in the net flux of CO_2 to the land for a given scenario of fossil fuel use and land use.

2. *We must predict more accurately the climatic effects of increasing atmospheric CO_2.* Quite clearly this is the major uncertainty in the assessment of the environmental impact of CO_2. Perhaps the only means that will provide the needed predictive power is a reliable model, one that can reproduce the important features of each regional climate when the driving variables of world climate are properly chosen.

Climate models have developed rapidly over the last two decades, and the most elaborate have reached the limits of capacity and speed of the largest and fastest computers available. Advances in computer technology now in sight may permit reductions in running time of perhaps a factor of ten, and Mitchell predicts (pers. comm.) that much more detailed global climate models will then be developed. It is his hope that insights thus gained will lead to simplified "smart" models that can make the needed prediction more elegantly and accurately. Many feel that improved models must include a better representation of the basic physical processes of climate, e.g. fluid dynamics, cloud formation, and cloud interactions. Such may come from an improved basic understanding, or perhaps these processes can be represented adequately by better empirical representations.

To support these development efforts and also to validate properly a reliable climate model, a more extensive observational network—including satellite monitoring as well as surface-based measurement—will be needed that provides more detailed and accurate worldwide meteorological data. The need for climate prediction is so great and the difficulty of achieving it so formidable that a much larger climate study effort should be undertaken; a broad program that includes all aspects of climatology. It should certainly include numerical modeling, physical modeling, basic studies of fluid dynamics, studies of cloud formation and interactions, systematic surface observations of climatic variables throughout the world, atmospheric monitoring by satellites, and statistical analysis of observational data. The staff for such a program should include, in addition to meteorologists and climatologists, representatives from the physical and engineering sciences. What seems most needed (S. Manabe, pers. comm.) for rapid progress in climate research are new ideas and insights that might replace the "brute force" methods of numerical computation with elegant simplifications—ideas and insights that are most likely to come from the bringing together of workers with diverse backgrounds.

3. *We must anticipate the consequences of climate change.* Ecological, economic, social, and political impacts must be foreseen quickly and accurately enough to guide remedial actions. The sooner specific climate changes and their effects can be foreseen, the more likely it is that effective actions can be taken. Assessments and supporting research of such a highly interdisciplinary nature and scope will probably require more effective information handling and modeling plus methods for validating models and scenarios that will enhance credibility.

In short, much of the problem is to develop and then test and use the *means* for credible assessment of impacts. Biophysical ecology (Gates and Schmerl 1975) and physiology provide valid principles for estimating how organisms can adapt. Models for species populations should be modified for crops and natural communities so that shifts in life zones and rates of production can be developed for test regions and eventually larger areas of continents and oceans. Beyond demonstrating that models are consistent with data from which they are formulated and tuned, testing their consistency with independent experience is needed for suggesting the kinds of perturbations to be expected from a known or hypothetical climate change.

If the present predictions (Fig. 7) are correct, not long after the year 2000 the warming effect of increased atmospheric CO_2 could become conspicuous above the "noise level" from other causes of climate fluctuation. However, the momentum of societal fuel-use patterns may make it difficult then to adjust from fossil energy

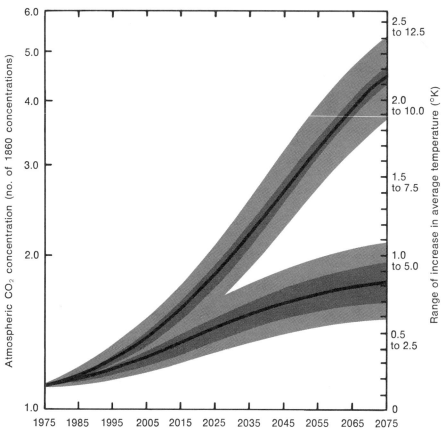

Figure 7. The projected growth in atmospheric CO_2 and the possible increase in the average surface temperature of the Earth are shown for the next 100 years. The solid curves represent the limiting scenarios in Figure 6 with 50% of the fossil-fuel flux balanced by ocean and/or land uptake of CO_2. The outer bands represent the effect of 40% to 60% uptake. The inner bands represent the effect of a ±2 Gt/yr variation in the net flux to the land. The range of the increase in average temperature corresponds to 1 to 5° K per doubling of the CO_2 concentration.

to nonfossil energy quickly enough to avoid eventual severe consequences. Hence the time available for action may be quite limited.

Quite clearly we must improve our predictions of the consequences of increased atmospheric CO_2. The largest uncertainty is the specific effect of a given increase on the regional climates of the world. As a consequence, a first priority should be given to the study of possible climate changes. A better understanding of the carbon cycle is also needed to project better the rate of increase of atmospheric CO_2. Finally, we must learn to project the impact of the climatic changes on man, his environment and his society.

As the potential consequences of various scenarios of energy development become more clearly foreseeable, these must be included in the cost-benefit analyses. Depending upon the severity of our energy problems, it may be expected that

nonfossil fuel options, such as fusion and breeder reactors for central station generation of electric power and wind, solar, and geothermal energy for dispersed sources, will be increasingly brought into use. One nonfossil fuel option being more actively considered is the use of cultivated and waste biomass as fuel, perhaps with conversion to methanol, ethanol, methane, and/or hydrogen (Pollard 1976). This could become an attractive "solar energy" conversion method that recycles atmospheric CO_2.

While actions that reduce the impact of climate change such as the establishment of food reserves and the diversification of agriculture could be effective even if taken unilaterally by individual nations, other actions that reduce the rate of production of anthropogenic CO_2 depend strongly on multinational cooperation to be effective. If the severe economic and political repercussions that are likely on a world scale are to be avoided, a technological commitment must be made in the next few years and a world strategy arrived at with enlightenment and wisdom. Though humanity may not be able to foresee the consequences of "the great experiment" clearly enough to control them, we cannot afford not to try!

References

Allen, L. H., Jr., S. E. Jensen, and E. R. Lemon. 1971. Plant response to carbon dioxide enrichment under field conditions: A simulation. *Science* 173:256.

Averitt, P. 1975. World estimated total reserves of coal. *USGS Bull.* 1412.

Bazilevich, N. I. 1974. Energy flow and biogeochemical regularities of the main world ecosystems. In *Proc. 1st Intl. Cong. of Ecol.*, p. 182. Wageningen, Netherlands: Pudoc.

Bolin, B. 1970. The carbon cycle. *Sci. Am.*, September, p. 125.

Bolin, B. 1974. Modeling the climate and its variations. *Ambio* 3:180.

Botkin, D. B., J. F. Jonak, and J. R. Wallis. 1973. Estimating the effects of carbon fertilization on forest composition by ecosystem simulation. In *Carbon in the Biosphere*, ed. G. M. Woodwell and E. V. Pecan, p. 328. USAEC Conf. 720510.

Broecker, W. S. 1974. *Chemical Oceanography*, p. 25. Harcourt Brace Jovanovich.

Broecker, W. S. 1975. Climate change: Are we on the brink of a pronounced global warming? *Science* 189:460.

Broecker, W. S., and Y-H. Li. 1970. Interchange of water between the major oceans. *J. of Geophys. Res.* 75:3545.

Callendar, G. S. 1958. On the amount of carbon dioxide in the atmosphere. *Tellus* 10:243.

Charlson, R. J., and M. J. Pilat. 1969. Climate: The influence of aerosols. *J. of Appl. Meteorol.* 8:1001.

Duncan, D. C., and V. E. Swanson. 1965. Organic-rich shale of the United States and world land areas. *USGS Circ.* 523.

Gates, D., and R. Schmerl. 1975. *Biophysical Ecology*. Springer Verlag.

Gribbin, J. 1976. Antarctica leads the ice ages. *New Sci.* 69:695.

Holland, H. D. 1972. The geologic history of sea water—An attempt to solve the problem. *Geochem. et Cosmochem. Acta* 36:637.

Hubbert, M. K. 1974. Estimate of the ultimate world production of petroleum liquids. Senate Com. on Int. and Ins. Affairs, Committee Print Ser. No. 93-40 (92-75).

ICAS. 1974. Report of the ad hoc panel on the present interglacial. NSF: Federal Council for Science and Technology Interdepartmental Committee for Atmosphere Science, ICAS 18b-FY75.

Keeling, C. D. 1973a. Industrial production of carbon dioxide from fossil fuels and limestone. *Tellus* 25:174.

Keeling, C. D. 1973b. The carbon dioxide cycle: Reservoir models to depict the exchange of atmospheric carbon dioxide with the oceans and land plants. In *Chemistry of the Lower Atmosphere*, ed. S. I. Rasool, p. 251. Plenum.

Keeling, C. D. In press. Impact of industrial gases on climate. In *Energy and Climate: Outer Limits to Growth.* Natl. Acad. of Sci.: Geophys. Res. Bd., Geophys. Study Com.

Keeling, C. D., R. B. Bacastow, A. E. Bainbridge, C. A. Ekdahl, Jr., P. R. Guenther, L. S. Waterman, and J. F. S. Chin. 1976. Atmospheric carbon dioxide variations at Mauna Loa Observatory, Hawaii. *Tellus* 28:538.

Lieth, H., and R. H. Whittaker. 1975. Primary productivity of the biosphere. *Ecol. St.* 14. Springer Verlag.

Machta, L., K. Hanson, and C. D. Keeling. 1976. Atmospheric carbon dioxide and some interpretation. Office of Naval Res. Conf. on the Fate of the Fossil Fuel Carbonates, Honolulu, Hawaii, January 19–23.

Mitchell, J. M., Jr. 1961. Recent secular changes of global temperature. *Ann. of the NY Acad. of Sci.* 95:235.

Mitchell, J. M., Jr. 1972. The natural breakdown of the present interglacial and its possible intervention by human activities. *Quat. Res.* 2:436.

Mitchell, J. M., Jr. 1975. A reassessment of atmospheric pollution as a cause of long-term changes of global temperature. In *The Changing Global Environment*, ed. S. F. Singer, p. 149. Boston: D. Reidel.

Oeschger, H., U. Siegenthaler, U. Schotterer, and A. Gugelmann. 1975. A box diffusion model to study the carbon dioxide exchange in nature. *Tellus* 27:168.

Olson, J. S. 1970. Carbon cycles and temperate woodlands. In *Analysis of Temperate Forest Ecosystems*, ed. D. E. Reichle. Springer Verlag.

Pollard, W. G. 1976. The long-range prospects for solar-derived fuels. *Am. Sci.* 64:509.

Reiners, W. A., L. H. Allen, Jr., R. Bacastow, D. H. Ehalt, C. S. Ekdahl, Jr., G. Likens, D. H. Livingston, J. S. Olson, and G. M. Woodwell. 1973. A summary of the world carbon cycle and recommendations for critical research. In *Carbon and the Biosphere*, ed. G. M. Woodwell and E. V. Pecan, p. 368. USAEC Conf. 720510.

Revelle, R., and H. E. Suess. 1957. Carbon dioxide exchange between the atmosphere and ocean, and the question of an increase in atmospheric CO_2 during the past decades. *Tellus* 9:18.

Rotty, R. M. 1976. Global carbon dioxide production from fossil fuels and cement, A.D. 1950–A.D. 2000. Office of Naval Res. Conf. on the Fate of Fossil Fuel Carbonates, Honolulu, Hawaii, January 19–23.

SCEP. 1970. Man's impact on the global environment: Assessment and recommendations for action. In *Study of Critical Environment Problems.* Cambridge: M.I.T. Press.

Schneider, S. H. 1975. On the carbon dioxide–climate confusion. *J. of Atm. Sci.* 32:2060.

Schneider, S. H., and C. Mass. 1975. Volcanic dust, sunspots, and temperature trends. *Science* 190:741.

Sillén, L. G. 1963. How has sea water got its present composition? *Svensk Kem. Tidskrift* 75:161.

Strickland, J. D. H. 1965. Production of organic matter in the primary stages of the marine food chain. In *Chemical Oceanography*, ed. J. P. Riley and G. Skirrow, p. 478. Academic Press.

Wangersky, P. J. 1972. The cycle of organic carbon in sea water. *Chimia* 26:559.

Whittaker, R. H. 1975. *Communities and Ecosystems*, 2nd ed. Macmillan.

"Oh, for Pete's sake, let's just get some ozone and send it back up there!"

PART 4 *Changing the Water*

G. Evelyn Hutchinson

Eutrophication

Marginalia

The scientific background of a contemporary practical problem

During the past few years the word *eutrophication* has continually cropped up in the daily press and in popular articles on the environment in magazines. It has usually been supposed to describe the process by which a beautiful lake or river became converted into a body of water covered with decomposing blue-green algae. That the word should mean the process of becoming well fed (*1*) merely illustrates once again the horrid dichotomy between starvation and excess that is apt to characterize much of contemporary society. It has therefore seemed timely to examine what the word may mean and how the ideas that it is used to express have developed during the sixty-six years since the German adjectival form *eutrophe* was first introduced into scientific discourse.

What do we mean by eutrophication? The word is due to C. A. Weber (*2*), who, in 1907, described the nutrient conditions determining the flora of German peat bogs as "nährstoffreichere (eutrophe) dan mittelreiche (mesotrophe) und zuletzt nährstoffearme (oligotrophe)," a sequence that expressed the changes as a bog built up and was raised above the surrounding terrain, so being more and more easily leached of its nutrients.

At first the bog vegetation was what Weber called *eutraphent*, requiring high concentrations of essential elements in the soil solution; at the end of the process an *oligotraphent* flora

G. Evelyn Hutchinson, Sterling Professor of Zoology Emeritus, Yale University, is well known to American Scientist *readers for his occasional articles on a wide diversity of topics. Address: Osborn Memorial Laboratory, Yale University, New Haven, CT 06520.*

covered the bog, composed of species tolerating very low nutrient concentrations. In Weber's case the process that took place in going from a less elevated, less leached to a more elevated, more leached bog would now be called oligotrophication, if anyone had occasion to use the word.

In 1919 Einar Naumann (*3*), who knew of Weber's work, employed the terms in a discussion of the phytoplankton of Swedish lakes. He originally used them to describe water types, so that springs, streams, lakes, or bogs could contain oligotrophic, mesotrophic, or eutrophic water, according to the concentration of phosphorus, combined nitrogen, and calcium present. Originally no estimates, however, could be given as to what these concentrations were. Naumann throughout his works gives the impression that he liked to draw limnological conclusions, expressible in schematic terms, merely from looking at lakes. Weber's original words *oligotrophic* and *eutrophic* were, in fact, now redefined for limnologists in terms of the appearance of a lake in summer. A lake containing eutrophic water is "*sehr stark getrübt oder sogar vollständig verfärbt*" as the result of a very dense population of algae. The unproductive oligotrophic lake did not support such a population and in consequence remained much less turbid and either blue, if it were unstained by peat, or brown in peaty montane areas. Even today, transparency and color are the simplest indicators of the nutrient condition of a lake, though of course they must be used with great discretion if no other information is available.

Much of the work that was being done by other limnologists in the first third of the twentieth century contributed to the development and ul-

timate confusion of Naumann's typological scheme.

The great difference between the lakes of the lands bordering the Baltic and those of more mountainous districts, notably the Swiss Alps, had been known for some time. Wesenberg-Lund (*4*), perhaps the greatest of limnological naturalists, in the general part of his work on the biology of the fresh-water plankton of Denmark, had discussed the biological characteristics of the Baltic lakes, of which the phytoplankton consisted largely of diatoms and blue-green algae.

At the same time the English algologists W. and G. S. West (*5*) were studying the lakes of northern and western Britain, finding a diversified desmid flora in the phytoplankton. Teiling (*6*) observed comparable assemblages in the mountains of Scandinavia and spoke of a Caledonian type of phytoplankton in contrast to the Baltic type. It was reasonable to regard these two types of plankton as regional expressions of the eutrophy of the waters of the Baltic Lakes and the oligotrophy of those of the mountainous parts of Europe.

Lake types

A few years after the publication of Wesenberg-Lund's monumental study, August Thienemann (*7*) began an investigation of the lakes of the Eifel district in Germany. These lakes occupy explosion craters, locally termed *Maare*, which were formed late in the Pleistocene, and vary greatly in depth. In considering Thienemann's work it must be borne in mind that any lake in a temperate region that is deep enough—in most cases over 10 m deep—develops what is called thermal stratification. The deep water remains cold and is moved only by feeble currents set up by oscillations, or seiches, while the upper five to ten meters becomes heated, but remains turbulent. The upper region is known as the *epilimnion;* since it is illuminated it supports a crop of algae. The lower region is known as the *hypolimnion;* it is usually too dark for much algal growth. The two parts of the lake are separated by a thermocline, best described as the surface of maximum rate of change of temperature with respect to depth. The intermediate region containing the thermocline is often called the *metalimnion.*

Thienemann found that in the bottom of the deeper lakes of the Eifel the hypolimnetic water retained most of its oxygen and the bottom mud was inhabited by a variety of animals intolerant of low oxygen concentrations, while in the shallower lakes the hypolimnion tended to run out of oxygen, and the inhabitants of the bottom, though often very numerous, were limited to relatively few species that could tolerate low oxygen concentrations and that indeed often contained haemoglobin. The two types of lake in the Eifel in fact differed in their bottom faunas in the same kind of way

as the lakes of the Baltic area were found to differ from those of more montane regions.

Thienemann came to regard the deeper lakes as oligotrophic and the shallower as eutrophic. Ideally, no doubt, an oligotrophic lake was a deep lake containing oligotrophic water with little plankton, much oxygen on the bottom during summer stratification, deep-water fish such as char and whitefish, and a diversified bottom fauna not limited to species tolerant of very low oxygen concentrations. A eutrophic lake, similarly ideally, was a shallow lake containing eutrophic water, rich in plankton, losing much of its hypolimnetic oxygen in summer, without char and whitefish, and with a bottom fauna composed of vast numbers of a few species of animals that can tolerate very low oxygen concentrations. To limnologists working in the 1930s, these lake types were what the words oligotrophy and eutrophy seemed to imply.

A bewildering array of terms ending in -trophy began to appear to characterize what Naumann (8) called asymmetrical, as opposed to harmonic, conditions. The best known, but in some ways the least fortunate, of these terms is *dystrophy,* applied to waters

and lakes much colored by humic material; in the present article these additional complications will not be considered.

Unfortunately it is obvious that if a moderately nutritive or mesotrophic water is present in a very deep lake, dying phytoplankton, feces, and other organic detritus produced in the illuminated waters of the epilimnion, in the course of a season, will not be sufficient to deplete the deeper part of the hypolimnion of its oxygen, though this may happen if the lake is quite shallow (Fig. 1). The concepts of oligotrophy and eutrophy, applied to lakes rather than to waters, thus may lose their trophic implications (9), though the two types of lake remain. By merely filling up with sediment an oligotrophic lake seems to become eutrophic in a certain sense; its deep-water chemistry and benthic fauna change, and a record of these changes is preserved in the sediments laid down at the bottom of the lake. In order to resolve this difficulty, Lundbeck (10) considered a very deep lake containing mesotrophic or eutrophic water, with much oxygen in the hypolimnion and an "oligotrophic" benthic fauna, to be secondarily or morphometrically oligotrophic. The problem, however, is by

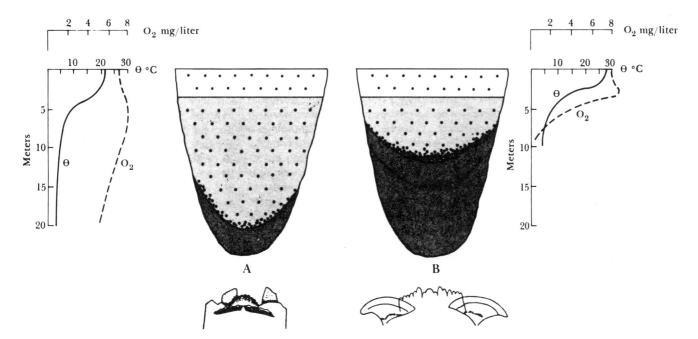

Figure 1. Some classical limnological theory, illustrated by diagrammatic representation of two lakes filled with water supplying a moderate amount of nutrients. In the deep lake, on the left, the sedimenting dead plankton and detritus fall through a large volume of water. The uptake of oxygen is from a large hypolimnetic volume, and the bottom water remains fairly well supplied with the gas. In the lake on the right, which may be regarded either (broken-line bottom of sediments) as a shallow contemporary or (solid-line bottom) a later stage of the deep lake, the hypolimnion is too small to supply appreciable oxygen, and falling organic particles produce deoxygenated water at the bottom. The hypolimnetic uptake per unit area may be the same in the two cases. The curves give typical late-summer temperatures (θ) and oxygen (O_2) concentrations. The figures of fossils show the front of the head of a typical "oligotrophic" midge (*left*) and a eutrophic one (*right*) (from Deevey 1942, ref. *15*).

no means laid at rest by this terminological device, for it is obviously important to know if the primary nutritive type of eutrophy is really independent of the secondary morphometric type.

Strøm (11) pointed out that in a shallow, more mature basin the ratio of water volume to sediment surface is less than in a deep basin, and thus the potential amount of nutrient material that can diffuse from mud to water is greater in shallow than in deep lakes. Pearsall (12), moreover, in the course of his classical studies on the basins of the English Lake District, divided the lakes into what he called unevolved and evolved. The former (Wastwater, Ennerdale, and to some extent Coniston) would ordinarily be regarded as oligotrophic, while the evolved type would be now regarded as mesotrophic (Windermere) or quite eutrophic (Estwaite).

Though some of the difference is due to morphometry, Pearsall thought that the main effects, which are very striking when either the phytoplankton or the flowering plants of the littoral zones are studied, were due primarily to the erosion in the drainage basin depositing lesser or greater amounts of silt, which is likely to be a source of potassium and phosphorus, if not other plant nutrients. Though Theinemann's two lake types clearly could be produced by morphometry alone with a common water type in each, it is evident that this will not necessarily happen. A small shallow lake may come to contain water richer in nutrient elements than does a large deep lake.

Subsequent work has developed in two initially quite different directions, though recently these diverse approaches have begun to converge. The first direction is historical and has involved trying to learn from lake sediments what changes have actually occurred in lakes over long periods of time. The second approach has been more geochemical and physiological, studying not merely the concentrations of nutrient materials in waters but also the ways in which different kinds of planktonic algae utilize them.

Historical studies

On the historical side, it was early shown by Lundqvist (13) in Sweden that lake sediments often exhibit a stratigraphic sequence in which very inorganic silt or clay is overlain by more organic sediments. It was, moreover, noted by Gams (14) in a section of this sort in Austria that the older, less organic sediments might contain fossils of midge larvae belonging to genera characteristic of oxygen-rich water, while later in more organic sediments the fossilized head capsules belonged to genera tolerating and mainly found in water containing very little oxygen.

Deevey (15), in a classic extension of this work, also found that the midge larvae, fossilized in the early sediments of what are now mesotrophic or eutrophic lakes in Connecticut, belonged to genera characteristic of oxygen-rich water. These were later replaced by midge larvae—usually the deep-red "blood worms"— of the genus *Chironomus*. It is fortunate that a rough but generally adequate determination can be made from nature of the antennary insertion on the head capsule which is easily fossilized. This is an interesting case of an apparently recondite taxonomic detail having wide biological significance. It should be noted that in one of the Connecticut localities studied by Deevey the oligotrophic indicator occurred in relatively inorganic sediments of a lake which was but 11 meters deep, though at the present time any lake of that depth in the same general area would have eutrophic indicator species. It would seem, therefore, that oligotrophy really did precede eutrophy and that in at least some basins it was real oligotrophy, in which little organic matter was contributed to the sediments of even quite shallow lakes, and not merely a very great capacity of the large hypolimnion to supply oxygen.

Subsequent work tended to show that, in many small lakes of temperate, formerly glaciated areas, a succession from more inorganic sediment, containing oligotrophic-indicator fossils, to a more organic sediment, containing eutrophic-indicator fossils, is usual. Moreover, once organic sedimentation has become established, the sediment laid down did not vary much in composition. This suggested that after an oligotrophic initial phase, a sort of steady state or *trophic equilibrium* was established. Material eroded or generated in the basin and washed into the lake produced a fairly constant nutrient supply characteristic of the landscape. This permitted the development of organisms, and a fraction of the organic matter so produced, along with inorganic material eroded in the basin, formed the characteristic organic sediment laid down, at least in eastern North America, century after century until the coming of European colonists in the seventeenth century or later. The organic content thus expressed a *trophic potential*, which might be more oligotrophic in some areas, more eutrophic in others. If the lake remained undisturbed, it appeared to remain in a steady-state condition for a very long time—in Linsley Pond for at least seven millennia.

The initial oligotrophic phase might be explained in various ways. Low postglacial temperatures may be involved. A deceptively attractive hypothesis was initially put forward by Hutchinson and Wollack (16), who postulated a process of internal differentiation in the lake, by which decomposition of a small amount of organic matter in the earliest sediments reduced the pH and promoted the solution of phosphate. This increased production of phosphate stimulated the growth of more phytoplankton so that more organic detritus fell to the bottom and, decaying, liberated still more phosphorus. The whole process continued autocatakinetically until the full nutrient potential was realized.

Simpler, less formally elegant alternatives, however, exist and are widely believed to be more probable. Livingstone (17), in particular, has emphasized that the greater erosion of glacial till in immediate postglacial times would rapidly bury any organic matter that was formed and prevent regeneration of the nutrients it might contain. The various vegetational changes which doubtless affected lakes by the amount and kind of leaf fall into the lake from the trees surrounding it may also be reflected in the distribution of organic matter in the sediment profile. At the time when the basic work on this matter was done, radiocarbon dating had not been invented; it is anyhow not directly applicable to the least organic deposits at the bottom of a lake profile. The rates of accumulation of inorganic sediment are uncertain, and the quantitative aspects of the whole process need modern reinvestigation.

Whatever the exact nature of the change from quite inorganic to relatively organic sediments in the lakes of glaciated temperate regions, such lakes have also yielded some quite definite information on the initial effects of man on the lacustrine ecosystem.

In the Linsley Pond profile, it will be noted that right at the top the organic nitrogen falls off sharply. This is undoubtedly due to the fact that most soils contain much less organic matter than do eutrophic lake sediments. As soon as clearing and plowing of the basin began soil would be eroded and carried into the basin, diluting the more organic material being deposited there. A study of the diatoms indicates that striking changes took place while this top layer of more mineral sediment was deposited. *Asterionella* makes its appearance, as it does in other profiles showing human disturbance. The reason for this is unknown, but the changes that are observed certainly indicate that the lake was beginning to respond to the results of European colonization.

Although we have been discussing the change from an oligotrophic to a eutrophic condition, it is unlikely that the supposedly eutrophic sediments, laid down before appreciable human disturbance, often indicate a degree of eutrophy that today would be mentioned in the newspapers. What contemporary popular writing means by eutrophy is usually something much more extreme than the conditions in Linsley Pond before soil began to erode into the lake. Eutrophy in a New England lake before 1650 probably meant good fishing; now it is apt to mean a thick scum of blue-green algae.

Some mineralized lakes in closed basins, notably in Central Africa (*18*), have a naturally dense blue-green algal flora dominated by *Spirulina*, *Arthrospira*, or *Nodularia*. The histories of a few lakes where records of water blooms go back some centuries—such as Llangors in Brechnocshire, Wales, to 1188 (*19*)—have as yet not been studied by modern methods, though such an investigation would be of great interest. There are a few cases known of lakes suddenly becoming eutrophic in Naumann's sense, producing a dense water bloom when none had been observed in earlier years. Pennak (*20*) records a remark-

able case in Colorado in a lake that appeared to have been uninfluenced by man. On the whole, such occurrences are exceptional. Eutrophication may be a natural process in temperate North America, as apologists for its unnecessary acceleration often insist, but the kind of eutrophication which seems most natural is the increase in organic production up to a steady state that may persist for a very long time.

When we leave the glaciated humid temperate regions and start investigating lakes in which the erosion of a large amount of unconsolidated till did not contribute to the early sedimentary history, we admittedly find a less clear-cut pattern. There seems to be no inevitable change from oligotrophy to eutrophy, apparently because trophic equilibrium was established in a very short time.

The best example is provided by Lago di Monterosi (*21*), north of Rome on the Via Cassia. This little lake occupies a shallow *Maar*, or explosion crater, which was probably formed about 26,000 years ago, shortly before the last glacial maximum (Würm III) in the Alps, at a time when the Roman Campagna had a cold dry climate, probably not

unlike parts of Central Asia today. For twenty thousand years, during a time when the climate ameliorated and forest was established around the basin, the lake was shallow and quite unproductive; a mineral sediment was deposited slowly on its floor. Such change in productivity as occurred seems to have been for a time in the direction of increasing oligotrophy, presumably as the most easily leached nutrients in the volcanic ash of the basin were removed, used, and then lost to the lake sediments.

Suddenly an event occurred which raised the water level, produced a bloom of blue-green algae, probably largely *Aphanizomenon*, and led to a rapid sedimentation of both organic and inorganic matter. The changes that took place are exactly what one would have expected from the work of Bormann and Likens (*22*) on the effects of deforestation at Hubbard Brook—namely a greater flow of water into the lake as transpiration in the catchment area is reduced, a greater deposition of sediment, a greater concentration of alkaline earths and alkalies in the incoming water, showing as an increase in the exchangeable calcium, magnesium, and, a little later, potassium in the sediment, and a great increase in organic

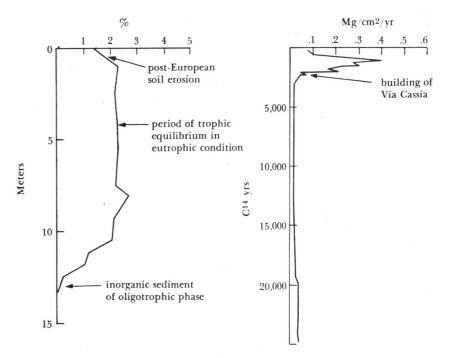

Figure 2. (*Left*) Nitrogen content of a core in the sediment of Linsley Pond, Conn. Subsequent C[14] studies showed the 10 m level here to be about 8,000 years old (from Hutchinson and Wollack 1940, ref. *16*). (*Right*) Rate of deposition of organic nitrogen in the sediment of Lago di Monterosi plotted against age in C[14] years. Note the eutrophication beginning with the building of the Via Cassia (from Cowgill and Hutchinson 1970, ref. *21*).

productivity as measured by nitrogen deposition. Since phosphorus is quite plentiful as apatite in the sediments, nitrogen and conceivably carbon are likely to have been limiting. Increase in combined nitrogen and alkaline earth bicarbonate probably caused the sudden increase in the productivity of the lake.

This all happened sometime between about 390 and 150 B.C. The most probable date for the building of the Via Cassia by the Romans was 171 B.C. We believe that the dramatic eutrophication that is recorded in the sediments is due to cutting of woodland on one side of the lake along the line of the road. Here, in the most striking possible way, the process was not natural, but completely artificial. It seems first to have involved an algal bloom, then a more balanced ratio of increasing inorganic and organic sedimentation, and after about A.D. 650 a slight reversal of the process, though the lake is still somewhat eutrophic.

Frey (23) had already shown that much earlier clearing in the Neolithic could have had an important effect on certain Austrian lakes. These cases are very instructive in showing that quite striking and at the time probably undesirable changes can occur as the result merely of clearing. Some of the alleged natural eutrophication of lakes observed all over North America is probably partly due to this.

Another dramatic example has just come to light through the research of Waldemar Ohle (24), of Plön, reported in an article on the history of the Grosser Plöner See in Holstein, to limnologists a very celebrated lake. Study of the sediments indicates here a slow increase in organic sedimentation from postglacial times to the Middle Ages. Suddenly, in or about A.D. 1256, there was a dramatic tenfold increase in the rates of both inorganic and organic sedimentation, not unlike what happened in Lago di Monterosi, which has persisted into modern times. The chief cause of this sudden change in medieval times seems to have been the artificial flooding of very shallow land when German colonists began to enter this previously Slavonic territory. Once again, the really extreme *Rasante Eutrophierung*, or Galloping Eutrophication, is a man-made phenomenon.

Nutrition of phytoplankton

The problems of the nutrition and production of phytoplankton began to be studied effectively during the decade after Naumann's original conception of oligotrophic and eutrophic waters. Three advances in method made this possible. Firstly, the development of various colorimetric techniques for analyzing nutrients in really minute quantities permitted some idea of the true quantitative difference between the nutrient potential of various lake waters.

There were, of course, difficulties in interpretation right from the beginning. In temperate latitudes in the spring the growth of large algal populations usually start as the light increases in water containing a relatively high concentration of nutrients. By relatively high is meant a few milligrams per cubic meter, or parts per billion, of phosphate phosphorus and rather over ten times this amount of nitrogen as nitrate or ammonia. As the season developed, however, it became increasingly difficult to detect changes in the nutrient content, particularly in the case of phosphorus, that were related to the conspicuous changes in algal populations. As Pearsall (25) pointed out, the bluegreen algae, which are the most conspicuous and often the most tiresome indicators of what is usually thought of as eutrophication, often seemed to appear when the phosphate content of the water had become vanishingly small and the combined nitrogen lower than at other seasons.

The second major technical advance in the study of eutrophication was the introduction of methods of measuring phytoplankton productivity. The first experiments in lakes were made by Winberg (26) in the USSR; rather later Riley (27) independently started an investigation in Connecticut. The technique used is to fill bottles, one clear and the other black, with water collected at any level, and then suspend the bottles from a raft at the level from which their contents were derived. After a suitable time, preferably twenty-four hours, the bottles are retrieved and the oxygen concentrations determined. Ideally the difference between the bottles should indicate the photosynthetic production of oxygen. If a number of depths from the surface downward are studied, a graph of photosynthetic production

per unit volume plotted against depth can be constructed and, by measuring the area that it encloses, the integral, giving photosynthetic production per unit area per day, can be easily calculated.

Riley's bottles were exposed for about a week, a period that is certainly much too long. Though his absolute values are probably somewhat in error, the pattern of variation that he observed is probably valid. He found that at the surface the gross productivity as measured by the difference in oxygen content of clear and black bottles was positively correlated with chlorophyll, as a measure of the producing organisms, and with temperature but not with illumination. When, however, the production of oxygen is integrated over all depths and expressed per unit area, the significant correlations are only with light and temperature.

These seemingly curious results are probably due to bright light being inhibitory at the surface, though on dull days the light flux was probably insufficient to saturate the photosynthetic machinery. When the whole water column is considered, a light flux that is inhibitory at the surface is optimal at some greater depth, and for almost any possible light flux and a given phytoplankton density, the greater the flux the greater the photosynthesis over the entire range of depths. The absence of an effect of chlorophyll on the productivity per unit area is doubtless partly due to shading and partly to production of organic coloring matter when the plankton is dense and in part moribund. Riley could find no direct effect of nutrients on oxygen production in his bottles, though the chlorophyll in the open water of the lake was positively related to the phosphate present during the previous week.

Though a very large amount of work has subsequently been done on the primary productivity of lakes, mainly using the fixation of C^{14} rather than O_2 production as a measure, no one seems to have attempted quite so elaborate a study of the environment of productivity. This is probably because it has been widely believed that, given a certain chlorophyll content and light flux, under specified physical conditions the productivity is determined. This is by no means certain. Further work using more modern techniques than were available to Riley, but adopting his overall system of observation, might be unexpectedly rewarding.

From the standpoint of the present review, the most important contribution of precise measurements of productivity lies in the demonstration, as in Rodhe's excellent work (28), that extreme oligotrophic lakes are actually very unproductive—in Swedish Lapland as low as 20 mg m^{-2} day^{-1} carbon fixed—while eutrophic lakes are very productive—as high as 2,000 mg m^{-2} day^{-1} carbon fixed in central Sweden at the height of summer.

A third and very simple though extremely important way of proceeding was to introduce nutrient substances in an appropriate form into bottles suspended in the lake and then estimate the production of plankton as compared with a control bottle. In this way it was easily possible to show that, though the addition of either nitrate or phosphate caused some increase in the phytoplankton of Linsley Pond (29), the two together were needed to produce a really dramatic increment. Methods of this sort, often using photosynthesis studied by C^{14} fixation as a measure of algal activity, have become commonplace in the study of eutrophication. They have been particularly successful in the hands of C. R. Goldman (30), whose work is discussed below. In order to understand their meaning we should have some idea of what is meant by a limiting factor.

Limiting factors

The materials dissolved in lake water which constitute the food of the phytoplankton have three ultimate geochemical sources. Some—notably carbon as carbon dioxide, nitrogen as N$_2$, or as small quantities of combined nitrogen in rain or as larger amounts biologically fixed in rivers—come from the atmosphere, though only for nitrogen is this the main reservoir.

Others—notably sulfur, the halogens, probably boron, and some CO$_2$—have been derived from the ocean and carried either in gaseous form or as aerosols in the atmosphere, from which they are washed by rain. The distinction between these elements

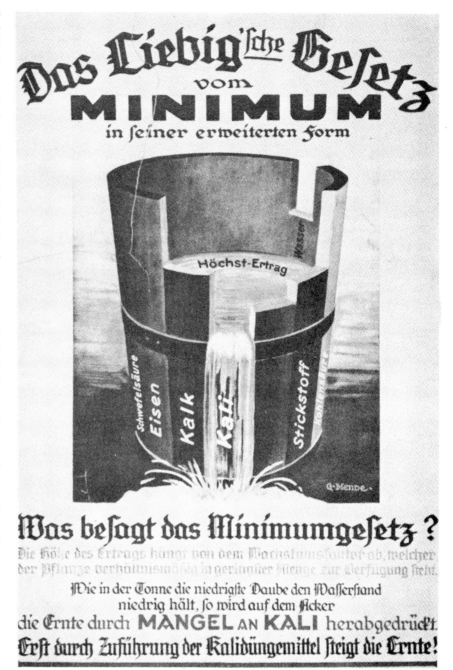

Figure 3. Liebig's Law of the Minimum used as an advertisement of potassium as a fertilizer (after Browne).

and those of the first group is rather artificial, though useful. It is, however, certain that in contrast to nitrogen, the reservoirs of water, sulfur, boron, the halogens, and carbon, apart from the functionally important fraction held in plants and soils on land, are oceanic. At the present time, of course, much sulfur is added from the lithosphere by industry.

The third group, consisting of phosphorus and all the biological cations and trace metals, comes from the lithosphere.

It is generally considered reasonable to start any investigation by assuming that what is usually called Liebig's Law of the Minimum holds at least approximately (31). The law, seemingly not fully formulated by its author, states that the total crop of any organism will be determined by the abundance of the substance that, in relation to the needs of the organism, is least abundant in the environment. An early, though post-Leibigian, didactic analogy, in which the level of the water in an open barrel composed of staves of different lengths is determined by the shortest stave (Fig. 3), was popular on the European continent during the first third of this century and may have some value today when ecological education has to be undertaken in spite of great intellectual and moral resistance. Liebig was, of course, aware that his implicit law did not necessarily apply to multispecific associations. One of his statements will appeal particularly to the limnologist (32):

33. When a given field contains a certain amount of *all* kinds of mineral plant-food in *equal* proportion, and in suitable form, it will become unproductive of a single species of plant, so soon as, in consequence of continuous cropping, any single kind of plant-food, e.g. soluble silica, is so far exhausted that its quantity is insufficient for a new crop.

34. A second plant which does not require this ingredient (silica e.g.), will yield one or more crops on the same soil, because the other, for it necessary, ingredients, although in changed proportions (i.e. not in equal quantities) are yet present in quantity sufficient for its perfect development.

After the second, a third kind of plant will flourish in the same field, if the remaining soil-ingredients be enough for its wants: and if, during the growth of these kinds of plants, a new supply of the wanting plant-food (soluble silica) has been made available by weathering, then, the other conditions being as before, the first plant will again flourish.

If the word *lake* were substituted for *field*, and *water* for *soil* in this passage, we should have, through the curious chance that the author used soluble silica for his example, an excellent description of what happens in a lake with a large spring diatom bloom.

It is easy to see that if we limit ourselves to the elements obtained primarily from the lithosphere, phosphorus is most likely to be limiting. In Table 1 the ratio of the mean concentration in the accessible crust to that of phosphorus is entered in column (1) for the partially or wholly non-atmophil elements of atomic number less than 43 (33). In column (2) the same is done for the composition of the average nonmarine, in practice terrestrial, plant. In column

(3) the ratio (1)/(2) can be used as a measure of the limiting nature of the element. If the value is greater than (1) the element will only be limiting relative to phosphorus when peculiar conditions determining solubility or availability exist.

It will be seen in Table 1 that if the partially atmophil elements of largely marine origin are excluded, the only ratio below unity is for selenium, which may be in part atmophil and anyhow is quite inadequately known. The reason for phosphorus occupying this position is fairly obvious. It is a critical element in constructing both the metabolic and the informational machinery of organisms, but as an element of odd atomic number it is much rarer than its neighbors, silicon and sulfur, while in the earth it may well have been partly lost, as iron phosphide, to the metallic core and is not made easily available at the surface as the atmophil elements are. It must be remembered that however important phosphorus may be, variations in the conditions of solubility or availability may at times make very abundant elements such as silicon or iron almost unobtainable.

Among the elements which have their main functional reservoir in the sea, none seem to be of great importance

Table 1. Liebigian table of elements derived primarily from lithosphere, or in parentheses from ocean, giving ratio of element to phosphorus in mean accessible crust (1), in mean terrestrial vegetation (2), and the ratio of (1) to (2) in (3). Where an entry in (3) is greater than unity the element is, on geochemical grounds only, less liable to be limiting than phosphorus.

	(1) In lithosphere per gram P.	(2) In terrestrial plants per gram P.	(3) Ratio (1)/(2)
Li	0.019	0.000043	440
Be	0.0027	<0.000043	>60
(B	0.0095	0.022	0.43)
F	0.595	<0.017	>35
Na	22.5	0.52	43
Mg	22.2	1.39	16
Al	78.4	0.22	360
Si	268.1	0.65	410
P	1.0	1.0	1.0 by definition
(S	0.25	1.48	0.17)
(Cl	0.12	0.87	0.14)
K	19.9	6.1	3.3
Ca	39.5	7.8	5.1
Sc	0.021	0.000003	7,000
Ti	5.43	0.00043	12,600
V	0.13	0.0007	186
Cr	0.095	0.0001	950
Mn	0.90	0.27	3.3
Fe	53.6	0.061	880
Co	0.024	0.00022	110
Ni	0.071	0.0013	55
Cu	0.052	0.0061	8.5
Zn	0.067	0.0435	1.5
Ga	0.014	0.000026	540
Ge	0.0014	<0.0002	>7
As	0.0017	0.000087	20
Se	0.00005	0.00009	0.56
(Br	0.0023	0.0065	0.35)
Rb	0.086	0.0087	10
Sr	0.357	0.0113	32
Y	0.031	0.00026	119
Zr	0.157	0.00028	560
Nb	0.019	0.00013	150
Mo	0.0014	0.00039	3.6

in determining phytoplankton productivity in fresh water.

The purely atmophil elements include the hydrogen and oxygen of water, which only become limiting, though very seriously so, when the water dries up, and in addition to them nitrogen and carbon. Both of the two last named elements are obviously of great importance in determining the fertility of water, but they raise special and different questions.

The enormous supply of nitrogen, around 700 gr per cm² of the earth's surface, is unavailable to almost or quite all eukaryote organisms, except technologically to Homo sapiens and, by symbiotic methods, to legumes and a number of other plants. Among the prokaryotes the capacity to split the N_2 molecule and form $-NH_2$ is very widespread. It is best known in a few eubacteria, such as Clostridium spp, Azotobacter, and the symbiotic Rhizobium, in the purple bacteria, and in many filamentous and a few coccoid blue-green algae, organisms which being prokaryote are much more like bacteria than other algae. The process is always a costly one, occurring at the expense of the products of photosynthesis and so often associated with periods of illumination.

Molybdenum is an essential element in the enzymatic machinery, and since it is a quite uncommon element and is easily associated with ferric hydroxide in wet oxidizing environments, it may become limiting in lakes, as Goldman (30) has shown. There is some evidence that as phosphorus increases in a lake, so can the fixation of nitrogen. This is to be expected and emphasizes that in natural conditions the limitation by phosphorus may be more fundamental over a long period of time. It is important to remember that, although most natural fixation of nitrogen is biological, at the present time artificial fixation is of the same order of magnitude as natural. No other element as yet is involved in any artificial cycle which approaches in magnitude a widespread natural one (34).

It was early apparent, particularly from the work of Pearsall (25) that the supplies of phosphorus and combined nitrogen, which usually increase during the dark winter months, are depleted in the spring as the phytoplankton increases. Deevey (35)

found that the crop of phytoplankton present in summer was highly correlated with the nitrate present in the same localities under the ice in winter. Edmondson (36) found a comparable correlation with phosphorus in Lake Washington, in Seattle.

During the early summer when the nutrients are largely depleted, a population of some species of Dinobryon often appears; this colonial flagellated yellow alga seems to be oligotraphent. Then as the water warms up, in truly eutrophic lakes, the population of bloom-forming blue-green algae begins to develop. This may happen without any previous increase in nutrients, so we have, as has already been noted, the paradoxical situation that the algae which seem to be the indicators of eutrophy appear at the time when there is the least available plant food in the water.

Pearsall tried to avoid the paradox by supposing that accumulation of organic matter in the water was involved. No clear evidence exists that the common bloom-forming species actually require organic compounds in their nutrition. Fogg (37) suggests that the apparent correlation with high organic content is due to the fact that waters containing such material tend to have a high oxygen demand. This would lead to a reduction in oxygen content in stratified water. He believes that blooms are apt to begin in such water, well below the surface, and that the algae involved are somewhat microaerophile. One is tempted to wonder whether this is reminiscent of their Precambrian origin. It has also been believed that bacterial decomposition of organic matter may provide additional CO_2 for algal photosynthesis (38).

Part of the parodox of the eutrophic algae developing best when the nutrient concentrations are lowest is resolved by the experiments that started in the late 1940s when radiophosphorus became available (39). These showed that the rate at which events occurred in the warm, illuminated surface waters of a lake in summer was much faster than had been expected. Rigler (40) found that the mean life of inorganic phosphate added to lake water was only a few minutes. Such inorganic phosphate as can be detected represents a steady state between uptake and various kinds of loss.

The matter has most recently been studied by Lean (41), whose paper appeared while this article was being written, and who finds that a phytoplankton population can keep the soluble inorganic phosphorus as low as 0.09 γ per liter; a low molecular-weight phosphorus compound is continually being excreted and then condensed into a colloidal component with the loss of a good deal of the phosphorus, which returns to ionic form. These discoveries suggest that the algae that appear in such quantities in very eutrophic lakes in summer are extremely efficient at taking phosphorus up from very dilute solutions and can probably outcompete other species for the minute but continuous supply regenerated at the mud-water interface of the littoral zone. This, of course, is likely to be particularly true where the more successful competitor also fixes molecular nitrogen.

Little is yet known about the kinetics of uptake in the species that are ecologically and economically most important, but the very interesting work of Fuhs, Demmerle, Canelli, and Chen (42) shows that in two species of the diatom Thalassosira the maximum rate of uptake of phosphorus per unit area of the cell is three and a half times as great in the large T. fluviatilis as in the smaller T. pseudonana, while the very much smaller bacteria studied has an even greater capacity to take up phosphorus. Differences of this sort are obviously of great importance in regulating the qualitative nature of the biota in a nutrient-limited environment.

Thomas (43), studying the nutrient contents in summer of a large number of lakes in Switzerland, came to the conclusion that the oligotrophic lakes were limited by phosphorus and often contained an excess of nitrogen; in eutrophic lakes the elements were both reduced to low levels together. Enrichment experiments often show like effects. Powers, Schults, Malueg, Brice, and Schuldt (44) found that the water of the very oligotrophic Waldo Lake in Oregon responded to phosphorus but not to nitrate added singly, though there sometimes was a further response if both nutrients were added simultaneously. The more eutrophic Triangle Lake responded a little to nitrate, phosphate, and bicarbonate, but the only striking effects were due to mixtures of phosphate and nitrate. In a third very eutrophic lake the phytoplankton did not respond significantly to any addition.

Though these results tend to agree with those of Thomas, it is clear that when more complicated enrichment experiments are done, more complicated situations are likely to be uncovered. Goldman (30) has found that the first limitation in many oligotrophic lakes is due to deficiency in various trace elements. In certain lakes in the South Island of New Zealand he found that on various occasions Mo, Co, Mn, Zn, Fe, $NaNO_3$, S as SO_4, and P as PO_4 might be limiting; the elements most frequently involved were cobalt and molybdenum. Very occasionally even low magnesium concentrations may determine the phytoplankton production, at least in short-term experiments.

In considering nitrogen there may be something of a paradox to resolve, though the data are so far inadequate to establish this. Since a major source of combined nitrogen is biological fixation, which is an expensive process requiring much energy, one would expect nitrogen to become less important as a limiting factor as the blue-green algal population became greater in increasingly eutrophic lakes, because they often fix nitrogen at the same time as capturing solar energy. Actually, such evidence as is available suggest that the opposite occurs, as has just been noted, nitrogen not being limiting in many oligotrophic lakes, while both elements are required in biologically equivalent amounts to raise production in eutrophic lakes.

The lack of limitation in very oligotrophic lakes is reasonable. Rain always contains at least a little nitrate and ammonia. These materials are probably derived largely from organic sources, in dust or at the sea surface, though some nitrate may come from NO or NO_2 in the atmosphere. Rain falling in a barren mountain valley may thus contain a little combined nitrogen before it has had a chance to acquire any detectable phosphate. The lake into which the rain runs as a stream is therefore more likely to be deficient in phosphorus or other contributions from the lithosphere than in combined nitrogen. The equivalence of the two main nutrient elements at the eutrophic end of the spectrum of productivity may indicate a neat regulation of the nitrogen to the greatly increased phosphorus supply.

The problem of carbon as a limiting factor has provided much argument recently. There is a priori no reason why in certain cases waters should not contain more phosphorus and nitrogen than are biologically equivalent to the photosynthetically fixable carbon. If we accept for blue-green algae a ratio of C:N:P of about 50:8:0.1 and inquire how much nitrogen and phosphorus are biologically equivalent to the carbon of the CO_2 in equilibrium with the air, we find that for 0.62 mg CO_2 per liter or 170 γ C per liter, we should need 32 γ N and 0.1 γ P. Such quantities would suggest that sometimes carbon and sometimes nitrogen, but more rarely phosphorus, would be limiting.

However, if all the carbon were used, more can diffuse into the water from the air (45), more nitrogen can be fixed in the free water by organisms such as *Anabaena*, but new phosphorus can only come from the mud-water interface of the littoral zone. There is evidence that it is in fact obtained in this way, but in any stratified lake the sources of supply would seem less than for the two substances derived from the atmosphere across the whole surface of the lake. It has been suggested that when photosynthesis is very active the bacterial decomposition of organic matter advected into the lake is an important source of carbon dioxide. The observations on which this idea was based are certainly scientifically respectable (38), but they were made in rather soft waters, and in spite of the glee with which they were received by the manufacturers of phosphate detergents, it is very unlikely that they are of significance in the harder waters in which serious algal blooms usually develop.

Various plants, including at least some of the significant bloom-forming algae, can use the HCO_3 ion as a source of carbon in photosynthesis, as most angiosperms of medium-hard waters also are able to do. All the evidence in fact seems to indicate that a low CO_2 content, especially in the presence of bicarbonate, limits the species characteristically producing the extreme blooms of hypereutrophic water far less than other algae. Shapiro (46) even found that the addition of CO_2 favored green algae in competition with Myxophyceae.

All the available evidence suggests that when a water develops a massive bloom as the result of pollution, it is due to the increased supply of combined nitrogen and phosphorus, and since most filamentous blue-green algae fix their own nitrogen, phosphorus is likely to be more important than nitrogen. Trace elements may play a part; they are apparently more likely to affect the qualitative aspects of the algal population than its total quantity, as Patrick (47) and her associates are finding in their remarkable work on the algae settling on glass slides under seminatural conditions that permit the experimental manipulation of the nutrient supply.

As Edmondson (36) has triumphantly shown in the case of Lake Washington, the best way to avoid the pollution of a lake is to put the excess nutrients elsewhere. Where this is impossible, shifting the population from blue-green algae to diatoms may well prove possible by the addition of manganese, which Patrick and her coworkers show favors diatoms at the expense of blue-green algae. A comparable situation, though one probably less easily controlled, is found when a blue-green bloom appears in still eutrophic water which has been depleted of silica by diatoms; Schelske and Stoermer (48) find this is an important aspect of the present biology of Lake Michigan.

Two less chemical aspects of the production of undesirable eutrophy may be mentioned in conclusion. One of the reasons why blue-green algae are so conspicuous is that they are apt to float at the surfaces of lakes, because of the presence of gas-filled vacuoles, commonly called pseudovacuoles. In a remarkable series of studies by Fogg and by Walsby and their associates (49), it has been shown that the production of the gas-filled vacuole is dependent on photosynthesis, but that the rising turgor which results from the accumulation of the products of photosynthesis can collapse the vacuole. The mechanism normally leads to the poising of the alga in an optimal environment in which growth occurs fast enough for the products of photosynthesis to be used and the osmotic pressure of the cell to be kept

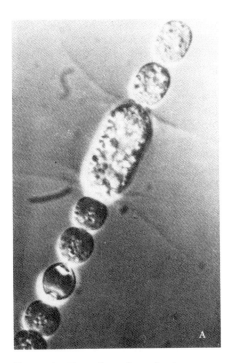

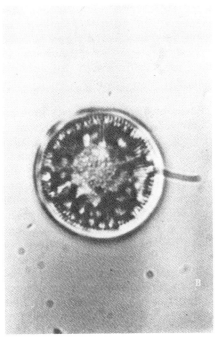

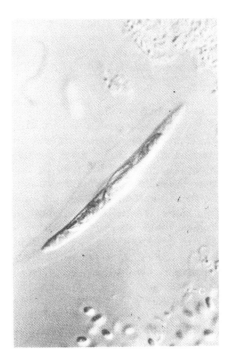

Figure 4. Algae from Porter's three categories. *A*, the blue-green *Anabaena*, in general not eaten. *B*, the diatom *Cyclotella*, eaten and usually digested. *C*, the gelatinous green alga *Elaktothrix*, eaten but passed through *Crustacea* intact (all from photographs by K. G. Porter, ref. *48*, x ca. 2,500).

suitably low. Under some conditions the mechanism appears to break down, producing the moribund scum at the end of a bloom.

A second well-known biological feature of the blue-green algae is their inedibility, due no doubt to their shape, the gelatinous texture of the coccoid species, and possibly to some chemical properties. Porter (*50*) has recently studied the edibility of phytoplanktonic organisms in a mesotrophic lake in Connecticut, in which a considerable variety of species may co-occur. By studying the effect of removing or enriching the crustacean zooplankton in large submerged plastic bags, it is possible to divide the algae into three groups (Fig. 4) reacting differently to predation. The blue-green algae, along with desmids and dinoflagellates, are in general unaffected. The larger diatoms, cryptomonads, and other small flagellates are eaten and digested; their populations are suppressed. The larger, gelatinous green algae, though eaten, pass unharmed through the crustacean gut and actually increase in proportion in the waters enriched in crustacea. This selective effect of the zooplankton is probably of considerable significance. The evolution of inedibility which plays a large part in the current development of evolutionary ecology may also be of great interest to the aquatic engineer.

References and notes

1. The etymology is discussed by O. R. Holmberg and E. Naumann. Die Trophie Begriff in sprachlicher Hinsicht. *Botan. Notiser.* 1927:211–14. The two most important contemporary collections of studies on eutrophication are *Eutrophication: Causes, Consequences, Correctives*, National Academy of Sciences, Washington, D.C., vii, 661 pp., 1969; *Nutrients and Eutrophication*, Amer. Soc. Limnol. Oceanogr. Special Symposia I (ed. G. E. Likens), 328 pp., 1972.

2. C. A. Weber. 1907. Aufbau und Vegetation der Moore Norddeutschlands. *Beibl. Bot. Jahrb.* 90:19–34. (Suppl. to *Bot. Jahrb.* 40)

3. E. Naumann. 1919. Några synpunkte angående planktons ökôlogi. *Med. sarskilâ hänsyn till fytôplankton. Svensk. bot. Tidskr.* 13:129–58. See also: Ziel und Hauptprobleme de regionale Limnologie. *Botan. Notiser*, 1927:81–103.

4. C. Wesenberg-Lund. 1908. *Plankton investigations in the Danish Lakes.* General Part: The Baltic fresh water plankton, its origin and variation. Copenhagen. 389 pp.

5. W. and G. S. West. 1909. The British fresh water plankton, with special reference to the desmid plankton and the distribution of British desmids. *Proc. Roy. Soc. B*81:163–206.

6. E. Teiling. 1916. En Kaledonisk fytoplankton formation. *Svensk Bot. Tidskr.* 10:506–19.

7. A. Thienemann. 1918. Untersuchungen über die Beziehungen zwischen dem Sauerst offgehalt der Wassers und der Zusammensetzung der Fauna in norddeutchen Seen. *Arch. Hydrobiol.* 12:1–65.

8. E. Naumann. 1932. Grundzüge der regionalen Limnologie. *Binnengewässer* 11: 1–176.

9. A. Thienemann. 1921. Seetypen, *Naturwiss.* 9:343–46. See also: Die Binnengewässer Mitteleuropas. *Binnengewässer* 1: 1–255, 1925.

10. J. Lundbeck. 1934. Über den primar oligotrophen Seetypus und den Wollingster See als dessen mitteleuropaischen Vertreter. *Arch. Hydrobiol.* 27:221–50.

11. K. M. Strøm. 1930. Limnological observations on Norwegian Lakes. *Arch. Hydrobiol.* 21:97–124.

12. W. H. Pearsall. 1921. The development of vegetation in the English Lakes, considered in relation to the general evolution in glacial lakes and rock basins. *Proc. Roy. Soc.* 92B:259–84.

13. G. Lundqvist. 1927. Bodenablagerungen und Entwicklungstypen der Seen. *Binnengewässer* 2, 124 pp.

14. H. Gams. 1927. Die Geschichte der Lunzer Seen, Moore und Wälder. *Int. Rev. ges. Hydrobiol. u. Hydrogr.* 18:304–87.

15. E. S. Deevey. 1942. Studies on Connecticut lake sediments III, The biostratonomy of Linsley Pond. *Amer. J. Sci.* 240: 233–64, 313–24.

16. G. E. Hutchinson and A. Wollack. 1940. Studies on Connecticut lake sediments. II. Chemical analyses of a core from Linsley Pond, North Branford, Conn. *Amer. J. Sci.* 238:493–517.

17. D. A. Livingstone. 1957. On the sigmoid growth phase in the history of Linsley Pond. *Amer. J. Sci.* 255:304–73.

18. L. C. Beadle. 1932. Scientific results of the Cambridge expedition to the East African lakes, 1930–1. The waters of some East African lakes in relation to their fauna and flora. *J. Linn. Soc. (Zool.)* 38: 157–211. P. M. Jenkin. 1936. Reports on the Percy Sladen expedition to some Rift Valley lakes in Kenya in 1929. VII. Summary of the ecological results with special reference to the alkaline lakes.

Am. Mag. Nat. Hist. ser. 10, 18:161–81. P. M. Jenkin. 1957. The filter feeding and food of flamingoes (Phoenicopteri). *Phil. Trans. Roy. Soc.* 240B:401–93. G. E. Hutchinson, G. E. Pickford, and J. F. M. Schuurmann. 1932. A contribution to the hydrobiology of pans and other inland waters in South Africa. *Arch. Hydrobiol.* 24:1–154.

19. B. M. Griffiths. 1939. Early references to water blooms in British lakes. *Proc. Linn. Soc. Lond.* 151:12–19. See also: Giraldus Cambrensis, *Itinerarium Kambriae*, Ed., J. F. Dimock, London, 1868, Lib. 1, Cap. II.

20. R. W. Pennak. 1949. An unusual algal nuisance in a Colorado mountain lake. *Ecology* 30:245–47.

21. U. M. Cowgill and G. E. Hutchinson. 1970. Chemistry and mineralogy of the sediments and their source materials. *In* Ianula: An account of the history and development of the Lago di Monterosi, Latium, Italy. *Trans. Amer. Phil. Soc.* n.s. 60 (pt 4):37–101. C. E. Goulden. The fossil flora and fauna (other than siliceous fossils, pollen and chironomid head capsules), *id.* 102–11. G. E. Hutchinson and U. M. Cowgill. The history of the lake: A synthesis, *id.* 163–70.

22. F. H. Bormann, G. E. Likens, D. W. Fisher, and R. S. Pierce. 1969. Nutrient loss accelerated by clear-cutting of a forest ecosystem. *Science* 159:882–84. G. E. Likens, F. H. Bormann, and N. M. Johnson. 1969. Nitrification: Importance to nutrient losses from a cutover forested ecosystem. *Science* 163:1205–06.

23. D. G. Frey. 1955. Langsee: A history of meromixis. *Mem. Ist. ital. Idrobiol. de Marchi.* Suppl. 8:141–61.

24. W. Ohle. 1972. Die Sedimente der Grossen Plöner Sees als Dokumente der Zivilisation. *Jahrbuch f. Heimatkunde (Plön)* 2:7–27.

25. W. H. Pearsall. 1932. Phytoplankton in the English lakes. II. The composition of the phytoplankton in relation to dissolved substances. *J. Ecol.* 30:241–62.

26. G. Winberg. 1934. Versuch zur Studium der Photosynthese und der Atmung des Seewassers Mitteilung I. (Russian, German summary.) *Trudy Limnolog. stants. Kossino* 18:5–24.

27. G. A. Riley. 1940. Limnological studies in Connecticut. III. The plankton of Linsley Pond. *Ecol. Monogr.* 10:279–306.

28. W. Rodhe. 1969. Crystallization of eutrophication concepts in Northern Europe. In *Eutrophication: Causes, Consequences, Correctives* (see n. 1): 50–64.

29. G. E. Hutchinson. 1941. Limnological studies in Connecticut. IV. Mechanisms of intermediary metabolism in stratified lakes. *Ecol. Monogr.* 11:21–60.

30. C. R. Goldman. 1972. The role of minor nutrients in limiting the productivity of aquatic ecosystems. In *Nutrients and Eutrophication* (see n. 1): pp. 21–34.

31. The history of the Law of the Minimum has been discussed by C. A. Browne (Liebig and the Law of the Minimum, in *Liebig and after Liebig*, ed., F. R. Moulton, *Publ. Amer. Assoc. Adv. Sci.* 16:71–82, 1942), who showed how the concept developed gradually. The earliest writer whom he quotes as indicating that a soil "may often be unproductive because it is deficient in one single element that is necessary as a food for plants" is C. Sprengel in his *Die Bodenkunde oder die Lehre vom Boden*, Leipzig, 1837. Sprengel had earlier published a paper (Von den Substanzen der Ackerkrume und des Untergrundes v.s.w. *J. für technische und ökonomische Chemie* (Erdmann) 2:423–74, 1828) in which he gave a list of twenty elements occurring in plants, including manganese, copper, which he suspected to be an analytical contaminant, barium in *Astragalus* and zirconium (!) in black pepper. Liebig's most formal statement, quoted by Browne from the seventh edition of *Die Chemie in ihren Anwendung auf Agricultur und Physiologie* (II, p. 223, Braunschweig, 1862) in translation, is: "Every field contains a maximum of one or more and a minimum of one or more different nutrients. With this minimum, be it lime, potash, nitrogen, phosphoric acid, magnesia or any other nutrient, the yields of crops stand in direct relation." Dr. Margaret Rossiter, the chief authority on Liebig in this country, tells me she believes no very formal statement of the law appears anywhere in the author's writings. The analogy of the barrel, due to Dobeneck, is later, but was popular in agricultural teaching throughout Europe in the earlier part of this century, as Dr. Luigi Provasoli tells me. Browne mentions other analogies, all of which were put forward to help farmers with little scientific knowledge.

32. J. von Liebig. 1855. *The Relations of Chemistry to Agriculture and the Agricultural Experiments of Mr. J. B. Lawes.* Translated by Samuel W. Johnson at the author's request. Albany, N.Y., p. 23.

33. The data for the lithosphere are from S. R. Taylor, 1964, Abundance of chemical elements in the earth's crust: A new table. *Geochim. Cosmochim. Acta.* 28:1273–85. Almost all the data for terrestrial plants are from H. J. M. Bowen, 1966, *Trace Elements in Biochemistry.* London and New York: Academic Press, ix, 241 pp.

34. C. C. Delwiche. 1970. The nitrogen cycle, *Scientific American* 223(3):136–46. P. S. Nutman. 1971. Perspctives in biological nitrogen fixation. *Science Progress* 59:55–76.

35. E. S. Deevey, Jr. 1940. Limnological studies in Connecticut. V. A contribution to regional limnology. *Amer. J. Sci.* 238:717–41.

36. W. T. Edmondson. 1972. Nutrients and phytoplankton in Lake Washington. In *Nutrients and Eutrophication* (see n. 1), pp. 172–93.

37. G. E. Fogg. 1969. The physiology of an algal nuisance. *Proc. Roy. Soc. Lond. B* 173:175–89.

38. P. C. Kerr, D. L. Brockway, D. F. Paris, and J. T. Barnett, Jr. 1972. The interrelation of carbon and phosphorus in regulating heterotrophic and autotrophic populations in an aquatic ecosystem, Shriner's Pond. In *Nutrients and Eutrophication* (see n. 1), pp. 41–62. H. L. Allen. 1971. Phytoplankton photosynthesis, micronutrient interactions, and inorganic carbon availabilities in a softwater Vermont lake. In *Nutrients and Eutrophication* (see n. 1), pp. 63–83.

39. G. E. Hutchinson and V. T. Bowen. 1947. A direct demonstration of the phosphorus cycle in a small lake. *Proc. Nat. Acad. Sci. U.S.* 33:148–53. G. E. Hutchinson and V. T. Bowen. 1950. A quantitative radiochemical study of the phosphorus cycle in Linsley Pond. *Ecology* 31:196–203. C. C. Coffin, F. R. Hayes, L. H. Jodrey, and S. C. Whiteway. 1949. Exchange of materials in a lake as studied by the addition of radioactive phosphorus. *Can. J. Res.* D27:207–22. F. R. Hayes, J. A. McCarter, M. L. Cameron, and D. A. Livingstone. 1952. On the kinetics of phosphorus exchange in lakes. *J. Ecology* 40:202–16.

40. F. H. Rigler. 1956. A tracer study of the phosphorus cycle in lake water. *Ecology* 37:550–62. See also: The phosphorus fractions and the turnover time of inorganic phosphorus in different types of lakes. *Limnol. Oceanogr.* 9:511–18, 1964.

41. D. R. S. Lean. 1973. Phosphorus dynamics in lake water. *Science* 179:678–80.

42. G. W. Fuhs, S. D. Demmerle, E. Canelli, and M. Chen. 1972. Characterization of phosphorus-limited plankton algae (with reflections on the limiting nutrient concept). In *Nutrients and Eutrophication* (see n. 1), pp. 113–33.

43. E. A. Thomas. 1969. The process of eutrophication in Central European lakes. In *Eutrophication, Causes, Consequences, Correctives* (see n. 1), pp. 29–49, and many papers referred to therein.

44. C. F. Powers, D. W. Schults, K. W. Malueg, R. M. Brice, and M. D. Schuldt. 1972. Algal responses to nutrient additions in natural waters. II. Field experiments. In *Nutrients and Eutrophication* (see n. 1), pp. 141–56.

45. S. D. Morton, R. Sernau, and P. H. Derse. 1972. Natural carbon sources, rates of replenishment, and algal growth. In *Nutrients and Eutrophication* (see n. 1), pp. 197–204.

46. J. Shapiro. 1973. Why blue-green algae? *Science* 179:382–84.

47. R. Patrick, W. B. Crum, and J. S. Coles. 1969. Temperature and manganese as determining factors in the presence of diatoms or blue-green algal floras in streams. *Proc. Nat. Acad. Sci.* 64: 472–78.

48. C. L. Schelske and E. F. Stoermer. 1972. Phosphorus, silica, and eutrophication of Lake Michigan. In *Nutrients and Eutrophication* (see n. 1), pp. 157–71.

49. A. E. Walsby. 1970. The nuisance algae: Curiosities in the biology of planktonic blue-green algae. *Water Treatment and Examination* 19:359–73. G. B. Fogg and A. E. Walsby. 1971. Buoyancy regulation and the growth of planktonic blue-green algae. *Mitt. Internat. Verein. Limnol.* 19: 182–88. A. E. Walsby. 1971. The pressure relation of gas vacuoles. *Proc. Roy. Soc. Lond. B* 178:301–26. M. T. Dinsdale and A. E. Walsby. 1972. The interrelations of cell turgor pressure, gas vacuolation, and buoyancy in blue-green algae. *J. Exper. Bot.* 23 (75):561–70.

50. K. G. Porter. In press. Selective grazing and differential digestion of algae by zooplankton. I am greatly indebted to Mrs. Porter for the opportunity to study this paper and for the photographs comprising Fig. 4.

Problems in Implementing U.S. Water Quality Goals

Walter E. Westman

Recent estimates of the cost of water pollution clean-up may prove unnecessarily high when some key assumptions are reexamined

Commenting on progress in cleaning up the Connecticut and Hudson rivers, former President Gerald Ford told a gathering, "The salmon are back. They cough a lot, but they have reappeared" (*Time*, July 14, 1975). Sewage-treatment plant construction in the United States currently is the single largest discretionary public works item in the federal budget. Sewage-treatment plant construction grants for FY75 were $1.9 billion, with estimated expenditures of $2.4 and $3.8 billion in FY76 and FY77 respectively. Public works expenditures on the Federal-Aid-to-Highways program are higher ($4.8, 6.6, and 7.0 billion in FY75–77 respectively), but these are funded from nondiscretionary Highway Trust Funds. The financing of sewage-treatment plants is approaching that for the combined costs of hydroelectric dams, flood control projects, and public power plants (estimated $3.9 billion in FY77).

The National Commission on Water Quality (NCWQ) has estimated that total governmental expenditures as high as $594 billion will be needed to meet the 1983 goals for municipal waste and stormwater treatment set by the 1972 Federal Water Pollution Control Act Amendments (FWPCA).

Walter E. Westman served as full-time Ecological Adviser to the U.S. Subcommittee on Air and Water Pollution in 1971 while it was drafting the Federal Water Pollution Control Act Amendments discussed in this article. He holds a Ph.D. degree from Cornell University in community and ecosystem ecology. The present article was written while Dr. Westman was Visiting Lecturer in Environmental Planning and Management in the School of Architecture and Urban Planning at U.C.L.A. Address: Department of Geography, University of California, Los Angeles, CA 90024.

It is expected that, when all the figures are in, 400–1,000 man-years will have been employed during 1975 and 1976 in preparation of areawide wastewater-treatment management plans (Centaur Management Consultants 1975), involving $200 million in federal money. In November 1975 the staff of the NCWQ issued a major report, mandated by Congress, to evaluate the social, economic, and environmental effects of achieving or not achieving the effluent limitations and goals for 1983 set forth in the FWPCA. In this article, I examine the effectiveness with which key elements of our nation's water quality goals are being implemented, the extent to which the NCWQ accurately reflects them, and some possible directions that future implementation strategy could follow to increase the speed and cost-effectiveness with which we approach the FWPCA goals.

The 1972 FWPCA (Public Law 92–500) provided both a novel philosophy and a changed strategy for implementing water pollution control in the United States. The philosophical position before the 1972 Act was man-centered, seeking to adjust pollution control levels to those necessary to maintain water quality suitable for particular human uses. Dubious assumptions about the origin, nature, and fate of pollutants and about the capacity of water bodies to assimilate wastes underpinned the 1965 Water Quality Act. By contrast, the FWPCA of 1972 recognized that some wastes are never assimilated by water bodies, that downstream water quality is affected by both point (localized) and nonpoint (dispersed) source inputs, and that the stream-segment use-classification approach was oversimplified and unenforceable. The Congress judged that in the

long term a single goal could cater to all of man's desired water uses. This goal was the elimination of disposal of wastes into the waters and, in the interim, a return to waters capable of supporting balanced populations of aquatic life and recreation in and on the water. By aiming to restore the "integrity" of the aquatic ecosystem, the Act adopted a philosophy of relying on nature's ability to maintain clean waters, rather than on man's technological ability to "manage" them in some partially degraded state.

The legislation was also a shift in strategy, from the 1965 Act's emphasis on estimating effluent discharges allowable to meet desired water quality goals in receiving waters, to an approach that was aimed at the elimination of discharge of wastes wherever possible, through the use of closed-cycle technology or land disposal of wastes. Failing elimination of discharge, treatment of discharges was to meet certain standards: for industry, best practicable control technology currently available by 1977 and best available technology economically achievable by 1983. Publicly owned treatment works were required to provide secondary treatment by 1977, and best practicable waste-treatment technology (subsequently defined by the Environmental Protection Agency [EPA] as secondary treatment) by 1983. The goal set was the elimination of discharge of wastes into water by 1985. The detailed basis for these shifts in policy was discussed in my 1972 *American Scientist* article. Here I shall address the following questions concerning progress to date in implementing the 1972 FWPCA Amendments:

- Do current implementation policies

provide the most cost-effective and timely means for pollution reduction?

• Is areawide waste-treatment management planning likely to achieve the goals intended by Congress?

• Is the current monitoring program adequate and appropriate to meet the objectives of the FWPCA?

• Are alternative technologies for achieving elimination of discharge being explored and encouraged adequately?

• How effectively are water conservation and reuse practices. being encouraged?

• Are coastal waters and the oceans being protected adequately by the current manner of implementation of the legislation?

Are implementation policies cost-effective?

The NCWQ Draft Report acknowledges that only half the municipalities and a somewhat larger proportion of industrial dischargers are likely to meet the Act's 1977 objectives on schedule. The NCWQ Report further notes that even when municipal and industrial point discharges are eliminated entirely, discharges by nonpoint sources and stormwater outfalls will continue to prevent achievement of the Act's goals. A federally sponsored study in the Delaware River estuary (Enviro-Control 1974) shows that 40–80% of the total annual BOD (biological oxygen demand) and COD (chemical oxygen demand) load that enters receiving waters from a city comes from sources other than the treatment plant. In addition, toxic material from urban runoff exceeds that from typical industrial discharges, and the load of pathogens exceeds that from the chlorinated effluent of treatment plants (see also Colston 1974).

A key problem in effective implementation of the Act to date— and one highlighted by the NCWQ—is the historical asynchrony that has developed between implementation of sections of the Act dealing with point source treatment alone (Sec. 201) and point and nonpoint source management considered jointly (Sec. 208).

Sec. 201 of the Act provides 75% federal matching funds for the construction of facilities for the treatment or recycling of wastewaters from point sources. Sec. 208 of the FWPCA provides for areawide waste-treatment management planning by a regional agency to create an integrated program of treatment of point and nonpoint sources of wastewater. A recent court decision (Natural Resources Defense Council and Environmental Defense Fund vs. Environmental Protection Agency, June 1975, District of Columbia—the so-called "Smith case") has interpreted Sec. 208 to apply to all portions of the country. Although in 1973 the EPA immediately began the process of soliciting and reviewing proposals from municipal dischargers for the construction of treatment facilities under Sec. 201 and continued the process of reviewing industrial permits for discharge begun in 1969, it was not until 1975 that the first planning for areawide waste-treatment management began in earnest, and the first Sec. 208 plans are not expected to be completed till mid-1977. The effect has been to encourage the treatment of municipal and industrial wastes by giving them higher priority than nonpoint sources of wastes. Such an implementation strategy preempts consideration of the possibility that, when municipal, industrial, stormwater, and other nonpoint sources are viewed jointly, a different set of priorities might achieve pollution reduction in a more timely and cost-effective manner.

This is not the only aspect of the Act, and of the EPA's water quality strategy, to discourage cost-effective implementation of the Act's goals. Three additional factors conspire to aggravate the problem.

Treatment of urban runoff is discouraged. The FWPCA program, while providing 75% federal matching funds for treatment plant construction, has been interpreted by the EPA to exclude matching funds for programs to decrease sewer infiltration, to improve sewer inspection, cleaning, and maintenance programs, or to improve street-sweeping programs. Further, no funds will be provided for the treatment of stormwater except when it is diverted to sewage-treatment plants, and no funds will be provided for construction of new stormwater pipes to accomplish this

task. The net effect is to provide strong incentives to municipalities to plan for construction of conventional sewage-treatment plants and to neglect treatment of stormwater and nonpoint sources of urban pollution. Yet those sources normally account for a significant fraction of total pollution loads, and can be cheaper to treat, through management strategies, than sewage waste.

Optimal strategies for stormwater treatment are neglected. Strategies for partial treatment of stormwater and nonpoint sources of pollution may be more cost-effective than sewage treatment. For example, the Enviro-Control study (1974) showed that the storage of the first one-third to one inch of rainwater in the sewer system itself or in storage lagoons, followed by treatment of a storm's runoff, halved the cost of BOD removal while increasing the level of BOD removal threefold. Yet in the EPA's *Guidelines for Areawide Waste Treatment Management Planning* (1975) there is no mention of the possibility of treating only a portion of the stormwater load. No mention is made of alternative, low-cost methods of stormwater treatment, land treatment, biological treatment such as percolation through managed bullrush swamps (Josephson 1975), or other alternatives. As a result, the EPA discourages stormwater treatment altogether. To quote from its *Guidelines* (1975) p. I–5:

Priorities should focus on problems that can be most effectively solved within existing technological capabilities. For example, renovating urban stormwater systems may be a low priority due to the high capital costs. On the other hand, establishing a treatment works program may be a very high priority.

Pollution sources are not ranked by severity. At no time in plotting its implementation strategy has the EPA apparently asked whether achievement of the objectives of the Act would best be served by first controlling those pollutants that cause the most damage, and, if so, how it might be accomplished. The EPA has provided no incentive to municipalities or Sec. 208 planners to rank major pollutant categories (toxic materials, nutrients, pathogens, nonnutrients) by volume and toxicity and to examine the major sources of each to determine which sources are best controlled first, and to what degree. In fact, the EPA gave low priority to the control of toxic substance discharges until a court decision late in 1976 (Natural Resources Defense Council vs. EPA) forced acceleration of the program. At the time of issuance of the NCWQ Report, the EPA had failed to issue any pretreatment or effluent discharge standards for toxic pollutants. An attempt to rank needs for pollution control by pollutant category may help to refine further the question of which pollution sources should be controlled first. A careful assessment of the degree of treatment needed at each source to optimize overall pollution reduction within funding limits could then enhance cost-efficiency.

One may point to a variety of possible causes for existing cost-inefficiencies in strategy implementation: the widespread bias toward construction of well-known hardware on the part of both municipalities and their engineering consultants; the aggravation of this tendency by both the speed with which Sec. 201 grants were to be applied for and the discouragement of management strategies other than construction of municipal treatment plants through lack of federal matching funds for these projects; the lack of synchrony between the Sec. 201 construction grant program and areawide waste-treatment management planning (Sec. 208); the existing biases of state statutes against land disposal of sewage wastes; and a historical lack of appreciation of the toxicity and volume of total pollution loads contributed by stormwater and nonpoint sources.

One effect of this implementation strategy has been to foster a very discouraging picture for implementation of water quality goals. By viewing the solution to water pollution problems as a stepwise process involving construction of treatment plants for municipal and industrial wastes first (at monumental costs), and construction of treatment plants for nonpoint sources of pollution at a later date, disconcerting cost estimates and discouraging prospects for water clean-up can be projected. The NCWQ estimates that, to reach the 1983 goals of secondary treatment for sewage and stormwater, construction costs for public works will be $242–594 billion (medium estimate: $357

billion)—not including costs for treatment of nonpoint sources. These figures are enough to scare any politician and average taxpayer into paroxysms of capitulation on earlier commitments to clean water.

It is my thesis that these cost estimates are considerably higher than they would be if we were to approach the implementation of the FWPCA by (1) making further grants for treatment plant construction and further industrial permit requirements contingent upon completion of Sec. 208 plans for each region, with the EPA Administrator empowered to make exceptions only when a strong case can be made for an early judgment; (2) encouraging Sec. 208 planners to examine the major sources of pollutants, considering jointly municipal, industrial, stormwater, and nonpoint sources, and to approach the control of these with a priority designed to control the largest amount of the most highly damaging pollutants first, regardless of source; (3) encouraging the use of land disposal to achieve secondary treatment of wastes where feasible and cost-effective, instead of limiting land disposal to tertiary treatment schemes; (4) encouraging the use of management strategies and alternative technologies for treatment of all or parts of wastewater categories. The latter could include the holding of the first one-third to one inch of rain for treatment; the use of more efficient street sweepers to capture the finer particles (<250 microns), which contain the great bulk of toxic materials (Sartor and Boyd 1972); the use of biological treatment ponds, natural lagoons, and groundwater recharge where feasible for stormwater and other wastewater treatment; the encouragement of more open space and more porous paving materials in cities, to provide increased opportunities for on-site infiltration of rain and to decrease urban runoff and its associated waste load; and the active encouragement of water conservation programs to reduce wastewater volumes.

A clear inference from the NCWQ Staff Report is that Congress will have to postpone its deadlines in the FWPCA for achievement of various levels of treatment if it is not to prosecute the tens of thousands of municipalities and industries that will not meet the 1977 deadlines. Indeed,

the NCWQ recommended postponements in its report to Congress in March 1976. This fact, rather than being a source of unmitigated despair, can be seen as an opportunity for Congress to adjust deadlines to make them achievable within the context of completed Sec. 208 plans, which have already begun the process of integrating the various wastewater-treatment problems discussed above. Apart from this change in the law, some variant of which appears inevitable, the remaining responsibility for cost-efficient implementation of the water clean-up program lies with the EPA and with consultants who are preparing Sec. 208 plans. While Sec. 208 planning has the potential to address the major priority questions outlined here, it remains to be seen how effectively the plans will deal with these problems.

Will plans achieve congressional goals?

A survey completed in July 1975 provides a rather discouraging picture of current areawide waste-treatment management (Sec. 208) planning (Centaur Management Consultants 1975). Few personnel hired to conduct Sec. 208 planning appear trained to consider the feasibility of unconventional strategies, and alternative technologies, in meeting FWPCA objectives. Equally, few appear trained to appreciate the ecological processes shaping the needs for control of various categories of pollutants that migrate in a complex fashion through ecological systems. About 58% of the Sec. 208 planning in the nation is being contracted out by the designated agencies (which are predominantly regional councils of government). Of the contractors, 45% are engineering firms principally involved in facilities design. Many of the other contractors deal with aspects of Sec. 208 planning other than pollution control per se, such as legal requirements, citizen participation, and management of personnel.

While it is not possible to say from this breakdown alone what the quality of the completed tasks will be, the survey indicated that some Sec. 208 agencies were not even aware of the requirements of the FWPCA. About one-third of the agencies surveyed were unaware that they had the power to incur indebtedness and to refuse wastes from sources not complying with Sec. 208 plan requirements. Fifty-five agencies appeared unaware of the mandated public review process, expressing the feeling that local review of their plan would jeopardize meeting the 24-month planning deadline.

I have already indicated some of the ways in which the EPA's *Guidelines for Areawide Waste Treatment Management Planning* (1975) bias planners toward conventional technologies. Additional weaknesses of the document include (1) failure to provide adequate guidance for estimating contributions from nonpoint sources (except for a single overly simplistic formula, discussed below), and actively discouraging the agencies from using more sophisticated models for this purpose (EPA *Guidelines*, p. 1II–8); (2) failure to encourage consideration of pollutants in terms of their toxicities to aquatic life in order to set up priorities for source control; and (3) failure to explain the potential of biological systems for monitoring and treatment.

Compounding these difficulties has been the declining federal funding for Sec. 208 planning, from an authorization of $150 million in 1975 to $53 million in 1976. No further authorizations have yet been made, although it seems reasonable to expect them to be forthcoming in view of the Smith case and delays in implementation of the Act's requirements.

Is the monitoring program adequate?

Of the various criticisms that could be leveled at the current water-quality monitoring program, four of the most severe are (1) the failure to encourage and enforce Sec. 308 of the FWPCA, which requires each discharger to conduct biological monitoring in receiving waters wherever appropriate; (2) the lack of an organized monitoring program to distinguish between the contributions of pollutants from point and nonpoint sources; (3) the lack of sufficient monitoring of stormwater and groundwater, and inadequate designs for offshore monitoring; (4) the lack of adequate staff to check on the accuracy of reports from point dischargers.

Biological monitoring—the use of organisms in the receiving waters as indicators of the extent of pollution—was recommended by Congress as an efficient means to obtain an integrated measure of the effects of pollutants on aquatic life (Westman 1972, 1974). The failure to pursue the requirement for biological monitoring in receiving waters is almost certainly due in part to the lack of biologically trained personnel at the monitoring site, as well as a long-standing bias toward monitoring of physical and chemical rather than biological parameters of water quality. It was precisely this bias that legislators were attempting to reverse when they wrote Sec. 308 (and Sec. 504, which defines "biological monitoring") to require "where appropriate" the direct monitoring of the effects of each point discharge on aquatic organisms in the receiving waters. The Act is explicit and detailed in its requirements: effects are to be measured on aquatic life actually in receiving waters (not in laboratory tanks), and in addition monitoring to detect "accumulation of pollutants in tissue . . . [in] organisms representative of appropriate levels of the food chain" (Sec. 504) is to be conducted.

To date the EPA has issued no guidelines on how to conduct biological monitoring, nor is its Office of Research and Development conducting any research on the subject. The EPA draft research plan for the next five years calls for no funds to develop or apply such methodologies; the Fish and Wildlife Service of the Department of Interior is likewise not working on developing such systems. The NCWQ report continues the pattern of neglect by failing to mention the issue at all.

This lack of implementation cannot be blamed entirely on a lack of methods for accomplishing the task. The literature on sophisticated methods of biological monitoring for water pollution is at least a quarter-century old (Patrick 1949), and a recent volume of the American Society for Testing and Materials (Cairns and Dickson 1973) has made the literature part of standard methodology. A nationwide survey of the extent to which biological monitoring is being carried out is currently being conducted by Oak Ridge National Laboratory on contract to the EPA, and details of the extent of implementation are not yet available. A case I know of, however, may illustrate some of the implementation problems to be expected.

The Tapia treatment plant, at Las Virgenes, on the outskirts of Los Angeles, currently maintains a "biological monitoring" facility to test the impact of its periodic discharges into nearby Malibu Creek on resident aquatic life. The monitoring facility consists of two aspects: a basket in the stream, in which trout are maintained for 96-hour periods, and a series of "bioassay" tanks in which trout of two size classes (but no larval stage) are exposed to effluent. There are no representatives of other trophic levels in the tanks. In all cases, the fish are fed with commercial fish food purchased at the local pet store before the 96-hour test period begins. If there were any bioaccumulative toxins (various metals and synthetic organics widely found in domestic sewage, even with no industrial hook-ups [Van Loon 1974]) in the effluent, this monitoring set-up would certainly provide no opportunity for the food-chain concentration to occur.

As discussed at length elsewhere (e.g. Westman 1974), such bioassay tests do not take account of the toxicity of receiving waters to various life stages (especially the highly sensitive juvenile stages), of chronic low-level exposure over longer time periods (Congressional Research Service 1975), or of synergistic or ecological interactions. The results are of highly questionable value as indicators of in-stream tolerances by all native species to the mixture of pollutants present in the stream in varying concentrations over the seasons and years and to the more subtle effects on shifting competitive balances among species within the aquatic ecosystem. Though Cairns (e.g. Cairns et al. 1970) and others have done much to develop biological monitoring techniques usable by the nonscientist, it is probably the case that, until funding is provided for some biologically trained personnel to sample at the local level, biological monitoring techniques will not be implemented in an appropriate fashion. That the EPA has not yet issued guidelines for biological monitoring aggravates the inadequacies of implementing this kind of monitoring.

The traditional physical and chemical

parameters for monitoring have been shown by many investigators to be particularly inadequate indicators of pollution impact on aquatic organisms (e.g. Westman 1974). It is impossible to predict, for example, what the level of a bioaccumulative pesticide in the eggshell of a predatory bird will be, based on the concentration of the pesticide in water. Likewise, it is easier to detect a carcinogen in water by observing a tumor in a fish than by analyzing for 30,000 suspected carcinogens in water.

The lack of data on pollutant contributions from nonpoint sources is particularly acute. The consultants to the NCWQ found that many communities in their regional studies could not provide any data on nonpoint source contributions, and others "used only generalized information to determine the possible magnitude of nonpoint problems" (NCWQ 1975, p. VI–14).

It is difficult to obtain accurate data on the quality of urban flows that are not captured in stormwater pipes. Nevertheless, it seems worthwhile to attempt to correlate data on the quality of surface water and groundwater with nearby major nonpoint sources, in view of the importance of these sources to total loads. Until such data are obtained, the process of planning truly cost-effective management practices will be severely hampered. Indeed, it is almost certainly the current lack of such data that contributes to the neglect that nonpoint source pollution has suffered in management plans.

In the EPA's *Guidelines for Area-wide Waste Treatment Management Planning* (1975), use of computer models for estimating nonpoint sources is discouraged due to the two-year time limit on such planning and the scarcity of such models. The EPA *Guidelines* recommend instead the use of an arithmetic formula which assumes that all detected material at the end of a stream segment that was not present at the beginning of the stream segment, and that did not sink or decay in the interim, must have been contributed by nonpoint sources of pollution. The formula takes no explicit account of accumulation of materials into the biota (particularly important for heavy metals, which are a major component of urban runoff), of in-stream chem-

ical transformations, of temporal (diurnal, seasonal) variations in load, or of dissolution of materials from sediment. The formula is certainly an improvement over having no data at all, but it is some indication of the level of approximation with which we are still dealing in estimating pollution from what may be an area's largest source.

The current level of monitoring of dischargers for compliance with permit provisions is very low. According to the NCWQ Report (p. V–29), the EPA only began to shift manpower from permit issuance to compliance monitoring in mid-1975, and many states that have been delegated the monitoring responsibility are not expected to take it on until early FY77. These plans reflect in part the fact that most permits have only been in effect since mid-1974. However, an attitude survey conducted by the NCWQ indicates that federal and state officials are likely to implement fully the mandatory requirement of the FWPCA Amendments for swift enforcement actions for permit compliance only slowly, if at all: 69% of interviewed state water pollution control agency officials and 62% of EPA officials agreed strongly with the statement that "control of water pollution is largely a process of bargaining, negotiation and compromise between the regulated and regulator for enforcement of the law" (Table V–9).

Are alternative technologies explored?

The NCWQ Report documents a number of instances in which the speed of preparation of proposals for construction of treatment works and the small number of consulting engineers familiar with alternative technologies and management strategies for wastewater treatment and reduction have resulted in reliance on conventional technology. I will consider here land treatment, one of the most important alternative technologies, relied upon heavily by Congress in its thinking during the formulation of the FWPC Act.

Table V–25 of the NCWQ Report indicates that as many as 38 states require secondary pretreatment before land may be irrigated by sewage wastes for various purposes. The

NCWQ Report asks (p. I–12): "What is the impact of rigid adherence by many States to the requirement for secondary treatment as a prerequisite to land application of wastewater from publicly owned treatment works?" This is an extremely important question, since on it hangs much of the basis for the large cost estimates for achieving the 1977 and 1983 objectives. And yet the NCWQ Report does not provide any data to permit readers to decide whether in fact secondary-level pretreatment is necessary before land disposal and, if so, in what proportion of instances. The Report considers land disposal to be "similar to secondary treatment but serving as a more efficient 'pretreatment' system for add-on innovative technologies which must also be employed for achieving elimination of discharges" (p. I–77). But the Report does not give any quantitative comparative cost estimates of achieving secondary treatment of wastes by land disposal or by mechanical means, although it lists the costs of the former as "low" in Table II–49.

The NCWQ Report presents two reasons why it did not consider land disposal as an option for achieving secondary treatment. First, many states do not allow it—but the reader is not told whether this prohibition is based on historical attitudes toward earlier approaches to land disposal or on current assessments of the risks. Second, effluent not given secondary pretreatment will "clog the soil" (p. II–153)—but this phenomenon will vary from soil to soil, and it will also vary with the overlying vegetation, the nature and flow rate of effluent, and other factors. The Werribee farm in Australia, for example, used the overland-flow technique to treat 96% of the wastes of the city of Melbourne (2 1/2 million people), including one-fifth industrial wastes, successfully for 70 years without secondary pretreatment. The farm raises cattle and sheep for human consumption, at a total net cost to the citizen for sewage purification of $1.07/year. Not a single case of illness due to consumption of meat from this operation has been reported (Melbourne and Metropolitan Board of Works 1971).

Until the question of the feasibility and cost of using land disposal technologies for meeting secondary-treatment requirements is widely and seriously addressed, cost estimates for meeting 1977 and 1983 goals of secondary treatment for municipal dischargers will remain perhaps unnecessarily inflated.

Is water conservation encouraged?

Pages V–71–76 of the NCWQ Report discuss progress to date in implementing Sec. 201(d) of the Act, which requires the administrator to encourage the reclaiming and recycling of wastewater as part of the requirements of construction grants. The NCWQ Report offers some insight into the nature of hindrances to encouraging wastewater recycling. Among them were the requirement of the FWPCA that water reuse should produce revenue for the treatment facilities, the relatively low priority for water reuse given by EPA, historical or legal constraints, and public health uncertainties (NCWQ 1975, pp. V–75–76). The Report also cites some figures to document the extremely low level of participation in recycling programs in the country—e.g. only 357 locations in the United States as of 1975 were directly reusing municipal wastewater, exclusive of groundwater recharge. The Report, however, does not pursue the implications of these findings, nor are they mentioned in the summary chapter.

A second, closely related issue is water conservation and wastewater source reduction. Considerable savings in costs of wastewater treatment could be realized by reducing the volume of wastewater generated. Sec. 104(o)(1) of the FWPCA Amendments requires the administrator to conduct research and investigations "on devices, systems, incentives, pricing policy, and other methods of reducing the total flow of sewage, including, but not limited to, unnecessary water consumption in order to reduce the requirements for, and the costs of, sewage and waste treatment services." Not only is progress on this point to date not evaluated; more significantly, the NCWQ Report fails to provide scenarios on what kinds of cost savings in treatment-plant construction could be achieved by various levels of water conservation practices. At a time when such calculations are becoming commonplace for energy conservation, it would not seem unreasonable to expect similar

considerations to be highlighted in the wastewater area. Until such figures are available, however, we can only speculate on the nature of the impacts (see e.g. Washington Suburban Sanitary Comm. 1974).

Are coastal waters adequately protected?

Sec. 403 of the FWPCA Amendments sets out detailed criteria for formulation of guidelines for the issuance of ocean discharge permits. This, and relevant passages of PL 92–532 (Marine Protection and Sanctuaries Act), were the basis for the EPA guidelines on ocean dumping in 1973 (Federal Register 38(198):28610–21). The guidelines continue to generate much controversy, many thinking the guidelines insufficiently stringent, others viewing them as too strong. Certainly the guidelines are lax by ecological standards, as they, for example, allow the dumping of solid wastes containing up to .75 mg/kg of mercury, and up to 1.5 mg/kg (= c. 1,500 micrograms/liter) mercury in liquid effluents. Maximum permissible levels of mercury in edible portions of fish flesh have been set at .5 mg/kg by the Food and Drug Administration, and an average total level in seawater not exceeding .05 micrograms/liter is recommended by the Committee on Water Quality Criteria (1972). Such levels for ocean dumping leave completely open the question of the extent to which such toxic heavy metals will bioaccumulate as they are transferred along the food chain.

The NCWQ Report presents a discussion (pp.IV–75–78) of effects of ocean outfalls from municipal treatment plants in selected areas of the country for which some long-term data exist. The discussion is completely qualitative, however, and draws heavily from such sources of data as the Southern California Coastal Water Research Project (SCCWRP), which is directly funded by the municipal agencies that are discharging their wastes offshore. The Report states (p. IV–77): "The assimilative capacity of deep, circulating marine systems seems to be such that introduction of municipal sewage effluents does not increase regional concentrations of most potential pollutant materials beyond natural background levels." But mercury and cadmium are elements that cannot be

further degraded. Where do they go? How do we know what the background levels are? How do we know what the assimilative capacity of the deep ocean is when our general state of knowledge of deep oceans is widely recognized to be extremely limited? The NCWQ Report provides no tables or figures to support its contention.

Another statement in the NCWQ Report is that (p. IV–76) "several fish diseases—including a fin rot condition and a skeletal disorder—appear at unusually high frequencies near some outfalls, but it is unclear whether the disorders are caused by the effluents or the unusual crowding of fishes near the outfalls." The Report fails to pursue this comment to its obvious next question: Is the crowding of fish near the outfall due to the presence of the outfall? It would seem a gross neglect of ecological concepts to claim that ocean discharge could not be blamed for the fish disorders simply because the adverse effects were due to physical and behavioral phenomena rather than directly to chemical phenomena. The fish could be crowded near the outfall, for example, to feed (ultimately) off the plankton which themselves may be thriving from the nutrients in the effluent.

Unfortunately, this example of incomplete analysis is not an isolated one in the literature. Indeed, a disturbing observation about the literature and the public testimony on effects of sewage discharges on the marine environment is the degree to which it has been generated by scientists whose research has been funded by organizations which appear to have a vested interest in showing that ocean discharges are not harmful to the marine environment. For example, major articles on ocean dumping (Bascom 1974; Heckroth 1973) generalize widely about effects of ocean outfalls based on SCCWRP data, and testimony to the Senate Public Works Committee on the FWPCA Amendments (1971, p. 2119 ff.) by scientists from the Franklin Institute on an ocean dumping site off Delaware and New Jersey was based on work sponsored by the Philadelphia Water Department, which is a major user of the site under study. What Congress needs, rather, are large-scale studies, covering whole ocean circulating systems and extending over long terms—sponsored, for example, through joint cooperation of the National Oceanic and Atmospheric Agency and the EPA. To date, no such large-scale, long-term monitoring studies of ocean discharges by agencies that have no vested interest in the outcome are being conducted, to the best of my knowledge.

The path ahead

I have outlined in this paper some of the reasons why I believe the NCWQ estimates of costs for achieving U.S. water quality objectives are so high. I have also pointed out that the current delay on the part of dischargers in meeting FWPCA Amendments deadline objectives may provide a useful opportunity to reorder the sequence of tasks for pollution clean-up so that Sec. 208 plans can identify the most critical sources for control, and the most cost-efficient strategies for control, before further funds are converted to concrete.

Nevertheless, I have noted that at present Sec. 208 planning is proceeding at a pace and with a personnel that may not guarantee that effective, integrated, and innovative plans are drawn up for the regions. To permit the synchronization of planning stressed above, the logical next step for the NCWQ or the EPA is to attempt to evaluate the extent to which short-term delays in planning and implementing of the objectives of the Act are likely to result in long-term net benefits in both pollution control strategy and ultimate cost savings. The agencies should also determine the extent to which such savings will be diminished by increases in real costs due to delay.

I have criticized the NCWQ Report in places for not pursuing its questions far enough, but these criticisms should not mask the fact that the Report represents an outstanding contribution to the quest for better policy formulation and implementation. It amasses a large volume of data essential to evaluating properly the monumental public works undertaking involved and succeeds in highlighting many important issues.

If there are recurrent themes to be identified in the persistent problems of water pollution control, they are those associated with the tendency of our policy implementers to turn first to conventional high-level technology for solutions to our technologically generated problems. Nevertheless, the problems run deeper, to sources widespread and not easily remedied: mistrust between levels of government; differences in orientation and values between the professionals involved (sanitary engineers, planners, ecologists); and tendencies toward conservatism in the operation of bureaucracies. There are historical factors delaying consideration of land treatment of waste waters and the recognition of the need for treatment of stormwater and nonpoint sources of pollution. And there is the political fact that construction of sewage-treatment plants can be more readily perceived as creating jobs than can more complex forms of waste-treatment management.

Through its implementation of the FWPCA Amendments the United States remains committed, nevertheless, to one of the most ecologically enlightened and ambitious programs in the field of environmental management. Many countries are watching the progress of this approach with intense interest. Yet there is a danger that this country may falter in its commitment because of apparently insurmountable costs in meeting the objectives of Congress. One of the major challenges to environmental planners in the coming decade will be to demonstrate cost-effective routes toward achievement of these objectives. Only in this way can there be assurances that, if we retreat from the program goals, we have not done so because of inadequate coordination of existing skills and resources.

References

Bascom, Willard. 1974. The disposal of waste in the ocean. *Sci. Am.* 231:16–25.

Cairns, John, Jr., Kenneth L. Dickson, Richard E. Sparks, and William T. Waller. 1970. A preliminary report on rapid biological information systems for water pollution control. *Water Poll. Contr. Fed. J.* 42:685–703.

Cairns, John, Jr., and Kenneth L. Dickson, ed. 1973. *Biological Methods for the Assessment of Water Quality.* Philadelphia: Am. Soc. for Testing and Materials Tech. Publ. 528.

Centaur Management Consultants, Inc. 1975. *National Profile of Section 208 Areawide Management Planning Agencies.* Washington, DC: EPA Contract No. 68–01–3195.

Colston, Newton V., Jr. 1974. *Characterization and Treatment of Urban Land Runoff.* Washington, DC: EPA 670/2–74–096.

Committee on Public Works, U.S. Senate. 1971. *Hearings on Water Pollution Control Legislation. Part 5. Ocean Dumping.* Washington, DC: U.S. Government Printing Office, Serial No. 92–H10.

Committee on Water Quality Criteria. 1972. *Water Quality Criteria, 1972.* Washington, DC: Environmental Studies Board, Nat. Acad. Sci.–Nat. Acad. Engr.

Congressional Research Service. 1975. *Effects of Chronic Exposure to Low-level Pollutants in the Environment.* Washington, DC: U.S. Government Printing Office. Serial 0. 60–7520.

Enviro-Control, Inc. 1974. *Total Urban Water Pollution Loads: The Impact of Stormwater.* Washington, DC: Council on Environmental Quality, EPA and HUD.

Heckroth, C. W. 1973. Special report: Ocean disposal—good or bad? *Water and Wastes Engr.* 10(10):32–38.

Josephson, Julian. 1975. Green systems for wastewater treatment. *Environ. Sci. and Tech.* 9:408–09.

Melbourne and Metropolitan Board of Works. 1971. *Melbourne and Metropolitan Board of Works Farm.* Werribee, Victoria, Australia.

National Commission on Water Quality. 1975. *Staff Draft Report.* Washington, DC.

National Commission on Water Quality. 1976. *Report to the Congress.* Washington, DC: U.S. Government Printing Office.

Patrick, Ruth. 1949. A proposed biological measure of stream conditions, based on a survey of the Conestoga Basin, Lancaster County, Pennsylvania. *Proc. Acad. Nat. Sci. Phila.* 101:277–341.

Sartor, James D., and Gail B. Boyd. 1972. *Water Pollution Aspects of Street Surface Contaminants.* Washington, DC: EPA R2–72–081.

U.S. Environmental Protection Agency. 1975. *Guidelines for Areawide Waste Treatment Management Planning.* Washington, DC.

Van Loon, J. C. 1974. Mercury input to the environment resulting from products and effluents from municipal sewage treatment plants. *Environ. Poll.* 7:141–47.

Washington Suburban Sanitary Commission. 1974. *Water Conservation/Wastewater Reduction, Customer Education and Behavioral Change Program.* Washington, DC.

Westman, W. E. 1972. Some basic issues in water pollution control legislation. *Am. Sci.* 60:767–73.

Westman, W. E. 1974. Bioassays and biological monitoring. In *A Compilation of Australian Water Quality Criteria*, ed. B. Hart. Canberra. Australian Water Resources Tech. Paper No. 7.

Robert Dolan
Alan Howard
Arthur Gallenson

Man's Impact on the Colorado River in the Grand Canyon

The Grand Canyon is being affected both by the vastly changed Colorado River and by the increased presence of man

Man-made landforms are found throughout the United States; however, some of the most extensive and persistent scars of large-scale environmental modification are found in the American Southwest. The sparse vegetation and generally slow pace of geomorphic processes leave the landscape much as man leaves it—here he is a significant agent of geologic change.

Agriculture, mining, highway construction, and earthmoving associated with rapid urban growth contribute measurably to erosion and siltation. The large reservoirs on the major rivers of the Southwest serve as sediment sinks for much of the eroded material, disrupting the sediment budgets of the drainage systems below the dams. In this

Robert Dolan will be remembered as the senior author of "Man's Impact on the Barrier Islands of North Carolina," which appeared in American Scientist *in March 1973. Alan Howard, who is also in the Department of Environmental Sciences at the University of Virginia, received his doctorate in 1970 from The Johns Hopkins University. His research interests are in fluvial geomorphology and arid-zone landforms. Arthur Gallenson has been with Grand Canyon Expeditions, Kanab, Utah, for seven years. Before becoming a Colorado River Guide, he completed graduate degree work in geology.*
This research was supported by the Office of Natural Sciences, National Park Service, Washington, D.C. The authors wish to acknowledge the valuable discussions of their colleagues during the course of a float trip in 1973: Yates Borden (project leader), Fred Borden, Jack Rogers, Charles Strauss, Brian Turner, Harmer Weeden, and Roy Johnson, to whom they are especially indebted for providing information on common riverfront species and for discussions about vegetational responses to the regulation of the river. Address for Drs. Dolan and Howard: Department of Environmental Sciences, University of Virginia, Charlottesville, VA 22903.

paper we will describe the environmental impact that a recently completed dam-reservoir system is having on one of the largest rivers in the Southwest, the Colorado. The reach of the Colorado that we investigated extends 280 miles from the Glen Canyon Dam to Lake Mead—an area known as the Grand Canyon (Fig. 2).

The problem

When Major J. W. Powell made his historic trip down the Grand Canyon in 1869, the Colorado River system was one of the last unexplored regions in the United States. In fact, the area was considered so remote and primitive that J. C. Ives, another early explorer of the Southwest, described it in these terms:

Ours has been the first, and will doubtless be the last, party of whites to visit this profitless locality. It seems intended by nature that the Colorado River, along the greater portion of its lonely and majestic way, shall be forever unvisited and undisturbed [1].

Ives's prediction was off considerably: the National Park Service reports that the forty-millionth visitor will enter Grand Canyon National Park sometime during the present decade.

Even disregarding the environmental changes caused by forty million visitors, the Colorado River today is vastly different from the river Powell explored in the mid-1800s. Powell's Colorado remained fundamentally unchanged until Hoover Dam was completed in 1935; and, although the Hoover Dam reservoir (Lake Mead) extended into the lower reaches of the Grand Canyon,

the upper reaches of the canyon remained in an essentially natural state until the Glen Canyon Dam reservoir (Lake Powell) was completed in 1963. Since then, the flow of the Colorado in Marble Canyon and Grand Canyon has been almost completely dependent upon the release of water from Lake Powell (Fig. 2). Virtually all the sediment that formerly passed through these canyons is now trapped in the reservoir, and the frequent high water (flash flood) that is associated with the rivers of the Southwest is now totally controlled. The environmental responses to these changes have been both rapid and significant.

Before Glen Canyon Dam existed, the river gained volume from the spring snowmelt in the headwaters, reached maximum flow in May or June, and then receded during the remainder of the year. Flash flooding in the late summer often resulted in a second peak. During periods of high water, when the river had the greatest transport capability, large quantities of sand and silt were carried through the canyon, scouring the channel. As the water receded in the summer, the river lost both competence and capacity and deposited much of its silt and sand load along the channel. The river bars and terraces (colloquially

Figure 1. This steep beach face near Nankoweap Rapids in Marble Canyon was produced by rapid undercutting of fine-grained terrace deposits. Such examples of very rapid erosion are uncommon; elsewhere the widespread removal of pre-dam fluvial deposits by backcutting becomes apparent only through photographic comparison of the present riverfront with pre-dam conditions. (Photo by Alan Howard.)

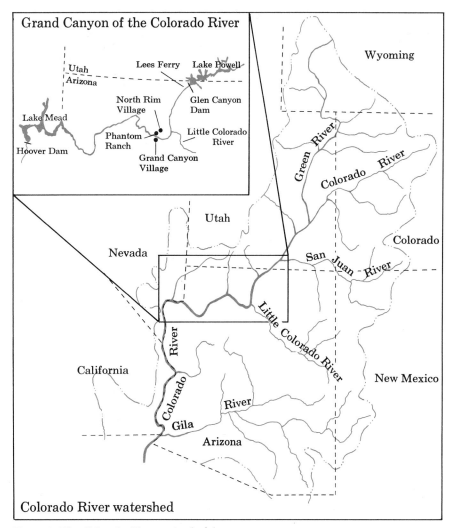

Grand Canyon of the Colorado River

Colorado River watershed

Figure 2. The Colorado River watershed in the vicinity of the Grand Canyon. (USGS base map.)

The environmental changes presently occurring along the Colorado channel might elicit only limited interest if man's use of the river were to continue as it was during the pre-dam era; however, the number of people taking Colorado River boat trips has increased dramatically in recent years. The 200th person to make the river-run did so in the early 1950s; since then, more than 100,000 people have made the trip. Because of this increase in human traffic, conservation groups and the National Park Service came to the conclusion that the river's "carrying capacity" might have been reached or perhaps exceeded, and in 1971 Grand Canyon National Park started limiting boat trips to approximately 10,000 persons a year (2).

Thus the two questions of importance for management of this unique landscape are (1) In what manner and how rapidly is the Grand Canyon adjusting to the new river regime? and (2) Is the increased use of the river by man influencing these adjustments?

Pre-dam hydrology and fluvial morphology

From the Glen Canyon Dam to Lake Mead, a distance of 280 miles, the Colorado River falls from 3,000 to 850 feet above sea level. The average gradient is over 7 feet a mile, or about 25 times that of the Mississippi (3). The 161 rapids of the Colorado, among the river's major visitor attractions, account for a significant amount of the decrease in elevation along its length. The twenty largest rapids, with drops of up to 40 feet, account for approximately 20 percent of the fall between Lees Ferry and Lake Mead. The depth of the river averages about 50 feet, and widths of 200 to 300 feet are common (4). The river is less than 80 feet wide at its narrowest point.

Prior to construction of the Glen Canyon Dam, the Colorado River's mean annual flood height was about ten times the present median discharge (Table 1). Floods exceeding 100,000 cubic feet per second occurred every few years. The two highest floods of record were approximately 300,000 cfs, in 1884,

called beaches) were thus periodically eroded and replenished with sediment.

With the present controlled flow, the higher terraces are no longer flooded, and the lower terraces and bars are eroding (see Fig. 1). At the same time, elimination of high-water discharges has resulted in the rapid development of dense flood-plain vegetation in areas which were formerly inundated (Fig. 3), and wind deflation is removing large quantities of fluvial sediment above the current high-water levels.

Table 1. Pre- and post-dam statistics for the Colorado River

	Lees Ferry Gauging Station		Grand Canyon Gauging Station	
	Pre-dam	Post-dam	Pre-dam	Post-dam
Median discharge (cfs)	7,400	12,200	8,200	12,800
Mean annual flood (cfs)	86,000	27,000	86,000	28,000
10-year recurrence interval flood (cfs)	123,000	30,000	122,000	40,000
Discharge equaled or exceeded 95% of time, based on average daily flows (cfs)	3,600	5,500	4,000	5,900
Median sediment concentration (ppm)	1,500	7	1,250	350
Sediment concentration equaled or exceeded 1% of time (ppm)	21,000	700	28,000	15,000

Data based on U.S. Geological Survey records.

Figure 3. Beachfront along a wide, calm section of the Colorado at low water. Note the dense vegetation and eroded, silty fluvial deposits to the left at the level of high water. The rubber raft is one of the larger motorized rigs. (Photo by Alan Howard.)

and 220,000 cfs, in 1921. Sediment concentration during flood peaks varied by more than an order of magnitude, depending upon whether the runoff source was the spring meltwaters in the headwaters of the system or summer thunderstorms over the Colorado plateau.

The river averaged 140 million tons of suspended sediment a year between 1935 and 1948 at the Grand Canyon Gauging Station, near Phantom Ranch (5). The total amount of sediment deposited in Lake Mead over this same period corresponded very closely to the total suspended sediment measured at the gauging station (5), indicating that most of the sediment transported through the Grand Canyon and deposited in Lake Mead was suspended and that the bed load was very small. Under natural conditions the river averaged 0.38 million tons a day; the maximum recorded was 27.6 million tons on 13 September 1927, with a discharge of about 125,000 cfs (5).

Most pre-dam fluvial deposits along the channel are fine-grained terraces, although bars of pebble- to cobble-sized particles do occur locally and may underlie the finer sand and silt terraces. Floods with low-sediment concentration resulted in the net erosion of these fine-grained terraces, whereas the occasional summer peaks resulted in deposition. This alternating erosion and deposition produced a time-varying, fluvial-terrace morphology. Measurements of pre-dam flood-terrace heights taken in 1973 indicate that the terraces in the narrower portions of the canyon are 18 and 30 feet above the present high water. The height of these terraces corresponds to the pre-dam mean annual flood of 80,000 cfs (Fig. 4) and the frequent 120,000 cfs peaks.

A conspicuous line of hardwood vegetation (Fig. 4, Zone C; see also Fig. 5) is associated with the higher terraces. Below them, there was little permanent vegetation under pre-dam conditions, because the cycle of erosion and deposition during floods presented an unstable substrate, either uprooting or burying seedlings. Furthermore, growth of phreatophytes on higher terraces was discouraged by the vertical distance to the water table during summer low water.

Pre-dam flood terraces were deposited in zones of reduced river velocity, such as in the mouths of tributary canyons, in alcoves along the banks, on point bars in the wide sections of the river, and as narrow deposits bordering especially wide, straight stretches of the river. The most common physiographic context for promoting pre-dam flood terraces occurred at the rapids. Almost all of the rapids are formed at

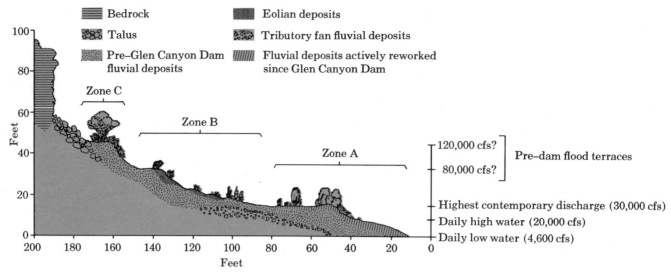

Figure 4. The cross section shows an idealized river deposit under post-dam conditions. The characteristics of the vegetation, sediments, and human use of the 3 zones are listed in Table 2.

points where the river is constricted by the debris fans of tributary washes (Fig. 6). Immediately above and below the falls, a lower-velocity reverse eddy caused deposition of fluvial terraces that mantled the debris fans.

Effects of Glen Canyon Dam

The regulation of flow by Glen Canyon Dam has resulted in a slight increase in median discharge and a great decrease in the number of flood peaks (see Table 1). Since demands for hydroelectric power determine the schedule of discharges, the discharge varies by a factor of about 5 over a 24-hour cycle, resulting in a vertical daily variation of the river by as much as

Table 2.   Characteristics of beach zones in Figure 4

	Zone A	*Zone B*	*Zone C*
Substrate	Post-dam fluvial sediments	Pre-dam fluvial sediments reworked by eolian processes	High pre-dam flood terraces and eolian deposits
Dominant grain size of substrate	Fine sand	Fluvial: fine sand and silt Eolian: fine sand	Fluvial: fine sand and silt Eolian: fine sand
Vegetation density	Sparse to dense	Sparse to dense	Dense
Common species on fine-grained fluvial deposits	*Pluchea sericea* (arrow weed) (S) *Tamarix pentandra* (tamarisk) (SE) *Salix exigua* (coyote willow) (S) *Cynodon dactylon* (Bermuda grass) (E)	*Pluchea sericea* (arrow weed) (S) *Bromus rubens* (red brome) (E) *Alhigi camelorum* (camel thorn) (SE) *Salsola kali* (Russian thistle) (E) An unidentified composite	*Fallugia paradoxia* (Apache plume) (S) *Acacia greggii* (cat-claw acacia) (ST) *Prosopis juliflora* (honey mesquite) (ST) *Baccharis sarothroides* (desert broom) (S)
Human use	Mooring, bathing; high portion occasionally used for camping and thus for cooking, etc.	Camping, cooking, disposal of human wastes	Little use because of dense vegetation, distance from river, steep slopes
Undesirable human impact	Ephemeral but probably contributes to accelerated erosion	Accumulation of scraps and chemically treated human waste; damage to vegetative cover and soil leading to wind erosion; direct erosion by man along paths and on steep slopes	Little impact

(E) = exotic invader (S) = shrub (T) = tree
(Species identification by Roy Johnson)

Figure 5. The line of hardwood vegetation marks the pre-dam flood level (120,000 cfs?). The lower terrace is at the present high-water mark (24,000 cfs). (Photo by Robert Dolan.)

15 feet. The mean daily high discharged from the dam is about 20,000 cfs, and the daily low is 4,600 cfs, with extremes ranging from 2,000 to 27,000 cfs. Discharge during holidays and weekends is low in response to decreased power demand. Arrival of peak flow downstream is, of course, delayed because of the finite water velocity. (River guides, who carefully take these daily fluctuations into account because most major rapids are less dangerous during higher water, plan their trips to avoid following the weekend low water as it proceeds downstream.)

The effect of the Glen Canyon Dam on the Colorado's sediment load has also been dramatic. At Lees Ferry, the median suspended-sediment concentration has been reduced by a factor of about 200 (Table 1). Farther downstream, however, there is less reduction because of additional sediment from tributaries and from the continuing erosion of pre-dam terraces and of

the channel bed; at the gauging station near Phantom Ranch the factor of reduction is about 3½.

Changes in the hydraulic regime of the Colorado have markedly changed the alluvial morphology and the vegetation patterns along the river. The extensive pre-dam flood deposits have been eroded directly by the river and by the seepage of groundwater from terraces during daily low water. In many locations lateral erosion stops after the exposure of coarse fluvial gravels, fan deposits, or talus, which under present controlled discharges resist movement (Fig. 7). Even where the river deposits are not protected from lateral erosion by coarse debris, a dynamic equilibrium may be reached where episodes of deposition and erosion become roughly balanced. Photographic comparisons of pre-dam and post-dam beach morphology provide examples of both marked erosion (Fig. 8) and nearly indistinguishable change.

In the fall of 1972 and again in the spring of 1973, floods of the Little Colorado River produced discharges into the lower canyon of 34,000 cfs. Sediment contributed from this tributary and from bed scour built up 1 to 3 feet of fine sand and silt on the fluvial deposits not inundated by post-dam discharges of the main branch of the river (Fig. 9). This resulted in the lateral growth of bars and terraces by as much as several tens of feet. During the 1973 float trip, we saw that these flood deposits were being extensively eroded. A long-term balance between erosion and deposition is thus more likely to be established along the lower canyon, where the accumulated contribution of sediment from tributaries and from the continued erosion of canyon terraces is greatest.

The terrace and eolian deposits above the present high-water level (Fig. 4, Zones B and C) are primarily modified by the wind. Much of this sand will eventually be lost ei-

Figure 6. This oblique aerial view, looking upstream, shows the alluvial fan and terrace deposits at Soap Creek Rapids (Mile 11). The river above the rapids is approximately 200 feet wide. The triangular alluvial fan deposited by Soap Creek enters from the left, constricting the channel and forming rapids. Severe erosion since Glen Canyon Dam has removed most of the shorefront sand and silt. The terrace deposits covering the fan have also been reworked by the wind into sparsely vegetated dunes. (Photo by Alan Howard.)

ther back to the river or to the land areas well above the river, depending upon the prevailing wind directions.

The lack of occasional high water has allowed many plants to become more firmly established and to expand onto the remnant floodplain deposits. These recent invaders are densest on the steep, silty beaches and along wide, still-water stretches of the river where erosion is slowest. The most common of these plants is the tamarisk, an exotic shrub introduced from the Middle East to decorate the shores of Southwestern reservoirs (6). Although the tamarisk does help to hold some of the deposits in place, it often forms a veritable jungle along the river's banks. Other plants that have moved into reduced stress zones are the cattail, brittle bush, Russian thistle, mesquite, arrow weed, camel thorn, and sparse willow (Table 2). In addition to the rapid development of new plant communities along the banks, the shallow-water areas of the river channel are becoming covered with a thick green algal growth (Roy Johnson, pers. comm.), resulting from the reduced stress along the bed and the increased light penetration through the sediment-free waters.

Murphy (7) has reported that the

fish population is undergoing drastic changes in its species composition because of the changing river regime. Many endemic species (squawfish and bonytail chub) adapted to the turbulent, turbid waters are rapidly disappearing (8), and sluggish-water species (bass and baitfish) are now populating the newly created clear-water "tidal" habitat.

The river guides have raised a question concerning the long-term effects of the Glen Canyon Dam on the Grand Canyon rapids. As indicated earlier, the majority of the 161 Colorado River rapids were created when alluvial fan materials too large to be moved by the parent stream were deposited in the channel by flash flooding of the tributaries. These alluvial fans were continually altered by erosion and deposition as long as peak flows on the order of 50,000 cfs occurred (pre-dam); however, deposition of the large alluvial debris continues and is now unchecked by the balancing erosion of occasional major floods. The guides believe that some of the rapids are becoming more severe and therefore more dangerous. Increased exposure of boulders in the rapids by erosion of sand and small cobbles as well as cementation of boulders by travertine may add to navigation problems.

Quantification of erosion rates and of the balance between sediment losses and deposition is difficult. Base-line studies have not been made, and there is no systematic measurement program. This data gap can be partially bridged through photogrammetric comparison of pre-dam and post-dam aerial photography. A detailed comparison of this type is now being made by the authors. In addition, establishment of several field sites for continual monitoring of long-term changes in riverfront morphology and vegetation is expected within a year.

Man's use of the Colorado

Although hundreds of thousands of people visit the Grand Canyon's rims yearly, very few hikers reach the Canyon floor, and, until recently, even fewer people made boat

Figure 7. Beaches in the narrow Granite Gorge section of the river are small, infrequent, and very susceptible to erosion, which exposes the underlying coarse rock debris, making camping and mooring difficult. (Photo by Alan Howard.)

Figure 8. A comparison of Trail Canyon beach at Mile 219 under pre-dam conditions in 1932 (top) and post-dam conditions in 1969 (bottom) shows pronounced erosion. (1932 photo by John H. Maxson; 1969 photo by Art Gallenson.)

In the summer of 1973, our research team stopped at more than 100 campsites specifically selected to represent examples of the various beach types. We were unable to detect any significant degradation of the beaches and adjacent areas because of littering or waste disposal. National Park Service regulations require commercial outfitters to carry chemical toilets and to leave the beaches as clean as possible. Most comply and haul their trash and waste out of the canyon; however, the direct impact of thirty to forty people conducting the normal bathing, cooking, and camping routine was found to be significant. We noted that footpaths on some beaches had resulted in surface erosion of up to two feet, and a one-foot reduction was common. In addition, heavy foot traffic roughens surfaces that are periodically inundated, contributing to accelerated sediment losses during the following diurnal high water.

Some conservationists are convinced that this heavy commercial use is leading to irreversible erosion and even more rapid degradation of the river's deposits. In addition to the concern about erosion trends and ecological changes, the National Park Service is equally worried about overall degradation of the Grand Canyon "wilderness experience." Outboard motors are one of the major contributors to noise pollution. Also, since all the outfitters usually schedule their trips to coincide with the high-water periods, the more scenic stops tend to be congested and overused. Most of the outfitters disagree with this viewpoint, as one would expect, and, in fact, a recent study by Boster (9) shows that most people making river trips do not consider crowding to be a serious problem.

Figure 9. On a terrace deposited in 1973 as a result of flooding of the Little Colorado River, the 3-foot-thick deposits (vertical bank) partially buried the beachfront cottonwood (*right*) and willow (*left*). Subsequent lateral erosion has reexposed many of these plants' lower branches. The cottonwood, willow, and tamarisk are adapted to such episodes of alternating burial and erosion. (Photo by Alan Howard.)

trips down the Colorado. During the mid-1960s, however, when Marble Canyon and Grand Canyon were threatened by plans for two new hydroelectric dams, the battle between conservationists and the Bureau of Reclamation received national publicity, and before a ten-year moratorium was placed on the project, thousands hastened to travel through the Grand Canyon "before dam builders ruined it." Many celebrities also rushed to ride the rapids, providing additional publicity. By 1969, the Grand Canyon river trip had become one of the world's best-known white-water river trips, described by some as the finest wilderness experience in North America.

With the exception of a few National Park Service patrol boats and a very limited number of private white-water boats, the Grand Canyon float trips are conducted by a dozen or so commercial outfitters. The commercial boats are of two types: the smaller rowing rigs carry

from two to twelve passengers with a crew of one or two, and the larger outboard-motor-powered rubber boats can accommodate between seventeen and twenty passengers and a crew of two (see Fig. 3). The outfitters usually run two or more boats together, for a party of forty passengers, the maximum permitted by the National Park Service. These people remain together throughout the five- to eighteen-day trip.

The outfitters and their passengers must use one of the river bars, or beaches, for camping each night, and most parties stop at one of the beaches for lunch. This means that, at the more desirable campsites, between thirty and forty people may use the beaches each summer evening. Human impact includes occasional litter, burial of chemically treated waste, and the direct stress associated with people walking on the vegetation and unstable sedimentary deposits. Effects of this usage are summarized in Table 2.

The future

It is a much simpler task to list the environmental problems along the post-dam Colorado than it is to recommend specific solutions. It appears unlikely that anything can be done to increase the sediment yield or the flood stages of the upper Colorado River as long as the Glen Canyon Dam is in place. Diversion of waters from the upper reaches of the system to areas below the dam has been suggested as one possible solution; however, this would require such a major commitment of resources that it seems impractical at this time. Therefore, we must face the realization that we have created a new environment in the Grand Canyon and that the physical and ecological adjustments presently underway are inevitable.

The system is now so modified that the earlier natural state can no longer serve as the standard. For this reason our focus should be on the processes and rates of adjustment to the new river regime. To do this, new data and new investigations are needed. In the meantime, however, the National Park Service must face several difficult decisions concerning regulation of man's use of the river. If human impact on the physical environment is high compared to the post-dam degradation by fluvial and eolian processes, then low quotas are a certainty. If, on the other hand, the human impact is low compared to the post-dam erosion rates, then use may be restricted more by social concerns—for the quality of the wilderness experience, for example —than by environmental concerns. Since 1970 the National Park Service has been limiting use of the river to approximately 10,000 visitors a year; this level is probably the upper limit for the admittedly subjective criterion of a true wilderness experience.

Summary

The Colorado River in its natural state often discharged more than 80,000 cfs and carried an average of 0.38 million tons of sand and silt a day through the Grand Canyon. This high water scoured the bottom of the canyon and eroded and redeposited material on the river shores, keeping the river channel navigable for small boats and rafts. In 1963, the river was impounded by Glen Canyon Dam, and the water released by the dam is a turbid-free, powerful erosive agent. Daily the discharge varies from 4,000 cfs to about 20,000 cfs, creating many effects and problems.

The sediment-free water erodes the existing beach areas but does not resupply the sand lost either to the wind or directly into the river. The reduced discharge is less capable of clearing the river channel of flash-flood material brought in by tributaries, thus creating hazardous rapids and falls that may eventually become unnavigable. Diurnal variation in the river's discharge has led to ecological changes along the canyon bottom: exotic plants, for example, are rapidly displacing indigenous species. Increased use of the river by man in recent years appears to be contributing to the erosion problem; however, this impact has not been quantified.

At this time the future of the river bars and terraces is unclear. The system is rapidly approaching a new state at the present rate of change; and it is clear that Emory C. Kolb, one of the pioneer rivermen on the Colorado, was correct when he said, "No one will ever know the Colorado as it really was. It's too late" (10).

References

1. Robert Wallace. 1972. *The Grand Canyon: The American Wilderness.* New York: Time-Life Books, p. 23.

2. Mark A. Boster. 1972. *Colorado River Trips within the Grand Canyon National Park and Monument: A Socioeconomic Analysis.* Technical Report on Hydrology and Water Resources, Rept. #10. Tucson: Univ. of Arizona, p. 24.

3. Kenneth W. Hamblin and J. Keith Rigby. 1969. *Guidebook to the Colorado River,* part 2. Brigham Young Univ. Geologic Studies, vol. 16. Provo, Utah: Brigham Young Univ., p. 24.

4. Luna B. Leopold. 1969. The rapids and the pools: Grand Canyon. In *The Colorado River Region and John Wesley Powell.* Geological Survey Professional Paper 669-D. Washington: U.S. Gov't. Printing Office, p. 135.

5. W. O. Smith, C. P. Vetter, and G. B. Cummings. 1960. *Comprehensive Survey of Sedimentation in Lake Mead, 1948–1949.* Geological Survey Professional Paper 295. Washington: U.S. Gov't. Printing Office, p. 196.

6. David R. Harris. 1971. Recent plant invasions in the arid and semi-arid Southwest of the United States. In *Man's Impact on the Environment,* Thomas R. Detwyler, ed. New York: McGraw-Hill, pp. 469–70.

7. Ref. *3,* p. 13.

8. U.S. Fish and Wildlife Service. 1973. *Threatened Wildlife of the United States.* Bureau of Sport Fisheries and Wildlife, Resource Publ. 114. Washington: U.S. Gov't. Printing Office, p. 35.

9. Ref. *2,* p. 35.

10. Ref. *1,* p. 131.

"To think we used to complain about a little flotsam and jetsam."

PART 5   *Changing the Land*

Erosion of the Land

Sheldon Judson

What's happening to our continents?

Not quite two centuries ago James Hilton, Scottish medical man, agriculturalist, and natural scientist—now enshrined as the founder of modern geology—and Jean Andre de Luc, Swiss emigré, scientist, and reader to England's Queen Charlotte, carried on a spirited discussion concerning the nature and extent of erosion of the natural landscape. Dé Luc believed that once vegetation had spread its protective cloak across the land, erosion ceased. Not so, in Hutton's opinion. He argued (Hutton, 1795):

> According to the doctrine of this author (dé Luc) our mountains of Tweed-dale and Tiviotdale, being all covered with vegetation, are arrived at the period in the course of times when they should be permanent. But is it really so? Do they never waste? Look at rivers in a flood—if these run clear, this philosopher has reasoned right, and I have lost my argument. [But] our clearest streams run muddy in a flood. The great causes, therefore, for the degradation of mountains never stop as long as there is water to run; although as the heights of mountains diminish, the progress of their diminution may be more and more retarded.

We know today, of course, that vegetation plays an important role in the preparation of material for erosion. We know, also, that although vegetation may slow the removal of material from a slope, it does not stop it completely. Hutton's view is overwhelmingly accepted today. Erosion continues in spite of the plant cover, which, in fact, is conducive to certain aspects of erosion. The discussion now centers on the factors determining erosion, the nature of the products of this process, how these products are moved from one place to another, and at what rates the products are being produced. Hutton, in his day, had no data upon which to make a quantitative estimate of the rates at which erosion progressed. Today

Sheldon Judson, who is the Knox Taylor Professor of Geography in the Department of Geological and Geophysical Sciences of Princeton University, traces the course of erosion as it affects the continents on which we live. An undergraduate career in Princeton University was succeeded by A.M. and Ph.D. degrees (geology) at Harvard. Appointed instructor in Geology at the University of Wisconsin immediately thereafter (1948), he was promoted to Assistant Professor in 1949, becoming an associate professor three years later. He was called to Princeton in 1954. Many summers and leaves of absence have been spent in France and Italy making special studies of the geological antiquity of man.

we, unlike Hutton, measure rates of erosion for periods of a fraction of a man's lifetime, as well as for periods of a few hundreds or thousands of years of human history. In addition, radioactive dating and refined techniques of study in field and laboratory allow us to make some quantitative statements about the rates at which our solid lands are wasted and moved particle by particle, ion by ion, to the ocean basins.

This report sets forth some of what we know about these erosional rates. We will understand that erosion is the process by which earth materials are worn away and moved from one spot to another. As such, the action of water, wind, ice, frost-action, plants and animals, and gravity all play their roles. The destination of material eroded is eventually the great world ocean, although there are pauses in the journey and, as we will see later, the material delivered to the ocean must be in some way reincorporated into the continents.

Some modern records

Let us now examine some modern records of erosion of various small areas on the earth's crust, essentially determinations of rates at specific points. There is a large amount of information to be gleaned from agricultural, forestry, and conservation studies as well as from studies by geologists.[1]

Even a casual inspection of our cemeteries demonstrates that some rock goes to pieces at a measurable rate and that rocks have differing resistance to destruction. Figure 1 shows four marble headstones photographed in 1968 in the Princeton, N.J., cemetery. They indicate what can happen to marble in the 172 years involved. The marker erected in 1898 was still easily legible 70 years later, but the crisp, sharp outline of the stone carver's chisel was gone. The headstone erected 70 years earlier was still partially legible in 1968, but the stone put up in 1796 was completely illegible. In this instance the calcite ($CaCO_3$), which makes up the marble, was attacked by a carbonic acid formed by rain water and the CO_2 of the atmosphere. In general, marble headstones become illegible in the humid northeastern states after 150 to 175 years of exposure.

---

[1]Data on erosion are expressed in metric tons per square kilometer and as centimeters of lowering either per year or per thousand years. A specific gravity of 2.6 is assumed for material eroded from the land.

Figure 1. Marble headstones in the Princeton, N.J., cemetery. Headstone in lower left dated 1828. Headstone in lower right is dated 1796. All photographed 1968.

Figure 2. Slate headstone erected 1699. Photographed 1968. Cambridge Burying Ground, Cambridge, Mass. Compare with Figure 1.

In contrast to the marble headstones is the marker shown in Figure 2. The stone stands in the Cambridge, Massachusetts Burying Ground, and was erected in 1699 and photographed in 1968. It is made of slate, often used as a headstone material in many New England cemeteries until marble became fashionable at the turn of the nineteenth century. Unlike marble it is resistant to chemical erosion. Nearly 270 years after the stone was erected the inscription stands out clearly.

Graveyards do most certainly provide examples of the impermanence of rock material as well as of the relative resistance of different rock types. The earliest study in such an environment that I have seen was by Sir Archibald Geikie, in Edinburgh, published in 1880. More recent studies have been made of the rates at which erosion proceeds on tombstones. Thus, in an area near Middletown, Connecticut, it is estimated that tombstones of a local red sandstone are weathering at the rate of about 0.006 centimeters per year (Matthias, 1967). In general, however, a graveyard does not present the best conditions for the accumulation of quantitative data.

More reliable data seem to come from agricultural stations. Here is an example. A summary of measurements has been made at 17 different stations on plots measuring 6 by 72.6 ft and under differing conditions of rainfall, soil, slope, and vegetative cover (Musgrave, 1954). Periods of record in this instance vary between 4 and 11

years. On the average, erosion from plots with continuous grass cover annually lost 75 tons per square kilometer, a lowering of about 3 meters per 1000 years. This is a dramatic demonstration of the role of plants in affecting erosion. In this instance the rate of erosion increased 100 times between grass-covered plots and well-tilled row-crop plots.

Obviously climate will also affect the rate of erosion. For example, recent studies by Washburn (1967) in eastern Greenland show that seasonal freeze and thaw in a nearly glacial climate produce erosion rates ranging between 9 and 37 meters per thousand years. This contrasts with the rates in more temperate climates cited previously. In semiarid lands, where vegetation is discontinuous and rainfall low (± 25 cm per year) and unpredictable, the erosion rates are high, but not as high as those in the rigorous climate of northeastern Greenland. Studies of bristlecone pines in Utah and California have allowed an estimate of erosion rates on a time base of hundreds and even thousands of years (Eardley, 1967). Thus the pines, which may reach 4000 years in age, betray the amount of erosion during their lifetime by the amount of exposure of their root systems. The depth of exposed roots on living trees is a measure of the amount the land surface has been reduced since the tree began to grow (Figure 3). Rates of lowering in general vary with exposure (greater on north-facing slopes) and with declivity of slopes (greater on steeper slopes). On the average, the rate varies between about 2 cm per 1000 years on slopes of 5 degrees and 10 cm on slopes of 30 degrees. A total of 42 observations indicate a direct relation between the erosion rate and the sine of the slope.

A different sort of study, this one in the rain forest of mountains in New Guinea, has yielded the estimate that between 1 and 2 cm per 1000 years is lost from the area by landslides alone (Simonett, 1967). How much additional

Figure 3. Bristlecone pine in Cedar Breaks National Monument, Utah. This tree, 2840 years old, has a strip of living bark being cored through by man at left. Man on right points to level of ground surface when tree began to grow. Depth of exposure of roots indicates amount of lowering of land surface during the life of the tree. (Photograph courtesy of A. J. Eardley.)

Figure 4. Ruins of cistern built in the 2nd century A.D. for a Roman villa. The tape measures 1.30 m of exposed footings and thus the amount of erosion since construction.

material is lost through the agency of other processes is not known.

Archaeological sites may yield information on erosional rates and have, as in the case of the bristlecone pines, a fairly long time base. Data collected in Italy show that for the sites studied the range in rates is 30 to 100 cm per 1000 years (Judson, 1968). Figures 4 and 5 suggest the nature of some of the evidence. Figure 4 shows the remains of a Roman cistern built for a villa about 60 km north of Rome in the second century A.D. The rough-textured base of the wall is the footing for the structure. It was constructed by pouring concrete mixed with angular fragments of rock into a trench. The top of the footings marked the ground surface in the second century A.D. On top of the footing were built the cistern walls. Roughly finished blocks of stone were laid with some care, and groups of courses were separated by layers of tile. Since construction, erosion has exposed the footing, lowering the land surface a total of 1.30 m. Figure 5 shows a section of the Via Prenestina west of Rome. Some of the resistant basalt blocks are still in place. Others have

begun to move down the slope. When the road was constructed, it was level with the surface of the ridge along which it runs. The lithified volcanic ash that forms the ridge is less resistant to erosion than the second-to-third-century B.C. road. The slopes have eroded at the rate of 30 cm per 1000 years so that today the Via Prenestina stands elevated above the general land surface.

These are but a sample of the type of information that abounds in the literature on the rate of erosion. They are enough, however, to indicate how variable the rates can be when, as in the examples cited, the observation is for a single spot or limited area. Not only are they highly variable, but they can hardly be representative of rates of erosion over large areas. It is apparent that the material eroded in one spot may be deposited nearby, at least temporarily, and thus the net loss to an area may be little or nothing. Erosion is more rapid at some spots than others for any one of many different reasons. Material removed from its position at any single spot on the landscape follows a slow, halting, devious course as natural processes transport it from the land to the ocean.

Figure 5. The Via Prenestina led between Rome and Palestrina. This section, built about 200 B.C., lies 25 km from the center of Rome. When built it was flush with the surface of the hill. The road blocks of basalt, however, now stand as a low ridge because the less resistant lithified volcanic ash of the hill has been eroded away.

River records

When we ask now how much material is being lost by the continents to the ocean, the spot measurements such as those reported above are of little help. We need some method of integrating these rates over larger areas. One way to do this is to measure material carried by a stream from its drainage basin at the point where the stream leaves the basin. Alternatively, the amount of sediment deposited in a reservoir or in a natural lake over a specific length of time is indicative of the rate at which the land has been worn away in the basin lying upstream. The mass of sediments accumulated in unit time can be averaged out over the area of the contributing drainage basin to produce an erosion rate. Of course the erosion rate is not uniform over the entire basin, but it is convenient for our purposes here to assume that it is.

If we examine the solid load of a stream carried in suspension past a gauging station, we discover that the amount of material per unit area of the drainage basin varies considerably according to a number of factors. But, if we hold the size of the drainage basin relatively constant, we find pronounced correlation between erosion and precipitation. Figure 6 is based on data presented by Langbein and Schumm (1958) from about 100 sediment gauging stations in basins averaging 3900 sq km. It suggests that a maximum rate of erosion is reached in areas of limited rainfall (± 25 cm per year) and decreases in more arid as well as in more humid lands.

Considering small drainage basins (averaging 78 km²), Langbein and Schumm also show a similar variation in erosion with rainfall, but at rates which are 2 to 3 times as rapid as for the larger basins. In still smaller basins, erosion rates increase even more. A small drainage basin in the Loess Hills of Iowa, having an area of 3.4 km², provides an extreme example. Here sediments are being removed at a rate which produces a lowering for the basin of 12.8 m per 1000 years.

We have data based on river records for larger areas. Judson and Ritter (1964) have surveyed the regional erosion rates in the United States and have shown that, on the average, erosion is proceeding at about 6 cm² per 1000 years. Here too, as shown in Table 1, there are variations. These appear to be related to climate, as in the smaller areas already discussed. Greatest erosion occurs in the dry Colorado River basin. In examining the rates of regional erosion, we note that although erosion rates increase with decrease in discharge per unit area, they do not increase quite as rapidly as the major component, the detrital load, increases. This is so because the absolute dissolved load decreases with decreasing discharge per unit area. This inverse relation between solid and dissolved load is shown in Figure 7.

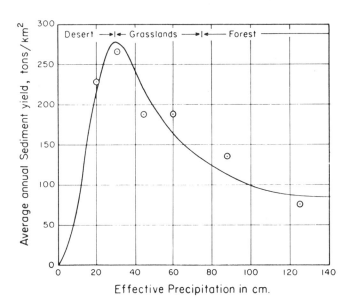

Figure 6. Variation of the yield of sediments with precipitation. Effective precipitation is defined as precipitation necessary to produce a given amount of runoff. (After Langbein and Schumm, 1958.)

Table 1. Rates of Regional Erosion in the United States. (After Judson and Ritter, 1964).

Drainage Region	Drainage[1] Area Km² ×10³	Runoff m³/sec	—Load tons Km²/yr— Dissolved	Solid	Total	Erosion cm/1000 yr	% Area sampled	Avg. years of record
Colorado	629	0.6	23	417	440	17	56	32
Pacific Slopes, California	303	2.3	36	209	245	9	44	4
Western Gulf	829	1.6	41	101	142	5	9	9
Mississippi	3238	17.5	39	94	133	5	99	12
S. Atlantic & Eastern Gulf	736	9.2	61	48	109	4	19	7
N. Atlantic	383	5.9	57	69	126	5	10	5
Columbia	679	9.8	57	44	101	4	39	<2
Totals	6797	46.9	43	119	162	6		

[1]Great Basin, St. Lawrence, Hudson Bay drainage not considered.

These data suggest that on the average the United States is now being eroded at a rate which reduces the land surface by 6 cm each 1000 years. Actually, the rate is somewhat less when we consider that the area of the Great Basin, with no discharge to the sea, is not included in these figures—and that for all practical purposes the net loss from this area is presently close to zero.

Effect of man

What effect does man's use of the land have on the rate at which it is destroyed by natural forces? Three examples are cited here.

Bonatti and Hutchinson have described cores from a small volcanic crater lake, Lago di Monterosi, 41 km north of Rome. (See Judson, 1968, note 3.) An archaelogical survey of the environs of the lake indicates that intense human activity dates from approximately the second century B.C., when the Via Cassia was constructed through the area. At this moment the cores indicate a sudden increase of sedimentation in the lake. The rate varies somewhat but continues high to the present. Extrapolation of the sedimentation rate in the lake to the surrounding watershed shows that prior to intensive occupation by man (that is, prior to the second century B.C.) the erosion rate was 2 to 3 cm per 1000 years. Thereafter it rose abruptly to an average of about 20 cm per 100 years.

Ursic and Dendy (1965) have studied the annual sediment yields from individual watersheds in northern Mississip-

pi. The results of their data are shown in Figure 8. These indicate that, when the land is intensively cultivated, the rate of sediment production and hence the rate of erosion is three orders of magnitude or more above that experienced from areas with mature forest cover or from pine plantations.

Wolman (1967) has described the variation of sediment yield with land use for an area near Washington, D.C. These data are summarized in Figure 9. They show that, under original forest conditions, erosion proceeded at the low rate of about 0.2 cm per 1000 years. With the rapid increase of farmland in the early nineteenth century the rate increased to approximately 10 cm per 1000 years. With the return of some of this land to grazing and forest in the 1940's and 1950's this high rate of erosion was reduced perhaps by one-half. Areas undergoing construction during the 1960's show yields which exceed 100,000 tons per square kilometer for very small areas, which approximate a rate of lowering of 10 m per 1000 years. For completely urban areas the erosion rates are low, less than 1 cm per 1000 years.

There is no question that man's occupancy of the land increases the rate of erosion. Where that occupation is intense and is directed toward the use of land for cultivated crops the difference is one or more orders of magnitude greater than when the land is under a complete natural vegetative cover such as grass or forest. The interventions of man in the geologic processes raises questions when we begin to apply modern rates to the processes of the past before man was a factor in promoting erosion.

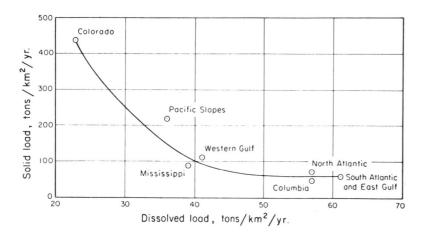

Figure 7. Relation by regions in the United States between solid load and dissolved load in tons/km²/yr. (After Judson and Ritter, 1964.)

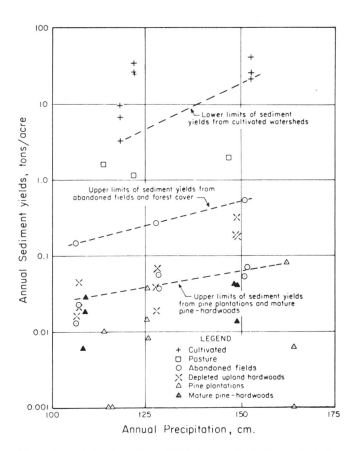

Figure 8. Variation in sediment yields from individual watersheds in northern Mississippi under different types of land use and changing amounts of precipitation. One ton/acre equals 224 tons/km². (After Ursic and Dendy, 1965.)

Ian Douglas (1967) postulates that man's use of the landscape has so increased the rates of erosion that they far exceed those of the past before man became an important geologic agent. He presents persuasive data and arguments to suggest that any computation of present-day erosion rates on a world-wide basis is unrepresentative of rates that predate man's tampering with the landscape. So, as we turn to the question of world-wide erosion, we will want to distinguish between present-day rates which are profoundly affected by man's activity and those of the immediate past before man introduced grazing, agriculture, and other activities.

Let us first attempt an estimate of erosion before man began to affect the process. It is estimated that approximately one-fourth of the United States is in cropland. If

this area is now undergoing a rate of erosion ten times that of its natural rate, then, for the United States as a whole, the increase of rate of erosion because of man's use of the land increases the rate of the removal of solid particles from the earth's crust by a factor of a little over three times. Assuming that this is correct and that the dissolved load does not change appreciably, then, as a first approximation, the present rates of erosion listed in Table 1 for the United States would be decreased to approximately 3 cm per 1000 years, which is about 78 tons per square kilometer per year. This figure would apply then to the area of the United States before the intervention of man with intensive agricultural practices.

Rates for entire earth

What can we say now about the rate of erosion for the entire earth? Presented in Table 2 are data for approximately 10 per cent of the earth's surface. The table includes erosional data for the drainage basins for the Amazon, the world's largest river; the Congo; and for that part of the United States covered in Table 1. Here, however, the data for the United States have been adjusted to account for the increased rates of erosion presumed to have occurred because of man's cultivation of the land. Neither the Congo nor the Amazon basins are significantly affected by man [in 1968]. For the 15 million square kilometers of these areas, the average rate of erosion is 3.6 cm per 1000 years, or 93 tons per square kilometer annually.

Let us accept the figures just given as representative of erosion rates prior to man's intervention in the process and use them to extrapolate to erosion rates for the whole area of the earth. The earth's land surface has approximately 151 million square kilometers, but much of this area has no streams that drain directly to the ocean. For example, a large area of the western United States is without direct drainage to the sea, as is a large percentage, about 50 per cent, of Australia. Areas of little or no drainage to the sea are estimated to occupy approximately one-third of the earth's surface. So for our purposes we estimate that 100 million kilometers of the earth's surface are contributing sediments directly to the sea by running water. In addition to this there is a certain amount of wind erosion, and part of the materials eroded by the wind are delivered to the sea. It is even more difficult to find data on the amounts of regional erosion by wind than it is for erosion by running water. We have some preliminary estimates for the amount of eolian material

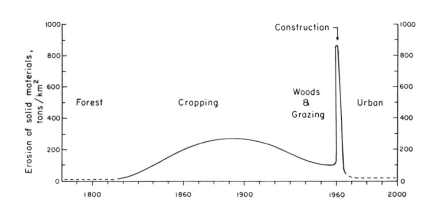

Figure 9. A sequence of land use changes and sediment yield beginning prior to the advent of extensive farming and continuing through a period of construction and subsequent urban landscape. Based on experience in the Middle Atlantic region of the United States. (After Wolman, 1967.)

Table 2. Rates of Erosion for the Amazon River Basin, United States, and Congo River Basin.

Drainage Region	Drainage Area Km² × 10⁶	Load, tons × 10⁶/yr Dissolved	Solid	Total	Tons Km²/yr	Erosion cm/1000 yr
Amazon River[1]						
Basin	6.3	232	548[2]	780	124	4.7
United States[3]	6.8	292	248[3]	540	78	3.0
Congo River[4]						
Basin	2.5	99	34[2]	133	53	2.0
Totals	15.6	623	830	1453	93	3.6

[1] From Gibbs, 1967.

[2] Solid load increased by considering bed load as 10% of suspended load.

[3] From Judson and Ritter, 1964. Solid load reduced to adjust for increased erosion because of man's activity.

[4] From Spronck, 1941, quoted in Gibbs 1967.

which has been dumped into the oceans. These lie between 1 and 0.25 mm per 1000 years.[2] Whatever the figure, wind erosion of the land is volumetrically unimportant when compared with the amount of material carried by the streams.

We can estimate, then, the amount of sediment carried as solids and as dissolved material from the continents to the ocean basins each year as 9.3×10^9 tons. This figure is based on the assumption that, on the average, 3.6 cm per 1000 years are eroded from the 100 million square kilometers of land which are estimated to drain into the oceans. Further, the figure attempts to eliminate the effect on the erosion rate of man's activity. If we include an estimate for the amount of erosion by wind action, then this figure increases by an amount approximating 10^8 tons. Glacier ice may add a similar amount.

We can now compare this estimate of the tonnage of eroded materials with other esimates in the following paragraphs and Table 3.

[2]Although data are very incomplete the interested reader will find some specific information in Bonatti and Arrhenius (1965); Delany, et al. (1967); Folger and Heezen (in press); Goldberg and Griffin (1964); Rex and Goldberg (1958, 1962); and Riseborough, et al. (1968).

Barth (1962) presents data on some geochemical cycles, indicating that weathering of the land produces on the average of 2.5 kg per cm² per million years. From this figure we calculate that the average tonnage per year of all material, dissolved and solid, would be 3.8×10^9 tons, which seems low. Strakhov (1967) quotes Lopatin (1950) to the effect that annual dissolved and solid loads of the rivers total 17.5×10^9 tons, of which 4.9×10^9 tons are dissolved material. Two other estimates on dissolved loads should be quoted. Clarke (1924) estimates 2.7×10^9 tons per year and Livingstone (1963) 3.9×10^9 tons per year. This last figure can be duplicated by extrapolation of the data in Table 3. Livingstone indicates that the figure might be high. Indeed new figures on the salinity and discharge of the Amazon River by Gibbs (1967) indicate that Livingstone's figure should be adjusted downward by 5 per cent.

MacKenzie and Garrels (1966) estimate that the rivers of the world carry 8.3×10^9 tons of *solid material alone* to the oceans each year. In arriving at this figure they adopted from Livingstone an average annual world-wide runoff of 3.3×10^{16} liters and an average suspended sediment concentration equal to that of the Mississippi River. If man's occupancy has indeed increased erosion rates as we have suggested, then this figure is high.

Table 3. Estimates of World-Wide Erosion Rates by Various Authors. (All material assumed to reach the oceans).

	10⁹ metric tons/yr
Carried by Rivers	
Dissolved Load	
Livingstone (1963)	3.9
Clarke (1924)	2.7
Solid Load[1]	
Fournier (1960) as calculated by Holeman (1968)	58
Kuenen (1950)	32.5
Schumm (1963) as calculated by Holeman (1968)	20.5
Holeman 1968	18.3
MacKenzie and Garrels (1967)	8.3
Combined Solid and Dissolved Loads	
Lopatin (1950)[1]	17.5
Judson (this paper)[2]	9.3
Barth (1962)[2]	3.8
Carried by Wind from Land	
Calculated from various sources	0.06-0.36
Carried by Glacier Ice	
Estimated	0.1

[1] Does not include bed load.

[2] Solid load includes both suspended and bed load.

Kuenen (1950) gives an estimate for solid load of 32.5×10^9 tons per year, a high estimate, the basis for which is not clear.

Even higher is the estimate of 58×10^9 tons of suspended load calculated by Holeman (1968) from data in Fournier (1960). Douglas (1967) points out that the data presented by Fournier seem to be strongly influenced by man's activity. Holeman also extrapolates data of Schumm (1963) from selected drainage basins in the central United States to obtain a figure of 18.3×10^9 tons of suspended sediment per year. These data, too, are affected by man. Holeman, himself (1968), presents suspended sediment data for rivers draining 39 million square kilometers of the earth's surface and extrapolates this to the approximately 100 million square kilometers of land surface draining to the ocean. He obtains a figure of 18.3×10^9 tons per year of suspended sediments carried annually to the oceans. The figure is strongly affected by data from the Asiatic rivers, particularly those of China, India, and the Southeast. These provide 80 per cent of the total sediment from 25 per cent of the land area in Holeman's figures. These are the same continental areas where the world's population is most concentrated and where the largest areas of intensive agriculture are located.

Let us now estimate the present rate of erosion. In this the major component is the suspended load carried by rivers. Of the data available, Holeman's appear to be the most inclusive and reliable. Allowing the bed load to be 10 per cent of suspended load and adding these two figures to the dissolved load as calculated by Livingstone, then the total material delivered annually to the sea by rivers at the present is 24×10^9 metric tons. This is about two and one-half times the rate that we estimated existed before man started tampering with the landscape on a large scale (see Table 4).

Returning now to our estimate of the material produced by erosion before the serious intervention by man, we should be able to check our figure by comparing it with the amount of material deposited annually in the oceans. Thus far our only way of determining annual sedimentation rates over large areas is to average them out over the last several thousand years. Because man has only recently become a world-wide influence on erosion, this averaging serves to curtail his impact on the rate of accumulation of the sedimentary record.

Table 4. Mass of Material Estimated as Moved Annually by Rivers to the Ocean Before and After the Intervention of Man.

	10^9 metric tons
Before man's intervention	9.3
After man's intervention	24

What figures do we have on sedimentation in the oceans? Large areas of the ocean floor and the rates at which sedimentation takes place there are but dimly known at the present. We have data from coring of the ocean bottom, but our data are scanty at best. In considering the tonnage which settles annually to the ocean floors, we should distinguish between the deep oceans and the shallower oceans. As far as sedimentation goes, there is probably a difference between those ocean floors lying below 3000 m and those above 3000 m. For the deep seas—those below 3000 m—current figures suggest something like 4.2×10^{-4} gm per cm^2 per year.[3] Spread over the nearly 280,000,000 km^2 of area for the deep sea, this amounts to 1.17×10^9 tons of sediments per year. Estimates for the shallower waters are probably less reliable than for the deep waters. For those waters shallower than 3000 m, about 72,000,000 km^2, I have assumed that between 10 and 20 cm of sediment accumulates every thousand years. Given a density of 0.7, there would be approximately 7 to 14×10^{-3} gm deposited for each square centimeter per year. This is equivalent to a total tonnage of between 5 and 10×10^9 tons per year. Totaling the tonnage for the deep and shallow waters, we have a range of 6.2 to 11.2×10^9 tons. Most of this is provided by the rivers. Wind provides an estimated 10^8 tons per year. The contribution of ice is also estimated as 10^8 tons. Extra-terrestrial material is estimated by various authors as between 3.5×10^4 to 1.4×10^8 tons per year (Barker and Anders, 1968). Table 5 compares the estimate of the amount of material deposited each year in the oceans with the esimate of the amount delivered by various agents annually to the oceans. In both estimates we have tried to eliminate the effect of man.

Whether we use the rate of erosion prevailing before or after man's advent, our figures pose the problem of why

[3] I use data from deep sea cores as reported by Ku, Broecker and Opdyke, 1968. In calculating weights of sediments from rates of sedimentation I have used a density of 0.7 per cm^3 (Ku, personal communication, 1968) and sedimentation rates which include original $CaCO_3$ content.

Table 5. Estimated Mass of Material Deposited Annually in the Oceans Compared with Estimated Mass of Material Delivered Annually to the Oceans by Different Agents.[1]

	10^9 metric tons/year
Estimated mass of material deposited in ocean	
Oceans shallower than 3000 meters	5–10
Oceans deeper than 3000 meters	1.17
Total	6.2–11.2
Estimated mass of material delivered to oceans	
From continents	
By rivers	9.3
By wind	0.06–0.36
By glacier ice	0.1
From extraterrestrial sources	0.00035–0.14
Total	~9.6

[1] Man's influence on rates of erosion is excluded from estimates.

our continents have survived. If we accept the rate of sediment production as 10^{10} metric tons per year (the pre-human intervention figure) then the continents are being lowered at the rate of 2.4 cm per 100 years. At this rate the ocean basins, with a volume of 1.37×10^{18} m³, would be filled in 340 million years. The geologic record indicates that this has never happened in the past, and there is no reason to believe it will happen in the geologically forseeable future. Furthermore, at the present rate of erosion, the continents, which now average 875 m in elevation, would be reduced to close to sea level in about 34 million years. But the geologic record shows a continuous sedimentary history, and hence a continuous source of sediments. So we reason that the continents have always been high enough to supply sediments to the oceans.

Geologists long ago concluded that the earth was a dynamic system, being destroyed in some places and renewed in others. Such a state would help resolve the problem of what happens to the sediments and why continents persist. Thus, although the sediments are carried from continents to oceans to form sedimentary rocks, we know that these rocks may be brought again to the continental suface. There they are, in turn, eroded and the products of erosion returned to the ocean. These sedimentary rocks may also be subjected to pressures and temperatures which convert them from sedimentary rocks to metamorphic rocks. If this pressure and temperature is great enough, the metamorphic rocks, in turn, will melt and become the parent material of igneous rock. These relationships are the well-known rock cycle, which has been going on as long as we can read the earth's rock record. In simplified form it is repeated in Figure 10.

Inasmuch as we have been talking about the sedimentary aspects of the rock cycle, we should ask how much time it takes to complete at least the sedimentary route within the whole cycle. Poldervaart (1954) gives the total mass of sediments (including the sedimentary rocks) as 1.7×10^{18} tons. Taking the annual production of sediments as 10^{10} tons, then one turn in the sedimentary cycle approximates 1.7×10^8 years. At the present rates, then, we could fit in about 25 such cycles during the 4.5 billion years of earth history.

Accepting Poldervaart's figure of 2.4×10^{19} tons as the mass of the earth's crust, then there has been time enough for a mass equivalent to the earth's crust to have moved two times through the sedimentary portion of the cycle.

We began this review with a brief examination of the homely process of erosion. As we continued we found that man has appeared on the scene as an important geologic agent, increasing the rates of erosion by a factor of two or three. We end the review face to face with larger problems. Regardless of the role of man, the reality of continental erosion raises anew the question of the nature and origin of the forces that drive our continents above sea level. In short, we now seek the mechanics of continental survival.

References

Barker, John L., Jr. and Edward Anders, 1968. Accretion rate of cosmic matter from irridium and osmium contents of

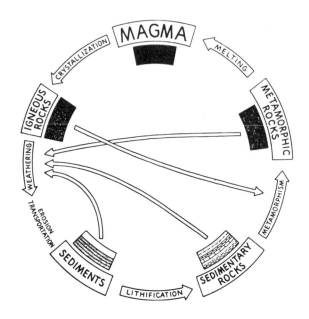

Figure 10. The rock cycle. (From Leet and Judson, 1965.)

deep-sea sediments. *Geochimica et Cosmochimica Acta, 32,* pp. 627–645.

Barth, T. F. W., 1962. *Theoretical Petrology.* 2nd edition. John Wiley & Sons, Inc.: New York and London, 416 pp.

Bonatti, E. and G. Arrhenius, 1965. Eolian sedimentation in the Pacific off northern Mexico. *Marine Geology, 3,* pp. 337–348.

Clarke, F. W., 1924. Data of geochemistry, 5th edition, *U.S. Geological Survey, Bulletin 770,* 841 p.

Delany, A. C., *et al.,* 1967. Airborne dust collected at Barbados. *Geochimica et Cosmochimica Acta, 31,* pp. 885–909.

Douglas, Ian, 1967. Man, vegetation and the sediment yields of rivers. *Nature, 215,* Pt. 2, pp. 925–28.

Eardley, A. G., 1967. Rates of denudation as measured by bristlecone pines, Cedar Breaks, Utah. *Utah Geological and Mineralogical Survey, Special Studies, 21,* 13 p.

Folger, D. W. and B. C. Heezen. (in press), Trans Atlantic sediment transport by wind. (abstract) *Geological Society of America.* Special paper.

Fournier, F., 1960. *Climat et Erosion,* Presses Universitaires de France.

Geikie, Archibald, 1880. Rock-weathering as illustrated in Edinburgh churchyards. *Proceedings, Royal Society, Edinburgh, 10,* pp. 518–532.

Gibbs, R. J., 1967. The geochemistry of the Amazon River system: Part I, *Bulletin, Geological Society of America, 78,* pp.1203–1232.

Goldberg, E. D. and J. J. Griffin, 1964. Sedimentation rates and mineralogy in the South Atlantic. *Jour. of Geophysical Research, 69,* pp. 4293–4309.

Holeman, John N., 1968. The Sediment Yield of Major Rivers of the World. *Water Resources Research, 4,* No. 4, pp. 737–747.

Hutton, James, 1795. *Theory of the earth.* Vol. 2, Edinburgh.

Judson, Sheldon, 1968. Erosion rates near Rome, Italy. *Science, 160,* pp. 1444–1446.

Judson, Sheldon and D. F. Ritter, 1964. Rates of regional denudation in the United States. *Journal of Geophysical Research, 69,* pp. 3395–3401.

Ku, Teh-Lung, W. S. Broecker, and Neil Opdyke, 1968. Comparison of sedimentation rates measure by paleomagnetic and the ionium methods of age determinations. *Earth and Planetary Science Letters, 4,* pp. 1–6.

Kuenen, Ph. H., 1950. *Marine Geology.* John Wiley and Sons: New York and London, 551 p.

Langbein, W. B. and S. A. Schumm, 1958. Yield of sediment in relation to mean annual precipitation. *Transactions, American Geophysical Union, 39,* pp. 1076–1084.

Leet, L. Don and Sheldon Judson, 1965. *Physical Geology.* 3d edition. Prentice-Hall, Inc.: Englewood Cliffs, N.J., 406 p.

Livingstone, D.A., 1963. Chemical Composition of Rivers and Lakes. *U.S. Geological Survey Professional Paper* 440-G., 64 p.

Lopatin, G. V., 1950. Erosion and detrital discharge. *Priroda,* No. 7. (Quoted by Strakhov, 1967.)

MacKenzie, F. T. and R. M. Garrels, 1966. Chemical mass balance between rivers and oceans. *American Journal of Science, 264,* pp. 507–525.

Matthias, George F., 1967. Weathering rates of Portland arkose tombstones. *Journal of Geological Education, 15,* pp. 140–144.

Musgrave, G. W., 1954. Estimating land erosion-sheet erosion. *Association Internationale d'Hydrologie Scientifique, Assemblee Generale de Rome, 1,* pp. 207–215.

Poldervaart, Arie, 1954. Chemistry of the earth's crust, in *Crust of the Earth.* Edited by A. Poldervaart. Geological Society of America Special Paper 62, p. 119–144.

Rex, R. W. and E. D. Goldberg, 1958. Quartz content of pelagic sediments of the Pacific Ocean. *Tellus, 10,* pp. 153–159.

Riseborough, R. W., R. J. Huggett, J. J. Griffin, and E. D. Goldberg, 1968. Pesticides: Transatlantic movements in the northeast trades. *Science, 159,* pp.1233–1236.

Schumm, S. A., 1963. The disparity between present rates of denudation and orogeny, *U.S. Geological Survey,* Prof. Paper 45411, pp. 1–13.

Simonett, David S., 1967. Landslide distribution and earthquakes in the Bewani and Torricelli Mountains, New Guinea, in *Landscape Studies from Australia and New Guinea,* Edited by J. N. Jennings and J. A. Mabbutt, Australian National University Press: Canberra, pp. 64–84.

Spronck, R., 1941. Mesures hydrographique effectuées dans la region divagante du Bief Maritime du Fleuve Congo. *Brussels, Institute Royale Colonial Belge Memoire.* 156 p. (quoted by Gibbs, 1967).

Strakhov, N. M. 1967, *Principles of Lithogenesis,* vol. 1. Translated from the 1962 Russian edition by J. P. Fitzsimmons. Oliver and Boyd: Edinburgh and London, 245 p.

Ursic, S. J. and F. E. Dendy, 1965. Sediment yields from small watersheds under various land uses and forest covers. *Proceedings of the Federal Inter-Agency Sedimentation Conference, 1963, U.S. Department of Agriculture,* Miscellaneous Publications 970, pp. 47–52.

Washburn, A. L., 1967. Instrumental observations of mass-wasting in the Mesters Vig district, northeast Greenland. *Meddeleser om Gronland, 166,* No. 4, pp. 1–296.

Wolman, M. G., 1967. A cycle of sedimentation and erosion in urban river channels. *Geografiska Annaler, 49-A,* pp. 385–395.

The Lessons of the Dust Bowl

William Lockeretz

Several decades before the current concern with environmental problems, dust storms ravaged the Great Plains, and the threat of more dust storms still hangs over us

The dust storms of the 1930s were the worst man-made environmental problem the United States has ever seen, whether measured in physical terms or by their human and economic impact. Indeed, at a time when we are so concerned about air pollution measured in parts per billion, it is hard to picture dust so thick that pedestrians could literally bump into each other in the middle of the day. The term *air pollution* scarcely begins to describe a cloud several miles high carrying hundreds of millions of tons of dust as far as several thousand miles.

Yet airborne dust was only one part—certainly the most spectacular part—of an even greater problem. For the blowing dust once was topsoil, and topsoil was the most valuable and productive resource of the area known as the Dust Bowl, which included considerable portions of Texas, New Mexico, Colorado, Oklahoma, and Kansas (see Fig. 1). Blowing soil came to symbolize dramatically the breakdown of an agricultural system that was the basis of the region's economy and social order. When the dust had settled, the region not only had to recover from staggering economic losses and human suffering but also faced the more far-reaching challenge of re-

William Lockeretz is a senior agricultural scientist at the Northeast Solar Energy Center. He was formerly in the Center for the Biology of Natural Systems at Washington University, where his work included a long-term research project on resource conservation in agricultural production. He received his B.S. from City College of New York and his M.A. and Ph.D. from Harvard. Address: Northeast Solar Energy Center, 470 Atlantic Ave., Boston, MA 02110.

structuring its fundamental economic activity to ensure that the problem would never recur. Unfortunately, new dust storms in the past few years—although not nearly as severe as those of the 1930s—suggest that even today this goal has not been fully achieved.

Those who experienced the dust storms generally said that they were almost beyond description. Soil conservationist Russell Lord (1938) called them "as nearly a literal hell on earth as can be imagined." During a bad dust storm, any semblance of normal activity was out of the question. Homes, barns, tractors, and fields were buried under drifts up to 25 feet high (Fig. 2). The sky could turn completely black in a matter of minutes, and at times dust obscured the sun for several days (Fig. 3). Some people actually thought they were seeing the end of the world.

Even wet towels stuffed in the cracks of windows could not keep the dust out, and from across the room an electric light might look no brighter than the tip of a cigarette. Everything in the house—even food in the refrigerator—was covered with dust. To be able to breathe, people covered their faces with wet cloths, but continuously breathing the damp air only aggravated the effects of the dust. Each storm was followed by many cases of serious lung damage, and some proved fatal.

Dust storms were extremely frequent on the Great Plains during the mid-thirties, although they were not always intense and long-lasting. There were an average of nine storms per month during the first four months of each year (the main dust storm season) from 1933 to 1936 at Amarillo,

Texas, and in one month there were dust storms on 23 days (Choun 1936). These storms lasted an average of about ten hours, and during about one-fifth of them visibility reached zero.

The record at Amarillo was not particularly unusual. At various times serious wind erosion, and sometimes full-blown "black blizzards," hit virtually every part of the Plains, not just the Dust Bowl. For example, the great dust storm of May 1934, which deposited large amounts of dust on the East Coast and the North Atlantic (Hand 1934; Mattice 1935), originated in the Dakotas and Nebraska. The most severe storms occurred from 1933 to 1938 on the Southern Plains, and from 1933 to 1936 in the north.

The economic and social consequences of the dust storms were aggravated by two other problems—drought and depression—that made recovery much more difficult. The severe and protracted drought that began in 1931 and precipitated the dust storms damaged crops even on fields that escaped blowing, not just on those that contributed to the storms. Moreover, because of the Depression, farmers got very low prices for whatever crops they were able to produce. It is hard to separate the interacting effects of the dust storms, drought, and depression, but we can say that the storms made an already distressing situation much worse.

Farmers bankrupted by dust storms joined the ranks of tenants and farm laborers who were displaced by machines ("tractored out") and who could find no other jobs in the depressed region (Stein 1973). The re-

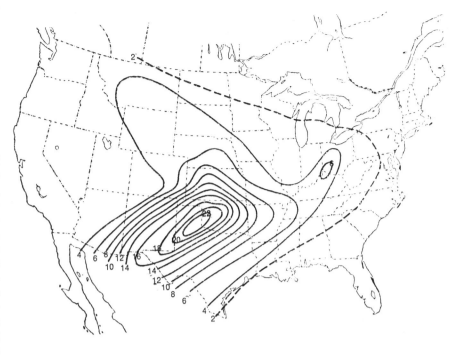

Figure 1. The contours indicate the number of days with dust storms or dusty conditions during March 1936. During the 1930s the main dust storm area shifted from month to month. The worst area on the Southern Plains during 1933–38 corresponds roughly to the 16-day contour on this map shifted about 200 miles to the northwest. (From Martin 1936.)

sulting movement of hundreds of thousands of Dust Bowl refugees to the West Coast—so vividly portrayed in *The Grapes of Wrath*—was without precedent in the country's history. Those who were able to remain faced equally discouraging prospects. In 1937 the Soil Conservation Service estimated that 43 percent of a 16-million-acre area in the heart of the Dust Bowl had been seriously damaged by wind erosion (Joel 1937), a major resource loss for a region almost entirely dependent on agriculture. In some Southern Plains counties, more than half of all farm families were on relief in 1935 (Kifer and Stewart 1938). The federally created Great Plains Committee, in a superb report called *The Future of the Great Plains* (1937), painted a disturbing picture of widespread rural poverty, a staggering burden of mortgages and debts, and increasingly frequent farm foreclosures.

Soil erosion

Soil is both an indispensable and a nonrenewable resource. Excluding fishing and some very intensive techniques with limited applications (like hydroponics), there is no way to obtain food without soil. Nor can we manufacture soil, and the natural processes that form it work very slowly. It takes many centuries to rebuild as much topsoil as a dust storm can remove in a matter of days or hours.

Soil erosion has been a problem in the United States since colonial times. In the older agricultural areas of the humid eastern part of the country, the major form of erosion is by water. In contrast, wind erosion is worst in semiarid, drought-prone areas with a

flat, treeless topography that offers no obstacles to the wind, and large portions of the Great Plains region are therefore highly susceptible (Kimberlin et al. 1977). Severe dust storms have been known since ancient times in North Africa, the Near East, and Central China (Idso 1976). On the Great Plains, in addition to the "dirty thirties," there have been several other periods of fairly serious dust storms in the century since settlement began. But no other dust storms in the country's history

reached the continental proportions attained during the 1930s.

Wind erosion is initiated by the force of the wind against individual particles at the soil surface. Very small particles get carried in suspension, while large ones simply roll or slide along the surface. But in a process called saltation, particles between .1 and .5 mm are lifted up to about a meter and are accelerated by the greater wind speed at that height before hitting the ground again. Be-

Figure 2. After a particularly bad dust storm, sand drifts could reach 25 feet in height and bury tractors, barns, and homes beneath them. (Photo courtesy of Resettlement Administration.)

Figure 3. "Black blizzards" were common in Kansas and the rest of the Dust Bowl during the 1930s. Several minutes after the start of a storm the sky would turn completely black, and the sun would be hidden from view for days at a time. (This photo and the one on the facing page are by courtesy of the Soil Conservation Service.)

cause their impact in turn loosens and dislodges more particles and damages or destroys plants, wind erosion is a cumulative process. Thus one effective erosion-control technique is to break the avalanching effect with strips of erosion-resistant plants perpendicular to the prevailing wind direction (Fig. 4).

The most effective method of prevention is an adequate cover, either of growing plants or residues from the previous crops (Woodruff et al. 1972). A good cover reduces wind speed at the surface and shields the soil from the wind's abrasive action. It also traps dust blown in from exposed soil and absorbs the impact of saltating particles. Also, plant roots help to bind the soil.

Erosion can be reduced by creating barriers that cut down the wind speed. Using rows of trees near buildings as windbreaks or shelterbelts is common even in humid areas. Unfortunately, trees do poorly in many parts of the Southern Plains. Tall annual crops such as sorghum offer some protection, but the rows must be fairly closely spaced. Mixing crops on a single field, which is also done in strip cropping, presents

problems for the farmer who wants to raise the single most profitable crop on as much land as possible. Single-crop farming was an important factor in creating the Dust Bowl, as will be seen.

Erosion is also minimized by maintaining a rough, cloddy surface to reduce surface wind speed. Large clods cannot be moved by the wind and also help protect more erodible soil components. The formation of stable clods is aided by returning organic matter to the soil. When some early Plains farmers burned grain straw to facilitate tillage, they accelerated the loss of humus and made the soil more erodible (McDonald 1938).

Because crops differ considerably in their tolerance of drought and their susceptibility to erosion, erosion control requires choosing an appropriate mix of crops, depending on the weather, soil moisture, and soil erodibility. The major Plains crops include grasses, close-planted small grains, and row crops. Perennial grasses offer year-round protection, even in a drought, if they are not overgrazed. However, grass provides no income for farmers who do not have cattle.

Winter wheat is the dominant small grain on the Southern Plains. Planted in late summer or early fall, it provides good cover in the fall, winter, and the following spring (when the erosion hazard is greatest), if a good stand is established and maintained, which may not be possible during a drought. By the 1930s it was already well known that when the soil moisture is below a certain critical level at planting time, crop failure will probably result (Rule 1939). However, economic factors sometimes encouraged or compelled Plains farmers to plant wheat anyway.

The sorghums, which are fairly drought-tolerant relatives of corn, are an important group of row crops in the Southern Plains. Sorghums were originally raised as livestock forages, although since the 1950s they have also been raised for grain. They leave a considerable amount of residue, which can be left to protect the field until after the main blowing season the following spring.

These crops differ in the relative timing of expenses and income. Wheat and grain sorghums provide a cash income in less than a year, but forage crops provide no return until

Figure 4. Wind erosion is common in semiarid, drought-prone areas with a flat, treeless topography. To prevent the wind from loosening and dislodging soil particles, a combination of windbreaks—created with trees or tall crops—and strip-cropping of erosion-resistant plants like grass perpendicular to the prevailing wind direction is used. Besides reducing surface wind speed, the grass catches blowing soil.

the cattle are marketed. The need for immediate cash made many Plains farmers specialize in wheat shortly before the dust storms of the 1930s.

Soils differ significantly in their susceptibility to erosion. Some Plains soils cannot be cultivated safely and are best kept permanently in grass. Of course, while rainfall is above average, even these soils can profitably grow crops. Some farmers overlooked their limitations and chose a cropping system for maximum return under the best weather conditions, rather than for protection during unfavorable ones. This practice has caused many problems in a region where growing conditions are so variable and unpredictable (Sears 1935).

Rainfall and yield

The successes and failures of Plains agriculture have been determined by variations in rainfall more than by any other physical factor. Seasonal temperatures generally are favorable for grain production. Many Plains soils are among the most fertile in the country, with newly turned sod giving high yields even without fertilization. The extensive tracts of level land so characteristic of the Plains are well suited to large-scale mechanization, with the result that when tractors and combine harvesters were introduced after World War I, wheat production costs in the Plains became the lowest in the country (Stephens 1937). But the average annual precipitation, between about 12 and 25 inches, depending upon the location, is roughly equal to or somewhat below the minimum needed for grain production. Therefore even relatively minor fluctuations in rainfall cause disproportionately large fluctuations in yield.

Yet great variations in precipitation, not just minor fluctuations, are the rule on the Plains. The concept of "average" is really only a mathematical construction, not a very useful predictor of actual precipitation in a particular year. For example, from 1875 to 1936 (roughly from the beginning of crop production to the drought that followed the most important period of conversion from native sod to cultivated crops) the average annual precipitation at Dodge City, Kansas, was 20 inches, just about enough to produce crops (Stephens 1937). But in one out of five years it was above 25 inches, while in one out of six years it was less than 15 inches. This range represents the difference between bumper crops and virtual crop failure. Periods of several consecutive years of subnormal precipitation are even more damaging, since they exhaust farmers' financial reserves and since the cumulative depletion of soil moisture and loss of cover increases soil erosion. The same precipitation data for Dodge City show five different times in 61 years in which annual precipitation stayed below the 20-inch average for at least three successive years.

Yet even these figures do not tell the whole story. Rainfall is helpful during the fall and spring growth periods of winter wheat, but heavy rains when the crop is nearing maturity in summer can seriously damage the crop. Year-to-year variations in the seasonal distribution of precipitation on the Plains compound the effects of variations in total annual precipitation (Thorntwaite 1936).

It is not surprising, therefore, that crop yields on the Plains have fluctuated sharply. For example, in Sheridan County in northwest Kansas, the fraction of wheat land that was actually harvested varied between 11

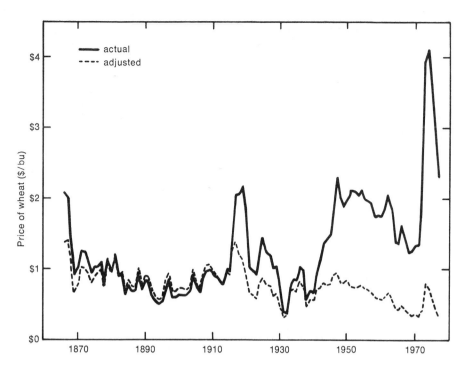

Figure 5. The national seasonal average price of wheat has varied sharply since the Civil War. The first three peaks correspond to major wars, while the most recent peak is related to grain sales to the USSR and to other aspects of the world grain situation. The deep valleys reflect the agricultural depression of the early 1920s and the Great Depression beginning in 1929. The adjusted price, which is in terms of the purchasing power of the farmer's dollar in 1910–14, shows a gradual decline along with these short-term changes.

percent and 99 percent from 1912 to 1934, and the yield per planted acre ranged from .3 to 21.3 bushels (Thornthwaite 1936). The economic effects of such yield variations were further aggravated by changing crop prices. The income of Plains farmers specializing in wheat depends directly on the price of that one crop. Such farmers do not have even the limited flexibility available to farmers of more diversified crops, who at least can adjust to changes in the relative prices of various crops and livestock, although not to changes in the overall price level.

Since the Civil War, the national annual average price of wheat has varied between $.38 and $4.09 per bushel (USDA 1967, 1977). These extremes mainly reflect cyclic changes, with only a very slight upward trend. Short-run changes have often been very sharp. The price of wheat has at least doubled within two years on three different occasions, and three times it has fallen by at least half (see Fig. 5). The price received by a farmer at a particular time and particular location has varied even more sharply than these national annual average figures indicate.

Since the price of wheat is determined not only by the quantity produced but also by nonagricultural factors such as wars, overseas demand, and general economic conditions, varia-

tions in the quantity produced have not always been offset by opposing changes in price. When severe drought occurred during a major national depression, as in the 1930s, the results were disastrous.

Plains agriculture: Feast or famine

Throughout its history of about a century, Plains agriculture has followed a boom-or-bust pattern. Before the arrival of the first settlers—the cattlemen—the undisturbed ecosystem changed in response to variations in weather, but the far-reaching alterations that accompanied each wave of settlement greatly magnified the impact of subsequent weather cycles.

In the area that was to become the Dust Bowl, the native vegetation was mainly sod-forming short grasses such as buffalo grass and blue grama. Although much sparser looking than the tall-grass prairies farther east, the short-grass plains supported an enormous number of grazing animals, including vast herds of bison. In the semiarid climate, the short grasses cured naturally, thereby providing high-quality forage throughout the winter (McArdle and Costello 1936).

This phenomenon was exploited by cattlemen, the first arrivals, who in-

troduced the longhorn breed from Mexico via Texas after the Civil War. Cattle ranged over vast unfenced areas, receiving virtually no attention except during roundups and trail drives. The cattle industry expanded feverishly in the early 1880s (Brisbin 1881), and aggressive promoters attracted speculative capital from as far away as Europe. But while it was highly romanticized in song and story, the open range actually represented only a transient phase. Overgrazing, the invention of barbed wire, dubious financial practices, the sudden collapse of the market, and devastating blizzards in 1886 and 1887 combined to end the open-range cattle industry (Webb 1931; Stewart 1936). From the mid-1880s on, cattlemen lost more and more of their range to newly arrived farmers, despite frequent fights to keep it, while fencing in the remaining land and managing it more closely. In its spectacular growth and equally spectacular collapse the industry foreshadowed the drastic cycles that were to become the pattern for Plains agriculture.

The conversion of the Plains from grassland to cultivated crops was accomplished by waves of optimistic farmers arriving during periods of favorable rainfall. But each such period was followed by serious drought, leading to dust storms, bankruptcies, foreclosures, and outmigrations. The economic, social, and technological factors that interacted with the physical environment to make the effects of the droughts so serious—and nothing less than catastrophic in the 1930s—became apparent almost from the earliest days of Plains agriculture.

Cultivation pushed into the Plains in the late 1870s on land distributed in 160-acre homestead units. Grazing cattle on only 160 acres was out of the question: only cultivation could possibly sustain a family. As long as rainfall was above average, there was a fair chance of success. But, with inadequate rainfall, crops failed, and, unprotected by crops, the soil could not withstand the region's high winds (McDonald 1938; Bennett 1939). Soon after they arrived many farmers were forced to leave the Plains during the first of what would be several periods of serious dust storms.

But the return of above-normal rainfall erased the memory of previous failures, and around 1900 another group was ready to try again. This time, the frontiersman's characteristic willingness to take risks was reinforced by the aggressive boosterism of various interest groups, especially the railroads. Having been granted alternate square miles of land in a checkerboard pattern out to 20 miles on each side of the line as payment for building railroads through the Plains, they were eager to bring in settlers to whom they could sell tracts of land and who would also generate increased traffic. Techniques like offering free one-way tickets to prospective settlers, reinforced by the promotional activities of state governments, newspapers, and speculators, proved quite effective.

The influx of farmers in the early twentieth century was further stimulated by the "dry farming" movement, which promoted special systems for areas with inadequate rainfall. The best-known proponent of dry farming, Hardy W. Campbell, advocated a firmly packed subsoil but a loose and finely divided topsoil, or "dust mulch," which he erroneously thought was necessary to minimize the loss of water from lower layers of soil. Campbell also recommended summer fallowing, which means raising a crop on alternate years only and cultivating the unplanted land several times during the summer to control weeds and to keep the surface in a condition to absorb the maximum amount of rain. The goal was to store up as much water as possible so that the next crop would have adequate moisture. Summer fallowing is still practiced by some Plains wheat growers, although most of Campbell's other techniques, especially the dust mulch, have long since been discarded. Modern summer fallowing, however, controls weeds either with herbicides or subsurface tillage, which, unlike the older cultivation methods, does not increase the soil's susceptibility to erosion.

Campbell's claim that these methods would ensure the Plains farmer protection against drought was widely publicized, often with a missionary zeal. Groups who wanted to have the Plains settled seized upon his work as an apparently scientific response to anyone who was concerned about the failures of previous Plains farmers (Hargreaves 1948).

At about the same time, the USDA set up several dry-land experiment stations in the Plains. The leader of this work, E. C. Chilcott, sharply criticized the exaggerated portrayals of any one dry-farming method as the panacea for Plains agriculture (Chilcott 1912). Unlike Campbell, USDA researchers recognized that a loose, finely divided topsoil was very susceptible to wind erosion, and they showed that the soil still could conserve moisture when left instead in a rough, cloddy condition. This principle was embodied in new soil-conserving tillage implements, especially starting in the 1930s (Chilcott 1937).

Along with the scientific and quasi-scientific precepts of the dry-farming movement, some utter nonsense also found acceptance. The saying "Rainfall follows the plow" reflected the theory that bringing more land under cultivation would make the Plains climate more favorable. An even more curious notion was that the telegraph lines and railroads then being built in the region would have the same effect. A particularly colorful rainmaking scheme was based on the belief that rainfall follows major military battles. C.W. Post, the breakfast cereal magnate, tried to make rain through a series of "battles," planned with military precision, in which he detonated large quantities of explosives (Johnson 1947).

The optimism of the early 1900s, founded on a mixture of science, pseudoscience, and hucksterism, was destroyed by the drought that hit the Southern Plains in 1910. This time the dust storms were quite severe, sometimes lasting several days and reducing visibility to near zero (Johnson 1947). In duration and intensity they anticipated some of the worst storms of the 1930s, although they never attained the same regional scale. Still, they were more than enough to cause widespread farm failures.

But once again the dust storms and drought did not convince everyone that it was dangerous to convert large amounts of grassland to cultivated crops without giving adequate attention to erosion. With the predictable eventual arrival of adequate rainfall, this time starting in 1914, came the almost equally predictable arrival of another wave of farmers determined to make plowed-under sod produce grain, regardless of whether the soil and climate were suitable for it.

By then, it was well known that cropping systems other than wheat monoculture offered better protection against drought and erosion. Nevertheless, the wheat boom that began around World War I was bigger by far than anything that had come before. The usual spirit of optimism and adventure was now strengthened by two very powerful forces: high prices and new technology. In 1919, wheat soared to a record average price of $2.16 a bushel, more than twice the 1910–14 average of $.87. This price would not be seen again for almost three decades and has never been equaled in terms of the purchasing power of the farmer's dollar (see Fig. 5). Such prices, if accompanied by good weather, held the promise of unbelievable profits, enough to pay off an entire farm in one year (Thorntwaite 1936).

Moreover, such profits could now be achieved on a vast scale. Tractors introduced around World War I could pull up to twelve disc plows at a time. The newly introduced combine harvester cut labor costs, reduced field losses, and allowed one man to handle a much larger acreage.

Some of the increase in wheat production occurred on large, highly mechanized farms developed with outside capital. The most spectacular example—the Thomas Campbell farm in Montana—capitalized at $2 million, produced 50,000 acres of wheat with 33 tractors, 50 gang plows, and 100 grain wagons (Fortune 1935). But many other farms were family-size operations run either by survivors of previous droughts or by new arrivals on still-available public land. Short-term economic considerations may have motivated some of these farmers, too, but others were interested in farming in a sustainable way so that they could pass a productive farm on to their descendants.

Unfortunately, economic necessity prevented many of them from carrying out this wish, since the favorable prices of World War I did not last very long. A serious agricultural depression began in 1921, dropping the average wheat price to $.97 by 1922. Traditional mixed farming could not hope to compete with large-scale wheat production that used the new mechanized methods and had the lowest costs in the country (Stephens 1937).

When favorable prices returned later in the decade (a high of $1.44 in 1925), weather, technology, and economic conditions coincided perfectly, and the wheat boom accelerated even more. The labor required to produce wheat on the Plains could be kept so low with the new machinery, and the necessary operations could be performed so quickly, that a person no longer even had to live on his farm. The so-called "suitcase farmer," based as much as several hundred miles away, could come to his farm for a few weeks each summer and live in temporary quarters (Hewes 1977). In those few weeks, he could harvest his previous winter wheat crop (assuming he had succeeded in raising one), till the ground, and seed the next crop. Many professional people and other city dwellers found in suitcase farming a nice opportunity of escaping from their normal routine each year as well as a way of putting their surplus capital to work in the hope of realizing handsome returns.

Economic factors dealt the first blow to the 1920s wheat boom. The Great Depression made wheat prices fall disastrously, down 62 percent in two years to an average of $.39 during 1931. Although yields remained fairly good at first, many Plains farmers were forced into heavy debt or had to become tenants. Paradoxically, the low wheat price actually encouraged wheat production, since farmers had to raise cash crops to have any hope of covering their operating costs, rent, interest on their newly acquired machinery, and mortgage payments on land bought at the inflated prices

prevalent during more favorable years. Wheat acreage continued to rise, with the result that when the next drought came it was devastating.

Economic forces and unheeded warnings

In a very narrow sense, the drought that started in 1931 caused the Dust Bowl disaster. But the drought would not have had such destructive consequences had Plains farmers not converted large areas of grassland to crops, especially wheat, without regard for the suitability of the soil and climate for such farming. I have already discussed some of the factors that caused this indiscriminate expansion of wheat farming. High wheat prices encouraged some farmers to take risks in the hope of reaping tremendous rewards, while intervening low prices forced even the more cautious farmers to work the land still more intensively just to survive economically, a dilemma poignantly described by Carlson (1935). The unsuitably small holdings that inevitably would be abandoned and made available to speculators at distressed prices, together with the land grants that the railroads wanted to sell quickly, stimulated speculation in Plains land. Real estate dealers and promoters seized the opportunity to capture windfall profits from the agricultural boom and rising land prices that accompanied each return of favorable weather. Rapid advances in agricultural technology allowed farmers to produce wheat on a large scale, at low costs, and with unprecedented "efficiency," if the term is not taken to include what would eventually happen to the soil. Finally, an indefatigable optimism helped people interpret each return of good rainfall as a sign that the Plains climate had improved permanently.

One factor that can be ruled out as a cause of the Dust Bowl phenomenon is inadequate knowledge. Almost from the time settlers began arriving on the Plains, some people foresaw the problems that were inevitable unless agriculture was carried out in a way compatible with the region's very stringent climatic conditions. In a famous report entitled *Lands of the Arid Region of the United States* (1878), J.W. Powell, of the U.S. Geological Survey, warned that the 160-acre limit on farm size under the

Homestead Act, which was originally established for the humid East, was completely inappropriate for the Plains. Powell's unheeded recommendation was for the limit to be increased to four sections (2,560 acres), so that an adequate income could be obtained from cattle grazing.

The chief hydrographer of the U.S. Geological Survey, F. Newell (1897), cautioned against interpreting a few years of above-average rainfall as indicating a permanent improvement in the Plains climate. He noted that the high fertility of the Plains soils made them very attractive as long as rainfall was favorable. But then the inevitable happens: "The following spring opens with the soil so dry that it is blown about over the windy plains. Another and perhaps another season of drought occurs, the settlers depart . . . and this beautiful land, once so fruitful, is now dry and brown." But the rain eventually returns, and with it, Newell predicted with remarkable prescience, "recurs the flood of immigration, to be continued until the next long drought. This alternation of feast and famine . . . bids fair to be repeated upon our Great Plains."

The causes and prevention of wind erosion were already understood before the World War I wheat boom. In 1912, E.E. Free had criticized the "dust mulch" theory of Campbell's dry farming system and instead had recommended a cloddy or granular surface. He had also suggested that new cultivation be done in stages, with strips of native vegetation left to protect newly seeded strips until they are established. However, this suggestion was not heeded by the farmers, who rushed to raise as much wheat as possible after the war.

Modern parallels

Because interest in the environment has increased so sharply in recent years, there is a tendency to forget that environmental problems have existed for a long time. It is interesting that contemporary observers who analyzed the dust storms in the 1930s in many ways anticipated current debates over today's environmental problems.

In its 1937 landmark report the Great Plains Committee clearly recognized that a complex set of causes lay be-

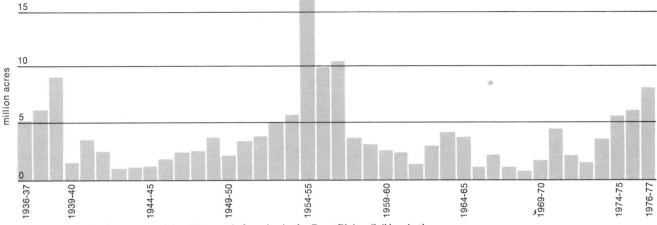

Figure 6. Although the dust storms of the 1950s were not as spectacular as those of the 1930s, more land was actually damaged annually by wind erosion in the Great Plains. Soil loss in the mid-1970s was on a scale comparable to that of the 1930s. (From *Soil Conservation* 1977.)

neath the Plains environmental problems and strove to understand how the climate, biota, and soils of the undisturbed Plains ecosystem interacted with the technological, economic, and social conditions that accompanied the settling of the Plains. The report could stand as a prototype of an environmental impact assessment, although this term would not come into common use for over three decades.

Together with several other deep-rooted attitudes that were identified as underlying causes of the dust storms, the Committee criticized the view that "an owner may do with his property as he likes." They commented that "all too frequently what appears to be of immediate good to the individual in the long run is not good for the people of the region," and noted that there is no "social accounting" adequate to deal with this problem. If we replace their clear language with the corresponding jargon of modern economics—"negative externalities"—we see that they identified what today is widely regarded as a key factor in many of our environmental problems.

H.H. Bennett (1939), the first head of the Soil Conservation Service, saw soil erosion problems as arising from "a false philosophy of plenty, a myth of inexhaustibility" in connection with apparently unlimited land and soil resources. The Great Plains Committee likewise challenged the belief that "resources are inexhaustible and can absorb an indefinite

population, and that settlement and development will continue into the distant future." The parallels to modern discussions of how we permitted ourselves to get into our current energy situation are obvious.

Bennett and the Great Plains Committee represented what might be considered a middle ground in analyzing the causes of the Dust Bowl. They recognized that some serious mistakes had been made and that major changes were needed to rehabilitate Great Plains agriculture, but they also were confident that rehabilitation was possible. Others expressed more extreme views on both sides.

To some people, the dust storms were primarily a natural phenomenon, with man an innocent and helpless victim—a view that was often promoted by the narrowest kinds of local booster and special interest groups. Kansas historian J.C. Malin (1947) criticized the "erroneous idea" that the plow caused the dust storms, noting the reports of dust storms by early explorers. He attributed this "error" to "the excesses of political agitation, the sensationalism of various types of social agitators, and the lack of historical perspective of the 1930s." Some participants in the more recent debates over environmental problems have similarly used the strategy of either denying that there is a problem or pointing to the problems encountered in the natural ecosystem. This approach is sometimes coupled with attacks directed

not at the problem but rather at those who say there is a problem.

Those who were at the other extreme also have their modern counterparts. One opinion held that any cultivation on a large scale was incompatible with the Plains environment and that the only solution was a massive reconversion to permanent vegetation (Thorntwaite 1936). Although the problem of wind erosion is still very much with us, and although after four decades there still is disagreement over just how much interference with the grass cover can be tolerated (Worster 1977), this view now seems too pessimistic. The most conservation-minded of today's Plains farmers have demonstrated that in much of the region crop production need not result in excessive erosion. The perceived need to abandon cultivation is somewhat analogous to the belief sometimes expressed today that the basic cause of our environmental problems is technology per se, not just misused or poorly planned technology.

The aftermath

Four decades of historical perspective have reinforced the middle-ground view, as represented by *The Future of the Great Plains,* for example. This position was that sustainable agriculture on the Plains required fundamental readjustments involving not just physical production practices but also the economic factors—land tenure, credit, and crop prices—that determined what production methods farmers would adopt. In the spirit of the New Deal, these changes were seen as requiring massive federal intervention, since the problems of the Dust Bowl were regional and beyond the ability of individuals or even states to solve for themselves.

This view was put into practice by the Soil Conservation Service, created in 1935 by a law passed unanimously by both houses of Congress shortly after Plains dust began settling in the Capitol during H.H. Bennett's Congressional testimony. Realizing that doing research on erosion control was not enough, the SCS actively encouraged and assisted farmers to adopt proved and available erosion-control methods. Through demonstration centers, conservation districts, and financial aid, Plains farmers were helped with shelterbelts, strip cropping, re-establishment of grass on damaged cropland, and new tillage methods (Rule 1939).

The new tillage methods made it possible for farmers to leave most of the residue of the previous crop on the surface as a "stubble mulch" while killing weeds and loosening the soil below to prepare the next seedbed. But while stubble mulching greatly reduced erosion, it was, unfortunately, not an adequate solution in many areas. Thus the Great Plains Committee recommended that some 15 million acres of Plains cropland be returned permanently to grass, a recommendation that obviously conflicted with the trend toward more cash grain production.

When favorable prices and good rainfall returned in the 1940s, once again some farmers ignored the lessons of previous droughts. As had happened twenty-five years earlier, the end of the drought came near the start of a world war, which increased demand and raised crop prices. By 1947, the price of wheat surpassed the 1919 record, and a new wheat boom was under way, accompanied in some circles by the usual bravado (*Fortune* 1948). In some areas nonresident owners who wanted to extend wheat production to unsuitable land organized to remove or weaken the successful land-use restrictions that resident farmers had imposed on themselves through Soil Conservation Districts (Finnell 1946; Johnson 1947).

Those who warned that the favorable weather was going to lead to a repetition of past disasters (e.g. Henson 1940 and Johnson 1947) were largely ignored, but their predictions proved correct. When drought returned in the 1950s, the dust storms were fairly severe, although they did not reach the scale of twenty years earlier because farmers were using improved tillage methods and at least in part had adopted other conservation measures. Still, from 1954 to 1956 some 10 to 16 million acres were damaged by erosion each year, a higher rate than in the 1930s (Fig. 6), and Great Plains cropland became a major source of air pollution (Hagen and Woodruff 1973). The USDA estimated that between 15 and 30 million acres under crops were unsuited for crop production and recommended that they be returned to grass (Muehlbeier 1958).

For almost two decades following the mid-fifties drought, erosion remained relatively low. Rainfall generally was fairly good. The government limited acreages of wheat and many other crops to help raise prices. New herbicides helped reduce erosion by permitting farmers to control weeds on summer fallow without cultivating the soil. The Great Plains Conservation Program that began in 1957 strengthened the efforts begun two decades earlier, although in 1972 it was estimated that about two-thirds of all land susceptible to wind erosion was still inadequately protected (Woodruff et al. 1972). With the introduction of center pivot systems, rotating sprinkler systems that irrigate 132-acre circles with almost no labor, irrigated hybrid sorghums on the Southern Plains and irrigated corn on the Northern Plains replaced much dry-land wheat and pasture. Unfortunately, irrigation sometimes introduced new erosion problems. Many shelterbelts have been removed to permit installation of center pivots (Sorenson and Marotz 1977), and the systems have permitted cropping of drought-susceptible sandy soils that erode readily if not enough crop residues are left.

Despite the steps taken toward erosion control, in 1976 and 1977 there were more dust storms, and erosion damage on the Plains reached levels comparable to the 1930s (see Fig. 6). Once again dust storms came when drought followed a rapid expansion of

crop production during favorable conditions. This time the expansion had not been stimulated by a world war, although the slogan "all-out food production" (Hueg 1975), adopted in response to the "world food crisis" in 1974, was somewhat reminiscent of "Wheat will win the war" of World War I days. But the slogan was undoubtedly not as significant as the price of wheat, which rose to an average of $4.09 in 1974. With acreage restrictions removed, 23 percent more winter wheat was planted in the Plains in the fall of 1974 than in 1972. But coincidentally with the return of drought, prices fell as rapidly as they had risen, bringing the latest wheat boom to a sudden halt. "All-out food production" had a remarkably short life. In 1977, some wheat land was once more taken out of production as part of the price-support program. Once again, conservation could be profitable, at least for a while.

It is hard to say how severe the next dust storms will be. That there will be another drought we can predict quite confidently, since drought is a physical phenomenon entirely outside our control. But how much damage it will do is very much within our control and therefore much harder to predict.

References

Bennett, H. H. 1939. *Soil Conservation.* McGraw-Hill.

Brisbin, J. S. 1881. *The Beef Bonanza.* Reprinted 1959. Univ. of Okla. Press.

Carlson, A. D. 1935. Dust blowing. *Harper's* 171:149–58.

Chilcott, E. C. 1912. Some misconceptions concerning dry farming. In *Yearbook of the Dept. of Agriculture 1911,* pp. 247–56. USDA.

———. 1937. Preventing soil blowing on the southern Great Plains. USDA Farmers' Bull. 1771.

Choun, H. F. 1936. Dust storms in the southwestern plains area. *Monthly Weather Rev.* 64:195–99.

Finnell, H. F. 1946. Pity the poor land. *Soil Conservation* 12:27–33.

Fortune. 1935. Grasslands 2: The broken sod. April, pp. 65–66, 185–90.

Fortune. 1948. The land of the big rich. April, pp. 98–103, 183–88.

Free, E. 1912. The Movement of Soil Material by the Wind. USDA Bur. of Soils Bull. 68.

Great Plains Committee. 1937. *The Future of the Great Plains.* 75th Cong., 1st Sess., H. R. Doc. 144.

Hagen, L. J., and N. P. Woodruff. 1973. Air pollution from dust storms in the Great Plains. *Atmos. Env.* 7:323–32.

Hand, I. F. 1934. The character and magnitude

of the dust cloud which passed over Washington, DC, May 11, 1934. *Monthly Weather Rev.* 62:157–58.

Hargreaves, M. W. M. 1948. Dry farming alias scientific farming. *Agr. Hist.* 22:39–56.

Henson, E. 1940. Borrowed time in the Dust Bowl. *Land Policy Rev.* 3:3–7.

Hewes, L. 1977. Early suitcase farming in the central Great Plains. *Agr. Hist.* 51:23–37.

Hueg, W. F., Jr. 1975. Agronomic research and production strategy for all-out food production. In *All-Out Food Production: Strategy and Resource Implications,* spec. publ. 23, Am. Soc. Agron.

Idso, S. B. 1976. Dust storms. *Sci. Am.* 235:108–14.

Joel, A. H. 1937. Soil conservation reconnaissance survey of the southern Great Plains wind-erosion area. USDA Tech. Bull. 556.

Johnson, V. 1947. *Heaven's Tableland: The Dust Bowl Story.* Reprinted 1974. Da Capo Press.

Kifer, R. S., and H. L. Stewart. 1938. *Farming Hazards in the Drought Area.* Research Monograph 16, Works Progress Admin. Reprinted 1971. Da Capo Press.

Kimberlin, L. W., A. L. Hidlebaugh, and A. R. Grunewald. 1977. The potential wind erosion problem in the United States. *Trans. Am. Soc. Agr. Eng.* 29:873–79.

Lord, R. 1938. To hold this soil. USDA misc. publ. 321.

McArdle, R. E., and D. F. Costello. 1936. The virgin range. In *The Western Range,* pp. 72–80. U.S. Forest Serv. 74th Cong., 2nd Sess., Sen. Doc. 199.

McDonald, A. 1938. Erosion and its control in Oklahoma territory. USDA misc. publ. 301.

Malin, J. C. 1947. *The Grassland of North America: Prolegomena to Its History.* Lawrence, KS: privately printed.

Martin, R. J. 1936. Dust storms of February and March 1936 in the United States. *Monthly Weather Rev.* 64:87–88.

Mattice, W. A. 1935. Dust storms, November 1933 to May 1934. *Monthly Weather Rev.* 63:53–55.

Muehlbeier, J. 1958. Land-use problems in the Great Plains. In *Yearbook of Agriculture 1958,* pp. 161–66. USDA.

Newell, F. 1897. Irrigation on the Great Plains. In *Yearbook of the Dept. of Agriculture 1896,* pp. 167–96. USDA.

Powell, J. W. 1878. *Report on the Lands of the Arid Region of the United States.* 45th Cong., 2nd Sess., Exec. Doc. 73.

Rule, G. K. 1939. Crops against the wind on the southern Great Plains. USDA Farmers' Bull. 1833.

Sears, P. B. 1935. *Deserts on the March.* Univ. of Okla. Press.

Soil Conservation. 1977. Severe wind erosion hits Plains. 42:22.

Sorenson, C. J., and G. A. Marotz. 1977. Changes in shelterbelt mileage statistics over four decades in Kansas. *J. Soil and Water Cons.* 32:276–81.

Stein, W. J. 1973. *California and the Dust Bowl Migration.* Greenwood Press.

Stephens, P. H. 1937. Why the Dust Bowl? *J. Farm. Econ.* 19:750–57.

Stewart, G. 1936. History of range use. In *The Western Range,* pp. 119–33. U.S. Forest Serv. 74th Cong., 2nd Sess., Sen. Doc. 199.

Thorntwaite, C. W. 1936. The Great Plains. In *Migration and Economic Opportunity,* ed. C. Goodrich, pp. 202–50. Univ. of Penn. Press.

USDA. 1967. *Agricultural Statistics.*

USDA. 1977. *Agricultural Statistics.*

Webb, W. P. 1931. *The Great Plains.* Ginn.

Woodruff, N. P., L. Lyles, F. H. Siddoway, and D. W. Fryrear. 1972. How to control wind erosion. USDA Agr.Inf. Bull. 354.

Worster, D. 1977. Grass to dust: Ecology and the Great Plains in the 1930s. *Environ. Rev.* 4:2–12.

PART 6 *Impacts on Communities of Organisms*

F. Herbert Bormann
Gene E. Likens

Catastrophic Disturbance and the Steady State in Northern Hardwood Forests

A new look at the role of disturbance in the development of forest ecosystems suggests important implications for land-use policies

Models of ecosystem development usually portray plant succession as an orderly progression of biological changes in an environment that is presumed to be more or less constant (Odum 1969; Woodwell 1974). Yet every terrestrial ecosystem is subject to a range of disturbances varying from those that barely alter the structure, metabolism, or biogeochemistry of the system to those that wholly or dramatically change it. Defining "disturbance" itself is something of a problem, because it is difficult to draw a line between endogenous disturbances, that is, events that come within the scope of normal plant succession (for example, the fall of old trees), and exogenous disturbances, events that might be considered to deflect the autogenic pattern (for example, severe fires or hurricanes).

F. Herbert Bormann is Professor of Forest Ecology at the Yale School of Forestry and Environmental Studies; Gene E. Likens is Professor of Ecology in the Division of Biological Sciences, Section of Ecology and Systematics, at Cornell University. For the last sixteen years they have been principal investigators in the Hubbard Brook Ecosystem Study, a multidisciplinary exploration of the structure, function, development, and biogeochemistry of the northern hardwood ecosystem. The work, based on observation of the Hubbard Brook Experimental Forest in New Hampshire and carried out in cooperation with the U.S. Forest Service, has involved more than sixty senior scientific collaborators. The findings outlined here first appeared in the authors' book Pattern and Process in a Forested Ecosystem, *recently published by Springer-Verlag. Address: F. Herbert Bormann, School of Forestry and Environmental Studies, Yale University, New Haven, CT 06511.*

A growing body of literature has emphasized the importance of fire and wind as common, widespread perturbations that historically have shaped the structure and function of North American forests. Several researchers, while recognizing the role of endogeneous disturbance, have suggested that the development of forest ecosystems rarely achieves a steady state, but is interrupted by catastrophic exogenous disturbances at irregular and relatively short intervals.

Loucks (1970), for example, has hypothesized that prior to settlement by Europeans, forests in Wisconsin burned repeatedly at short intervals ranging from several decades to about a century. These catastrophic disturbances presumably truncated the development of the ecosystem, in effect rejuvenating it and restarting it at an earlier developmental state. Recovery patterns for production, biomass, and some species and community changes are portrayed as wave phenomena, with the rhythmic rise and fall triggered by fires at relatively short intervals.

Loucks's hypothesis, however, neither allows for nor considers an autogenically derived "steady state," the concept that interests us here, but seems to imply that such a condition occurs only rarely and is characterized primarily by shade-tolerant plant species. Accurate fire histories for the western region of the Great Lakes states support the conclusion that a steady state, that is, a condition in which there is no net change in biomass over time, was seldom achieved in presettlement forest ecosystems (Frissell 1973; Heinselman 1973). A similar but less well-

documented finding resulted from studies in central New England, where evidence suggests that strong cyclonic winds regularly interrupt autogenic development before it reaches the steady state (Stephens 1955 and 1956; Raup 1957; Henry and Swan 1974).

Such conclusions raise fundamental questions about the usefulness of the steady-state concept in the interpretation and management of forest ecosystems. Is the steady state merely a theoretical concept with little or no reality in nature? Are forest ecosystems historically characterized by waveform phenomena triggered by random catastrophic disturbance at intervals much shorter than the time necessary to achieve a steady state? Has the historic pattern of exogenous events been substantially altered by the arrival of European man? By comparing the historical record of exogenous disturbance in northern hardwood forests of the White Mountains region of New England (Fig. 1) with the extensive data available for forests of the Great Lakes region, we suggest that the rapid waveform configuration of exogenous disturbances is not universal, and that an environment in which steady state could occur does in fact exist. In addition, we present here a model of ecosystem development, based on extensive study of northern hardwood forests after clear-cutting, which incorporates the element of endogenous disturbance. Our model differs in important respects from other models, and illustrates how a steady state might be achieved and what its characteristics might be.

The defense of the reality of the autogenically derived steady state is not

Figure 1. This general view of the White Mountains from the northwestern flank of Mt. Moosilauke shows the northern hardwood forest as it appears in the vicinity of the Hubbard Brook Experimental Forest.

merely an intellectual exercise, but serves a useful purpose. Ecology, like all other fields, is affected by the swinging pendulum of opinion. For decades Clementsian notions of succession and climax thoroughly dominated much ecological thinking and buttressed land-use policies that assigned disturbances a minor role in most naturally occurring ecosystems (Raup 1967). Quite properly, these ideas have come under attack, and the concept of catastrophic disturbance, particularly fire, as an integral part of the structure and function of temperate forest ecosystems has gained enormous ground. But the pendulum may swing too far toward catastrophic recycling at the expense of concepts which involve long-term autogenic development. This is not a trivial matter, because theories of ecosystem development are beginning

to play a major role in studies of evolution (Loucks 1970; Connell and Slatyer, unpub.; Smith, unpub.) as well as in decisions regarding the management of land (Kilgore 1973; Wood and Botkin, pers. comm.).

Exogenous disturbances: Fire

Effects of disturbance are extremely complex, since many factors, both biological and physical, may act to make trees more susceptible to the action of physical forces. These include biological processes such as competition, senescence, attack by insects or disease, and simple growth in size, as well as climatic fluctuations that are unfavorable to growth, such as hard frosts, severe drought, or prolonged periods of unfavorable weather. Physical disturbance itself

can make a tree more susceptible to subsequent disturbance by weakening its competitive position—by breaking its limbs and reducing its leaf area, or by decreasing its resistance to insects and disease.

Most agents of disturbance occur as a continuum—for example, winds may range from mild breezes to hurricane force—and consequently it is often difficult to find the exact point of division between endogenous and exogenous disturbances. We consider disturbance to be endogenous if it results in the localized fall of individual trees which have been weakened or killed during the process of growth, or autogenic development; the fall of these trees might be caused by their own weight, usual winds, or normal loads of ice or snow. Whatever the final cause that tips them over,

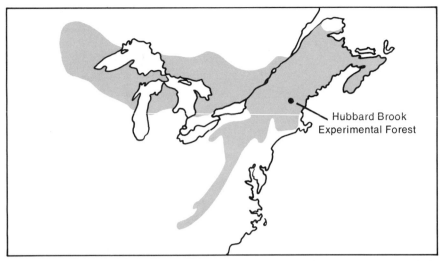

Figure 2. The northern hardwood forest stretches from Minnesota to the Atlantic Ocean. It is composed of a variety of trees, including coniferous and deciduous species, but is often dominated by a mixture of hemlock, sugar maple, beech, and yellow birch. Hubbard Brook Experimental Forest contains a typical range of these species.

their fall is inevitable even in the most protected of locations. Endogenous disturbance is an integral part of the developmental process of an ecosystem.

Exogenous disturbance, by contrast, results from forces external to the developmental process, such as intense fire or wind or clear-cutting by man. Fire and wind, the disturbances we will focus on here, not only hasten the death or fall of trees weakened in the developmental process but damage or kill trees that were reasonably healthy prior to the event. These disturbances also affect, in a fairly massive way, a variety of ecosystem processes, including energy fixation, decomposition, nutrient cycling, hydrology, and erosion.

Catastrophic fires, both natural and manmade, have been common for thousands of years throughout the northern hardwood forest (Fig. 2) and the boreal forest along its northern border (MacLean 1960; Heinselman 1973; Rowe and Scotter 1973). Heinselman's detailed study of the Boundary Waters Canoe Area in northwestern Minnesota indicates a natural "fire rotation," or time interval between fires, of 100 years before European settlement began: on average, an area equivalent to the whole area was burned over every 100 years. Between 1681 and 1894, 83% of the area burned in nine fire periods. Collectively, these data suggest that only a relatively small proportion of

the transitional forest is free from fire for periods exceeding several hundred years.

Old stands of white pine occur throughout the Great Lakes region and are generally thought to have originated after intense fires (Graham 1941; Maissurow 1941; Hough and Forbes 1943; Chapman 1947). Frissell (1973) reported that fires occurred, on average, every 10 years between 1650 and 1922 in Itasca Park in central Minnesota. In common with Heinselman's findings, Frissell found that fires often resulted in subsequent establishment of stands of pine uniform in age and in a presettlement mosaic of largely even-aged stands dating from different fires. Based on a study of fire scars, Lutz (1930) identified 40 fires between 1687 and 1927 at Heart's Content in northwestern Pennsylvania. Five of these fires—those in 1749, 1757, 1872, 1903, and 1911—were considered to be severe, and two were thought to be associated with drought years.

The record of fires in northeastern forests based on even-aged stands, fire scars, or charcoal is far less complete than that for the Great Lakes region. Cline and Spurr (1942) suggest that more or less even-aged stands of old-growth white pine in southwestern New Hampshire originated from fires. More recently, Henry and Swan (1974), working in the same area, were able to assign one of these fires to the year 1665.

In evaluating the frequency of fires in presettlement times, it is important to keep in mind that Indians often deliberately set fires to clear land for agriculture and other purposes. Judging from early historical writings, such fires were common in southern and central New England and westward to Pennsylvania (Lutz 1930; Day 1953; Spurr 1956b; Thompson and Smith 1970). In northern New England, however, historical evidence for the deliberate use of fire by Indians seems to be lacking (Day 1953; Brown 1958), perhaps because the usual incentives for burning were absent there. Indian populations in the mountainous regions were small and migratory, and agriculture was not as widely practiced. Travel, by canoe rather than overland in the summer and by snowshoe in the winter, was not hindered by underbrush, nor was deer hunting, which took the form of stalking or stillhunting rather than driving.

In the vicinity of the Hubbard Brook Experimental Forest in New Hampshire, where we conduct our studies, Indians apparently spent the autumn, winter, and spring months in the river valleys, planting crops in early spring before migrating to the coast for the summer, at the end of which they returned to carry out their harvest (Likens 1972). In river valleys surrounding Hubbard Brook, early explorers noted small stands of white pine (Brown 1958), which may have originated after abandonment of Indian garden sites or after fire had been used to clear the land. An early traveler, Peter Kalm, reported extensive Indian fires along the southern Champlain Valley of New York and Vermont in 1750 (Benson 1937). However, comments by land surveyors from 1783 to 1787 on the nature of the land along survey lines of township borders in the presettlement forest of northern Vermont include no mention of fire or fire scars (Siccama 1971).

Although fires were probably common in presettlement times throughout much of New England and adjacent Canada, within the northern hardwood forests of the White Mountains there is very little evidence, vegetational or historical, that fire was widespread. Certainly there are no fire histories comparable to those found by Heinselman (1973) and Frissell (1973) in Minnesota.

After 1869, with the introduction of large-scale logging in the White Mountains, the frequency of fires increased drastically. For the most part these fires burned over slash-filled areas left by logging operations. Since the advent of fire protection, fire is once again a relatively rare occurrence in the White Mountains.

Wind as disturbance

Unlike fire, wind is relatively independent of control by man. In a study of land survey records, Stearns (1949) reported considerable wind damage to presettlement northern hardwood forests in northeastern Wisconsin. Surveyors' maps made in about 1859 show areas of blowdown from one to several square kilometers in size, and the surveyors recorded many instances of blowdown in small areas. In nearby Menominee County, Wisconsin, 80 million board feet (1 board foot = 2,359 cm^3) of drought-weakened timber blew down between 1930 and 1937 (Secrest et al. 1941). These data emphasize the importance of wind in the western extension of the northern hardwood forest, but because of marked differences in topography and wind patterns it is difficult to relate them directly to forests in northern New England.

New England forests are subject to three major classes of destructive wind storms: tropical cyclones (hurricanes), extra-tropical cyclones, and localized intense winds associated with storm fronts and thunderstorms (Smith, M.S. diss.). Since 1492, northern New Hampshire and Vermont have been struck by severe hurricane-force winds only twice, in 1815 and again in 1938. A hurricane in 1788 seems to have been confined to southeastern Vermont and central New Hampshire (Ludlum 1963).

The effects of the 1938 hurricane are reasonably well known from survey records of the U.S. Forest Service (see Spurr 1956a; Smith, M.S. diss.). In Connecticut, Rhode Island, Massachusetts, and Vermont, out of a total forest area of about 5.3 million ha, we estimate that about 4.5 million ha were in the zone affected by the hurricane. Nearly 3 billion board feet of timber were blown down, and 243,000 ha were severely damaged, representing only about 5% of the affected zone. Although many stands were completely destroyed or lost patches

of trees, within the 4.5 million ha region most stands escaped with injury only to isolated trees. Most observers agree that topography was a major factor in limiting damage from this hurricane (Smith 1946). In the White Mountains, damage was principally confined to defective trees or sites exposed to wind, while most old-growth and even-aged northern hardwoods were relatively unaffected (Jensen 1939).

The fact that there have been only two severe hurricanes during 487 years and that the greatest devastation was restricted to particular sites close to the paths of these storms suggests that hurricanes are not a major recycling factor for most of the hardwood forest of northern Vermont and New Hampshire. This area also seems to be at low risk from large-scale storms, including extra-tropical storms (Smith, M.S. diss.).

Intense, relatively localized winds associated with frontal showers and thunderstorms may be a more important factor than large-scale storms because of their much greater frequency and because they probably affect a larger total area. There are almost no precise data on these winds, but our observations of northern hardwood forests in the White Mountains over the last 20 years suggest that single trees and some small- to moderate-sized patches of trees are commonly lost to windthrow.

Apparently there was relatively little loss to wind in the presettlement forests of northern Vermont. Only 5 of 163 comments about vegetation along land-survey lines mention windfalls (Siccama 1971). Lorimer (1977) reports that in surveys of northeastern Maine covering the period from 1793 to 1827, windfalls covered only 2.2% of the total surveyed distance. Most of these windfalls were confined to conifer forests, with only a few occurring in mixed or hardwood stands.

A 500-year history of a 0.4-ha plot in the Harvard Forest in central Massachusetts has been reconstructed by a careful analysis of windthrow mounds, fallen trees in all stages of decay, and living trees (Stephens 1955 and 1956). About 14% of the area of the plot was covered with mounds and pits. The analysis indicates that

four of six windthrow events could be considered major—one in the fifteenth century and the three others, in 1815, 1936, and 1938, that correspond to dates of major hurricanes.

Henry and Swan (1974) applied Stephens's methodology of analyzing mounds to a 0.04-ha plot in Pisgah Forest in southwestern New Hampshire. To optimize the conditions for reconstructing forest history, the plot was chosen in an area where rotting material was abundant. Henry and Swan concluded that a severe fire in about 1665 resulted in a more or less even-aged conifer forest, which grew without major disturbance for 262 years. Between 1897 and 1938 four wind storms, culminating in the 1938 hurricane, completely destroyed the larger trees and initiated new growth.

These studies emphasize the frequency and magnitude of wind as a disturbing force in forest ecosystems of central New England, but it should be borne in mind that the amount and frequency of disturbance per unit of land reported is very much a function of the study site selected by the investigator. Nevertheless, windthrow mounds are a widespread phenomenon. Their prevalence in a northern hardwood forest in Pennsylvania led Goodlett (1954) to single out windthrow of individual trees or small groups of trees as an important factor in maintaining shade-tolerant species in the presettlement northern hardwood forest. Stephens (1956), in an 8,000-km journey to the Cumberland and Smoky mountains, south through the southern Piedmont, west to the Ouachita and Boston mountains and back to Massachusetts, found mounds and pits of uprooted trees practically everywhere. Lutz (1940) also determined that windthrow is a universal phenomenon in forest regions and that, over long periods of time, the soil under forest stands is repeatedly subjected to disturbance when trees are uprooted. This conclusion applies quite well to the Hubbard Brook Experimental Forest in the White Mountains and is reflected in the pit-and-mound topography mapped on one of the experimental watersheds (Bormann et al. 1970). We should point out, however, that many of the mounds noted in our study and others could equally well have resulted from the fall of trees due to endogenous causes.

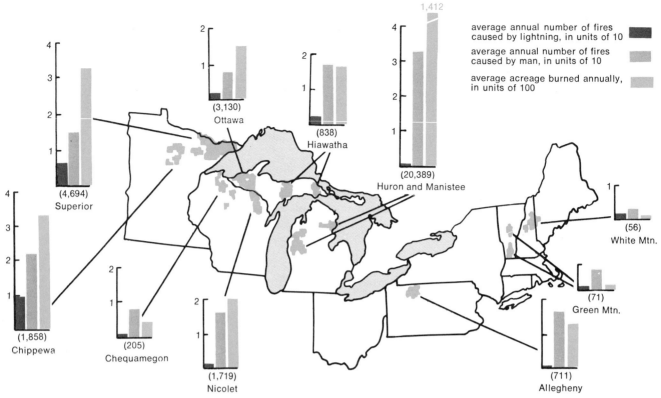

Figure 3. Fire statistics for the eleven national forests in the northern hardwood region from 1945 to 1976 point up the difference in incidence of fires between the western and eastern parts of the region. The numbers in parentheses represent the largest acreage burned in each national forest in a single year. All data are per million acres of national forest land. (Data calculated from U.S. Forest Service Annual Fire Reports; primary data supplied by Junius Baker, Jr., U.S. Forest Service.)

It seems reasonable to conclude that presettlement northern hardwood forests in the White Mountains were subjected to frequent disturbances by wind, but mostly on a modest scale. However, stands of trees on exposed sites might have suffered extensive wind damage at fairly frequent intervals.

Disturbance intervals

In contrast to the 100-year natural fire rotation period estimated by Heinselman for the Boundary Waters Canoe Area of northern Minnesota, the natural fire or cyclonic wind rotation for much of the White Mountains region in presettlement times and later seems to have been many centuries or even a millennium. Our conclusion is based on the convergence of several lines of evidence.

First, Indian populations, elsewhere a significant factor in presettlement fires, were sparse and had little incentive to clear land by burning. Second, the lower elevations of the White Mountains region are among the lowest wind-risk areas in New England (Smith, M.S. diss.), and the

area also seems to be relatively resistant to fire. Many factors—such as recurrence of severe drought years, frequency of lightning, vigor of the vegetation, propensity to accumulate burnable matter, and human activities—determine the susceptibility of a forested ecosystem to intense fires. Although it is difficult to combine these factors into a meaningful index of fire susceptibility, extensive records of fires on national forest land from 1945 to 1976 (the period most reliably documented) suggest that forests in the White and Green mountains are among the least burnable in the northern hardwood region (Fig. 3).

Fires occur at the rate of 4.3 per 405,000 ha per year in the White Mountain National Forest, with about one third of these ignited by lightning. This is the lowest ignition rate for any of the eleven national forests located in the northern hardwood region. Still more interesting is the fact that on average only 3 ha/405,000 ha of the White Mountain National Forest actually burn each year—the smallest area burned per year among the eleven forests. With the exception of the Green Mountain

National Forest (4 ha/405,000 ha) and Chequamegon National Forest in Wisconsin (17 ha/405,000 ha), the average area burned annually in the White Mountain National Forest is 15 to 40 times lower than that of other forests. It is more than two orders of magnitude lower than the area burned in national forests in lower Michigan, and about 40 times lower than that burned in national forests in Minnesota, one of which contains the Boundary Waters Canoe Area. The single largest area burned in the White Mountain National Forest in any year is 23 ha/405,000 ha, which is from one to two orders of magnitude smaller than areas burned in the other forests, with the exception of the Green Mountain and Chequamegon national forests.

The principal cause of fire in the northern hardwood region is man and his activities (Haines et al. 1975). The White Mountain National Forest receives more than twice as much recreational use per unit area as forests surrounding the Great Lakes. Given this heavy use by man, the lowest annual ignition and burn rates, and the smallest single area burned in any one year, it would appear that a combination of meteorologic, biologic, and topographic factors make the White Mountains forests less susceptible to fire.

Some of these factors can be tentatively identified. Vulnerability to fire or wind is determined by a number of physiographic and biologic characteristics, causing some areas to be more resistant than others to catastrophic damage. Given the well-watered, rugged landscape of the White Mountains, for example, it seems reasonable to think that many areas would be protected from the easy sweep of fire or from intensive cyclonic winds.

Moreover, the composition of an ecosystem contributes to the vulnerability to fire and wind of given portions of the ecosystem at a given time. Some species are more flammable than others, and the accumulation and spatial distribution of organic fuel is an important factor. Similarly, susceptibility to wind damage may be related to the size of individual trees, to whether the trees are deciduous or evergreen, and to the structure of the stand. Although we do not yet have specific information on susceptibility to fire for the various developmental stages of northern hardwood forests, a number of ecologists and foresters are of the opinion that most northern hardwood forests are relatively resistant to fire (Chittenden 1905; Bromley 1935; Hough 1936; Egler 1940; Stearns 1949; Winer, Ph.D. diss.); in fact, they have been called "asbestos forests." On the other hand, it would seem that as northern hardwood stands become composed of larger and older trees their vulnerability to wind would increase. Toppling of large trees in an area might be coupled with an increase in the susceptibility of the area to fire.

In addition, the degree to which ecosystems are vulnerable to fire is related to the rate at which biological decomposition reduces the fuel load of dead wood or organic matter on the mineral soil surface (Wright and Heinselman 1973). In some systems, litter production is so much greater than decomposition that fuel accumulation apparently reaches enormous proportions (Bloomberg 1950). In humid temperate and tropical systems characterized by intense fungal and bacterial activity, decomposition can reduce susceptibility

to fire by a rapid turnover of litter, and the amount of dead wood and forest floor material present at any one time is minimal. Our studies indicate that the northern hardwood forests in the White Mountains follow this pattern (Bormann and Likens 1979).

Steady state reexamined

Given the fact that ecosystems sufficiently free of exogenous events to allow progression to a steady state do seem to exist, it is appropriate to look more closely at the idea of the steady state itself, and to consider in more detail both how such a state might develop and what its characteristics might be.

The idea of the steady state is one of the most controversial of ecological constructs. Woodwell and Sparrow (1965) define the steady state as a condition in which there is no net change in total biomass over time, with annual ecosystem respiration approximately equaling annual gross primary productivity (GPP). Changes in total biomass within the ecosystem are governed by relationships between the four major biomass compartments (green-plant living biomass, dead wood, organic matter composing the forest floor, and organic matter in the mineral soil).

In defining our own idea of the steady state, we have proposed a biomass accumulation model for ecosystem development distinguished by four phases following a major exogenous disturbance such as clear-cutting: reorganization, aggradation, transition, and steady state. The model illustrates one pathway by which an aggrading northern hardwood forest might develop into a steady-state ecosystem. It should be stressed that our treatment is a theoretical one derived from a logical assemblage of information on natural history and biogeochemistry; it is not based on actual measurements of extant steady-state ecosystems.

Following a major exogenous disturbance such as clear-cutting, we posit an orderly pattern of autogenic development which given sufficient time and a fairly constant macroenvironment can lead to a steady-state condition. The amounts of organic matter in the forest floor and in dead wood level off about midway through

the aggradation phase (i.e. input $\simeq$ output). If we assume that organic matter in the mineral soil behaves in the same way, a steady state according to the Woodwell-Sparrow definition would be realized if the green-plant living biomass became stabilized. Our analyses indicate that stabilization in the amount of living biomass would be achieved several centuries after clear-cutting. However, a steady-state concept based on the premise that ecosystem respiration equals GPP should be considered at best approximate. In a strict sense there can be no absolute steady state but only a system undergoing slow long-term change.

In nature, of course, departures from this inherent tendency toward order are caused by fortuitous events—the exogenous disturbances we have been considering—which introduce an element of disorder into the pattern. These exogenous events complicate the interpretation of developmental relationships of the northern hardwood ecosystem. Thus, while it is easy to recognize extant ecosystems that correspond reasonably well to our proposed reorganization and aggradation phases, it is difficult to find stands that conform exactly to our transition and steady-state phases, although there are a few candidates, notably Charcoal Hearth and Bowl forests in New Hampshire.

The difficulty of identifying such stands with certainty arises from several causes. Because of human activity, stands containing old-aged trees (that is, trees more than 200 years old) are fairly rare, and their history of disturbance is often unknown. Furthermore, the age of the individual trees in itself is insufficient evidence to place a stand within the developmental sequence; old-aged trees can be found in the late aggradation and transition phases as well as in the steady-state phase. Also, the age of northern hardwood species is often impossible to determine because the centers of old-aged trees, necessary for dating, have become rotten.

Steady state and the biomass curve

A widely accepted model of primary and secondary ecosystem development (Margalef 1968; Odum 1969;

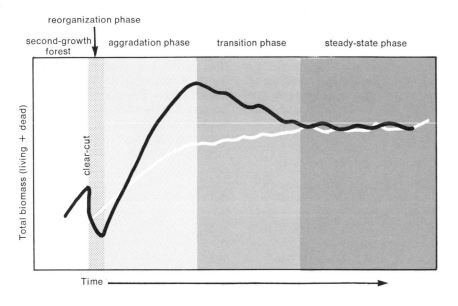

Figure 4. Two models of ecosystem development following clear-cutting, based on total (living plus dead) biomass accumulation, show differences in projected recovery and stabilization patterns. The simple asymptotic model (*white line*) assumes that biomass slowly increases until the steady state is achieved; maximum biomass occurs during the steady-state phase. Our model (*black line*) delineates four phases of biomass decline and recovery, with a sharp drop in the reorganization phase and maximum accumulation of biomass occurring prior to the steady state.

Whittaker and Woodwell 1972; Whittaker et al. 1974; Whittaker 1975) is characterized by an asymptotic curve of biomass accumulation culminating in a steady state or "climax" condition at maximum levels of biomass (Fig. 4). Our reasoning, however, suggests that an asymptotic curve of biomass accumulation is insufficient to portray the developmental potential of the northern hardwood ecosystem following a substantial exogenous disturbance such as clear-cutting.

Our model of biomass accumulation (Fig. 4) departs from the asymptotic model in several significant ways. The standing crop of total biomass after cutting declines (reorganization phase), steadily increases to a maximum (aggradation phase), erratically declines (transition phase), and finally stabilizes with somewhat irregular oscillations about a mean (steady-state phase). This developmental pattern reflects the initial even-aged condition of the cut-over northern hardwood ecosystem and the gradual change to an all-aged condition, which we term the shifting-mosaic steady state. The biomass accumulation pattern we propose and the conditions that underlie its expression lead to conclusions about ecosystem energetics, structure, nutrient cycling, and stability quite different from those arising from the assumption of an asymptotic curve of biomass accumulation.

Thus far, we have considered the northern hardwood ecosystem as an

integrated unit equal to or greater than some minimum area necessary to maintain the integrity of the ecosystem as a functioning unit. However, considerable variation may exist within that unit. The forest that develops after clear-cutting might be considered one large even-aged patch resulting from exogenous disturbance. In time individual trees or groups of trees fall down, creating smaller patches of younger vegetation. Eventually the whole forest will be composed of patches of varying size and age. Although the discussion that follows is based on the simulated behavior of 10 × 10-m plots, we believe it provides a logical approximation of the natural situation.

An individual plot will never exhibit a prolonged steady state in which biomass accumulation will approximate zero. That is, assuming no outside disturbance, it is highly probable that an individual plot would ultimately be dominated by a large old tree. Eventually the old dominant will die and fall over. When it does, it will create a local disturbance, depositing in a small area a heavy concentration of dead biomass which decomposes fairly rapidly. Disturbance and increased decomposition promote an increase in available water and nutrients (Bormann and Likens 1979). Rapid revegetation by numerous small trees, each with relatively small living biomass, follows these changes. As time passes, the plot undergoes thinning, living biomass accumulation occurs as the vegetation develops, and the biogeochemistry of the

plot returns to conditions similar to those found during the aggradation phase. Eventually the plot again comes to be dominated by one or two massive trees and the cycle repeats itself.

Since an event such as clear-cutting imposes an even-aged condition on the ecosystem, the behavior of most plots is synchronized for about a century and a half afterwards. During the aggradation phase, as thinning continues and as the density of dominants declines, plots tend to be occupied by fewer and larger even-aged trees which date to the clear-cutting. Thus, maximum living biomass for the entire developmental sequence is attained at the end of the aggradation phase, when a majority of plots support anywhere from one to several more or less even-aged trees of massive size. Forest structure at this stage might be considered as roughly equivalent to that of an old forest plantation where spacing has been adjusted to maximize living biomass accumulation. Interestingly, this type of massive, more or less even-aged successional forest seems to be equated with the "virgin," "climax," "pristine," or steady-state forest in the minds of many novelists, conservationists, foresters, and ecologists.

The end of the aggradation phase, when the ecosystem is dominated by old even-aged trees, must be considered a period of instability in the developmental sequence. The populations of even-aged dominants do not live forever; hence the biomass peak is followed by a period of decline of living biomass (the transition phase), which results as even-aged dominants die out and are replaced by patches of young vegetation growing up from the forest floor. This leads to a drop in total living biomass as the much lower weights of these patches are averaged into the whole.

The steady state is achieved after the progressive elimination of these old even-aged dominants and with the development of dominants of all ages on the plots that compose the ecosystem. Dead biomass, which is temporarily increased by accelerated input from the living biomass compartment during the transition phase, eventually comes into balance at a lower level. Thus total biomass in the steady-state phase is less than that at the end of the aggradation phase.

Since the developmental phase of the ecosystem is determined by the state of the naturally occurring patches comprising the ecosystem, we used JABOWA, our forest growth model (Botkin et al. 1972a and b), to simulate on a computer the behavior of living biomass in individual plots in order to gain a more detailed view of the developmental process.

Based on the projected values for living biomass, we assigned plots to three states or conditions. Plots in state A (<0.6 t of biomass/100 m²) may be dominated by herbs, shrubs, or young forests, e.g. one hundred trees 4 cm in diameter at breast height (dbh) or three 18-cm-dbh trees = 0.6 t/100 m². Plots with a living biomass ranging from 0.6 to 4.9 t/100 m² were assigned to state B, indicating that they might be dominated by many small trees, a few intermediate-sized trees, or a larger tree, e.g. four 38-cm-dbh trees or one 67-cm-dbh tree = 4.9 t/100 m². State C (>4.9 t/100 m²) plots may be dominated by one or two massive trees, e.g. two 69-cm-dbh trees or one 92-cm-dbh tree = 10.6 t/100 m². The plots in the various states are dynamically related to each other.

The percentage of plots in states A, B, and C and the trends of the states through time define the position of the ecosystem along the temporal scale of development (Fig. 5). This pattern of plot distribution during the reorganization and aggradation phases results because the majority of plots progressively accumulate bio-

mass and tend to follow the developmental sequence state A → state B → state C, while relatively few plots lose biomass and drop to a lower state. This pattern is largely a consequence of even-agedness, fairly long potential lifespans for some dominants, and natural thinning.

Shifting-mosaic steady state

In most discussions of steady-state or "climax" ecosystems (e.g. Vitousek and Reiners 1975), the condition of the steady-state ecosystem is loosely defined by one or two parameters for the ecosystem as a whole, such as the assumption that biomass accumulation equals zero or that GPP equals total ecosystem respiration. More often than not, authors are extremely vague or totally unconcerned about the detailed structure of the steady-state ecosystem or the means by which the steady state might perpetuate itself through time. Yet such information is basic to any analysis of the energetic, biogeochemical, or stability relationships integral to the steady-state condition. Visualizing the steady state is not an easy task, and it is with some trepidation that we attempt an approximate characterization of what a hypothetical northern hardwood forest steady state might be like, and how it might perpetuate itself.

Based in part on JABOWA simulations, we suggest that a steady state is achieved several hundred years after clear-cutting, when the standing crop of total biomass begins to oscillate

about a mean. The proportions of the ecosystem in states A, B, and C remain more or less constant with time (Fig. 5), but the state of any individual plot may change as it gains or loses biomass. For example, new plots in state A arise when gaps are created by the fall of large trees. We term this dynamic but relatively unchanging condition the shifting-mosaic steady state.

Several factors suggest that in a real steady-state ecosystem the proportion of total area in state A patches would be several times greater than that projected by the JABOWA simulations, where mortality rates are based strictly on deaths reflecting competition between trees (Botkin et al. 1972a and b). Deaths from the crushing effects produced by the fall of massive trees are not included, although we know from observation that such endogenous events may clear areas equivalent to three to five times a JABOWA-sized plot (up to 500 m²). Also excluded from JABOWA calculations are local forces of disturbance that operate in any forest ecosystem: localized attacks by insects or disease, lightning, or increased attrition of trees surrounding gaps resulting from snow, ice, and winds.

Taking this into account, the shifting-mosaic steady state may be visualized as an array of irregular patches composed of vegetation of different ages. In some patches, particularly those where there has been a recent fall of a large tree, total respiration would exceed GPP, while in other

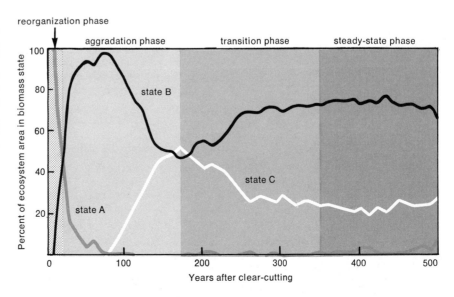

Figure 5. The percentages of the ecosystem area in states A (<0.6 t of biomass/100 m²), B (0.6 to 4.9 t/100m²), and C (>4.9 t/100m²) vary after clear-cutting, tending to stabilize with time. This pattern is based on computer calculations involving two hundred 10 × 10-m plots.

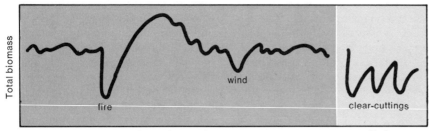

Figure 6. Naturally occurring castastrophic perturbations such as fire and large-scale winds take place only at fairly long intervals in much of the White Mountains region. In presettlement times, erratic biomass fluctuations as shown probably predominated over much of the landscape. Such a pattern differs markedly from that produced in some areas by modern land management, which regularly harvests by clear-cutting at 60- to 70-year intervals.

patches the reverse would be true. For the ecosystem as a whole, the forces of aggradation and of decomposition would be more or less balanced, and gross primary production would approximately equal total ecosystem respiration. Over the long term, nutrients temporarily concentrated in small areas in fallen trunks would be made available to larger areas by root absorption and by redistribution through fall of litter. The forest stand would be considered all-aged and would contain representatives of most species, including some early-successional species, on a continuing basis.

Probability for a steady state

Loucks's hypothesis that forest ecosystems are periodically destroyed and restarted by fire at intervals so short that an autogenically derived steady state is rarely achieved seems reasonable for large areas of vegetation dependent on fire for renewal. However, we would suggest that it cannot be generally applied to northern hardwood ecosystems of the White Mountains. During presettlement times there may have been some fire-prone areas where return periods of fire were short enough to truncate autogenic development regularly, and over millennia the whole region might have been recycled. However, modern fire records for the province of New Brunswick, Canada, indicate fire rotation periods of about 650 to 2,000 years for various forest types in which northern hardwood species are important (Wein and Moore 1977), and similar estimates derived from the modern fire record for the White Mountain National Forest yield incredibly long fire

rotation periods. Consequently, it seems that fairly large areas of presettlement hardwood forest within these humid and rugged mountains have been free of catastrophic disturbance for periods of time sufficient to allow achievement of a steady state in the course of ecosystem development.

The presettlement northern hardwood landscape might be conceived of as a collection of ecosystems in various stages of development. Some areas, particularly those susceptible to fire or wind, might have been regularly recycled by catastrophic disturbance, but substantial areas might have supported ecosystems approaching the steady state. We say "approaching" because small-scale exogenous disturbances which kill or maim healthy trees—wind, snow, and ice—seem unavoidable when the area being considered is extensive and the time period long. These minor disturbances might more appropriately be considered within the pattern of autogenic development.

In attempting to construct a broader picture, we suggest that it might be useful to consider catastrophic recycling and the autogenically derived steady state as components of a two-dimensional geographical space. Because of modest levels of exogenous disturbance or long periods of time between large-scale disturbances prior to colonization by Europeans, forested regions of the humid temperate mountains of the northeastern United States might be considered as centers where the probability of achieving steady-state conditions through autogenic development is highest, while in almost every direction away from these centers cata-

strophic recycling takes on increasing importance.

In recent years, however, the intervention of man in the White Mountains has appreciably increased the area occupied by even-aged forests. In presettlement forests, relatively large areas were probably in an all-aged condition. Many stands were composed of patches in all stages of development.

Major exogenous disturbances by man—notably clear-cutting, intense fires, and land clearing and abandonment—have removed living biomass and often resulted in the establishment of even-aged stands (Gilbert and Jensen 1958). Man might therefore be thought of as an organizing force imposing synchrony on the previously asynchronous patches of the presettlement steady-state ecosystems. The second and third generation clear-cuts now occurring in the northern hardwood forest tend to truncate the trend toward asynchrony in the developing forest ecosystem. Thus management of the northern hardwood forest by clear-cutting produces a pattern of recycling through time quite similar to that proposed for natural ecosystems subjected to severe exogenous disturbances at short intervals (Fig. 6). In areas naturally prone to disturbance, paradoxically, suppression of fire disrupts the short-term recycling thought to be characteristic of these areas in presettlement times. This type of management allows progress toward the steady state, and helps to bring about a condition seldom achieved previously.

References

Bensen, A. B., ed. 1937. *Peter Kalm's Travels in North America,* Vol. 1. Dover.

Bloomberg, W. G. 1950. Fire and spruce. *For. Chron.* 26: 157–61.

Bormann, F. H., and G. E. Likens. 1979. *Pattern and Process in a Forested Ecosystem.* Springer-Verlag.

Bormann, F. H., T. G. Siccama, G. E. Likens, and R. H. Whittaker. 1970. The Hubbard Brook Ecosystem Study: Composition and dynamics of the tree stratum. *Ecol. Monogr.* 40:377–88.

Botkin, D. B., J. F. Janak, and J. R. Wallis. 1972a. Rationale, limitations, and assumptions of a northeastern forest growth simulator. *IBM J. Res. Devel.* 16(2):101–16.

———. 1972b. Some ecological consequences of a computer model of forest growth. *J. Ecol.* 60:948–72. IBM Research Report No. 15799.

Bromley, S. W. 1935. The original forest types of southern New England. *Ecol. Monogr.* 5:61–89.

Brown, J. W. 1958. Forest history of Mount Moosilauke. I: Primeval conditions, settlements and the farm-forest economy. II: Big logging days and their aftermath (1890–1940). *Appalachia* 24(7):23–32, 221–33.

Chapman, H. H. 1947. Natural areas. *Ecology* 28:193–94.

Chittenden, A. K. 1905. *Forest Conditions of Northern New Hampshire.* USDA Bureau of Forestry Bull. No. 55.

Cline, A. C., and S. H. Spurr. 1942. *The Virgin Upland Forest of Central New England.* Harv. For. Bull. No. 21.

Connell, J. H., and R. O. Slatyer. Mechanisms of succession in natural communities and their role in community stability and organization. Unpub.

Day, G. 1953. The Indian as an ecological factor in the northeastern forest. *Ecology* 34:329–46.

Egler, F. E. 1940. Berkshire plateau vegetation, Massachusetts. *Ecol. Monogr.* 10:145–92.

Frissell, S. S., Jr. 1973. The importance of fire as a natural ecological factor in Itasca State Park, Minnesota. *Quat. Res.* 3(3):397–407.

Gilbert, A. M., and V. S. Jensen. 1958. *A Management Guide for Northern Hardwoods in New England.* Northeastern Forest Experiment Station Paper No. 112, Upper Darby, PA.

Goodlett, J. C. 1954. *Vegetation Adjacent to the Border of the Wisconsin Drift in Potter County, Pennsylvania.* Harv. For. Bull. No. 25.

Graham, S. A. 1941. Climax forests of the upper peninsula of Michigan. *Ecology* 22:355–62.

Haines, D. A., V. J. Johnson, and W. A. Main. 1975. *Wildfire Atlas of the Northeastern and North Central States.* USDA Forest Service General Technical Report NC-16.

Heinselman, M. L. 1973. Fire in the virgin forests of the Boundary Waters Canoe Area, Minnesota. *Quat. Res.* 3(3):329–82.

Henry, J. D., and J.M.A. Swan. 1974. Reconstructing forest history from live and dead plant material: An approach to the study of forest succession in southwest New Hampshire. *Ecology* 55:772–83.

Hough, A. F. 1936. A climax forest community on East Tionesta Creek in northwestern Pennsylvania. *Ecology* 17:9–28.

Hough, A. F., and R. D. Forbes. 1943. The ecology and silvics of forests in the high plateaus of Pennsylvania. *Ecol. Monogr.* 13:299–320.

Jensen, V. S. 1939. *Edging White Pine Lumber in New England.* USDA Forest Service. Northeastern Forest Experiment Station Tech. Note No. 26.

Kilgore, B. M. 1973. The ecological role of fire in Sierran conifer forests. *Quat. Res.* 3(3):496–513.

Likens, G. E. 1972. Mirror Lake: Its past, present and future? *Appalachia* 39(2):23–41.

Lorimer, C. G. 1977. The presettlement forest and natural disturbance cycle of northeastern Maine. *Ecology* 58:139–48.

Loucks, O. L. 1970. Evolution of diversity, efficiency and community stability. *Amer. Zool.* 10:17–25.

Ludlum, D. M. 1963. *Early American Hurricanes, 1492–1870.* Boston: American Meteorological Society.

Lutz, H. J. 1930. The vegetation of Heart's Content, a virgin forest in northwestern Pennsylvania. *Ecology* 11:1–29.

———. 1940. *Disturbance of Forest Soil Resulting from Uprooting of Trees.* Yale Univ. School of Forestry Bull. No. 45.

MacLean, D. W. 1960. *Some Aspects of the Aspen-Birch-Spruce-Fir Type of Ontario.* Dept. of Forestry, Forest Research Division Tech. Note No. 94.

Maissurow, D. K. 1941. The role of fire in the perpetuation of virgin forests of northern Wisconsin. *J. Forestr.* 39:201–7.

Margalef, R. 1968. *Perspectives in Ecological Theory.* Univ. of Chicago Press.

Odum, E. P. 1969. The strategy of ecosystem development. *Science* 164:262–70.

Raup, H. M. 1957. Vegetational adjustment to the instability of the site. In *Proc. and Papers of the 6th Technical Meeting of the Internat. Union for the Protection of Nature, June 1956, Edinburgh,* pp. 36–48. London: Society for the Promotion of Nature Reserves.

———. 1967. American forest biology. *J. Forestr.* 65:800–3.

Rowe, J. S., and G. W. Scotter. 1973. Fire in the boreal forest. *Quat. Res.* 3(3):444–64.

Secrest, H. C., A. J. MacAlong, and R. C. Lorenz. 1941. Causes of the decadence of hemlock at the Menominee Indian Reservation, Wisconsin. *J. Forestr.* 39:3–12.

Siccama, T. G. 1971. Presettlement and present forest vegetation in northern Vermont with special reference to Chittenden County. *Amer. Midl. Natl.* 85:153–72.

Smith, D. H. Storm damage in New England forests. M.S. diss., 1946, Yale Univ.

Smith, F. E. Ecosystems and evolution. Presidential Address to the Ecological Society of America, August 1975, Corvallis, OR. Unpub.

Spurr, S. H. 1956a. Natural restocking of forests following the 1938 hurricane in central New England. *Ecology* 37:443–51.

———. 1956b. Forest associations in the Harvard forest. *Ecol. Monogr.* 26:245–62.

Stearns, F. S. 1949. Ninety years of change in a northern hardwood forest in Wisconsin. *Ecology* 30:350–58.

Stephens, E. P. 1955. Research in the biological aspects of forest production. *J. Forestr.* 53:183–86.

———. 1956. The uprooting of trees: A forest process. *Soil Sci. Soc. Amer. Proc.* 20(1):113–16.

Thompson, D. Q., and R. H. Smith. 1970. The forest primeval in the Northeast: A great myth? In *Proc. Tall Timbers Fire Ecology Conference No. 10, August 1970, Frederickton, New Brunswick, Canada,* pp. 255–65. Tallahassee, FL: Tall Timbers Research Station.

Vitousek, P. M., and W. A. Reiners. 1975. Ecosystem succession and nutrient retention: A hypothesis. *BioScience* 25:376–81.

Whittaker, R. H. 1975. *Communities and Ecosystems.* Macmillan.

Whittaker, R. H., and G. M. Woodwell. 1972. Evolution of natural communities. In *Ecosystem Structure and Function,* ed. J. A. Wiens, pp. 137–56. Oregon State Univ. Press.

Whittaker, R. H., F. H. Bormann, G. E. Likens, and T. G. Siccama. 1974. The Hubbard Brook Ecosystem Study: Forest biomass and production. *Ecol. Monogr.* 44:233–54.

Winer, H. I. History of the Great Mountain Forest. Ph.D. diss., 1955, Yale Univ.

Woodwell, G. M. 1974. Success, succession and Adam Smith. *BioScience* 24:81–87.

Woodwell, G. M., and A. H. Sparrow. 1965. Effects of ionizing radiation on ecological systems. In *Ecological Effects of Nuclear War,* ed. G. M. Woodwell, pp. 20–38. Brookhaven National Laboratory 917 (C-43).

Wright, H. E., Jr., and M. L. Heinselman. 1973. The ecological role of fire in natural conifer forests of western and northern North America: Introduction. *Quat. Res.* 3(3):319–28.

"There's a 60 percent chance of 20 percent acid rain and a 40 percent chance of 30 percent acid rain."

Stephen Berwick

The Gir Forest: An Endangered Ecosystem

Complementary studies of the major elements of an area—people, domestic and wild animals, and plants—suggest ways to preserve its ecological integrity

Accelerating use and resultant abuse of natural resources in the developing tropics lend an immediacy to attempts not only to survey problem areas in resource husbandry (see Talbot 1960, Eckholm 1975a and b) but to conduct intensive, area-specific research to identify the components of natural ecosystems, their interactions, and their resistance to a variety of disturbances or alterations. The demands on natural resources are exceptional in India, where over 80 percent of the human population of 613 million is rural, where the annual rate of population growth is 2.4 percent, and where the projected population in the year 2000 will be 1.06 billion (Myers et al. 1975). At a doubling time of 29 years, by the year 2000 India will have a population density of about 322 persons per square kilometer, compared to 28 per km^2 for the United States. Pressures to ex-

Stephen Berwick is Assistant Professor of Wildlife Ecology at Yale University. A graduate of the University of California at Berkeley, Dr. Berwick holds masters degrees from the University of Montana and Yale University, and a Ph.D. from Yale. His research centers on the ecology of ungulates, including their food habits, behavior, demography, and productivity. His work on mountain sheep in the Rockies and wildlife in India has also led to considerations of predator-prey systems, human ecology, land use, and disappearing ecosystems. Currently Dr. Berwick is conducting a cross-cultural analysis of the decision-making process.
The author would like to acknowledge the support of the Smithsonian Institution, the Bombay Natural History Society, Yale University, and the National Science Foundation. Among many others, credit is due to M. A. Berwick, D. Brewster, S. Chavan, Z. Futehally, K. T. B. Hodd, M. Huxley, P. Jordan, P. Joslin, N. Sanyal, and L. Talbot. Address: School of Forestry and Environmental Studies, Yale University, New Haven, CT 06511.

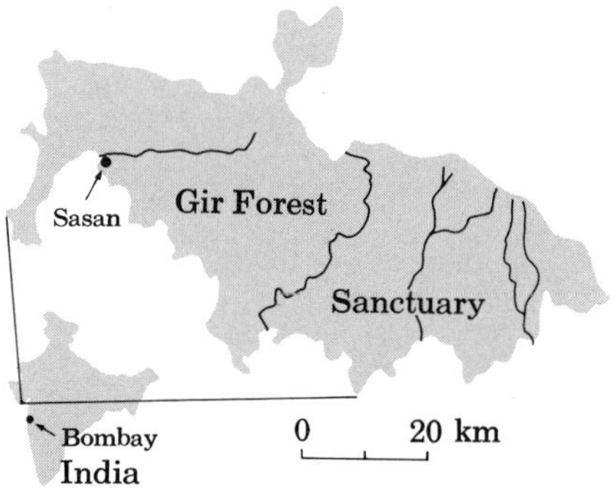

Figure 1. With an area of approximately 1,200 square kilometers, the Gir Forest, in the state of Gujarat, about 320 km northwest of Bombay, is the largest nature preserve in India. National parks in much of the world do not fulfill international standards because of the conspicuous effects of human inhabitants, but without such "pragmatic" preserves few essentially wild ecosystems would remain in many parts of India and other countries.

ploit certain resources such as wood and dung for fuel (as opposed to fossil fuels) will increase with the population. The wildlife resource is, of course, intimately related to the integrity of the land. About 75 percent of the world's mammals currently considered to be in danger of extinction are so classified primarily because of man's activities (Fisher et al. 1969). Although one of the legacies of the British raj in India was depleted numbers of some game due to overhunting, habitat alteration now seems to be the critical limiting factor.

A paradigm of the problems associated with wildland alteration and biological impoverishment is to be found in the Gir Forest, in the state of Gujarat in northwestern India (Fig. 1). The purpose of the research described in this paper is to present baseline data and derivative analyses necessary for the con-

servation of systems like the Gir and to demonstrate one way in which the problems endemic to such a broadly typical situation were approached.

The Gir Forest is unique as the home of the 177 remaining Asiatic lions (*Panthera leo persica*) (Figs. 2 and 3), a race of lions that once ranged through semiarid regions from Greece to Bihar, in eastern India (Talbot 1960). The Gir, with an area of about 1,200 km^2, is also the largest biologically intact, contiguous tract of land in India reserved primarily for the conservation of its native wild fauna. This sanctuary harbors remnant populations of many wild ungulate species that once constituted the magnificent faunal wealth of India—the spotted deer (*Axis axis*), sambar deer (*Cervus unicolor*), Indian gazelle (*Gazella gazella bennetti*), nilgai antelope (*Boselaphus tragocamelus*), wild boar (*Sus scrofa*), and the world's only four-horned antelope (*Tetracerus quadricornis*).

Although the Gir is protected as a wildlife sanctuary, several human activities have an impact on the precarious ecological balance of the area. The custodians of the forest, the Gujarat State Forest Department, permit logging, primarily of teak, which yields an annual income of about $60,000; this revenue, like that from all other uses of the for-

Figure 2. The Asiatic lion (*Panthera leo persica*), which once ranged from Greece to eastern India, now numbers only 177 individuals, all of which live in the endangered Gir Forest. (All photos are by the author unless otherwise indicated.)

est, is of minor importance. Silvi-cultural policy dictates the replant-ing of clear-cut areas to teak, a practice that promotes a mono-culture of a plant that is among the least preferred foods of the wild herbivores. Also, the creation of a homogeneous biotic landscape from a once diverse forest characterized by many ecological checks and bal-ances means that small perturba-tions such as infestations of insect pests can cause large-scale destruc-

the Gir each year to see the lions, which are attracted by baits offered daily (Joslin 1969). The great ma-jority of tourists are from Gujarat, although the state and federal gov-ernments are attempting to attract foreigners with their valuable cur-rency through publicity campaigns and the construction of a new forest guesthouse.

Agriculture is advancing to the boundaries of the Gir and has even

Figure 3. Once a nocturnal predator, the Asi-atic lion now hunts during the daylight hours when the numerous cattle of the Maldhari herdsmen are easy prey. This lioness, blind in her right eye, has killed a buffalo for her-self and her cubs. The rumen (*lower left-hand corner*), the contents of which do not appeal to the lions, is one of the few parts of the prey left uneaten.

tion of the single "crop" species—teak. Now, as is typical of artificial monocultures, from a cornfield in Iowa to a stand of Douglas fir in the Pacific Northwest, the monotonous teak stands in the Gir Forest are subject to regular and often near total defoliation by two species of caterpillars.

Tourism is becoming increasingly important: about 8,500 people visit

encroached into the sanctuary ille-gally along the flatter, more fertile river bottoms. In fact, the lion pop-ulation declined from about 250 in 1965, when 46 percent were found in forests outside of but adjacent to the sanctuary, to 177 in 1968, when 17 percent were found outside the sanctuary (Joslin, pers. comm.). The decrease in lions coincides with the loss of habitat; the density of lions within the sanctuary has remained constant and probably could not be increased without fostering artificial and zoolike conditions.

By far the greatest human impact on the Gir Forest is made by the Maldhari herdsmen, who live and graze their 25,000 cattle within the Gir (Fig. 4). This practice is particularly harmful because about half the grazing takes place during the monsoon (June–October), when the

percent of the diet of the 177 remaining lions consists of domestic buffalo and cattle (Joslin, pers. comm.)—a direct result of the high numbers and availability of domestic livestock grazing beyond the protection of the Maldhari settlement.

The shift from feeding on native wild prey to preying on domestic animals has required a behavioral adjustment for the lion, which is

soil is wet and compactable and the new growth of grasses is physiologically most vulnerable. Occasionally, as the Maldhari lead their livestock through the stunted teak forests to the hillsides where the more palatable grasses are found, a lion will emerge from the shrubs and kill a buffalo or cow. In fact, by identifying the hair found in lion droppings and by cataloging lion kills, it has been determined that about 75

now a daytime hunter instead of the nocturnal predator of wildlife of earlier times. The result is a formidable array of new competitors such as the Maldhari, who own the livestock; the hide and meat collectors, who drive the lions from the kill and strip it of skin and choice steaks before the lion gets so much as a single bite in over 25 percent of the kills (Joslin, pers. comm.) (Fig. 6); and a vulture population that

Figure 4. A small Maldhari village is completely dependent on the surrounding Gir Forest. Shelters for the six or seven families that make up the settlement are built of grass, mud, and poles; livestock is protected by acacia thorn fences. The approximately 185 cattle and buffalo, which provide the milk products for the settlement, live on the grasses and water of the sanctuary.

can consume the entire carcass of a 300-kilogram adult buffalo in less than half an hour. Because the lions are displaced from more than 50 percent of their kills by the new competitors, they have to make more kills to secure food, which brings them into even more conflict with the Maldhari herdsmen.

To reduce the competition for the kills of the lion and to protect the Maldhari livestock by increasing the populations of wild ruminant prey species to a point where they might again serve as the primary lion prey, I began a 20-month study in 1970 of the factors that limit the

Figure 5. *Clockwise from left:* A nilgai antelope (*Boselaphus tragocamelus*), black buck (*Antilope cervicapra*), and chital, or spotted, deer (*Axis axis*) sample forage held by the author in an enclosure where the animals lived during an experiment to determine which forage was preferred by six species of deer and antelope. (Photo courtesy of Peter A. Jordan.)

numbers of wild deer and antelope. Why are there 4,000 spotted deer and not 5,000 or 3,000?

Research was directed toward (1) determining the numbers of both wild and domestic prey, (2) determining whether the numbers of wild prey could be increased so that they could replace the domestic prey in the diet of the lion, (3) measuring the existence and extent of habitat overutilization and destruction, and (4) in anticipation of one management option—the translocation of the Maldharis and their livestock—defining the role the Maldhari graziers play in the Gir ecosystem, their demographic and social

characteristics, and their utilization of forest resources.

Observers who had visited the Gir Forest before the ecological studies began unanimously ascribed the regulation of the herbivorous wild prey of the lions to the competition for forage from the hordes of Maldhari cattle (Wynter-Blyth 1952; Talbot 1960; Spillett 1968). Also, overuse of the land for grazing seemed to be leading to the elimination of the forest habitat of the prey—and, of course, of the lion and the Maldhari community as well—by a subtle phenomenon known as xerification—a drying up of the land due to overuse of many kinds, but most often by grazing (grass-eating) and browsing (shrub-eating) domestic animals.

Xerification, popularly known as "the march of the deserts," has been postulated as a primary cause of the decline of early civilization along the Tigris and Euphrates rivers (Lowdermilk 1953). It can be seen today in such places as eastern and sub-Saharan Africa (Talbot 1960), Mexico (Leopold 1959), the southwestern United States (Hastings and Turner 1965), and much of India, including the Gir. Less than a century ago, the forests of Gir covered more than twice the area they do today (Santapau and Raizada 1956). One reason for the loss of forested lands lies in the conversion of wildland to agriculture under the pressure of a human population that has quadrupled during this time (Government of India 1968). However, particularly in the hillier tracts more refractory to agricultural development, xerification seems to have ravaged the forest.

Maldhari ecology

The uses the Maldharis make of the forest influence its composition, structure, productivity, and capacity to sustain the spectrum of wild animals found there. It was therefore essential to investigate the different uses made of the resources and the effects of these activities on the rest of the system. Demographic and cultural trends also had to be evaluated to help predict the effects of resource utilization and the efficacy of any management suggestions. For example, in an area where artificial population control is virtually nonexistent, I wondered why family sizes are so small. Obviously, the future of the Gir ecosystem might turn on the density of its human occupants, their forms of resource utilization, and their cultural plasticity.

The Maldhari, a group of devout Hindu tribes, have been part of the Gir ecosystem for at least 125 years (Berwick and Berwick, in press). Thirty to forty Maldharis live together in a small settlement, known as a *ness,* which consists of six or seven houses, with an extended family of about six persons in each house. There are 136 nesses, or about 6,000 Maldharis, living within the Gir Forest. Although this figure is only about 4 percent of the average population density in the state of Gujarat, the Maldharis have a tremendous impact on the forest, primarily by grazing their 25,000 cattle—about 14 percent above the calculated carrying capacity of the forest for grazing animals. This figure does not include the 25,000–70,000 (depending on drought conditions) cattle and buffalo that seasonally invade the forest from hundreds of kilometers around (Grubh and Tolia, pers. comm.).

Because of the inaccessibility of the nesses, milk cannot be transported to market because it would soon spoil. The Maldharis therefore churn the milk into butter that they heat and clarify into a prized cooking oil called *ghee* (Fig. 7), which is sold to merchants in the nearest village, which may be 20 km away. Buffalo are the preferred class of stock because the butterfat content of their milk is several times that of cows' milk and produces more ghee. However, this system is disastrous ecologically, since buffalo consume much more forage per unit of milk produced than cattle. Furthermore, about half of the buffalo calves are males and economically useless, and since the Maldharis are loath to cull the animals, thousands of unproductive primary consumers roam the forest.

The Maldharis make other uses of the forest and its products. They construct dwellings of twigs, poles, grass, and mud and completely surround the ness with acacia thorn fences to enclose and protect the livestock at night from lions and

Figure 6. A Maldhari herdsman, who as a Hindu cannot handle the carcass himself, guards his buffalo from the lions while he waits for one of the *harijan*—or "children of god," as Gandhi called the untouchables—who acts as the hide and meat collector and with whom the herdsman has a contract to claim the kill. Now that the lions hunt in the daytime they must compete for their kills with vultures and with the harijan, which together take over half the kills.

Figure 7. A Maldhari woman and her daughter churn rich buffalo milk into butter, which they will heat and clarify into *ghee,* a cooking oil that is then sold to merchants in the nearest village. Even the closest village is too distant for the safe transport of fresh milk, although about three times as much income could be derived from selling milk instead of ghee.

leopards (*Panthera pardus*). Since the people move frequently (about one-third of the households move in a two-month period), this use of construction material is doubled or trebled annually.

A less obvious use of forest products is the mixing of topsoil and buffalo dung, which the Maldharis collect in large buckets from a 1-km radius around the ness and sell to nearby cultivators. This removes from the forest a nutrient package consisting of protein, carbohydrates, fats, and minerals that would normally be recycled by decomposer organisms such as bacteria back into the vegetation and, eventually, the herbivores. The Maldharis also use the forest as a source of herbs and fruits for medicine and food. They recognize at least 70 different plant species, 42 of which have uses other than for fodder, 27 for human medication for infections, dysentary, injuries, bites, and other ailments.

The Maldharis live very close to their environment—at the economic margins of existence. A lion kill of a milk buffalo may mean the loss of one-third of a family's annual income—money that would be used to buy food supplements for the livestock during the dry season, and sugar, grain, and potatoes to eat with the traditional milk products (Table 1).

Nutritional deficits greatly affect the survival of the Maldharis. Adults may receive only one-half to two-thirds of the daily caloric requirement recommended as adequate by FAO (Berwick and Berwick, in press). Weight fluctuations are often indicative of nutritional status, and significantly more people lose weight during the monsoon than during the winter or summer, supporting the observation that the monsoon is the harshest season for the Maldharis' health.

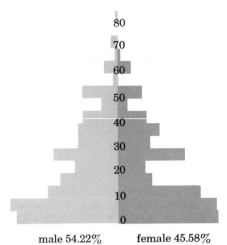

male 54.22%   female 45.58%

Figure 8. The structure of the Maldhari population (based on a sample of 771) reveals significant dips at certain ages, which seem to be related to droughts and disease. Instead of a steady expansion, the total population is slightly decreasing at its base owing to high mortality. Numbers in center refer to age groups.

Hygiene problems in the ness—contaminated drinking water, the proximity of buffalo dung to food and water, the use of dung as plasters to draw boils, unsterilized milk, and the proximity of animals to the people inside the living quarters—are also sources of mortality. The lack of medical attention due to the remoteness of the ness, particularly during the monsoon, when many nesses are virtually cut off from outside contact, is reflected in the forms of mortality and the manner by which mortality appears to regulate the growth of the Maldhari population in the Gir. Examination of the numbers of Maldharis in each age group (Fig. 8) indicates that there are significant population dips in certain ages which seem to correspond to two major smallpox epidemics, a drought, and a flood. There has also been a recent decrease in the 0–4 year age class. This may be a result of a 238 percent increase in malaria in the Gir area between 1966 and 1969 (Kosare, pers. comm.). The mosquito

vectors of malaria are evidently becoming refractory to repeated sprayings of DDT. There has also been a 38-fold increase in cases of smallpox between 1965 (n = 76) and 1968 (n = 2,905).

Our study also reveals that the sex ratio of males to females is exceptionally high among the Maldharis—much higher than for India as a whole or for a nearby agricultural village. The preponderance of males is particularly evident at the onset of child-bearing (15–24) years. All these factors tend to restrain population growth. The estimated life expectancy of Maldharis is about 24 years, approximating the all-India figure for 1891–1900 and well below the 41-year average for 1951–1960 (Government of India 1968).

Another indication of the direct and intimate effect the environment of the Maldharis has on maintenance of the population is that reproduction, as with the wild animals of the Gir, is seasonal, reflecting environmental exigencies such as the monsoon or the hot season. The highest number of births during the study period occurred in November, while there were no births at all in February or May. This places conceptions at an annual peak in February. It was found in Australia that human conception is most likely to occur and result in a living child when the mean monthly temperature is near 21°C (Mills in Macfarlane 1963), which is virtually the same temperature found at the Gir in February. Also, February is a time when the people have been living at the highest nutritional plane for several months. Likewise, November, when most births occur, is the most benign period in terms of nutrition and climate.

Animal ecology

To determine how many wild and domestic herbivores the vegetation of the Gir could support, primary productivity (the dry weight of plant tissue produced each year) had to be measured in order to find how much food was available at levels of consumption that would not permanently harm the plants. We constructed fenced, animal-proof exclosures and estimated herbaceous forage production from samples of grasses and weeds clipped

Table 1. Cost accounting for a Maldhari buffalo herd over the seasons (in rupees for 15 animals)

	Monsoon	*Winter*	*Summer*	*Total*
Income	4,400	1,400	1,300	7,100
Costs for supplementary feed	500	900	2,200	3,600
Wages for hired herdsman	—	—	—	500
Net income	3,900	500	−900	3,000

within the exclosures at the height of growth, just after the monsoon. Utilization was then measured by comparing the weight of vegetation inside the exclosures (ungrazed) to that outside the exclosures (grazed) after a year of grazing. These measurements indicate that, after one year of protection, production in "wildland," or relatively inaccessible areas usually over 2 km from a ness, is over twice that in chronically overgrazed areas, which are usually near a ness (4,139 kg/ha as compared to 1,909 kg/ha). Furthermore, we found that in relatively accessible sites (the flatter ridges and valleys) utilization of annual plant growth was between 80 and 90 percent (Fig. 9), whereas proper use would be about 25 percent (Stoddart and Smith 1955; Albertson 1959; Jameson 1962; U.S. Forest Service 1963).

In a similar manner, browse production and utilization were measured. In contrast to the extreme overuse of herbaceous plants, the browse is being underutilized: only about 33 percent of the annual production of twigs and leaves are being eaten (Table 2), whereas the plants could probably sustain use of nearly 50 percent (Garrison 1953).

The overgrazing has serious implications for the ecology of the Gir Forest. Nutritious perennial grasses are giving way to other, less palatable annual grasses that set their seed and die each year. Bare soil is exposed to the rain and wind. Compaction due to trampling under the feet of domestic animals is two times as great outside the experimental exclosures as inside. Water infiltration into the ground outside exclosures is one-sixth that inside (Hodd, pers. comm.). At this point the question must be asked: Who or what is causing this trend to erosion and xerification—wild animals, domestic animals, or both? Answering this question meant investigating the food habits of wild and domestic animals.

We compared the preferences wild and domestic animals exhibited for forage plants—browse and grass—confining our study to the hottest and driest season (March-May), because food competition due to shortage of forage was thought to be most critical then. This period was

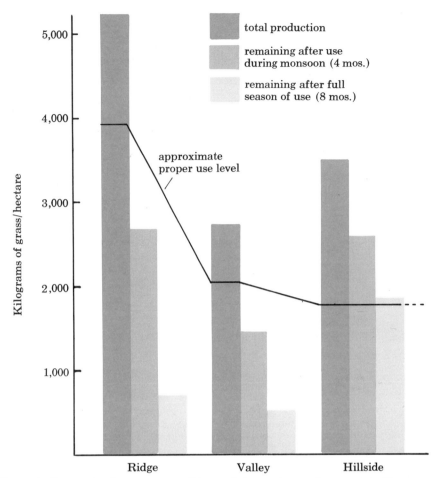

Figure 9. Grasses in the more accessible areas—the ridges and valleys—are grazed at far more than the proper use level. The more palatable and nutritious grasses disappear, soils become bare and compacted with consequent surface erosion, and the carrying capacity for grazers declines, resulting in a continual, long-term decrease in productivity.

also presumed to coincide with the time the forage was mature and least nutritious.

A stockade with pens and corrals was constructed to house 18 captive wild animals, representing six species of antelope and deer. They were offered a variety of fresh forages from the jungle, cafeteria style, and their selections were recorded (Fig. 5). The animals were then tamed to a leash and followed in the various habitats of the forest. Again

Table 2. Production and utilization of important browse species in the central Gir

Species	Total production[1]	Weight consumed[1]	Percent consumed[2]
Acacia catechu	131.87	37.96	28.79
Acacia leucophloea	388.81	150.63	38.74
Bauhinia racemosa	81.80	20.91	25.56
Emblica officinalis	270.88	90.93	33.57
Helicteres isora	711.54	103.62	14.56
Soymida febrifuga	366.15	199.22	54.41
Tectona grandis	923.39	439.90	47.64
Terminalia crenulata	71.36	9.72	13.62
Ziziphus mauritiana	114.11	39.24	34.39
Others	1,687.54	456.36	27.04

[1]In grams dry weight for a 13-hectare drainage (total g dry weight/m² = 35.64)
[2]Average amount of browse consumed = 33%

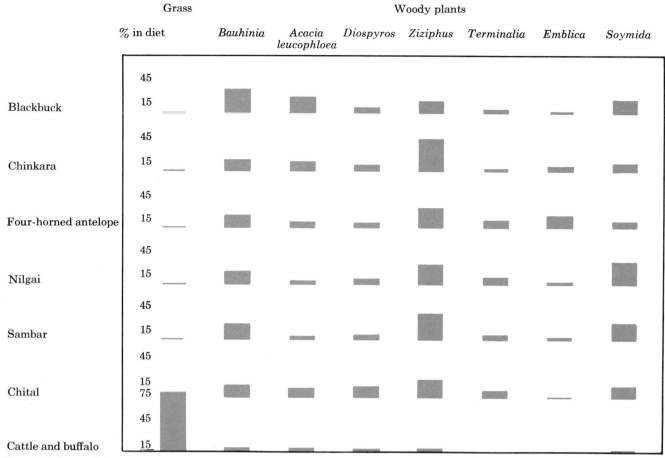

Figure 10. Seven of the twenty major woody species and grass were used in "cafeteria"-style experiments to find the type of forage preferred by the domestic animals and wildlife that constitute the prey of the lion. Results are unambiguous: domestic animals eat grass; wild prey eat browse.

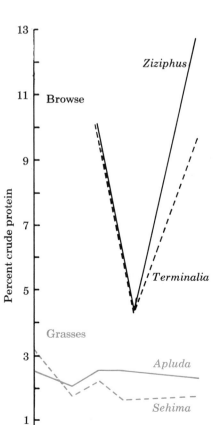

Figure 11. There is significantly more crude protein in the two representative browse plants than in the grasses during the hot, dry months of April and May. Lactating ruminants may need more than five times as much protein as the grasses they eat can provide, and their diets must be supplemented with costly peanut-cake and cottonseed, a system that is ecologically and economically untenable.

observations of the forage plants selected were recorded. Unlike plants offered during the cafeteria trials, those in the field were not equally available, and a relative forage preference index (RPI), similar to Krueger's (1972), was employed:

$$RPI = \frac{\% \text{ composition in diet} \times 100}{\% \text{ range frequency} \times \% \text{ range composition}}$$

In this way the availability and distribution of a forage plant are considered when calculating forage preference. Domestic buffalo and cattle were also followed in the field to observe forage preferences.

The cafeteria and field-feeding trials yielded similar, and striking, results: domestic cattle and buffalo distinctly prefer grass, while the six wild animal species as a group prefer an assortment of woody plants—roughly the same plants in the same proportions (Fig. 10). There is virtually no dietary overlap between the domestic animals and wildlife. Contrary to our initial hypothesis, competition during the hot, dry season between wild and domestic herbivores for a potentially scarce and, therefore, limiting resource is virtually nonexistent. Because the grass is overgrazed and domestic animals are solely responsible for grazing, it was conclusively established that the domestic herds are primarily responsible for the tremendous land abuse in the Gir Forest.

A glance at Figure 10 reveals that there appears to be considerable dietary overlap between the wild herbivores. An analysis of variance shows that the six animal species have similar and decided preferences among the various forage plants. Since all six species appear to have selected among the plants in a similar manner, this suggests that if niche separation exists, it is not based on forage preference during the hot, dry season.

This finding is an interesting contrast to the fine feeding differences reported for communities of African ungulates (Bell 1970; Talbot and Talbot 1962) and suggests that competition for forage plants has not been a major force in regulating populations and that some other factor may well be holding the large wild herbivores below carrying capacity. If coincident diets are characteristic of the wildlife in the more pristine tracts of the Gir Forest, such a phenomenon may reflect a condition that has existed for millennia in northwestern India, which seems to have been a center of autochthonous bovid evolution (Pilgrim 1941), with early Boselaphine forms similar to the four-horned antelope and nilgai, the African antelope, and the various forms of cattle.

By following the phenology of woody plants—that is, the yearly cycle of leafing, fruiting, and leaf fall—we found that 80 percent of the woody plants begin to grow and form leaves during the hot, dry season. This new, succulent growth is very high in nutrients such as protein (10–15 percent), whereas the grasses, dry at this time of year, are very low in nutrients (2 percent protein) (Fig. 11). Thus cattle and buffalo, which are obligate grazers, are living below minimum maintenance standards, which range between 6 and 11 percent protein for adult sheep and cattle (NAS-NRC 1970) and 7 and 8 percent for deer (Hill 1956). The livestock's food must therefore be supplemented with cottonseed and peanut-cake, which is a major expense for the Maldhari. The wildlife, on the other hand, as browsers, do very well during the hot, dry season. Ecologically and economically, the Gir Forest is not a good place for domestic cattle and buffalo, whereas the wildlife can thrive on the nutritious browse (Fig. 13).

Such investigations answered one of our original questions: Would wild prey increase if domestic livestock were removed to alleviate overgrazing? They would not. Since wild prey and domestic prey do not eat the same forage, removal of cattle

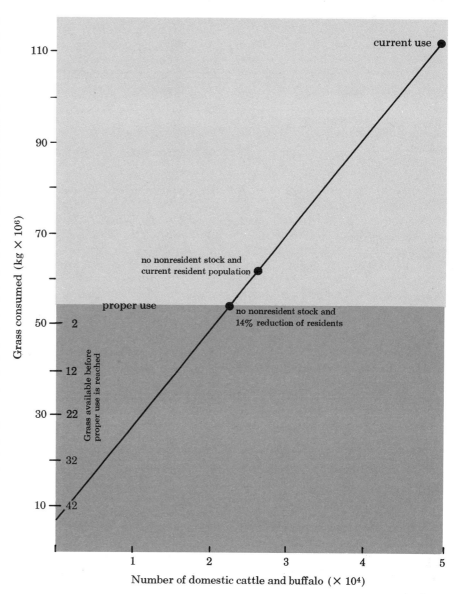

Figure 12. The stocking-rate model shows real and hypothetical populations of livestock and the amount of grass they would consume. The weight of grass left over below proper use level and available to a replacement population of grazers is indicated by the figures to the right of the y-axis.

and buffalo would not result in an increase of deer and antelope.

The question as to what *is* regulating the numbers of wild prey still remained to be answered. I regularly noted the presence of leopards in a 250-km^2 area in the Gir and calculated that there were about 100 leopards in the sanctuary, whose diet consisted of roughly 38 percent wild ungulates in addition to other animals such as the abundant langur monkeys (*Presbytis entellus*). Based on published rates of consumption (Schaller 1972), my own estimates of the numbers of leopards, census figures for the lions (Dalvi 1969), and their food habits (established by P. Joslin, who identified the hairs found in over 1,800

lion droppings), I calculated that these large predators require about 129,000 kg of wild prey each year. Then calculating the number and weight of deer and antelope that die each year, I found that virtually the same weight of prey dies and is replaced by new births in the population each year—approximately 123,000 kg—as is required by the predators. Predators thus account for nearly all the wild prey that die each year.

An analysis of breeding habits, censuses, life tables, and sex and age ratios showed that the wild ungulate populations were relatively stable. For example, of the 361 chital seen at the end of the hot, dry season (just prior to fawning, which occurs during the monsoon), 63 (17.5 percent) were fawns. Extrapolating this to the total population of 4,404 chital, there are 771 fawns that will become yearlings and enter the breeding population. Since 763 adults and yearlings die each year, the population can be considered stable.

Malnutrition is virtually nonexistent in wild prey of the Gir. This is in rather stark contrast to the typical conditions found in large North American herbivores such as deer, whose numbers often are limited by the nutritive quality of their forage resources—possibly because the full complement of natural predators has been eliminated by man, and cruder modes of population regulation such as malnutrition operate. At the Gir Forest, 77 percent of the predator-killed animals found were in good physical condition.

Thus it appears that the large predators limit the populations of wild prey at the Gir Forest. Other studies (Kruuk 1972; Mech 1966) indicate that such predation keeps herbivores below the point at which they would damage the plants that constitute their forage. Also, such high predatory pressure may promote a maximum diversity of prey species by making more resources available for additional species (Paine 1966).

There was above-average rainfall during our two years of intensive study, and we wondered how well our evaluations of the Gir ecosystem would hold up in an average year or, even more critical, in one of the frequent drought years. In 1973, when the monsoon rains failed, leading to the worst drought in over 70 years, I visited the Gir Forest. An estimated 70,000 head of cattle and buffalo invaded the Gir from hundreds of kilometers around, adding to the effects of over 25,000 resident cattle. They devastated the grass cover, and by the end of the hot, dry season, thousands of cattle and buffalo were dying. The lopping of branches off the trees and often the felling of whole trees to provide leaves for starving livestock compounded the problem of overgrazing and the disappearance of the forest. The wild herbivores, by comparison, consumed the newly green, nutritious browse and ap-

peared to be in excellent condition. Thus, while the predators and wild prey seemed to prosper, the subtle and insidious destruction of the forest by the agent of land abuse accelerated.

Conservation implications

The Gujarat State Forest Department is faced with a difficult dilemma. The Maldharis and their cattle and the migrant cattle are destroying the Gir. This is a long-term, insidious process not immediately evident but nevertheless progressing and virtually irreversible. With the loss of the forest will go its unique biota, including, of course, the last of the Asiatic lions. If the Forest Department could remove the Maldharis and their cattle, the forest could be preserved, but the major source of food for the lions would disappear, and the Maldharis—an exceptional human resource—would have to be relocated with unknown potential social consequences. Ninety families have recently been moved to areas many kilometers away, where new grazing systems will probably be instituted. The sociological effects of having the men spend more time in fields near home have yet to be evaluated. Problems associated with maintaining new dwellings in place of traditional huts, dealing more intimately with merchants, being exposed to modern communication and transport systems, and working tame rather than natural pastures, all constitute a nexus of relationships that could result in a new ecology for the Maldharis.

It seems clear that present livestock grazing must be substantially reduced in order to reverse deterioration of the soil-plant system and to restore the system's previously high level of plant productivity. Otherwise, the capacity of this unique wild area to support any type of life will continue to decline, and all natural elements will eventually be lost. Other important effects of overgrazing will soon become evident. For example, the hills of the Gir Forest are a vital watershed for the agricultural areas in the surrounding flatlands. As the soil becomes impervious to water and surface runoff and erosion accelerate, less water is stored in the ground, the

streams are not recharged and dry up quickly, and the water table drops. Also, siltation rates are increasing, which means that the dams planned for the major rivers draining the Gir Forest will quickly fill with silt, making the reservoirs short-lived and the dam construction uneconomical. Already one reservoir in Gujarat has silted in after one-eighth of its projected life span (Yuvraj Digvyjay Singh, pers. comm.).

At the same time, a major reduction in livestock would pose a serious food crisis for lions, since the wild herbivores are not grazers and thus are not likely to fill the grazing niche even if all livestock were removed. In anticipation of a substantial reduction of livestock—which is the only way the forest can be saved—a substitute grazer to serve as lion prey could be introduced. This animal should have the following characteristics: (1) Its principal year-round food must be grass—the wildland annual production of grass in the Gir is over 10 times the annual available production of browse plants (378 g/m²: 34 g/m²). (2) It must proliferate within all or most of the habitats of the Gir without help from man. Because the biomass (live weight) of domestic stock is about 16 times that of wildlife (Berwick and Jordan 1971), the substitute grazer should constitute a source of prey considerably greater than that of the present array of wild ungulates combined to provide an adequate food source for the lion population. (3) It must successfully sustain year-round predation by the lion. That such an animal can be found appears reasonable: it most likely would be a grass-eating bovid.

Any animal introduced into the Gir Forest should be a wild species native to the general region. Although there is no wild grass-eating bovid now extant in the Indian subcontinent apparently suitable for the semiarid Gir Forest, zebu cattle (*Bos indicus*) did evolve in this region and were presumably in contact with lions. Feral (domestic gone wild) cattle exist today in the wild elsewhere in western India, and they seem to meet the above criteria. With the elimination of grazing by domestic livestock and the cessation of fodder cutting,

Figure 13. A nilgai antelope and her calf pause in the broken woodland that forms a transition between teak (*Tectona grandis*) forests of the western Gir and open savanna woodlands of the eastern third of the sanctuary. Wildland tracts such as this contrast with the degraded, xerified regions or the agricultural tracts that abut the Gir.

about 52,000,000 kg of grass would become available to the feral cattle at proper use levels. If 89 percent (5.2 kg) of the daily diet of a feral cow were grass (an amount equivalent to the precentage of grass in the diet of domestic cattle; the remainder is browse), there would be enough fodder to support about 25,000 animals per year. This would provide about 800,000 kg of meat for lions and leopards each year, significantly more than the approximately 500,000 kg a year that these predators need. A properly stocked population of feral cattle should be more than adequate to support present lion and leopard populations.

Another, partial solution—which would save only the lion—is to trap some of the lions and introduce them elsewhere. Such a transplant was tried with one lion and two lionesses from the Gir Forest to a 96-km^2 sanctuary in the state of Uttar Pradesh (Negi 1969). This attempt failed, possibly because the area was too small to support such a large carnivore. Other transplants to areas once within the range of the Asiatic lion, such as Iran, are being considered.

An obvious difficulty is the future of the Maldharis if they must leave, and thus it is hard to choose any single solution. Rather, implementation of several plans seems to be the best strategy. If the Gir is to be saved as a wildlife sanctuary, domestic livestock must be reduced: specifically, no migrants should be allowed into the forest, and the number of resident cattle and buffalo should be reduced by 14 percent, down to the proper grazing level (Fig. 12). This is the biological reality dictated by a consideration of husbanding a productive ecosystem for years to come. Of course the political and emotional ramifications of turning back hordes of starving cattle and desperate herdsmen present the forest administrator with a wrenching decision. However, short of these measures, xerification of the Gir Forest and subsequent loss of all of its inhabitants, including humans, is ensured. To complement the Forest Department's policy of substantial removal of Maldharis, feral cattle could be introduced to help the wild community of browsing ungulates absorb more of the predation by lions and leopards.

That a more realistic perspective could be gained by looking at a complex ecosystem through simultaneous studies of people, predators, prey, plants, soils, scavengers, and other major elements of the ecosystem became obvious as we analyzed the data from the Gir. Priorities dictated the studies described in this paper; a clearer picture of the dynamics and resilience of the Gir ecosystem will emerge when other major elements such as nutrient recycling are investigated. However, only such a systems approach as we undertook would have revealed the nature of the problems and the interactions of the various compartments of the Gir that form an ecological gestalt. Through this understanding it seems possible that the Gir ecosystem can be managed back to ecological integrity. The old wildlife management tack of focusing on a single species, such as the Asiatic lion, quite likely would not have yielded the information necessary to understand and manage the Gir Forest as a whole system.

The problems of the Gir are not exclusively local in their general nature: they are quite typical of a set of land-use problems encountered throughout the semiarid tropics of the world, from which about 19 percent of the total terrestrial primary productivity (35,000 × 10^6 tonnes) of the earth comes (Rodin et al. 1975). The comprehensive approach to ecosystems analysis used by the Gir research project could serve as a model for similar problem areas elsewhere.

References

Albertson, F. W. 1959. *Improving Grasslands in India.* Manhattan: Kansas State College U.S. International Cooperation Administration, IICAK SC-1, 31 pp.

Bell, R. H. V. 1970. The use of the herb layer by grazing ungulates in the Serengeti. In A. Watson, ed., Animal populations in relation to their food resources, *Proc. Brit. Ecol. Soc. Sympos.* 10:25–46.

Berwick, M. A., and S. H. Berwick. In press. The ecology of the Maldhari graziers, Gir Forest, India. *J. Bombay Nat. Hist. Soc.*

Berwick, S. H., and P. A. Jordan. 1971. First report of the Yale-Bombay Natural History Society studies of wild ungulates at the Gir Forest, Gujarat, India. *J. Bombay Nat. Hist. Soc.* 68:412–23.

Dalvi, M. K. 1969. Gir lion census, 1968. *Indian Forester* 95:741–52.

Eckholm, E. 1975a. *The Other Energy Crisis: Firewood.* Worldwatch Papers 1. Washington, D.C.: Worldwatch Inst., 22 pp.

Eckholm, E. 1975b. The deterioration of mountain environments. *Science* 189:764–70.

Fisher, J., N. Simon, and J. Vincent. 1969. *Wildlife in Danger.* New York: Viking Press, 368 pp.

Garrison, G. A. 1953. Effects of clipping on some range shrubs. *J. Range Mgmt.* 6:309–17.

Government of India. 1968. *India 1968.* New Delhi: Publications Division, Ministry of Information and Broadcasting.

Hastings, J. R., and R. M. Turner. 1965. *The Changing Mile.* Tucson: Univ. of Arizona Press, 317 pp.

Hill, R. R. 1956. Forage, food habits, and range management of the mule deer. In W. P. Taylor, ed., *The Deer of North America.* Harrisburg, Pa.: Stackpole, pp. 393–414.

Jameson, D. A. 1962. Evaluation of the responses of individual plants to grazing. In *U.S. Forest Service Range Research Methods.* Misc. Publ. No. 940, U.S.D.A. Washington, D.C: U.S. Govt. Printing Office, pp. 109–16.

Joslin, P. 1969. The Asiatic lion: Conservation aspects of its ecology. *Proc. IUCN 10th General Assembly and 11th Technical Meeting* I:16.

Krueger, W. C. 1972. Evaluating forage preference. *J. Range Mgmt.* 25:471–75.

Kruuk, H. 1972. *The Spotted Hyena.* Chicago: Univ. of Chicago Press, 335 pp.

Leopold, A. S. 1959. *Wildlife in Mexico.* Berkeley: Univ. of California Press, 568 pp.

Lowdermilk, W. D. 1953. *Conquest of the Land through Seven Thousand Years.* Agriculture Information Bull. No. 99. U.S.D.A.-S.C.S. Washington, D.C.: U.S. Govt. Printing Office, 30 pp.

Macfarlane, W. V. 1963. Endocrine functions in hot environments. In *Environmental Physiology and Psychology in Arid Conditions.* Reviews of Research, UNESCO.

Mech, L. D. 1966. *The Wolves of Isle Royale.* Fauna Nat. Parks of the U.S., Fauna Ser. 7. Washington, D.C.: U.S. Govt. Printing Office, 210 pp.

Myers, P. F., L. F. Bouvier, and J. R. Echols. 1975. *1975 World Population Data Sheet.* Washington, D.C.: Population Reference Bureau, 1 p.

National Academy of Sciences-National Research Council. 1970. *Nutrient Requirements of Beef Cattle,* 4th ed. Washington, D.C. 55 pp.

Negi, S. S. 1969. Transplanting of Indian lion in Uttar Pradesh. *Cheetal* 12:98–101.

Paine, R. T. 1966. Food web complexity and species diversity. *Am. Natur.* 100:65–75.

Pilgrim, G. E. 1941. The dispersal of the Artiodactyla. *Biol. Rev.,* Cambridge 16:134–63.

Rodin, L. E., N. I. Bazilevich, and N. N. Rozov. 1975. Productivity of the world's ecosystems. In National Academy of Sciences, *Productivity of World Ecosystems.* Washington, D.C.: NAS, pp. 13–26.

Santapau, H., and M. B. Raizada. 1956. Contribution to the flora of the Gir Forest in Saurashtra. *Indian Forest Records* (new series), *Botany* 4:105–70.

Schaller, G. B. 1972. *The Serengeti Lion.* Chicago: Univ. of Chicago Press, 480 pp.

Spillett, J. J. 1968. A report on wildlife surveys in South and West India: Nov.-Dec. 1966. *J. Bombay Nat. Hist. Soc.* 65:1–46.

Stoddart, L. A., and A. D. Smith. 1955. *Range Management.* N.Y.: McGraw-Hill, 433 pp.

Talbot, L. M. 1960. *A Look at Threatened Species, Endangered Wildlife and Other Aspects of Conservation in the Middle East and Southern Asia.* London: Fauna Preservation Society, 137 pp.

Talbot, L. M., and M. H. Talbot. 1962. Food preferences of some East African wild ungulates. *E. Afr. Agric. and Forestry J.* 27:131–37.

U.S. Forest Service. 1963. *Region I: Range Analysis Field Guide.* FSH 2212.02 rl., p. 164.

Wynter-Blyth, M. A. 1952. The Gir Forest and its lions. *J. Bombay Nat. Hist. Soc.* 48:493–514.

"As I understand it, *they're* in danger of becoming extinct, too."

Gordon W. Thayer
Douglas A. Wolfe
Richard B. Williams

The Impact of Man on Seagrass Systems

Seagrasses must be considered in terms of their interaction with the other sources of primary production that support the estuarine trophic structure before their significance can be fully appreciated

Twelve genera of aquatic angiosperms are completely adapted to the marine environment, having a well-developed anchoring system and the ability to function normally and complete the generative cycle when fully submerged in a saline medium (den Hartog 1970). These seagrasses, which are widespread throughout the world, rank among the most productive systems in the ocean and constitute one of the most conspicuous and common coastal ecosystem types. Eelgrass, *Zostera marina*, one of these flowering seagrasses, supports characteristic floral and faunal assemblages and forms consistent and recognizable communities or ecosystems—regardless of the particular geographic location or species structure (Fig. 1).

Because of their shallow sublittoral and to some extent intertidal existence, seagrass systems are subject to stresses imposed by man's ever-growing use of the coastal zone. Our continued multiplicity of demands upon estuarine and coastal environments as producers of food, avenues of transportation, receptacles of wastes, living space, and sources of recreational or esthetic pleasure makes it imperative that we understand the functioning of these near-shore ecosystems. This knowledge is essential to enable proper evaluation of the respective roles of the various ecological components of the system, so that we can manage this environment wisely and derive the maximum benefits from each of the components.

The true importance of seagrass meadows to coastal marine ecosystems is not fully understood and is generally underestimated. The scientific literature on seagrass systems is extensive, and this paper makes no pretense of a complete review. Rather, what is attempted here is a brief and concise evaluation, on the basis of existing information, of the probable value of seagrass communities to man's total ecosystem and the impact of man's varied activities upon seagrass communities, with special reference to *Zostera marina* communities. For comprehensive reviews of seagrasses and research on these systems see den Hartog (1970), Zieman (1970), McRoy (1973), and Phillips (1974).

It is in the context of the total estuarine system that man's impact upon seagrass communities must be evaluated. The ways that eelgrass acts to affect the function of estuarine ecosystems may be summarized according to the scheme established by Wood, Odum, and Zieman (1969) for seagrasses in general:

1. Eelgrass has a high growth rate, producing on the average about 300–600 g dry weight/m²/year, not including root production.

2. The leaves support large numbers of epiphytic organisms, with a total biomass perhaps approaching that of the grass itself.

3. Although a few organisms may feed directly on the eelgrass and several may graze on the epiphytes, the major food chains are based on eelgrass detritus and its resident microbes.

4. The organic matter in the detritus and in decaying roots initiates sulfate reduction and maintains an active sulfur cycle.

5. The roots bind the sediments together, and, with the protection afforded by the leaves, surface erosion is reduced, thereby preserving the microbial flora of the sediment and the sediment–water interface.

6. The leaves retard currents and

Gordon W. Thayer, leader of the Ecosystem Structure Branch, Beaufort Laboratory, Southeast Fisheries Center, NMFS, NOAA, Beaufort, NC, received his Ph.D. in zoology in 1969 from North Carolina State University. His research interests include phytoplankton and nutrient relations, zooplankton-larval fish dynamics, and food-web dynamics of estuarine and coastal ecosystems, with emphasis on benthic and seagrass systems.
Douglas A. Wolfe, Director of the Ecology Division at AEFC, received his Ph.D. in physiological chemistry in 1964 from Ohio State University. His research interests span the fields of malacology, fatty acid biochemistry, radioecology, and trace metal dynamics and modeling in estuarine and coastal ecosystems. Both he and Dr. Thayer are adjunct associate professors at North Carolina State University.
Richard B. Williams is the Director of the Biological Oceanography Program of the National Science Foundation. He received his Ph.D. from Harvard in 1962 and was Leader of the Ecosystems Task at AEFC until 1972. His research interests have been in the fields of phytoplankton, marine angiosperm, and zooplankton ecology and radioecology. He has recently written several articles on computer modeling of ecological systems. This manuscript was supported through a cooperative agreement between the National Marine Fisheries Service and the U.S. Atomic Energy Commission. Requests for reprints should be sent to Dr. Thayer, Atlantic Estuarine Fisheries Center, Beaufort, NC 28516.

Figure 1. Beds of the temperate seagrass *Zostera marina* (eelgrass) in the Newport River estuary, Beaufort, N.C., stabilize the sediment and provide protection and food for a vast variety of invertebrates, fish, and shore birds. (Photo by Herb Gordy, AEFC.)

increase sedimentation of organic and inorganic materials around the plants.

7. Eelgrass absorbs phosphorus both through the leaves and the roots; it may be that the phosphorus absorbed through the roots is released through the leaves, thereby returning phosphate from sediments to the water column (McRoy and Barsdate 1970). Nitrogen also is taken up by the roots and transferred to the leaves and into the medium (McRoy and Goering 1974).

In addition to these intricate ecological functions, dried eelgrass leaves have been used by man as fuel, packing and upholstering material, insulation, fodder, and fertilizer, but the manufacture and use of eelgrass products have been local and intermittent.

Temperate eelgrass communities

Eelgrass occurs throughout the Northern Hemisphere in temperate marine coastal waters and is very important to the trophic function and overall productivity of the coastal zone. On the Pacific coast eelgrass communities are found from Port Clarence, Alaska, to Agiopampo Lagoon, Mexico (Phillips 1972); on the Atlantic coast eelgrass extends from Greenland to Cape Fear, N.C. Zostera is abundant along the English coastline, the Danish coastline, the Spanish coastline, along the northern Mediterranean coast into the Black Sea, in the Baltic and White Seas, and along much of the coastlines of the Yellow Sea and Sea of Japan. Den Hartog (1970) and Phillips (1972) have described the distribution of this species outside North America, and den Hartog noted that, although eelgrass probably is the best known of the marine angiosperms, there are only a small number of thorough studies on its ecology.

Eelgrass tolerates for brief exposures a wide range of salinities and temperatures—from about 10–40 ‰ (parts per thousand) and 0–40°C. Conditions conducive for growth and reproduction, however, are probably restricted to 10–30 ‰ and 10–20°C. The plant flowers only when the temperature is above 9–15°C, and seed germination is optimal at salinities of 4.5–9 ‰ (Arasaki 1950; Phillips 1974). Arasaki, however, noted that a salinity range of 23–31 ‰ is optimal for vegetative growth of eelgrass in Japan. All studies to date appear to be merely descriptive rather than experimental, and interactions of temperature and salinity have not been evaluated. Zieman (1970) has suggested that there is a temperature–salinity interaction for Thalassia testudinum, a tropical seagrass commonly called turtle grass (see Fig. 2). His work has shown that Thalassia is able to tolerate low salinities at low environmental temperatures but is unable to withstand low salinities when water temperatures are high. This also may be true for Zostera and other seagrasses. The effect of photoperiod has not been determined in conjunction with temperature and salinity.

The depth distribution of seagrasses depends upon a complex of interrelated ecological considerations: depth, waves, currents, substrate, turbidity, and light penetration. Mean low water is a realistic effective upper limit for most seagrasses regardless of other factors, but the lower limit is probably established by a combination of minimum light intensity required for growth and presence of suitable substrate: seagrasses may grow at 20–30 meters depth in clear water but be restricted to depths of less than one meter where wave action continually stirs up the bottom, producing high turbidity. Seagrasses can be found on many substrates, from coarse sand to almost liquid mud, but the normal substrate is a mixture of mud and sand in which a reducing environment prevails beneath the oxidized sediment surface. McRoy (1973) and Phillips (1974) have indicated that much more research is necessary on substrates, since it appears that seagrasses condition the substrate and become an integral part of it. Alteration of the substrate may render it unfit for continued colonization by seagrasses.

Productivity of seagrass systems has been widely measured, especially that of Zostera marina and Thalassia testudinum communities. Values for annual production of Thalassia range from 200 gC (grams of carbon) per m² to 3,000 gC/m², and annual values for Zostera range from about 5–600 gC/m² (Phillips 1974). Representative annual production values for eelgrass are 581 g dry weight/m² for Puget Sound, Wash. (Phillips 1974), and 10–58 g dry weight/m² for Great Pond, Mass. (Conover 1958). Recent studies at Beaufort, N.C. (near the southern edge of Zostera's range on the Atlantic coast), indicate mean annual production of about 340 gC/m² or about 690 g dry weight/m² (Dillon 1971). Associated with the Zostera in these grass beds are Halodule and Ectocarpus, which together contribute an additional 300 gC/m² annually (Dillon 1971).

Thus, on an areal basis, Thalassia and Zostera beds are more productive than the world averages for cultivated corn (412 gC/m²) or rice (497 gC/m²) or the U.S. average for hay fields (420 gC/m²) or tall-grass prairie (446 gC/m²) (Odum 1959). These seagrass production rates are higher, on an areal basis, than phytoplankton production in upwelling areas off Peru (Ryther 1969), one of the most productive sea areas in the world. Seagrass production is supplemented in these communities, or in estuaries in general, by the production of benthic microalgae, macroalgae, epiphytes, phytoplankton, and shore-based vegetation such as salt marsh.

Petersen (1918) recognized the importance of eelgrass to ecosystem function over half a century ago, when he attempted to synthesize a model of the trophic relations of the Kattegat region of Denmark. His calculations were made from available estimates of fisheries productivity, gut content analyses, data on the occurrence of other organisms, and, where necessary, an assumed 10% relationship between standing crops of succeeding trophic levels (see Fig. 3). The assumed conversion efficiency was not rigorously examined, nor were the standing crops of all species actually measured, and, most important, secondary production of the lower trophic levels and primary productivity of the plant component (though discussed and recognized as significant) were either not measured or not employed in the

Figure 2. Tropical turtle grass, *Thalassia testudinum,* in Puerto Rico offers shelter and food for sea urchins, *Diadema antillarum;* four-eye butterfly fish, *Chaetodon capistra-* *tum;* and tomtate (small striped fish), *Bathystoma aurolineatum.* (Photo by Douglas Wolfe, AEFC.)

calculations. Nonetheless, Petersen's calculations suggested that cod and plaice were dependent upon the *Zostera* community for food resources. Petersen's model was tested in the 1930s when there was a sudden decrease in *Zostera* abundance throughout much of its geographic range. Although this drastic decline did not result in as great a decrease in bottom fishes in the North Atlantic as would have been predicted from Petersen's calculations, Milne and Milne (1951, p. 53) stated that undoubtedly the eelgrass catastrophe caused a major decline in these fishes.

Since 1969, researchers at the Atlantic Estuarine Fisheries Center have been evaluating the trophic dynamics of a newly established eelgrass community near Beaufort, N.C. Their data on standing crops, summarized in Figure 4, have indicated that the majority of the animals collected depend upon plant and detrital material which is most

likely produced within the bed or at least entrained within the bed (Adams 1974; Thayer et al., in press). Further, their data suggest that for the macrofaunal community (epifauna, infauna, and fish) about 12% of the food energy consumed by the organisms is utilized for the production of their new tissue; the remaining food energy consumed is either excreted or lost through metabolic processes.

Marshall (1970) noted that approximately two-thirds to three-fourths of the *Zostera* decays into the sediment annually and that on southern New England shores *Zostera*, its epiphytes, and macroscopic algae contribute 125 gC/m²/yr as detritus. Thayer et al. (in press) indicate that as much as 45% of the plant production in eelgrass beds in North Carolina estuaries may be carried to adjacent systems, thus supplying detrital material to them. These eelgrass systems also maintain larger populations of in-

vertebrates and fishes than the adjacent estuary.

Of special importance is the recognition that, although the eelgrass community represents a distinct faunal assemblage, it is still only part of the overall estuarine system, and the primary production of phytoplankton, benthic macroalgae and epiphytes, and shore-based plants supplements the eelgrass to support not only the fauna of eelgrass communities but the faunal assemblages in other estuarine habitats as well (Fig. 5). Williams (1973) has estimated that in the shallow estuarine system near Beaufort eelgrass (though occupying only 17% of the estuarine area) supplies 64% of the combined total production of phytoplankton, smooth cordgrass (*Spartina alterniflora*), and eelgrass in this estuarine system; phytoplankton and cordgrass supply 28% and 8% of the total, respectively (see Fig. 5). Ferguson and Murdoch (in press) estimated that benthic microalgae account for about 6 gC/m²/yr, or only 3% of the total, with the percent contribution to the total of other sources being only slightly reduced. We have no information on organic production by macroalgae and the availability of dissolved organic material.

The detrital material which is exported from the grass beds probably is significant to the trophic function of estuarine complexes. Further, fishery organisms from this estuarine system utilize most of the primary productivity, based on best available estimates of trophic structure and efficiency (R. B. Williams, unpubl.). By far the predominant trophic pathway in this estuarine system is eelgrass (plus algae and *Spartina*) → detritus (including its associated microbial community) → herbivores → carnivores.

Environmental influences

Despite the extensive studies on seagrass productivity and on the temporal and spatial variability in biological composition of seagrass communities, little is known of the general principles of ecosystem function and the factors controlling the "ecological success" of the community. As a result, subtle changes which may be caused by human activities generally pass unnoticed or are ascribed to "natural variation,"

and only gross changes, such as total destruction of a bed, are described in the literature. Even then, direct causal relationships are not always established.

The species diversity of the community, together with temporal and spatial variation of biomass, render the seagrass community itself difficult to describe. When this dynamic community is considered as an integral part of the larger, complex estuarine ecosystem to which it belongs, it is not easy to design and carry out sampling programs adequate to define the effects of man's activities. Until recently, the need for such elaborate ecological research was not recognized.

Of the several human activities which affect, or can be inferred to affect, success of seagrass communities in estuarine and coastal ecosystems, only a few have so far been documented as actually being deleterious. In general, dredging and other disturbances of the bottom sediments or sedimentation rates can destroy several seagrass species. Additions of toxic materials have been shown to affect animal components of seagrass communities but not the seagrass itself; thermal wastes have been shown to affect both the animal components and, in the case of *Thalassia*, the grass itself. Commercial fishing on seagrass bottoms, like dredging, can disrupt the growth of the

plants. Although commercial harvesting of seagrasses is obviously an important influence, discussions of harvesting generally are concerned with production and profits, not with effects on the resource. All the potentially deleterious effects directly result from uncontrolled development in the coastal zone to satisfy the increasing needs of an expanding human population with an internally perpetuating value system originally developed under radically different ecological and technological constraints.

All seagrass beds appear to overlie anaerobic sediments. Thus dredging not only increases suspended material and accelerates sediment deposition but also causes changes in the redox potential of the sediment. Under these conditions eelgrass density may be reduced considerably. It is not known whether the reduction is caused by direct smothering of the grass, by decrease in available light due to increased turbidity, by a change in the redox potential of the surface sediment by rapid addition of oxidized materials, or by toxins released from the suspended sediments.

Odum (1963) studied the ecological effects of dredging on *Thalassia* and *Diplanthera (Halodule)* beds. During dredging, light penetration was much reduced and the productivity and chlorophyll content of the grasses diminished. During the fol-

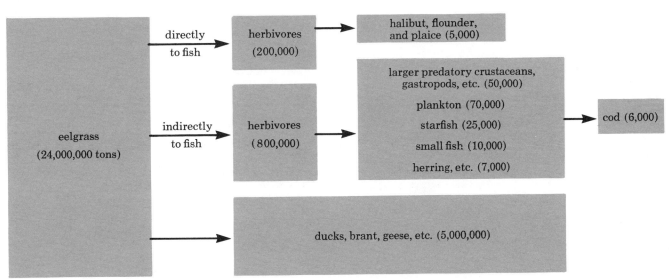

Figure 3. In 1918 C. J. G. Petersen estimated the relationship among standing crops of organisms supported by the eelgrass system in Denmark. Herbivores used *directly* as food for larger forms are small herbivorous animals eaten directly by the food fish such as halibut, flounder, and plaice; those used *indirectly* are consumed by crustaceans, small fish, etc., which in turn are utilized by food fish such as cod. Tons are nonmetric. (Data from Petersen 1918 and Milne and Milne 1951.)

lowing growing season, in areas not smothered by silt, however, plant production and chlorophyll content were greater than during the pre-dredging and dredging periods. The enhanced growth was attributed to redistribution of dredge spoil and, thus, possible increased availability of mineral nutrients.

Wood (1959) found that after removal of *Zostera* the bottom sediment became oxidized, and recovery of eelgrass was impaired. Odum (1963) noted that *Thalassia* was killed when buried beneath 30 cm of dredge spoil in Redfish Bay, Texas. Small *Zostera* areas cleared by hand, however, recovered completely within one season (Marshall and Lukas 1970). Briggs and O'Connor (1971) found that areas of Long Island Sound which had been used for deposition of dredge spoils lacked vegetation, especially eelgrass, though it was abundant at nearby sites where the bottom was undisturbed.

Clearing agricultural lands and channeling streams, thereby increasing the rate of erosion and thus causing high inputs of sediment into estuaries and coastal areas, might have effects on eelgrass similar to those noted for dredging. Stream diversion, on the other hand, would decrease input of freshwater and suspended sediments, with the probable net effect of increasing water clarity and promoting upstream penetration of saline waters. This might enhance the establishment of eelgrass over a wider area but, in other instances, might decrease the distribution of other species. For example, manatee grass, *Syringodium filiforme,* is found in Anclote Anchorage, Florida, only in areas where there are significant amounts of freshwater runoff.

The potential deleterious effect of freshwater diversion lies not only in decreased salinities but also in the accompanying diversion of mineral nutrients—nitrogen and phosphorus—usually introduced into estuaries in the freshwater runoff. Similarly, stream channelization promotes runoff and thereby decreases retention of detritus and valuable mineral nutrients, both in the agricultural lands of the coastal zone and in the recipient estuaries.

The addition of waste materials to estuarine ecosystems usually impinges more directly upon the animal components than upon the primary producers. The effects of pesticides and chlorinated hydrocarbons (Risebrough 1971), heavy metals (Merlini 1971), and petroleum derivatives (Radcliffe and Murphy 1969) have been well documented for many types of marine organisms, but their direct effects on eelgrass or other seagrasses are generally unknown. Studies by Parker (1962, 1966) have shown that sediments and *Thalassia* constitute the prime reservoirs for isotopes added to the system and that there can be a rapid flux between these two system constituents. Likewise, dissolved copper is removed from the overlying water by either the sediment or *Zostera* (Barsdate, Nebert, and McRoy, in press).

Other environmental disturbances

Spillage of crude oil from ship traffic in the English Channel was implicated as the cause of widespread reduction of eelgrass in England in the early 1930s (Duncan 1933), but a direct causal relationship was not established. On the south coast of Puerto Rico, however, oil spillage was shown to produce lasting damage to the tropical seagrass *Thalassia* (Diaz-Piferrer 1962). The role of seagrasses or their detritus in accumulating pesticides, PCBs, heavy metals, or petroleum derivatives and transferring these pollutants to other, more sensitive trophic levels has not been investigated, and literature showing other direct effects on seagrasses could not be found. Since eelgrass is capable of anaerobic respiration (McRoy 1966), direct effects of municipal organic wastes, other than those of sludge deposition, may be negligible initially. However, the length of time the plant can tolerate anoxic conditions is not known, especially under the decreased light penetration that may accompany discharges of sewage.

Since most seagrasses undergo normal seasonal fluctuations in production and abundance which are in part related to water temperatures, thermal pollution can have a critical effect. Numerous investigators (see Zieman 1970) have found

that *Thalassia* production shows a strong temperature dependency between 23–29°C and declines rapidly above 30° and below 20°. Data collected by Setchell (1929) from Mt. Desert Isle, Maine, suggest that 5–17° is the normal temperature range for *Zostera* and that above 20° it undergoes heat rigor. Dillon's studies (1971), however, indicate that near its southern boundary (Beaufort, N.C.) the upper temperature limit for *Zostera* is more nearly 30° and that temperatures above this are lethal to the plant. Thayer et al. (in press) have indicated that *Zostera* in the Newport River estuary near Beaufort began to die off when the temperature reached approximately 28° in August. Thus, there are upper and lower tolerance limits beyond which seagrasses may be destroyed, and their thermal limits may differ between north temperate and south temperate regions.

Discharges of heated water, though not documented for *Zostera,* are known to destroy tropical seagrass beds. At Turkey Point, in Biscayne Bay, Fla., *Thalassia* disappeared seasonally from the immediate vicinity of the thermal plume at the mouth of the discharge canal of the power station (Zieman 1970); there was also a loss of invertebrate fauna associated with the beds. Kolehmainen, Martin, and Schroeder (in press) have recorded decreased biomass of *Thalassia* in the area of the thermal plume issuing from a fossil-fuel power-generating plant in Quayanilla Bay, Puerto Rico, but were unable to determine whether this decrease resulted from elevated temperatures or increased scouring. Phillips (1974) warns that heated water released into eelgrass habitats could disrupt the reproductive cycle of *Zostera,* presumably interfering with the normal temperature-dependent periodicity of flowering and germination.

Effects of ionizing radiation are unknown, since background radiation levels have not been increased significantly in the environment, except perhaps at the Pacific Proving Grounds, where the effects of elevated radiation were accompanied and overshadowed by the effects of blast and massive sedimentation. As mentioned earlier, Parker (1962, 1966) has indicated that *Thalassia*

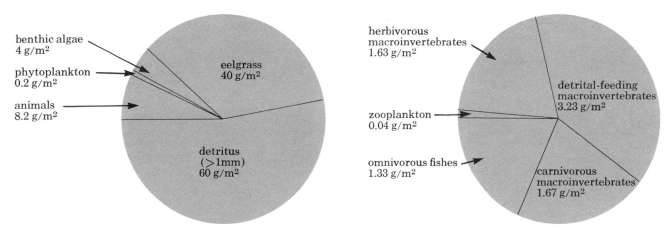

Figure 4. *Left:* Relation among standing crops and detritus in a 20,000 square meter eelgrass bed in the Newport River estuary, Beaufort, N.C. *Right:* Standing crops of animals in the eelgrass bed. Plants and detritus are in dry weights; animals in ash-free dry weight. (Data from Thayer et al., in press.)

takes up radionuclides, but seagrasses accumulate radioisotopes only to low levels (Polikarpov 1966), and the major role of seagrasses would be in conveying radioisotopes to other organisms in the community. Again, the efficiencies of these food-chain transfers simply are not yet known.

The activities of commercial fishermen using bottom trawls in the bays, sounds, and estuaries frequently conflict with the success of eelgrass and, consequently, of bay scallops. In North Carolina, where bay scallops generally occur in conjunction with eelgrass, scallops are usually harvested by bar dredges (25 kg maximum dredge weight) and hand rakes. Both methods uproot the grass, but dredging does so over large areas. Not only is the grass uprooted but the bottom sediments are stirred up, promoting oxidation of the sediments so that recolonization of *Zostera*—and bay scallops—probably is impeded (Thayer and Stuart 1974). On the Pacific coast, eelgrass renders oyster harvest difficult in many areas and may promote sedimentation to the extent that oysters cannot survive. In areas where oysters are of commercial interest, therefore, eelgrass is considered a pest that must be controlled (Thomas and Duffy 1968).

Esthetics are difficult to relate to other human activities or to the value of the seagrass community. Water-oriented recreation, with the exception of recreational fishing, however, is relatively incompatible with seagrass. Swimming beaches are made less attractive by the presence of a high-tide drift row of decaying grass, and water-skiing or swimming is unpleasant over the soft, muddy sedimentary bottoms characteristic of seagrass beds. The notion still prevails that the grass will pull people under. Fishermen, however, are cognizant of the importance of these grass beds for crustaceans, molluscs, and fishes. Numerous investigators have shown that seagrass beds generally have a denser faunal community than adjacent unvegetated bottoms. To those who view "naturalness" as an ideal state, seagrass meadows have a distinct esthetic value—attested to by birdwatchers and photographers—but this appreciation is currently enjoyed by only a small minority.

Consequences of seagrass destruction

The ecological consequences of seagrass destruction have been extensively documented during and since the sudden and drastic decline of eelgrass stocks on both sides of the Atlantic Ocean during the 1930s. Along most areas of the U.S. coast 99–100% of the standing stocks of eelgrass were destroyed in one year (Moffitt and Cottam 1941). This disturbance was characterized as "wasting disease" (Renn 1936), but its direct cause is still subject to question. The decline of fauna dependent upon *Zostera* was widespread, from small epifauna and infauna to fishes and waterfowl (Phillips 1974). These organisms are dependent on *Zostera* for food (detritus and its associated microbes, epiphytes, or epifauna), sediment stabilization, and protection afforded by the grass blades themselves. Perhaps the best documentation is in the literature on the sequence of events near Woods Hole, Mass. (Allee 1923; Dexter 1950). As the eelgrass declined, most of the animal species characteristic of the community disappeared. Many years later, when eelgrass became reestablished in limited areas, the entire community reappeared, but only in those areas where eelgrass was found.

Man's destruction of grass beds has often had similar effects. Flemer et al. (1967) noted a 71% reduction in average number of organisms in a Chesapeake Bay spoil area after dredging ceased. The area was soon repopulated by *Solen viridis* (green razor-shell clams), but thereafter population changes were erratic and total benthic biomass declined. Briggs and O'Connor (1971) noted that the diversity and density of species of fish generally decrease when vegetated areas are covered by dredge spoil. They further pointed out that some species may be entirely eliminated as a result of destruction of natural vegetation that provides both food and cover.

Taylor and Saloman (1968) estimated that the destruction of 1,100 tonnes (metric tons) of seagrass, primarily *Thalassia*, by burial and removal during dredging of Boca Ciega Bay, Fla., resulted in the immediate loss of approximately 1,800 tonnes of infauna. They also estimated that at least 73 tonnes of fishery products and 1,100 tonnes of

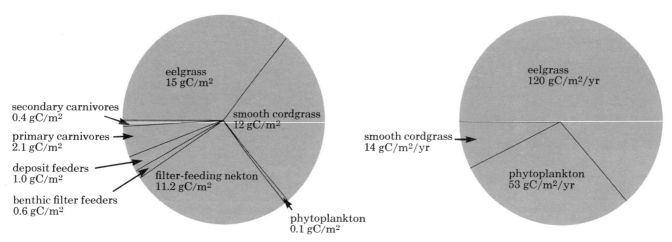

Figure 5. *Left:* Relation among standing crops (in terms of carbon) of organisms in the 400 square kilometer estuarine system near Beaufort, N.C. (Data from R. B. Williams, unpubl.) *Right:* Organic production (in terms of carbon) by the major plants in the estuarine system. (Data from Williams 1973.)

macroinvertebrate infauna were lost annually as a result of the dredging. This estimated loss of fishery production was based on standing crops of fishes collected in Texas grass beds, fish production estimates for Gulf coast estuaries, and the assumption that these values were representative for fishes utilizing grass beds in Boca Ciega Bay; macroinvertebrate production estimates were based on biomass data for the bay and an assumed invertebrate-production-to-biomass ratio of four.

Thus, the basic direct value of seagrass to its community is well established, and the potential value to top carnivores in the estuarine ecosystem can be estimated. These estimates must be put in a broader context, however, to enable proper evaluation of the real benefits of seagrasses to the estuarine ecosystem. We must consider the proportionate role of seagrasses in the energetic scheme of all estuarine and coastal productivity, upon which most of the fishery organisms used by man depend during some stage of their development.

In the area of Beaufort, productivity of eelgrass, phytoplankton, and cordgrass (*Spartina alterniflora*) has been evaluated; preliminary estimates of standing crop on a seasonal basis are available for benthic macroinvertebrates, zooplankton, and fish; and annual commercial yields of fish and shellfish are available (see Fig. 5).

A preliminary synthesis of the trophic structure (R. B. Williams, un-

publ.) suggests that a mean ecological efficiency of about 20% is required from the calculated sources of primary production to the annual production of fishery species in the Beaufort estuarine system —that is, an average of 20% of the material consumed at each trophic level is converted to tissue by the consumer organism. Respiration may account for about 75% of the assimilated energy for herbivores and detrital-feeding invertebrates (Teal 1962) and about 90% for fishes (Mann 1965; Adams 1974). Since assimilation may range from 20–60% of consumption for invertebrates (Miller and Mann 1973) and is about 80% for fishes (Mann 1965), most of the primary production is ultimately channeled into organisms used by man. While it is difficult to evaluate the utilization of different sources of primary production separately, the combined sources appear related directly to the fishery output of this estuarine system.

The relative contributions of seagrass would obviously vary between systems and species of seagrass, but the magnitude of Williams's estimate (64% of total productivity) suggests the importance of eelgrass to the total estuarine ecosystem. Synergism further amplifies the role of *Zostera*: loss of the seagrass results in increased turbidity which decreases the productivity not only of remaining *Zostera* but also of phytoplankton and benthic algae. On the other hand, redistribution of bottom sediments may enhance productivity by increasing availability of mineral nutrients. The

relative effects of these processes cannot now be quantified, but they should be considered carefully in developing priorities for man's ultimate use of the coastal zone.

References

Adams, S. M. Structural and functional analysis of eelgrass fish communities. Ph.D. thesis, 1974, Univ. North Carolina, Chapel Hill. 131 pp.

Allee, W. C. 1923. Studies in marine ecology. III. Some physical factors related to the distribution of littoral invertebrates. *Biol. Bull.* (Woods Hole) 44(5):205–53.

Arasaki, M. 1950. The ecology of Amano (*Zostera marina*) and Koamano (*Zostera nana*). *Bull. Jap. Soc. Sci. Fish.* 15(10):567–72.

Barsdate, R. J., M. Nebert, and C. P. McRoy. In press. *Lagoon Contributions to Sediments and Water of the Bering Sea.* Inst. Mar. Sci., Univ. Alaska, Occas. Publ. No. 2.

Briggs, P. T., and J. S. O'Connor. 1971. Comparison of shore-zone fishes over naturally vegetated and sand-filled bottoms in Great South Bay. *N.Y. Fish Game J.* 18(1):15–41.

Conover, J. T. 1958. Seasonal growth of benthic marine plants as related to environmental factors in an estuary. *Publ. Inst. Mar. Sci. Univ. Tex.* 5:97–147.

den Hartog, C. 1970. *The Sea-grasses of the World.* London: North-Holland Publ. Co. 275 pp.

Dexter, R. W. 1950. Restoration of the *Zostera* faciation at Cape Ann, Massachusetts. *Ecology* 31(2):286–88.

Diaz-Piferrer, M. 1962. The effects of an oil spill on the shore of Guanica, Puerto Rico. (Abstract.) Assoc. Island Mar. Labs., 4th Meeting, Curacao, pp. 12–13.

Dillon, R. C. A comparative study of the primary productivity of estuarine phytoplankton and macrobenthic plants. Ph.D. thesis, 1971, Univ. North Carolina, Chapel Hill. 112 pp.

Duncan, F M. 1933. Disappearance of *Zostera marina. Nature* 132(3334):483.

Ferguson, R. L., and M. B. Murdoch. In press. Microbial biomass in the Newport River Estuary, N.C. *Proc. Sec. Intern. Estuarine Res. Conf., Myrtle Beach, S.C.* Oct. 1973.

Flemer, D. A., C. Dovel, H. J. Pfitzenmeyer, and D. E. Ritchie, Jr. 1967. Spoil disposal in upper Chesapeake Bay. II. Preliminary analysis of biological effects. In P. L. McCarty and R. Kennedy, Chairmen, *Proc. National Symposium on*

Estuarine Pollution. Stanford, Calif.: Stanford Univ. Press, pp. 152–87.

Kolehmainen, S. E., F. D. Martin, and P. B. Schroeder. In press. Thermal studies on tropical marine ecosystems in Puerto Rico. *Symp. Physical and Biological Effects on the Environment of Cooling Systems and Thermal Discharges at Nuclear Power Stations*. Oslo: Intern. Atomic Energy Agency.

Mann, K. H. 1965. Energy transformations by a population of fish in the River Thames. *J. Anim. Ecol.* 34:253–75.

Marshall, N. 1970. Food transfer through the lower trophic levels on the benthic environment. In J. H. Steele, ed., *Marine Food Chains*. Berkeley: Univ. California Press, pp. 52–66.

Marshall, N., and K. Lukas. 1970. Preliminary observations on the properties of bottom sediments with and without eelgrass, *Zostera marina*, cover. *Proc. Natl. Shellfish Assoc.* 60:107–11.

McRoy, C. P. The standing stock and ecology of eelgrass, *Zostera marina*, Izembek Lagoon, Alaska. M. S. thesis, 1966, Univ. Washington, Seattle. 138 pp.

McRoy, C. P. 1973. Seagrass ecosystems: Research recommendations of the International Seagrass Workshop. *Inter. Decade Ocean. Explor.* 62 pp.

McRoy, C. P., and R. J. Barsdate. 1970. Phosphate adsorption in eelgrass. *Limnol. Oceanogr.* 15:6–13.

McRoy, C. P., and J. J. Goering. 1974. Nutrient transfer between seagrass *Zostera marina* and its epiphytes. *Nature* 248:173–74.

Merlini, M. 1971. Heavy-metal contamination. In D. W. Hood, ed., *Impingement of Man upon the Oceans*. New York: Wiley-Interscience, pp. 461–68.

Miller, R. J., and K. H. Mann. 1973. Ecological energetics of the seaweed zone in a marine bay on the Atlantic coast of Canada. III. Energy transformations by sea urchins. *Mar. Biol.* (Berl.) 18:99–114.

Milne, L. J., and M. J. Milne. 1951. The eelgrass catastrophe. *Sci. Amer.* 184(1):52–55.

Moffitt, J., and C. Cottam. 1941. *Eelgrass Depletion on the Pacific Coast and Its Effect on Black Brant*. U.S. Fish Wildl. Serv. Wildl. Leaflet No. 204. 26 pp.

Odum, E. P. 1959. *Fundamentals of Ecology*, 2nd ed. Philadelphia: Saunders. 546 pp.

Odum, H. T. 1963. Productivity measurements in Texas turtle grass and the effects of dredging on intercoastal channel. *Publ. Inst. Mar. Sci. Univ. Tex.* 9:48–58.

Parker, P. L. 1962. Zinc in a Texas bay. *Publ. Inst. Mar. Sci. Univ. Tex.* 8:75.

Parker, P. L. 1966. Movement of radioisotopes in a marine bay: Cobalt-60, iron-59, managanese-54, zinc-65, sodium-22. *Publ. Inst. Mar. Sci. Univ. Tex.* 11:102.

Petersen, C. J. G. 1918. The sea bottom and its production of fish food. A survey of the work done in connection with valuation of the Danish waters from 1883–1917. *Rep. Danish Biol. Sta.* 25:1–82.

Phillips, R. C. Ecological life history of *Zostera marina* L. (eelgrass) in Puget Sound, Washington. Ph.D. thesis, 1972, Univ. Wash., Seattle. 154 pp.

Phillips, R. C. 1974. Temperate grass flats. In H. T. Odum, B. J. Copeland, and E. A. McMahan, eds., *Coastal Ecological Systems of the United States: A Source Book for Estuarine Planning*, Vol. 2. Washington, D.C.: Conservation Foundation, pp. 244–99.

Polikarpov, G. G. 1966. *Radioecology of Aquatic Organisms*. New York: Reinhold. 314 pp.

Radcliffe, D. R., and T. A. Murphy. 1969. Biological effects of oil pollution: Bibliography. *Federal Water Poll. Cont. Admin. Res. Ser. DAST* 19.

Renn, C. E. 1936. The wasting disease of *Zostera marina* L. II. A phytological investigation of the diseased plant. *Biol. Bull.* (Woods Hole) 70(1):148–58.

Risebrough, R. W. 1971. Chlorinated hydrocarbons. In D. W. Hood, ed., *Impingement of Man upon the Oceans*. New York: Wiley-Interscience, pp. 259–86.

Ryther, J. H. 1969. Photosynthesis and fish production in the sea. *Science* 166:72–76.

Setchell, W. A. 1929. Morphological and phenological notes on *Zostera marina* L. *Univ. California Publ. Bot.* 14:389–452.

Taylor, J. L., and C. H. Saloman. 1968. Some effects of hydraulic dredging and coastal development in Boca Ciega Bay, Florida. U.S. Fish. Wildl. Ser., *Fish. Bull.* 67:213–41.

Teal, J. M. 1962. Energy flow in the saltmarsh ecosystem of Georgia. *Ecology* 43:614–24.

Thayer, G. W., S. M. Adams, and M. W. LaCroix. In press. Structural and functional aspects of a recently established *Zostera marina* community. *Proc. Sec. Intern. Estuarine Res. Conf., Myrtle Beach, S.C.* Oct. 1973.

Thayer, G. W., and H. H. Stuart. 1974. The bay scallop makes its bed of seagrass. U.S. Natl. Mar. Fish. Serv., *Mar. Fish Rev.* 36:27–30.

Thomas, M. L. H., and J. R. Duffy. 1968. Butoxyethanol ester of 2, 4-D in the control of eelgrass (*Zostera marina* L.) and its effects on oysters (*Crassostrea virginica* Gemlin) and other benthos. *Northeastern Weed Control Conf.* 22:186–93.

Williams, R. B. 1973. Nutrient levels and phytoplankton productivity in the estuary. In R. H. Chabreck, ed., *Proc. Coastal Marsh and Estuary Manag. Symp.* Baton Rouge: Louisiana State Univ., Div. Cont. Educ., pp. 59–o9.

Wood, E. J. F. 1959. Some east Australian seagrass communities. *Proc. Limnol. Soc. New South Wales* 84(2):218–26.

Wood, E. J. F., W. E. Odum, and J. C. Zieman. 1969. Influence of sea grasses on the productivity of coastal lagoons. *Lagunas Costeras. Un Simposio Mem. Simp. Intern. UNAM-UNESCO*, Mexico, D. F., Nov. 1967, pp. 495–502.

Zieman, J. C., Jr. The effects of a thermal effluent stress on the sea-grasses and macroalgae in the vicinity of Turkey Point, Biscayne Bay, Florida. Ph.D. thesis, 1970, Univ. Miami, Coral Gables. 129 pp.

Donald C. Rhoads
Peter L. McCall
Josephine Y. Yingst

Disturbance and Production on the Estuarine Seafloor

Dredge-spoil disposal in estuaries such as Long Island Sound can be managed in ways that enhance productivity rather than diminish it

For many millennia mankind has been disturbing natural ecosystems in order to enhance productivity. Primitive agriculturalists have employed slashing and burning; advanced cultures utilize selective timber cutting, plowing, and manipulation of water levels. Such practices show an appreciation of the fact that disturbances play an important role in maintaining parts of ecosystems at relatively high states of productivity. In the absence of disturbances, species interactions result in equilibrium associations of slow-growing, long-lived species. After disturbances, on the other hand, pioneering species with high growth rates and short generation times appear.

Scientific theories of ecological succession and its relation to productivity were developed decades ago for terrestrial ecology but have not been widely applied to understanding the dynamics of seafloor communities. Systematic study of the seafloor began in the early part of the nineteenth century, yet we still have little knowledge about how bottom-dwelling organisms respond to disturbances of any origin. But effective management of present and future uses of the seafloor demands an understanding of how disturbances affect seafloor productivity. In this article we approach the problem as it arises in the estuary, a habitat intensively disturbed by storms as well as by man.

At the present time, one of the most pressing estuarine management problems is related to the disposal of dredged sediment and sludge. Maintenance dredging is required to keep harbors navigable for commercial shipping and recreational boating. Channel dredging and other types of harbor excavations currently generate about 3.5×10^8 m^3/year of sedimentary spoil in the United States (Boyd et al. 1972). Much of this sediment is dumped onto the estuarine seafloor outside harbors, because onshore disposal is not always possible or desirable (Lee 1976), while dumping in deep water is very expensive and may have adverse ecological effects (Sanders 1977). But the oceans are a major source of food for mankind and have been looked to with increasing attention as terrestrial agriculture has come to be seen as inadequate to supply the world's food needs. Coastal zones yield about half of the world's harvest of fin fish, and intensive nearshore mariculture can produce up to 500,000 kg of shellfish tissue/ha/year (250 tons/acre/year) (Ryther 1969). Thus within the past few years the effects of disposal on harvested estuarine species has become a major concern.

In fact, dumping of dredged sediment in estuaries can be managed so that production of animals on the seafloor is enhanced rather than jeopardized. In this article we explore this proposal by examining the response of bottom communities in central Long Island Sound to physical disturbances. Chemical disturbance—that is, contamination by polluted spoil—is not dealt with here, though it is obviously a major concern, since a productive but contaminated food chain is clearly undesirable. Rather, we will focus on the influence of physical disturbance on ecological succession.

The estuary

Mid- to high-latitude estuaries are coastal bodies of water where fresh water from land drainage is mixed with seawater. Most estuaries are semienclosed by headlands or sandbars, which limit vertical mixing of the water column by open ocean waves. Vertically stratified flow is characteristic of such estuaries: a surface layer of fresh or brackish water moves seaward over a compensating landward flow of deeper saline water. This estuarine circulation pattern functions as a trapping mechanism for dissolved nutrients and pollutants and results in high sedimentation rates in navigation channels. Each year about 10^5 to 10^6 m^3 of sediment is dredged in Long Island Sound.

Dumping of dredged sediment is only one of the many sources of disturbances on the estuarine seafloor. Storm waves, tidal scour, seafloor mining, submarine construction, and raking or trawling activities of bottom fisheries all produce changes in bottom topography, alter sediment grain-size patterns, change sediment chemistry, and bury or otherwise re-

Donald Rhoads has been a professor of geology at Yale since he received his Ph.D. from the University of Chicago in 1965. He is interested particularly in skeletal growth of calcified marine invertebrates and the evolution of benthic communities. Peter L. McCall, who received his Ph.D. from Yale in 1975, is currently Assistant Professor of Geology at Case Western Reserve. His primary interests are in community structure and dynamics. Josephine Y. Yingst is a research associate in the Department of Geology and Geophysics at Yale. She received her Ph.D. in marine biology from the University of Southern California in 1975. She is primarily concerned with food-chain relations in detritus-based ecosystems. All three have been studying animal-sediment interactions in various aquatic environments. Address: Donald C. Rhoads, Department of Geology and Geophysics, Yale University, New Haven, CT 06520.

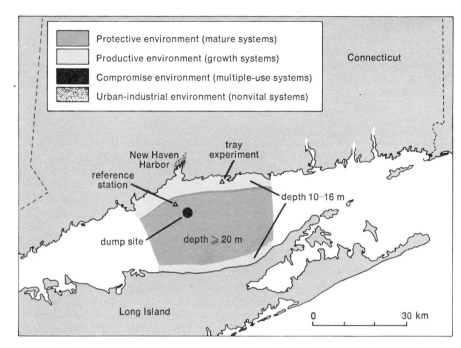

Figure 1. From the results of two experiments on the effects of physical disturbances in Long Island Sound, the estuarine ecosystem can be divided into the four interrelated kinds of environment outlined by Odum (1969) for terrestrial ecosystems. The innermost part of New Haven Harbor is a good example of a chronically polluted, nonvital urban-industrial environment. The tray experiment examined the naturally productive environment of nearshore bottoms shallower than 10–16 m, where seafloor erosion keeps the faunal associations at an early stage of succession. Protective environments on quiet-water bottoms deeper than 20 m were represented by the reference station; these areas are populated by mature communities, which are biologically predictable but not highly productive. Localized compromise systems within protective environments, such as the dredge-spoil dump site, can be achieved when human disturbances are managed so that productivity is both high and predictable (see Fig. 7).

move nutritionally important organic matter from the sediment–water interface. All of these forms of disturbance can produce major reorganizations of communities of bottom-dwelling species. Pelagic organisms—those living in the water column—may also be affected by seafloor disturbance, but organisms that spend most of their adult life associated with the seafloor, called *benthos* (new Latin from the Greek meaning "life of the deep"), are influenced over the long term and are therefore the focus of this article.

In 1969 E. P. Odum proposed a conceptual model for succession based mainly on an understanding of terrestrial ecosystems. This model can be used to examine marine ecosystems, because plant and animal species in a succession employ remarkably similar colonization strategies across very different habitats and in the face of disturbances of widely varying source and nature. This similarity in colonization strategies reflects an underlying pattern of evolutionary convergence in survival adaptations (see Hutchinson 1953; Margalef 1958 and 1963). One can rank most colonizing species according to their time of appearance in succession, their temporal and spatial persistence, and their rates of population growth and decline (Table 1).

Three patterns of colonization of shallow-water marine sediments by invertebrate species can be identified

(e.g. Dean and Haskins 1964; Harrison and Wass 1965; Leppäkoski 1971; Saila, Pratt, and Polgar 1972; Scheibel 1974; Kaplan et al. 1975; Boesch, Diaz, and Virnstein 1976; Boesch, Wass, and Virnstein 1976; Oliver and Slattery 1976; Rosenberg 1976; and Wolff, Sandee, and de Wolf 1977). Group 1 colonizers, which arrive within a few days, reach peak abundances within a relatively short period of time. In the absence of further disturbance, Group 1 species experience high mortality and may disappear locally as a result of competition and/or predation. Group 3 colonizers may appear early in succession, but they maintain more or less constant, relatively low population densities. Individuals of these species persist over long periods of time. Group 2 species represent a mode of colonization intermediate to groups 1 and 3.

Two experiments

Between 1972 and 1976, two studies were conducted to explore the impact of disturbance on Long Island Sound, an estuary that is subject to extremely intense recreational and commercial use by the human populations surrounding it (Fig. 1). One study examined colonization of trays of defaunated mud simulating a condition following a severe natural disturbance (McCall 1977). The second study examined colonization of a newly deposited mound of material dredged from New Haven Harbor, including

both heavily polluted inner-harbor sediment and clean sand from the outer harbor. Comparison of patterns of colonization in the two experiments must be made with caution, but if the various factors affecting that comparison are kept in mind, the two studies can be used fruitfully together to compare the effects of man-induced physical disturbance to those of natural disturbance such as bottom erosion by currents.

The first experiment, which we call the tray experiment, was carried out between 17 July 1972 and 10 October 1973, a period of 382 days. The study site was located in 14 m of water, on a bottom frequently resuspended by storm disturbance (Gordon and Pilbeam 1975). Observations in the second experiment, the dredge-spoil experiment, were begun on 5 June 1974 and ended on 23 June 1976, a period of 792 days. The dump site was located in 20 m of water, where bottom sediments are resuspended to a depth of 1–3 mm by tidal scour but are rarely churned by storm turbulence (McCall, in press).

A sieve with a mesh size of 300 microns was used in separating the animals from sediment in the tray experiment; a sieve with a mesh size of 1,000 microns was used in the dredge-spoil study. Juvenile and young stages are not retained on the coarser screen; therefore estimates of when different species arrived and information about initial rates of growth are not as accurate as when a finer mesh is used. Abundances of very small pioneering species are probably underestimated by factors of 2 to 8, though the large mesh screen retains all larger later arriving species (McCall, 1975 diss.). Our data are confined to macrobenthos—benthos larger than 300 microns in their smallest diameter. Because both studies were conducted at depths where light is limiting for plant growth, only benthic animals were considered.

The tray experiment. Trays of sediment from which all macroscopic organisms had been removed were placed by scuba divers in a region of firm silty sand. Populations of organisms arrived in the trays in exponentially increasing numbers within 10 days after the start of the experiment (Table 2). Most of the organisms first entered as larvae settling from the water column. Early in the experiment, densities in the trays were nearly two orders of magnitude higher than those on the ambient seafloor, which was sampled by a ship-deployed grab. Either the empty habitat represented by trays when they were first set out was a more favorable environment for survival of larvae than the ambient seafloor or larvae were preferentially attracted to the trays. Between 5 and 7 months after the start of the experiment, faunal densities in the trays were similar to densities observed on the surrounding seafloor (Fig. 2).

The greatest number of species ever present in the trays was recorded 2 to 3 months after initial colonization, though the peak may have been as late as November or December, when no samples were taken. Most settlement of larvae in Long Island Sound begins in April and continues into November. During the winter of 1972–73, several species that survived on the adjacent seafloor disappeared from the trays, perhaps as a result of competitive interactions or winter mortality with no subsequent recruitment. It took 10–12 months before the species compositions of the trays and the natural seafloor were similar.

The dredge-spoil experiment. In this study, dredged sediment was dumped weekly at a buoy in the sound, on a mud bottom 20 m deep, between 6 October 1973 and 23 April 1974. Over 6×10^5 m^3 of channel sediment was deposited to form a pile 9 m high with a basal area of roughly 29,000 m^2. Dredging began in the most heavily polluted inner harbor and proceeded out toward the sound, so that at the dump site the most polluted sediment was buried below clean sand from the outer harbor. The last few barge loads produced a more or less continuous sand cap several centimeters thick over the surface of the dumped sediment. Within a few weeks, the sand cap was in turn covered with a layer of silty mud a few millimeters thick, which had been resuspended from the surrounding seafloor by tidal-current scour.

A reference station located 5.6 km northwest of the dump site, in 15 m of water, was established to describe the population of benthic organisms characteristic of the undisturbed

Table 1. A conceptual model of succession in ecosystems

	Early stages	Mature stages
organism size	small	large
life cycles of species	short	long
growth of individuals and populations	rapid	slow
ratio of gross production to standing-crop biomass	high	low
feeding mode or strategy*	suspension feeding and surface deposit-feeding dominate	subsurface deposit-feeding dominates
utilization of buried detritus	less important(?)	more important
symbiosis within system	undeveloped	developed
nutrient conservation within system	poor	good

NOTE: This model is modified from Odum 1969; we have chosen 8 of Odum's 24 attributes that are useful in interpreting our Long Island Sound data.
* We have adapted this attribute from Odum's table, which characterized early stages as linear grazing food chains and mature stages as weblike detritus food chains, to describe specifically benthic feeding modes.

Table 2. Colonizing species in the tray experiment classified by successional group

	Time to maximum abundance (days)	Maximum abundance (per m^2)	Dif. between max. abundance and min. abundance after peak (per m^2)
Group 1			
Streblospio benedicti (polychaete worm)	10	418,315	385
Capitella capitata (polychaete worm)	29–50	80,385	955
Ampelisca abdita (amphipod crustacean)	29–50	9,990	0
Group 2			
Nucula annulata (clam)	50	3,735	50
Tellina agilis (clam)	86	1,400	0
Group 3			
Nephtys incisa (polychaete worm)	175	220	120
Ensis directus (clam)	50–223	30	0

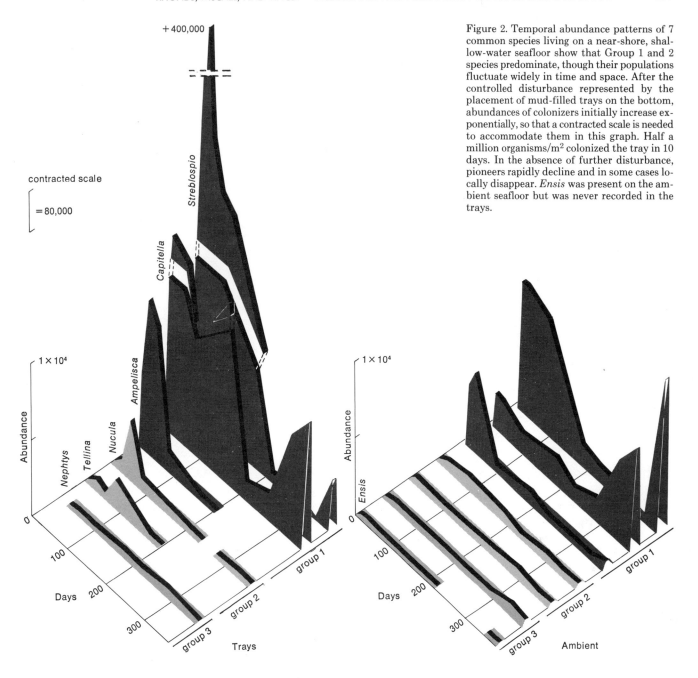

+ 400,000

contracted scale

= 80,000

1 × 10⁴

Abundance

Streblospio

Capitella

Ampelisca

Nucula

Tellina

Nephtys

100

Days

200

300

group 3

group 2

group 1

Trays

1 × 10⁴

Abundance

Ensis

100

Days

200

300

group 3

group 2

group 1

Ambient

Figure 2. Temporal abundance patterns of 7 common species living on a near-shore, shallow-water seafloor show that Group 1 and 2 species predominate, though their populations fluctuate widely in time and space. After the controlled disturbance represented by the placement of mud-filled trays on the bottom, abundances of colonizers initially increase exponentially, so that a contracted scale is needed to accommodate them in this graph. Half a million organisms/m² colonized the tray in 10 days. In the absence of further disturbance, pioneers rapidly decline and in some cases locally disappear. _Ensis_ was present on the ambient seafloor but was never recorded in the trays.

seafloor surrounding the dump pile. Samples were taken by diver-held box cores or the ship-deployed grab used in the tray experiment.

Because our information about colonization events was limited by sieve size, sampling area, and sampling frequency, we can only roughly estimate when faunal densities reached a peak on the dump (Fig. 3). This appeared to be in November 1974, approximately 200 days after dumping stopped. During the late fall of 1974 and winter of 1975, the dump maintained mean abundances of 1–2 × 10³ individuals/m⁻²—densities that were 2 to 10 times higher than those at the reference station.

the November peak, mean dump abundances steadily declined while those at the reference station generally increased. We estimate by extrapolation that the dump population dropped below densities at the reference station in late 1975. At the last sampling (May–June 1976), mean dump densities were about 4 times lower than those at the reference station. Again, in the absence of further disturbance, competitive interactions and predation probably account for the decreased density of organisms on the dump surface.

The greatest number of species appeared on the dump site between November 1974 and April 1975. The

wide range of values between duplicate samples during this period suggests a patchy distribution of colonizers on the disposal site. From November 1974 to January 1975, more species were found on the dump site than at the reference station. Although the numbers of species at the two sites converged in late 1975 and 1976, different species were found at the two areas. Indeed, throughout the 26 months of observation, distinctly different faunas were found at the dump and the reference station (Fig. 4).

The rate of colonization at the tray site was apparently a thousand times higher than the colonization rate at

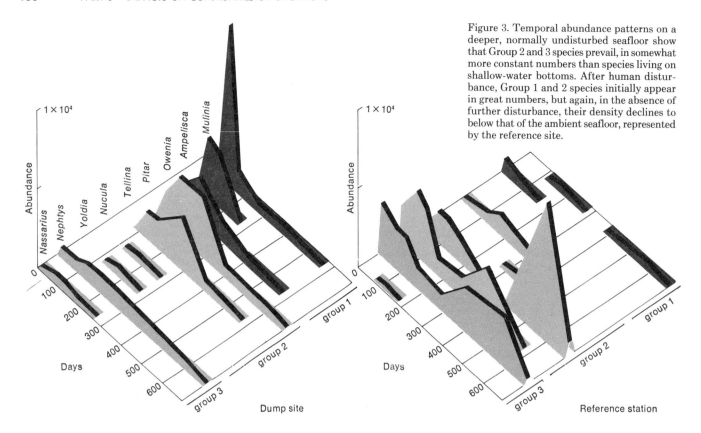

Figure 3. Temporal abundance patterns on a deeper, normally undisturbed seafloor show that Group 2 and 3 species prevail, in somewhat more constant numbers than species living on shallow-water bottoms. After human disturbance, Group 1 and 2 species initially appear in great numbers, but again, in the absence of further disturbance, their density declines to below that of the ambient seafloor, represented by the reference site.

the dump site. Only tens of days were required before peak densities were reached at the tray site, while several months were required to reach peak densities at the dump site. The fauna at the tray site became similar to the fauna on the surrounding bottom after about 200 days (as measured on the faunal similarity index, developed by Bray and Curtis, 1957, in Fig. 4).

Interpretation of these differences in patterns of colonization must take into account the limitations on comparison mentioned above. First, because the tray experiment was located on a shallow-water bottom disturbed by storms, Group 1 species were present nearby in high abundance and hence were able to populate the trays very quickly. The dredge-spoil dump was located several kilometers from these Group 1 populations, and thus it may have taken a longer time for the larvae of these pioneering species to disperse from shallow bottoms and settle onto the dump. Second, the 1 mm openings of the screen used in the dredge-spoil experiment delayed the record of the first appearance of settling organisms, and therefore the faunal densities of Group 1 species are underestimated, thus throwing off comparison with the results from the $300\ \mu$ screen used

in the tray experiment. Third, the numbers and kinds of larvae settling on the seafloor in Long Island Sound are highly variable from year to year (Yingst 1978). Therefore, overall rates of colonization might well be slower or faster in subsequent years.

It is possible that biogeochemical conditions at the dump surface influenced larval settlement and survival. Although highly contaminated sediment at the dump site was buried under a layer of relatively clean sediment, gravitational compaction of the deposit may have squeezed out soluble toxins from the sediment to the dump surface, inhibiting larval settlement. Newly deposited dredge spoil is, in any case, higher in soluble organic breakdown products, such as ammonia, and lower in fresh seawater constituents, such as sulfate, than the ambient seafloor (Rhoads, Aller, and Goldhaber 1977). We have no data to evaluate the effects of the chemical composition of the dump pile on colonization.

Colonizing species can be classified according to the three modes of colonization listed above on the basis of the temporal abundance patterns revealed by the experiments. Because the constellation of early colonizing

species varies with time and space, we have probably not identified all pioneering species in Long Island Sound. Nor, since we only have data for short-term recovery, have we necessarily documented all Group 3—or even later—species. Nevertheless, we can trace the broad outlines of the successional process from the data at hand.

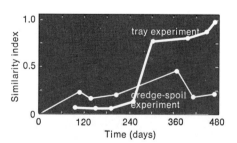

Figure 4. The Bray and Curtis faunal similarity index indicates similarity in faunal composition between an experiment site and its ambient environment (convergence = 1). Because the seafloor surrounding the tray site is perpetually in an early stage of succession, similarity is quickly reached after disturbance. Because, on the other hand, the seafloor surrounding the dump site is at a mature successional stage, the faunal composition of the dump will not match the ambient assemblage until the dump site has passed through earlier successional stages and the climax stage has had a chance to develop. This may require several years.

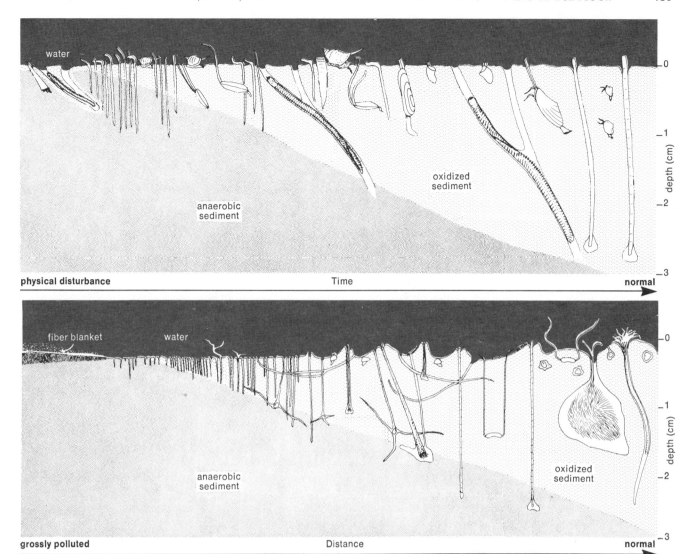

Figure 5. An interesting parallel is found between change in faunal composition over time after a singular physical disturbance, such as the dumping of dredge spoil, and that over distance from a chronic pollutant effluent such as the blanket of fiber from a cellulose factory. Immediately after disturbance or close to the source of pollution, a few species of abundant and productive polychaete worms are found. These are followed—in time or space—by suspension-feeding or surface-deposit–feeding molluscs, which are in turn replaced by less productive species that live deeper in the mud, feeding on buried detritus and oxygenating the sediment. Pioneering species at or near the surface may be more available as prey for foraging fish and crustaceans than deeply buried species of the mature stage. (Diagram of faunal changes over distance from pollutant effluent after Pearson and Rosenberg 1976).

Succession and productivity

Benthic assemblages on disturbed bottoms are dominated by species with short life spans, frequent reproduction, and high dispersability—characteristics well suited for the exploitation of continually changing habitats. Indeed, Levinton (1972, 1974) has suggested that suspension-feeding clams are evolutionarily preadapted for a colonizing life-style. In Long Island Sound, these assemblages are predominantly located on near-shore, current-scoured bottoms—like those studied in the tray experiment. In deep, quieter waters, they are confined to active dump sites. Most Group 1 and 2 species participating in the early stage of colonization feed on suspended or recently sedimented plankton and detritus, either at the sediment surface or by filtering overlying water.

Pioneering species have a negligible effect on sedimentary properties below the surface of the bottom (Rhoads, Aller, and Goldhaber 1977), in marked contrast to the intensive sediment-reworking activities of the equilibrium community. Because these suspension feeders usually live at, or near, the sediment surface, they are vulnerable prey. Pioneering species may therefore be especially important food sources for commer-cially exploited fish and crustaceans (Pearson and Rosenberg 1976; Virnstein 1977).

On mud bottoms later in succession, the fauna consists of species with longer mean life spans and lower recruitment rates that approximate death rates. The reference station for the dump site represents one such equilibrium stage, dominated by the clam *Nucula annulata* and the polychaete worm *Nephtys incisa*. Although these two species, and others associated with them, can participate in initial colonization of a disturbed bottom, they only reach equilibrium abundances in late successional stages. Most equilibrium species living on mud bottoms feed on buried detrital material.

We hypothesize that *Nucula, Nephtys,* and other species in this equilibrium community graze on buried particles coated with bacteria. Particle-feeding and burrowing mix the sediment to a depth of several centimeters. Respiratory activities pump water in and out of the bottom. Biological mixing and water exchange may stimulate microbial metabolic activity and turnover rates by mixing dissolved nutrients into the sediments and purging metabolites from the bottom. A kind of microbial gardening results (see Hylleberg 1975; Rhoads, Aller, and Goldhaber 1977). If our hypothesis is correct, the biological sediment mixing that results may serve to recycle nutrients efficiently.

Development of a microbial garden through biological sediment mixing probably requires a period of several years. Placement of dredged or other foreign material onto the bottom would be expected to destroy the preexisting system locally, and the new sedimentary deposit may not initially be capable of supporting deep-burrowing sediment feeders because of a limited microbial food source. Our hypothesis is supported by observations that, following disturbance, the seafloor becomes progressively populated by deeper-feeding benthos (Figs. 5 and 6). This phenomenon is not unique to our observations but has also been observed in studies of community structure along pollution gradients (Fig. 5). The difference in feeding types between the organisms found at the disposal site and those found at the reference site after almost 800 days might be explained by the lack of long-term biogenic processing of the dump surface required to develop a microbial garden. The establishment of an equilibrium community may require several years.

The attributes of our Group 1 and Group 2 colonizers are consistent with the modified version of Odum's model summarized in Table 1. Biomass of Group 1 species is 10 to 20 times higher than that of Group 3 species. Group 1 species have life cycles shorter than one year; Group 3 species, longer than one year. Both individual and population growth rates of Group 1 species are 10 to 100

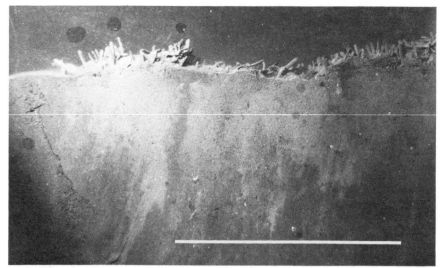

Figure 6. Details of organism–sediment interrelations can be examined by using an interface or profile camera (Rhoads and Cande 1971), which is lowered to the seafloor and cuts the bottom in a vertical plane, leaving local structures relatively undisturbed. White bars represent 10 cm. *Above:* a profile of a 10-m-deep bottom shows an early stage of colonization by small tube-dwelling crustaceans, *Ampelisca* *abdita.* Organisms are densely packed and feeding activity is confined to the sediment surface. *Below:* a profile from a 20-m-deep bottom shows the habitat of a mature community. Most organisms live and feed below the surface (see Fig. 5) and are therefore not visible. Note the deeply oxidized sediment profile characteristic of this stage.

times higher than those of Group 3 species.

The net increase in biomass between sampling intervals shows differences in productivity between early and late colonizers. Production estimates are shown in Table 3 for 11 colonizing species in the tray experiment over the first 86 days, the time interval it took to reach peak biomass for all macrofauna. The mean production rate (gm/m^2/day^{-1}) of early colonizers (groups 1 and 2) is higher by a factor of 10 than mean production rates of Group 3 species. However, the production to biomass (P/B) ratios over this short time interval do not show significant differences between

these groupings. Early colonizers are abundant and have high production rates, but their individual biomass values are low; the converse is true for Group 3 species, and hence P/B ratios are similar. Group 1 species can have several generations per year, however, and therefore the annual P/B for this group will be much higher than for Group 3 species over the long term.

Table 4 shows the estimated total production in the two experiments from their start to time of peak biomass. In the colonization trays production is about 0.1 gm/m^2/day. Over the same period ambient seafloor production is only about 50% of this value (0.05 gm/m^2/day). At the dump

Table 3. Life-history data for representative species colonizing the two experiment sites

	Maximum linear size (mm)	Biomass dry wt. (mg/ indiv.)	Genera-tions/year	Relative death rates	Estimated production* (gm/ m²/ day⁻¹)	Production/ biomass* ratio (P/B)
Group 1						
Streblospio benedicti	20 × 1	0.15–50	3–4	high	0.57	5.0
Capitella capitata	20 × 1	0.15–50	5–8	high	0.27	7.0
Ampelisca abdita	5–7	0.5–1	2	high	0.06	4.5
Owenia fusiformis	20 × 3	0.5–1	—	high	insufficient data	insufficient data
Mulinia lateralis	—	2–10	1–2	high	insufficient data	insufficient data
Group 2						
Nucula annulata	5–7	5–10	1?–2?	moderate	0.12	6.9
Tellina agilis	10	ca. 5	1?	moderate	0.04	3.0
Pitar morrhuana	10	ca. 10	1	moderate	insufficient data	insufficient data
Group 3						
Nephtys incisa	50 × 5	30–70	1	low	0.03	4.0
Ensis directus	50 × 10	100–300	1	low	0.05	5.6
Nassarius trivittatus	5 × 10	3–10	2	low	0.01	4.1

* Where values are given, they are estimates for species colonizing the tray experiment over the period to peak abundance, 0–86 days.

site we conservatively estimate a production rate of .04 gm/m²/day. Production at its reference station over the same period is about 16% of the dump production. The production difference between the trays and the ambient seafloor is less than the difference between the dump and its ambient seafloor because the seafloor near the tray experiment is naturally disturbed by bottom currents and therefore is dominated by productive Group 1 and 2 colonizers.

In summary, although the equilibrium community is less productive than a pioneering stage, it is more predictable in space and time, and its ecological role may be to recycle buried nutrients back into the water column. These attributes of a mature community are deserving of conservation and protection by man.

Managing disturbance

E. P. Odum (1969) has suggested that necessary human disturbance of ecosystems can be managed in such a way as to enhance productivity while maintaining a degree of environmental resiliency. He recommends a compromise system between the highly productive, variable, youthful stage and the stable but less productive mature stage. Such a compromise system will be more productive than

a mature stage, and the level of productivity will be kept predictable by managing disturbance. Natural disturbances produce local seafloor disasters in estuaries, and if we understand how benthic systems respond to these disasters, we can develop compromise systems when we create artificial disturbances by using estuaries for dredge-spoil disposal.

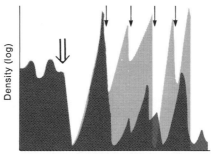

Time (years)

Figure 7. If a single massive disturbance (large arrow) takes place within a seafloor region normally populated by a mature community, that community is locally destroyed and is initially replaced by an explosive growth of productive opportunities. Subsequent population growth and productivity patterns are unpredictable over a time span of several years. If disturbance is regularly repeated (small arrows) after the initial recruitment period ends, however, the system can be maintained in a state of continuous recruitment and high productivity. This multiple-disturbance scheme is part of Odum's pulse-stability concept of managing compromise ecosystems.

To manage dredge disposal as part of a compromise system, four sets of biological information should be in hand: (1) how species in the system fit into the successional sequence; (2) rates of seasonal colonization and production; (3) effects of various spoil types on colonizers; and (4) the spatial distribution of the various potential colonizers on the estuarine seafloor. These data should allow determination of which parts of the ecosystem are most resilient, what the optimal timing of physical disturbance is to achieve the desired compromise system, and where in the system productivity can be most enhanced. Such data can be collected by making studies of the sort we have described at locations close to proposed or potential dump sites, and by regional benthic sampling.

Areas of the seafloor subject to chronic natural disturbance such as current scour or periodic sedimentation are among the most resilient parts of benthic ecosystems, because rapidly colonizing Group 1 and 2 species are likely to be present continuously (Copeland 1970; Holling 1973; Boesch 1974). For two reasons, however, dumping dredge material—particularly polluted spoil—in environments subject to frequent natural disturbance is not recommended. First, such areas are already at high levels of productivity, which dumping will do little to increase. Second, storms and heavy wave action make containment, stabilization, and management of the deposits impossible. Thus, for example, the current dump sites in the New York Bight—some of the world's largest and most active—are not amenable to the kind of management we suggest, because dump grounds are located on the open shelf and are exposed to ocean waves and storm surges. In protected estuaries and embayments comparable to Long Island Sound, we suggest that dredge materials be dumped at depths greater than 20 m to avoid dispersal by storm-generated currents. Resilience and productivity will have to be maintained by "pulsing" disturbance—that is, repeating physical disturbance at regular intervals (Fig. 7).

The timing of physical disturbance is critical in achieving a predictable compromise system, and the critical pulsing frequency of disturbances is system-specific. For the kind of ecosystem we have been examining, we recommend that dumping be done between January and April, a period of low recruitment and low bottom temperatures. From May through December, a period of intensive recruitment and population growth, dumping should cease so that full colonization potential can be realized. If disturbance in the area of the dump site is repeated every year, populations will be maintained in an exponential phase of growth. If the initial dump is relatively small, disturbance can be repeated beneficially by adding dredge spoil to the same site. If the first dump is large, however, additions to the pile would create a hazard for deep-draft vessels and would subject the top of the pile to natural disturbance from waves. In this case, disturbance can be repeated by moving subsequent dumps laterally, so that the pile grows sideways rather than vertically.

Deep-water locations where dumping can be effectively localized also hold the greatest potential for productivity enhancement (note production ratios in Table 4). The kind of enhanced productivity we are talking about is not directly utilizable by humans but may serve as a food resource for valuable commercial species such as lobsters, flounder, and other bottom-feeding fishes.

Table 4. Colonization data for the tray experiment and the dredge-spoil experiment

	Trays	Dump site
Site data		
ambient disturbance level	high	low
sieve size	300 μ	1000 μ
water depth	14 m	13–20 m*
Individual colonizers		
rate to peak abundance (no./m²/day)	47,000	11
time to peak abundance (days)	10–29	128–344
time to convergence with ambient abundance (days)	175–223	436–646
Species		
peak number	20	17
rate to peak number (no./m²/day)	0.22	0.05
time to peak number (days)	ca. 90	ca. 350
time to convergence with ambient number (days)	ca. 200	>800
Production †		
rate of production to time of peak biomass (gm/m²/day)	0.092	0.038
rate of production on undisturbed bottom over same period (gm/m²/day)	0.049	0.006
production ratio, disturbed/undisturbed bottom	ca. 2	ca. 6

NOTE: Readers interested in the data on which production values are calculated may obtain them by writing to the senior author.
* The top of the dump was at 13 m, the base at 20 m.
† These figures are based on 11 species at the tray site and 14 at the dump site, which account for >95% of the respective biomasses.

Although this article does not address the problem of chemical contamination, we can recommend following the procedure we used in the dredge-spoil experiment—that is, capping the material dredged from polluted inner harbors with cleaner material from outer-harbor regions. While there is still some question as to the effects of the composition of the buried material on colonization rates, this procedure may minimize contamination of

the food chain by biologically active pollutants.

The literature on systems ecology, population biology, and evolution contains a body of theory that can prove valuable in planning the use of our estuaries. We have tried to take a first step toward interpreting that theory in a way that will be useful to the people who have to make the decisions that will effect the future of these waters. But further information—both site-specific and general—is needed before intelligent decisions can be made.

Because the concept of succession has only recently been applied to benthic problems on muddy seafloors, we have a poor understanding of what a mature benthic community is, how it is formed and maintained, and what the threshold conditions are for its destruction. We do not know how long it takes a mature system that is stressed or destroyed to recover its original structure. Nor do we know how much of an estuary can be allocated for enhanced animal production without jeopardizing mature ecosystems in adjacent protective environments. W. E. Odum (1970) and Rosenzweig (1971, 1972) have pointed out that enrichment of exploited ecosystems has potentially destabilizing effects. Resolution of this question will require quantitative modeling of disturbance levels, patch distributions, and biological properties of patches (e.g. Levin and Paine 1974).

Even our hypothesis that enhanced Group 1 and 2 production increases commercial yields remains to be tested. In many cases, preferred prey species for secondary consumers such as crustaceans and bottom-feeding fishes are unknown; and an increased level of production of pioneering species will not necessarily have a beneficial effect on commercial fisheries. Research is required to evaluate availability, palatability, and caloric value of various pioneering species relative to potential prey species in mature systems.

One problem here is that, in a heavily used estuary like Long Island Sound, it is difficult today even to find a community at the mature successional stage described twenty years ago by Sanders (1956). Clearly, much of Long Island Sound is already a compromise system. Management decisions about the use of the coastal zone obviously cannot wait until all relevant research is completed. Such decisions are made every day, often without benefit of any data on site-specific problems. An appreciation of the complex workings of succession in benthic communities will at least serve to place the effects of human disturbance in perspective.

References

Boesch, D. F. 1974. Diversity, stability, and response to human disturbance in estuarine ecosystems. In *Proc. First Int. Cong. of Ecol.*, pp. 109–14. Wageningen, The Netherlands: Pudoc.

Boesch, D. F., R. J. Diaz, and R. W. Virnstein. 1976. Effects of tropical storm Agnes on soft-bottom macrobenthic communities of the Jones and York estuaries and the lower Chesapeake Bay. *Chesapeake Sci.* 17: 240–59.

Boesch, D. F., R. J. Diaz, and R. W. Virnstein. 1976. The dynamics of estuarine benthic communities. In *Estuarine Processes*, ed. M. Wiley, pp. 176–96. Academic Press.

Boyd, M. B., R. T. Saucier, J. W. Kelley, R. L. Montgomery, R. D. Brown, D. B. Mathis, and C. J. Guice. 1972. Disposal of dredge spoil. U.S. Army Engineer Waterways Experiment Station Tech. Rept. H-72-8.

Bray, J. R., and J. P. Curtis. 1957. An ordination of the upland forest community of southern Wisconsin. *Ecol. Monogr.* 27: 325–49.

Copeland, B. J. 1970. Estuarine classification and responses to disturbances. *Trans. Am. Fish Soc.* 99:826–35.

Dean, D., and H. H. Haskins. 1964. Benthic repopulation of the Raritan River estuaries following pollution abatement. *Limnol. Oceanogr.* 9:551–63.

Gordon, R. B., and C. C. Pilbeam. 1975. Circulation in central Long Island Sound. *J. Geophys. Res.* 80:414–22.

Harrison, W., and M. L. Wass. 1965. Frequencies of infaunal invertebrates related to water content of Chesapeake Bay sediments. *S. East. Geol.* 6:177.

Holling, C. S. 1973. Resilience and stability of ecological systems. In *Annual Review of Ecology and Systematics*, vol. 4, ed. R. F. Johnston et al., pp. 1–23. Annual Reviews, Inc.

Hutchinson, G. E. 1953. The concept of pattern in ecology. *Proc. Acad. Nat. Sci., Phil.* 105: 1–12.

Hylleberg, J. 1975. Selective feeding by *Abarenicola pacifica* with notes on *Abarenicola vagabunda* and a concept of gardening in Lugworms. *Ophelia* 14:113–37.

Kaplan, E., J. R. Welker, M. G. Draus, and S. McCourd. 1975. Some factors affecting the colonization of a dredged channel. *Mar. Biol.* 32:193–204.

Lee, G. F. (1976. Dredged material research problems and progress. *Env. Sci. Tech.* 10: 334–38.

Leppäkoski, E. 1971. Benthic recolonization of the Börnholm Basin (southern Baltic) in 1969–71. *Thalassia Jugoslavica* 7:171–79.

Levin, S. A., and R. T. Paine. 1974. Disturbance, patch formation, and community structure. *Proc. Nat. Acad. Sci.* 71:2744–47.

Levinton, J. S. 1972. Stability and trophic structure in deposit-feeding and suspension-feeding communities. *Am. Naturalist* 106:472–86.

———. 1974. Trophic group and evolution in bivalved molluscs. *Palaeontology* 17:579–85.

McCall, P. L. Disturbance and adaptive strategies of Long Island Sound infauna. 1975 diss., Yale University.

———. 1977. Community patterns and adaptive strategies of the infaunal benthos of Long Island Sound. *J. Mar. Res.* 35:221–66.

———. In press. Spatial-temporal distribution of Long Island Sound infauna: The role of bottom disturbance in a near-shore habitat. In *Estuarine Interactions*, ed. M. L. Wiley, pp. 191–219. Academic Press.

Margalef, R. 1958. Mode of evolution of species in relation to their places in ecological succession. *XV International Congress on Zoology*, section 10, paper 17, pp. 787–89.

———. 1963. On certain unifying principles in ecology. *Am. Naturalist* 97:357–74.

Odum, E. P. 1969. The strategy of ecosystem development. *Science* 16:262–70.

Odum, W. E. 1970. Insidious alteration of the estuarine environment. *Trans. Am. Fish. Soc.* 99:836–47.

Oliver, J. S., and P. N. Slattery. 1976. Effects of dredging and disposal on some benthos at Monterey Bay, California. U.S. Army Corps of Eng. Tech. paper 76-15.

Pearson, T. H., and R. Rosenberg. 1976. A comparative study of the effects on the marine environment of wastes from cellulose industries in Scotland and Sweden. *Ambio* 5:77–79.

Rhoads, D. C., R. C. Aller, and M. B. Goldhaber. 1977. The influence of colonizing benthos on physical properties and chemical diagenesis of the estuarine seafloor. In

Ecology of Marine Benthos, ed. B. C. Coull, pp. 113–38. University of South Carolina Press.

Rhoads, D. C., and S. Cande. 1971. Sediment profile camera for *in situ* study of organism-sediment relations. *Limnol. and Oceanogr.* 16:110–14.

Rosenberg, R. 1976. Benthic faunal dynamics during succession following pollution abatement in a Swedish estuary. *Oikos* 27: 414–27.

Rosenzweig, M. C. (1971. Paradox of enrichment: Destabilization of exploitation ecosystems in ecological time. *Science* 171: 385–87.

———. 1972. Stability of enriched aquatic ecosystems. *Science* 175:564–65.

Ryther, J. H. 1969. The potential of the estuary for shellfish production. *Proc. Nat. Shellfish Assoc.* 59:18–22.

Saila, S. B., S. D. Pratt, and T. T. Polgar. 1972. Dredge-spoil disposal in Long Island Sound. U. of R. I. Marine Tech. Rept. no. 2.

Sanders, H. L. 1956. Oceanography of Long Island Sound, 1952–54, 10: The biology of marine bottom communities. *Bull. Bingham Oceanogr. Coll.* 15:345–414.

———. 1977. Potential effects of dumping dredge spoil into the deep sea, recommendation 5. Testimony before the Senate Subcommittee on Antitrust and Monopolies. 95th Cong., 1st sess., 11–13 Aug.

Scheibel, W. 1974. Submarine experiments on benthic colonization of sediments in the western Baltic Sea, 2: Meiofauna. *Mar. Biol.* 28:165–68.

Virnstein, R. W. 1977. The importance of predation by crabs and fishes of benthic infauna in Chesapeake Bay. *Ecology* 58: 1199–217.

Wolff, W. J., A. J. J. Sandee, and L. de Wolf. 1977. The development of a benthic ecosystem. *Hydrobiologia* 52(1):107–15.

Yingst, J. Y. 1978. Patterns of micro- and meiofaunal abundances in marine sediments measured with the adenosine triphosphate assay. *Mar. Biol.* 47:41–54.

"Never mind the weather report—
what's the eutrophication report.?"

Grover S. Krantz

Human Activities and Megafaunal Extinctions

Man's modification of the environment may have caused the demise of some large Pleistocene mammals

One of the most vexing and most discussed problems that researchers in both paleontology and archeology are concerned with is that of the extinction of large animals in the Late Pleistocene. For all the efforts to clarify the cause or causes, there remain two sharply opposed schools of thought. Some authorities hold that the hunting activity of prehistoric man directly eliminated many species; others believe their disappearance is primarily a result of abrupt climatic changes. Both views are well represented in the recent volume edited by Martin and Wright on *Pleistocene Extinctions* (1967). The present paper offers a new interpretation of the data, which might have had a place in that book had the study been undertaken a few years earlier.

Man may well have caused many of these extinctions, I believe, but not by the direct means of physical elimination through excessive predation. I shall describe below three possible indirect means: (1) competition for a particular food supply, (2) causing one herbivore to exterminate other herbivores, and (3) agricultural practices altering ecological relationships. The first and third methods have been touched upon by others, while the second, to the best of my knowledge, is set forth here for the first time.

First let us examine the evidence that prehistoric man may have hunted out

After getting his M.A. in anthropology at the University of California, Berkeley, Grover Krantz worked for six years at the Lowie Museum of Anthropology in Berkeley as preparator and technician. He has taught physical anthropology courses, and completed the requirements for the Ph.D., at the University of Minnesota. His teaching and research center on the origin and evolution of man. Address: Anthropology Department, Washington State University, Pullman, Wash. 99163

these animals. The most convincing argument is the coincidence in time of the arrival of man with these extinctions, or, as in Africa and South Asia, the supposed first development of big game hunting. Martin (1967: p. 111) gives the approximate dates for these events in each area as follows:

Africa, South Asia	40,000 to 50,000 years B.P.
Australia	13,000 years B.P.
Northern Eurasia	11,000 to 13,000 B.P.
North America	11,000 B.P.
South America	10,000 B.P.
West Indies	"Mid-Postglacial"
New Zealand	900 B.P.
Madagascar	800 B.P.

Another argument advanced against any nonhuman or natural cause is the lack of replacment of the extinct forms by ecological equivalents. Martin (1958) and Jelinek (1967) see this as indicating human agency, which alone could eliminate a species leaving its ecological niche open. However, Guilday (1967) shows how the same phenomenon can occur under the stress of temporary climate change, as in the altithermal.

The last major argument is not so much support for man's being the exterminating agency as denial of the most obvious alternative explanation—climatic change. The nearly perfect coincidence of so many mammal extinctions in Northern Eurasia, North and South America, and Australia with the final withdrawl of the Wisconsin-Wurm ice sheet has led many authorities to conclude that abrupt changes in climate were the major causal factor (Guilday 1967; Slaughter 1967; Hester 1967; and Kowalski 1967). This conclusion has been challenged by those who point out that no comparable extinctions occurred at the ends of any of the previous glacial

advances (Edwards 1967: p. 144; Jelinek 1967: p. 193; and Martin 1967: p. 81).

Other, less often stressed, arguments include the comparative absence of extinctions among smaller mammals in the Late Pleistocene as well as no notable loss of plant species (Martin 1967: p. 78 and Leopold 1967). Had climatic change been the predominant factor, it is argued, plants and small mammals ought to have suffered to some degree as well.

The above arguments could be extended and documented at length, but the same question always arises: some new factor must have been present at each time and place of massive extinctions—and the only new factor that appears to be consistently present was man. The conclusion seems inevitable that prehistoric man must have hunted and killed these animals on such a scale that they were totally eliminated.

However reasonable this conclusion may appear in the light of one class of evidence, it fails utterly when questioned from another angle: just how was it possible for prehistoric hunters to accomplish this feat? Even Martin acknowledges the problem, stating (1967: p. 115), "We must beg the question of just how and why prehistoric man obliterated his prey," and further, "The thought that prehistoric hunters ten to fifteen thousand years ago exterminated far more large animals than has modern man with modern weapons and advanced technology is certainly provocative and perhaps even deeply disturbing." It is more than disturbing, it is impossible.

In order to clarify this problem somewhat one must consider the presumed causes of extinctions, in particular the predator-prey relationship.

When a hunting species specializes in taking a particular species as its food source, the population of the hunter is directly dependent upon that of its prey. Only a certain number of individuals of a prey species can be "harvested" without altering its population level. This "harvest," in turn, will support only a certain population of the hunting species. If the prey declines in numbers, so will the hunters, who can exist only in proportion to their food supply. Normally a stable balance is maintained easily and automatically. Some arctic species undergo drastic fluctuations in population, with cycles of several years' duration. Here too, the numbers of the hunting species rise and fall correspondingly, always in response to the availability of the prey.

This relationship still holds true even if the hunter is dependent on a particular prey species only during one brief season of the year. However great a variety of food they may consume in all other seasons, the hunter's population will be limited to those who can be fed in the season of scarcest game.

Clearly no extinctions will occur under these circumstances. The scarcer the prey, the scarcer the hunter, and predation pressure eases off automatically.

If the hunter species is less particular and takes its food from a number of game sources in all seasons, then a slightly different relationship follows. Should one of the prey species be hunted until its numbers are significantly reduced, individuals of this species will be less often encountered. If the hunter is to maintain his population independent of this reduction in one kind of prey, he must concentrate correspondingly more on other species. As the hunter takes what are available of his several game species, those fewest in number will be the least often met and least often taken, thus tending automatically to be preserved from extinction.

Vulnerability to predation is thus not an inevitable or even a likely cause of a species' demise. Extinction threatens only if the numbers are so reduced that mating encounters utilize but a small portion of their reproductive potential. It is only with the advent of "civilized man" that this becomes a reasonable possibility.

These predator-prey relationships hold when primitive man is the predator, and in some respects even more surely. Man's hunting practices are entirely learned by each generation from the preceding one. Any break in this cultural continuity would leave man without any instinctive behavior to depend upon. Also, the special activities and knowledge required for hunting each species of game will differ somewhat from those needed for every other. Should one game animal become scarce and thus more rarely encountered, human hunters, in concentrating more on other species (or upon vegetable gathering), will quickly lose the learned skills pertinent to taking the scarce game. Unlike inherent behavior programming, learned skills can disappear in a generation, and even seriously deteriorate in just a few years if not reinforced by practice.

In addition to the above points, nonliterate hunters are also known for deliberate game conservation beyond the automatic system which applies to other carnivores (see Heizer 1955 for numerous examples). All primitive hunters are quite aware of the importance of females and young for future game supplies and will often treat them accordingly—something no natural carnivore will do.

The seeming wastefulness of cliff drives may not be as significant as may appear. In the first place, such drives are not known to have been used earlier than 9,000 years ago (Hester 1967: p. 181), somewhat too late to be involved in most of the major extinctions. Also, such stampedes are not age-selective in their destruction; they take young and old alike, a point which will be seen later to have some significance.

Direct evidence also exists that, in North America at least, early hunting man did not significantly prey upon those animals he supposedly exterminated. Many archeological kill sites which are now well documented include the remains of animals killed by Paleo-Indians in the Late Pleistocene. These data, summarized by Hester (1967: p. 180), show that only two genera were hunted in significant numbers, mammoth and bison, one extinct and the other not. In 25 of the 34 documented sites bison was the exclusive or predominant game found, mammoth ran a poor second as the sole or major game in 7, and at only 2 were various other animals emphasized. The virtual absence of most extinct animals from kill sites has been noted as a serious objection to the idea of man's role in their demise (Jelinek 1967: p. 198; and Guilday 1967: p. 137).

At this point we seem to be faced with two "facts" that are reasonably well proven. First, the advent of big-game–hunting man alone correlates with the times of massive extinctions. Second, hunting man could not and did not exterminate these animals. These two "facts" appear to be contradictory. Other researchers have proceeded on the assumption that if one of these "facts" is true the other must somehow be explained away or ignored.

I shall attempt to show here that there is not necessarily any contradiction between the two "facts." At the root of the matter is the assumption made by most authorities that man could have exterminated a species *only* by directly destroying virtually all of its individuals. There are other methods.

Modern studies of ecology indicate that the major, if not the sole, cause of extinction is the removal of some essential aspect of the environment, and not predation. This sort of thing has been suggested but little explained by some who refer simply to the "indirect" influence of man (Simpson 1965: p. 228) or to the upset of a nicely balanced state of nature (Romer 1933; and Colbert 1942). The problem at hand is thus changed to answering the question: What actions of man could have so altered the "balance of nature" as to deprive numerous species of some ecological necessity?

Direct Competition

One distinct category of extinctions was, in a sense, caused by man: the extermination of certain large carnivorous mammals. Several writers have pointed out how difficult it would have been for early man to seek out and destroy such dangerous animals as extinct lions, cave hyenas, and saber-toothed cats (Eiseley 1943a; and Butzer 1964: p. 400). It is all the more unlikely that man could have directly eliminated any such carnivores in view of the predator-prey relationships noted above, considering the carnivores as prey and man as the predator.

At least two writers saw why these carnivores disappeared, though without suggesting the hand of man in the process. Guilday (1967: p. 122) and Vereshchagin (1967: p. 392) noted that with the loss of their large herbivorous prey the carnivores similarly vanished. Edwards (1967: p. 146) quite simply explains that as man can be a more efficient predator, the others are eliminated by direct competition (see also Martin and Guilday 1967: p. 33–34 on *Smilodon*). This becomes a case of ecological replacement: man need not kill a single animal to eliminate the species; he needs merely to deprive them of their normal food supply by getting it first. This would be especially effective at times of seasonal crisis, like northern winters, when food resources are reduced to a minimum and competition is most intense.

Probably most large carnivore extinctions since the Middle Pleistocene were caused by the direct competition of man's increasing hunting abilities. The early disappearance of saber-tooths from most of the Old World was not from actual extinction of their prey species, some of which still exist, but rather from a scarcity of these individual animals (young, lame, ill, and aged) which they normally preyed upon. These were being increasingly taken by early human hunters. The late occurrence of *Machairodus* in the latest glacial stage in Britain (Flint 1957: p. 456) indicates their survival only in the coldest northern climates, which man could not inhabit up to that time. Hunting man and sabertooths competed so closely that when the former was present these great cats were not. Similarly, *Smilodon* vanished as soon as big game hunting began in the New World, and shortly before its prey species died out.

Indirect Causes

So far I have discussed the role human agency may have played in extinctions by somehow removing the food of a species. The next method to be described is even less direct: man may have caused certain herbivores to exterminate other species with similar ecological requirements. In this section I will concentrate mainly on the well documented extinctions which occurred in North America at the end of the Pleistocene. These include many grazing mammals which did not significantly compete with early man for food resources.

The number of genera (33) named by Martin (1967) as recently becoming extinct in North America by "over-

kill" is perhaps exaggerated. Mason (1962: p. 243) lists only 15 genera with a total of 20 species, and Newell (1963: p. 48) gives 12 genera and a total of only 16 species. Removing carnivores from these lists will reduce Martin's list by 4 genera, Mason's by 2, and Newell's by 1.

The accuracy of these figures is perhaps worthy of a short digression. They are based essentially on a comparison of living fauna with the fossil fauna of the Upper Pleistocene. Earlier extinctions are based on comparisons of one fossil fauna with another fossil fauna. Since living and fossil animals have generally been classified according to different procedures and by different people, there is good reason to question any comparison of one with the other. Kurtén has noted (1968: p. 40) that the tendency now in paleontology is to "recognize broad, inclusive species with a span of morphological variation similar to that found in related species today," but that this has not been the practice in the past. There were probably far fewer extinctions at the end of the Pleistocene than is usually supposed because there were actually not so many species which could become extinct.

It is likely that the American bison was a single species at any one time, and that changes observed are a combination of evolutionary change and movements of subspecies in response to climate shifts (Eiseley 1943b; and Cornwall 1968: p. 184). In my opinion *Canis dirus* is probably not specifically distinct from the living timber wolf except possibly as an ancestral species. The number of species of elephants reported in the literature is probably also too many.

In spite of all such reservations it is still clear that a number of distinct types of large herbivores did become extinct within a short period of time. These include mammoth, mastodon, horse, camel, several ground sloths, at least one pronghorn, and possibly some cattle.

The archeological record in North America of early man's associations with these mammals, as noted above, is most informative. Only the mammoth and, especially, the bison occur in great numbers as the victims of hunting activities of Paleo-Indians. The absence, in most cases, of the remains of horse, camel, mastodon, or pronghorn from kill sites and their

occurrence in natural deposits hardly support the contention that man killed them off. In order for man, or any other predator, to destroy a species he must dispatch the vast majority of the individuals himself, and almost all of these at an early age prior to their reproduction. Clearly this did not happen, as the species in question are well represented by adult animals in deposits unrelated to any human activity.

If one accepts the archeological and paleontological evidence at face value, an interesting conclusion seems to be indicated: that heavy hunting by early man *preserved* at least one type while unhunted species became extinct. This is just the opposite of over kill as it has been presented. It appears that while man preyed heavily on the bison it *increased* in numbers and range. To suggest that hunting by man actually *caused* such an expansion of the bison may seem odd, but this can be demonstrated to be a likely possibility. The demonstration involves principally a comparison of human predation practices with those of other carnivores. Demographic data on age distributions within a prey population often show sharp differences depending on the type of predator that is chiefly concerned.

No satisfactory detailed figures seem to be available for bison, but the fate of other animals in similar circumstances illustrates the point quite well. Large natural carnivores prey mainly on two age categories of their game, with clear seasonal emphases. In the warmer half of the year, beginning with foaling or calving, the young herbivores are the major part of their diet. In the colder months it is mainly the oldest individuals, especially diseased and injured ones, that are taken. At all times it is the prey that is easiest to catch that is eaten.

This kind of seasonal variation in predation habits can be shown on a graph of age distributions of the prey population. A "survivorship curve" would show how many individuals remain at the end of each year from an original 100 percent born in a given spring. Data for a typical large herbivore survivorship curve under natural predation come from a recent study of the wolves and moose of Isle Royale in Lake Superior (Mech 1966). Here, well over half (62%) of each year's crop of young moose is taken by the wolves in that year before winter sets in. After that, the young adults can better defend themselves and rarely fall victim for the next several years. Finally with increasing age the moose are again unable to escape the wolves.

In his work on the wolves of Mt. McKinley, Murie (1944) found the bighorn sheep had a similar survivorship distribution, as based on ages of collected skulls. Murie's figures did not show as large a proportion of first-year kills; but it is clear, as he notes, that skulls of very young sheep would be more apt to disintegrate or be eaten than older skulls. With some correction for this factor, the age distribution of these sheep agrees with that for Mech's moose.

Other data which are less easily graphed all indicate a massive carnivore kill of each year's young, followed by a plateau of little predation, and finally the gradual elimination of the aging animals. In terms of the yearly cycle, it is during the winter that hunting man, if present, is pressing hardest for largely the same victims in lieu of significant vegetable foods. Competition with man in this season alone could be sufficient cause for local disappearance of those carnivores whose prey happened to be the same as man's.

In the absence of the natural carnivores, the herbivorous species would have a survivorship curve which follows mainly from human predation. This becomes a rather different picture, especially after the development of projectile weapons with which a man can dispatch adult animals almost as easily as young ones. Human hunters may also, in many cases, emphasize the young and aged game, but generally not to the same degree as most carnivores. Data on human game kills tend to indicate a more nearly equal take at all ages of the prey species. If such predation is severe enough, the surviving numbers of reproducing adults may be no more than when natural carnivores are involved, but in many instances this is not what happens.

Age distribution of prey populations under human predation is clearly shown in one case. Bourlière (1956: p. 293) records the extensive take of chamois by one hunter in the Alps and Pyrenees. Here there is no killing of the youngest animals, but the rest of the survivorship curve is distinctly different from that resulting from

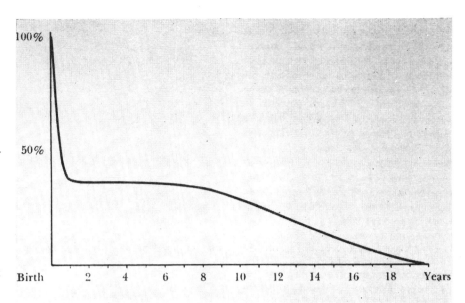

Fig. 1. Typical survivorship curve of large herbivore under natural predation.

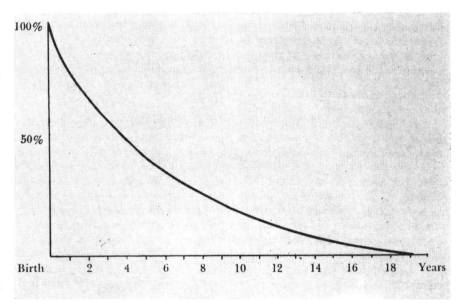

Fig. 2. Typical survivorship curve of large herbivore under human predation.

carnivore kills. There is no leveling off or plateau at the young adult stage.

This chamois curve representing the take of one hunter also shows the age distribution of the population from which they were taken according to availability. The age distribution was caused, in turn, by this and previous hunting which also took animals at all ages with no emphasis on the young and aged and no avoidance of young adults. The curve might be completed by adding an estimate, probably high, of 20 percent more as having died in their first year.

Other recent data on age distributions of human kills include Friley on otter (1949a) and on beaver (1949b). These records are graded not by age in years but rather by degrees of maturity; still they indicate the same curve of survivorship, with no plateau at any stage. More data, especially on kills by primitive hunters, would be useful to illustrate this point.

Some archeological data are also available on the proportions of young individuals recovered from occupation and butchering sites of ancient man. Butzer (1964: p. 382) records 19 percent as being "juveniles" among the reindeer taken at the Lake Mousterian site of Salzgitter-Lebenstedt. Soergel (1922, as cited by Butzer 1964: p. 388) mentions proportions of immature individuals of numerous species of game ranging from 25 to 35 percent in various European Paleolithic sites. In America, Hester (1967: p. 181) notes that Paleo-Indians took game of all ages with no particular emphasis. While some of these figures indicate a rather high mortality of young game animals, they are all still far below the over 50 percent which is indicated for natural carnivores.

A comparison can now be made of the two survivorship curves with natural carnivore predation (based on Mech and Murie) and with human predation (based on Bourlière, Friley, and others). The wide variation possible in each of these curves could, in some instances, negate the observations that follow. In general, however, the difference between human and other carnivore predation practices tends to cause a marked contrast in the age distributions of the prey population.

Most conspicuous is the difference in numbers of surviving young adults. Under human predation these individuals, the major breeding stock, are far more numerous because their numbers were not so drastically depleted when they were still immature. The numbers of surviving older adults might be greater under natural predation, but this would not generally be enough to outweigh the breeding potential of the younger ones. It can thus be seen that when natural predators are replaced by hunting man the most likely expectation is an *increase* in the population of the prey. If all else remains equal, this prey species ought then to exert considerable population pressure against any competing species in the area with similar ecological requirements.

A general picture of a series of biological events can now be suggested:

1. Human hunters enter an area and specialize in taking a particular species of game animal.

2. The local carnivore (or carnivores) specializing in the same prey are starved out during winter competition and become extinct.

3. With man taking proportionally fewer of the young, the prey species expands in numbers and presumably in territory.

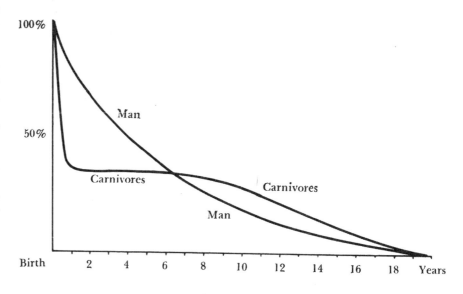

Fig. 3.   Superimposed survivorship curves showing differences between natural and human predation.

4. Other herbivores are exterminated by pressure from the "favored prey" through competition for such things as food under stress conditions.

5. Still other carnivores may next become extinct as their prey disappears, if they cannot depend on the expanding type.

Of course, some rather close predator-prey relationships must already have been in existence for this sequence of events to occur. If the predator which man competes with has another major food supply during seasons of stress, it will not become extinct. If other competing carnivores are taking significant numbers of the young of this game species, its population will not expand. Even with only moderate predator-prey specializations the chain of events outlined should occur to some degree.

In the case of the prominent faunal extinctions in North America, a reconstruction of the particular events, according to this scheme, might have been the following:

1. The first hunting by man with projectile weapons in North America began about 12,000 years ago (Haynes 1967), with emphasis on killing mammoths and especially bison.

2. The saber-toothed cats which depended upon the same two species, especially on the aged animals in winter, were competed out of existence.

3. Bison greatly increased in numbers because their young were no longer being killed by sabertooths. (That this

did not apply to the mammoth will be discussed below.)

4. Bison exterminated many other species which were in close ecological competition. Thus the demise of such other plains herbivores as horse, extinct pronghorn, various cattle, camel, and perhaps also the mammoth.

5. The jaguar, presumably a predator on horse, camel, or cattle (or all of them), then disappeared from the area.

The above is probably a minimal description of events. Other species may have been involved through ecological relationships which are not obvious to this writer.   In environments other than the plains, Paleo-Indians might have had other game specializations with similar effects on still other species. The extinction of the woodland mastodon suggests competition from other animals which have survived, but there are no data on this comparable with that on plains Paleo-Indian activities.

Just why the American mammoth disappeared remains a problem. Ecological pressure from bison seems the most reasonable explanation, while climate change may have been a major factor as well, and human predation no more than a minor factor.

Some light may be thrown on the reason for the American mammoth's extinction by a set of figures given by Soergel in 1922 (quoted by Zeuner 1963: p. 17) on the age distribution of fossil elephants of Pleistocene Europe. From Soergel's data two survivorship curves can be drawn—one from first

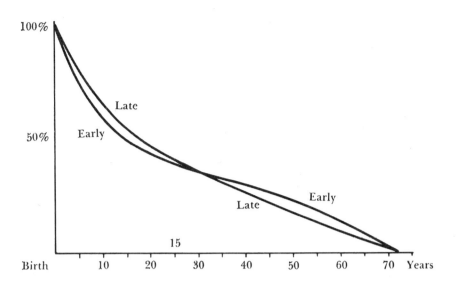

Fig. 4. Survivorship curves of Pleistocene European elephants under human predation (late), and presumed natural predation (early).

interglacial fossils and the other from fossils of third interglacial times. Zeuner assumes man was responsible for most of the kills in each group, but I suggest that sabertooths were the earlier predator. It is an educated guess that only a small difference would exist between the ability of man and of sabertooths to kill elephants; thus one might expect a close similarity in the two survivorship curves. Yet there is a noticeable difference, the earlier predation pattern being more like the natural one, with a greater "take" of young animals and a slight tendency to level off in most of the adult years.

Unlike most herbivores, elephants begin breeding at a relatively late age—about sixteen years. While there is some separation between the two curves, representing more elephants alive in early adulthood under human predation, this is more than canceled by the late onset of reproduction. These rather scanty data suggest that elephants, unlike the bison, would *not* increase in population after human predation replaced that of saber-tooth cats.

In Europe a chain of events similar to that conjectured for North America seems to have occurred, though with less drastic consequences in terms of numbers of kinds of animals exterminated. Throughout the Upper Paleolithic there was an increase in emphasis on reindeer hunting in Western Europe and a decrease in hunting mammoth and woolly rhinoceros. By the

last stage, the Magdalenian, there was an almost total concentration on reindeer as the game animal. One might conclude that man gradually shifted his hunting emphasis solely according to availability of game species. It seems more likely that the increasing abundance of reindeer was largely a result rather than a cause of man's concentration on this species.

In discussing the Meiendorf site of 13,500 B.P., Butzer (1964: p. 410) stated this proposition indirectly: "There is no ready explanation why bison and woolly mammoth should be completely absent in the Hamburg area other than by reason of deliberate specialization on reindeer by prehistoric man." Perhaps this was not intended to mean that man's specialization on one species was the *cause* of the absence of others in the area (not just the site), but that is what I am suggesting.

In some European regions a corresponding emphasis on horse hunting seems to have occurred. If we could identify the natural predators involved we might find a similar situation. The same events may have occurred in Australia, but adequate archeological data are lacking. Gill (1955), in reviewing the situation, was able to conclude only that man could not have been the direct cause of the extinctions. Here, annual variation in rainfall, rather than winter cold, is the probable source of the stress season during which one species eliminates another by taking its food sup-

ply. The aborigine's concentration on kangaroos and wallabies might have relieved other predation pressure and permitted these medium-sized marsupials to exterminate other larger species. More evidence is needed to pursue the Australian situation any further.

Agricultural Man

The third method by which man has been able to exterminate species without direct killing is by agriculturally related practices. Three of Martin's associations between the advent of man and the disappearance of big game animals are the more recent cases of the West Indies, New Zealand, and Madagascar (see also Hooijer 1967; Battistini and Vérin 1967; and Walker 1967). In each case, the human population at the time of extinctions was of the Neolithic type, with the subsistence economy based on agriculture. There is little doubt that these people were responsible for the disappearance of numerous species, but not necessarily in the sense of hunters destroying their prey.

There are several ways in which man, since the Neolithic revolution, has upset natural environments. Farming may remove local vegetation which was a food supply for some animals. Fencing will restrict some animals' movements as well as deny them access to the planted crops. Forest clearing will remove habitats as well as certain food sources, substituting others. Draining swamps and irrigating dry lands likewise alters vegetation and environment. Stock raising introduces major competitors for certain food resources. The physical presence of man with his activities and constructions can interfere with mating, nesting, or maternal behavior, or simply induce animals to leave an area to avoid such disturbances.

The possibility that some of these agricultural activities have caused exterminations has been pointed out by Guilday (1967: pp. 122, 126, 138) for much of the megafauna in North Africa and the Middle East, and by Hester (1967: p. 178) for North America since European colonization.

In addition to his great ability to affect native fauna indirectly, the agriculturalist differs from the hunter in his lack of dependence upon that fauna. The extinction of numerous large native herbivores will have little or no ill effect on the farmer who depends on his crops and/or herds; he may even welcome their disappearance. The hunter, on the other hand, would perish without them.

While many writers have missed the point by emphasizing the Paleo-Indian's dependence on big game hunting to account for his supposed destructiveness, Edwards (1967: pp. 147–48) realized that only by re-acquiring plant-gathering habits would primitive man have been able to afford the luxury of exterminating his game. This, of course, does not explain how such extermination was possible on a hunting and gathering level, but it does illustrate the point that man can destroy only what he does not depend upon, without destroying himself in the process.

The recent destruction of megafauna in New Zealand, Madagascar, and the West Indies followed from the activities of agricultural man rather than of hunters. This points up a meaningful dichotomy of human societies in terms of their effect on the environment. The contrast between "prehistoric" and "modern" man in this connection is not of much value. The "modern" Plains Indians and African Bushmen have had a very different effect on their environments than did the simple grain farmers of the Eastern Mediterranean some eight or ten thousand years ago. Agriculturally based societies differ from one another only in the degree to which they disturb the natural environment, while they all differ in kind from hunting and gathering societies.

There are some additional peculiarities of agricultural societies, in terms of size of population and commerce, which open up the possibility, at least, that they could have exterminated certain species by direct overpredation. Given a farming subsistence base, almost any area will support and feed a population ten to a hundred times larger than it could maintain by hunting and gathering alone. With such numbers available, especially for seasonal hunting, serious decimation of nonessential animal populations is certainly possible.

Even more important, perhaps, are such things as fur trapping, ivory hunting, sport and trophy collecting, and other ventures mainly for the commercial market. Items in this broad category will have an exchange value based, in part, upon their scarcity. Hunters may thus concentrate on certain animals not for their own use but for sale or trade with agriculturally based peoples. In these cases a decline in the supply of a particular animal may raise its price and serve to increase predation pressure. Just as the African elephant now has the added threat of ivory hunters, it may be possible that the last Siberian mammoth was killed for the Chinese ivory market.

Let me add that the above arguments are not proposed as the entire explanation of megafaunal extinctions. Climate change cannot be ignored, because the combination of an unusually abrupt end to the last glaciation with the subsequent altithermal warming may have been unique in the Pleistocene. Human agency, by the means suggested here, is proposed to account for extinctions only where climate change is an inadequate explanation.

Bibliography

BATTISTINI, R., and P. VÉRIN. 1967. Ecological changes in Protohistoric Madagascar, in Martin and Wright, pp. 407–24.

BOURLIÈRE, FRANÇOIS. 1956. *The Natural History of Mammals.* New York: Knopf.

BUTZER, KARL W. 1964. *Environment and Archeology.* Chicago: Aldine.

COLBERT, EDWIN H. 1942. The association of man with extinct mammals in the Western hemisphere, in *Proceedings, Eighth American Scientific Congress,* 2: 27.

CORNWALL, I. W. 1968. *Prehistoric Animals and Their Hunters.* London: Faber & Faber.

EDWARDS, WILLIAM ELLIS. 1967. The Late-Pleistocene extinction and diminution in size of many mammalian species, in Martin and Wright, pp. 141–54.

EISELEY, LOREN C. 1943a. Archaeological observations on the problem of postglacial extinction, in *American Antiquity,* 8: 209–17.

——— 1943b. Did the Folsom bison survive in Canada? in *Scientific Monthly,* 56: 468–72.

FLINT, RICHARD F. 1957. *Glacial and Pleistocene Geology.* New York: Wiley.

FRILEY, C. E., JR. 1949a. Age determination, by use of the baculum in the river otter, *Lutra c. canadensis,* in *Journal of Mammology,* 30: 102–10.

——— 1949b. Use of the baculum in age determination of Michigan beaver, in *Journal of Mammalogy,* 30: 261–67.

GILL, EDMUND D. 1955. The problem of extinctions, with special reference to Australia's marsupials, in *Evolution,* 9: 87–92.

GUILDAY, JOHN E. 1967. Differential extinction during Late-Pleistocene and Recent times, in Martin and Wright, pp. 121–40.

HAYNES, C. VANCE, JR. 1967. Carbon-14 dates and early man in the New World, in Martin and Wright, pp. 267–86.

HEIZER, ROBERT F. 1955. Primitive man as an ecologic factor, in *Kroeber Anthropological Society Papers,* 13: 1–31.

HESTER, JAMES A. 1967. The agency of man in animal extinctions, in Martin and Wright, pp. 169–92.

HOOIJER, D. A. 1967. Pleistocene vertebrates of the Netherlands Antilles, in Martin and Wright, pp. 399–406.

JELINEK, ARTHUR J. 1967. Man's role in the extinction of Pleistocene faunas, in Martin and Wright, pp. 193–200.

KOWALSKI, KAZIMIERZ. 1967. The Pleistocene extinction of mammals in Europe, in Martin and Wright, pp. 349–64.

KURTÉN, BJORN. 1968. *Pleistocene Mammals of Europe.* Chicago: Aldine.

LEOPOLD, ESTELLA B. 1967. Late-Cenozoic patterns of plant extinction, in Martin and Wright, pp. 203–46.

MARTIN, PAUL S. 1958. Pleistocene ecology and biogeography of North America, in *Zoogeography,* C. L. Hubbs, ed., American Association for the Advancement of Science, Publication 51, pp. 375–420.

——— 1967. Prehistoric overkill, in Martin and Wright, pp. 75–120.

MARTIN, PAUL S., and JOHN E. GUILDAY. 1967. A Bestiary for Pleistocene biologists, in Martin and Wright, pp. 1–62.

MARTIN, PAUL S., and HERBERT E. WRIGHT, JR., eds. 1967. *Pleistocene Extinctions,* vol. 6, Proceedings of the Eighth Congress of the International Association for Quaternary Research. New Haven: Yale University Press.

MASON, R. J. 1962. The Paleo-Indian tradition in Eastern North America, in *Current Anthropology,* 3: 227–78.

MECH, L. DAVID. 1966. *The Wolves of Isle Royale,* Fauna of the National Parks of the United States, Fauna Series 7. U.S. Government Printing Office.

MURIE, A. 1944. *The Wolves of Mount McKinley,* Fauna of the National Parks of the U.S., Fauna Series 5. U.S. Govt. Printing Office.

NEWELL, NORMAN D. 1963. Crises in the history of life, in *Human Variations and Origins,* W. S. Laughlin and R. H. Osborne, eds. San Francisco: Freeman. (*Scientific American,* Feb. 1963.)

ROMER, ALFRED S. 1933. Pleistocene vertebrates and their bearing on the problem of human antiquity in North America, in *The American Aborigines,* ed. by D. Jenness, pp. 76–77.

SIMPSON, GEORGE G. 1965. *The Geography of Evolution.* Philadelphia: Chilton Books.

SLAUGHTER, BOB H. 1967. Animal ranges as a clue to Late-Pleistocene extinction, in Martin and Wright, pp. 155–68.

VERESHCHAGIN, N. K. 1967. Primitive hunters and Pleistocene extinction in the Soviet Union, in Martin and Wright, pp. 365–98.

WALKER, ALAN. 1967. Patterns of extinction among the subfossil Madagascan Lemuroids, in Martin and Wright, pp. 425–32.

ZEUNER, F. E. 1963. *A History of Domesticated Animals.* London: Hutchinson.

James E. Mosimann
Paul S. Martin

Simulating Overkill by Paleoindians

Did man hunt the giant mammals of the New World to extinction? Mathematical models show that the hypothesis is feasible

Sometime toward the end of the Rancholabrean faunal age, around 11,000 years ago, a remarkable number of large mammals vanished from North America. North of Mexico, the losses included 3 genera of elephants, 6 of giant edentates, 15 of ungulates, and various giant rodents and carnivores (Martin 1967). Two-thirds of the Rancholabrean megafauna disappeared, leaving bison, musk-ox, wapiti, moose, mountain goat, mountain sheep, deer, and pronghorn to represent the "native" fauna of the continent. Discounting climatic change or other natural catastrophes as typical of the ice ages and thus not unique to the time of late-glacial extinction, we seek other causes for the phenomenon.

In his review of the radiocarbon chronology of extinction, Martin (1967, 1973) emphasized that there is no clear-cut case of loss of any

James E. Mosimann heads the Laboratory of Statistical and Mathematical Methodology in the Computer Division at the National Institutes of Health, where he has been since 1963. Paul S. Martin is Professor of Geosciences at the University of Arizona, where he has been since 1957. Mosimann and Martin were both students at the Museum of Zoology, University of Michigan, receiving their Ph.D. degrees, respectively, in 1956 and 1955. Martin has spent postdoctoral years at Yale and the Université de Montréal. His studies on extinction have taken him to South America, Africa, Madagascar, and New Zealand. Mosimann has taught biostatistics at the Université de Montréal, the University of Arizona, and the American University. He has been a postdoctoral fellow in biostatistics at the Johns Hopkins University and is a fellow of the American Statistical Association. Requests for reprints should be addressed to Paul S. Martin, Department of Geosciences, University of Arizona, Tucson, AZ 85721.

Rancholabrean animals prior to 12,000 years ago. Furthermore, no alleged postglacial survival of an extinct genus has been documented adequately. No extinct genera of the megafauna have been found in cultural deposits of the last 10,000 years. A careful effort at determining the time of extinction of the Shasta ground sloth (*Nothrotheriops*) by radiocarbon dating of its extraordinary dung piles indicated survival until 11,000 years ago, but not later (Long, Hansen, and Martin 1974).

The only event unique to the period around 11,000 years ago, when extinction actually occurred, was the arrival in the hemisphere of prehistoric big game hunters. For this reason, Martin has attributed the extinction to excessive human predation, termed *overkill.*

The concept of overkill is not new. For decades it was considered and commonly rejected, especially by those archaeologists and paleontologists best acquainted with the field evidence (for example Colbert 1937; Eiseley 1943; Simpson 1961). While willing to grant human predation a minor role in the extermination, the experts concluded that the human population was never sufficiently numerous in any area to have much impact. To the best of our knowledge, no one has sought to determine how many hunters would be sufficient, and how visible such a population might be in the fossil record.

There is an additional problem. In Eurasia, where abundant archaeological evidence links Paleolithic hunters with large mammals over hundreds of thousands of

years, only a few genera actually became extinct (Reed 1970). Paradoxically, in America, where many genera of large mammals vanished, archaeological associations are rare and kill sites are known only in the case of mammoth (Wendorf and Hester 1962; Hester 1967; Krantz 1970). The 5 mammoth sites that have been dated by the radiocarbon method are remarkably similar in age (range 11,160 to 11,310, average 11,250 years ago; see Haynes 1970). Many more kill sites are known for *Bison,* a genus that survived, than for mammoth and all other extinct genera combined. In the words of Krantz (1970, p. 166), "The absence, in most cases, of the remains of horse, camel, mastodon, or pronghorn from kill sites and their occurrence in natural deposits hardly support the contention that man killed them off." We believe we can resolve the paradox.

Following the scenario for the discovery of America offered by Martin (1973), we assume that the first people to enter the New World came from Asia by land, not by boat, on the only available corridor, the Bering bridge. We visualize a rapid crossing from Siberia in the late-glacial period, around 12,000 years ago. The Paleolithic invaders tracked herds of prey eastward through unglaciated parts of Alaska to an ice-free corridor that led east of the Canadian Rockies and south to the heart of the continent. These people came from a long lineage of skillful hunters with hundreds of thousands of years of Paleolithic experience behind them. They were expert at tracking, killing, butchering, and preserving meat from large mammals. It appears that they ate little else.

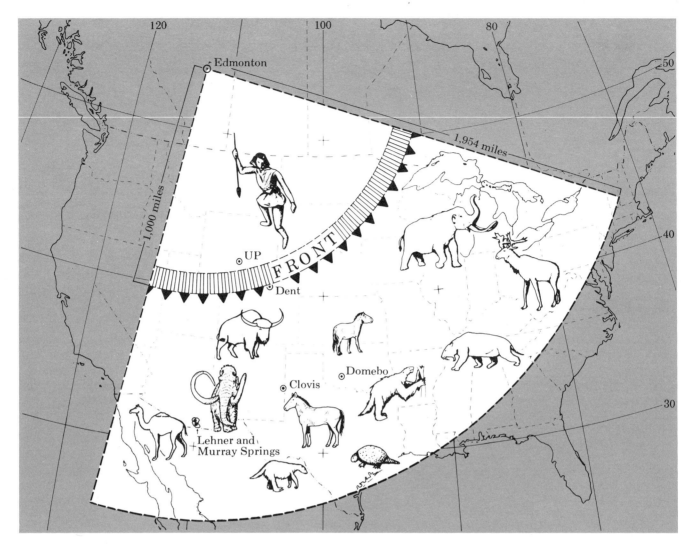

Figure 1. An essential feature of the overkill scenario is the concept of the "front." Upon reaching a certain critical density, the population of hunters, newly arrived in the New World, expands southward in a quarter circle whose center is represented by Edmonton, Alberta. As long as some prey remains in the area of human occupation, the front advances smoothly. When the local herds are exhausted, it advances in a jump. The range available to the hunted is steadily reduced. The width of the front prevents survivors from "leaking" back into unoccupied areas behind the front. In the position shown, 1,000 miles from Edmonton, the front has begun to sweep through the region of radiocarbon-dated Paleoindian mammoth kill sites. Depending on the simulation strategy, these sites will be overrun in 40–170 years. By the time the front has reached the gulfs of Mexico and of California (radius of circle = 1,954 mi) the herds of North America have been hunted to extinction.

The American megafauna had not experienced human predation before. For a brief period, at least until they learned fear, the large animals were easy prey. But could the hunters actually trigger massive extinctions? And how could they do this without leaving a good deal of fossil evidence of their bloody passage—evidence that would be highly visible in the fossil record of the New World?

The overkill scenario

In modeling extinction, we consider the size of the megafauna prior to human invasion, the maximum rate of biomass replacement when large animals experience heavy predation, and the rate of population growth of the invaders. The small band of invaders must grow rapidly into a population large enough to destroy millions of large animals and, in the process, many species, in the least amount of time. It is not necessary that the hunters actually eat all or even any of their prey.

These conditions can be accommodated by computer simulation. To specify a simulation, we provide estimates of the following parameters: initial prey biomass, N; prey carrying capacity, K; prey replacement or growth rate, A; initial human density, M; ceiling human density, L; maximum human growth rate, C; and prey destruction rate, G. Using this input, our computer programs display the year-by-year growth of the hunters, their rate of advance, their density on a front, and the front's width and position. These parameters determine the time until extinction of the megafauna and the total number of animal units consumed.

We begin our simulations with the arrival from Alaska of 100 hunters of both sexes. We locate them at Edmonton, Alberta, around 11,500 years ago. The human population grew at a logistic rate to a maximum locally. Overall, it increased at an exponential rate, with the surplus distributed into new lands available to the south.

Climates beyond the melting ice sheet were slightly cooler than at present. Range carrying capacity in the first 3 million square miles available to the hunters may have been somewhat greater than later in the postglacial period or at present. While we acknowledge their importance in an ideal model, we do not attempt to treat the age structure of the prey, to consider the possible effect of prey preferences, or to incorporate the inevitable local differences in carrying capacity at the time of invasion. Presumably midcontinent savannas supported much larger herds of game than did the tundra, desert, or closed-canopy forest.

We are unaware of any firm evidence to show that the New World herds of mastodon, mammoth, camels, horses, ground sloths, and brush oxen were genetically senescent, disease-ridden, or failing reproductively at the time. We assume that megafaunal biomass was high when the hunters arrived. With a few possible exceptions, all members of the Rancholabrean megafauna, some 49 genera in North America alone, representing over 100 species of large mammals, were available to the hunters as prey.

Assuming that the invasion of a new and favorable habitat would provide a major stimulus to population growth among the hunters, and based on historic analogy (Birdsell 1957), we consider a growth rate of 3.5 percent annually, or a doubling every 20 years, to be entirely feasible. The mean rates that we actually obtain are less—2.4 percent, or a doubling in 30 years. We also simulate with lower human growth rates.

Following Martin (1973), we incorporate a geographic dimension, the sweep of a "front" (Fig. 1), based on analogy with other successful invasions. For example, Caughley (1969) finds that populations of alien mammals in New Zealand increase at the highest rate along their perimeter. As resources are depleted, a steady state population of much lower density persists

while the more rapidly growing peripheral population moves on. Zaret and Paine (1973) describe the devastating effect of an Amazonian cichlid fish recently introduced in Gatun Lake. They report that the alien fish have not diffused haphazardly but have moved as a wave, with a leading edge composed of subadults. In our case, we consider only the dynamics of the expanding population, ignoring the fate of any persistent human populations surviving behind it.

In our simulations, we restrict the hypothetical prey of the hunters to those species of large mammals which became extinct. We ignore natural herbivore losses to native predators, parasites, or disease. We assume that prey biomass was high, either 75 million animal units, by analogy with African game parks, or 150 million animal units, the modern livestock plus wild game biomass of the region (see Martin 1973). An animal unit is defined as 1,000 pounds, or 450 kilograms, of biomass of large mammals.

Any realistic scenario must accommodate the fossil record. We are impressed with the following: (1) the scarcity of Paleoindian kill sites clearly associating extinct genera of the New World megafauna with their supposed destroyers; (2) concordance in age of the known kill sites, which are of mammoth only; (3) simultaneous or near-simultaneous disappearance of all extinct species around 11,000 years ago, with undeniable survival into the last 10,000 years of certain species of bison only; and (4) lack of substantial evidence for any population of big game hunters in North America prior to 12,000 years ago. To be realistic, our simulations must display the rapid removal of a great number of large mammals in a very short time by a human population barely visible to archaeologists.

The simulation model

Our simulation program, coded in double precision BASIC for the IBM 370, uses discrete time models. It was developed from Budyko's model (1967, 1974) of mammoth overkill in the Old World. For convenience in modeling, the area occupied by large mammals is treated

as a quarter circle whose apex lies at Edmonton and whose radii (1,954.4 mi) run southwest and southeast to an arc intersecting the Gulf of Mexico and the northern part of the Mexican Plateau (see Fig. 1). The area, 3 million square miles, is equivalent to the United States minus Alaska. In these 3 million square miles are large herbivores, the prey, at an average biomass of K animal units per square mile. This initial value is also the carrying capacity, and prey biomass is not allowed to exceed K. Up to this ceiling, the prey biomass reproduces (replaces) itself at rate A. Thus, for example, if N_t is the biomass surviving predation, then $N_{t+1} = \min(K, (1 + A) N_t)$.

A founding population of 100 people arrives at Edmonton, Alberta. They distribute themselves in the quarter circle within 100 miles of Edmonton, resulting in an initial human density of $M(0) = .0127$ persons per square mile. The human population now increases, consuming large herbivores, and it expands southward until the quarter circle of 3 million square miles is filled. We allow the southward movement of the people to occur either by a smooth advance or a jump advance. When some prey remains in the area of human occupation, a smooth advance occurs. When no prey remains, a jump advance occurs.

As long as some prey remains, the human population increases geometrically at rate $C > 0$. Multiplication of $(1 + C)$ times the number of people at time t gives the number of people at time $t + 1$. When no prey remains, a jump advance occurs and there is no change in the number of people from t to $t + 1$.

Let M be the density (persons per square mile) of people in the occupied area at time t. Let N be the prey biomass (animal units per square mile) in the same area at time t. Let G be the destruction rate (average number of animal units destroyed per person per year). A simulation proceeds as follows. First $N - GM$ is calculated. This gives the prey biomass remaining after predation by man. If $N - GM > 0$, then the human population expands southward in a smooth advance. If $N - GM \leq 0$, then prey in the occupied area is exhausted and a jump advance occurs. Thus, the following sequence is repeated: (1) calculation of the human density M and the prey biomass N in the area occupied by humans at time t; (2) determination of the prey biomass, $N - GM$, after destruction; and (3) calculation of a smooth or jump advance.

At time t there is a density of M people over Y square miles occupied, giving MY people. With an ample supply of food, people multiply geometrically, and at $t + 1$ there are $(1 + C) MY$ people occupying $Y + \Delta Y$ square miles. The new area occupied, ΔY, is determined as follows. Within any given area the human density is allowed only a logistic increase up to a ceiling density (L). Let $Z = (1 + C) MY$. The logistic increase from t to $t + 1$, readily obtained from Pielou's results (1969, p. 22), is pZ, where $p = L/(L + CM)$. Thus pZ people are allowed to stay, and $(1 - p)Z$ people must migrate south. The distance they migrate is determined so that the density of those staying equals the density of those migrating, $(pZ)/Y = (1 - p)Z/\Delta Y$, which implies that $\Delta Y = (CMY)/L$. The distance the front must move to give this value of ΔY is

$$R = -D + (D^2 + 4\Delta Y/\Pi)^{1/2} \quad (1)$$

Here D is the distance from Edmonton at time t, and $R + D$ is the distance at $t + 1$. The human density in the overall area of $Y + \Delta Y$ square miles is a "logistic" density, but the overall increase is geometric.

No smooth advance of over 20 miles is allowed. Should R be greater than 20, then R is set equal to 20 and ΔY is calculated from

$$\Delta Y = (\Pi/4) R(2D + R) \quad (2)$$

Finally, at some time there is no further area to occupy, $(D + R \geq 1,954.4)$. Then $R = 1,954.4 - D$ and ΔY is determined from Eq. 2. Once the entire 3 million square miles is occupied, the subsequent human growth is logistic. Extinction may or may not occur.

The prey biomass available to humans is readily determined. After

prey reproduction at rate A, there is a biomass of $(1 + A)(N - GM) > 0$ in the original area of Y square miles. There is a biomass of K in the newly occupied area of ΔY square miles. Multiplication of each biomass times its associated area gives the total animal units available. Division of this total by $Y + \Delta Y$ gives the new biomass N, at $t + 1$.

The jump advance occurs when the supply of prey is exhausted in an area, which is then evacuated by people because they can no longer obtain their preferred food. In our models, this evacuated area is never reoccupied by the prey. Thus, not only do people kill the large mammals, but they also reduce the environment for them. During the year in which a jump occurs, the human population is presumed to be under stress and does not increase.

The initial jump is determined in a special manner. At time t the occupied quarter circle is Y square miles in area and its perimeter is D miles from Edmonton. This distance is increased by $R = 20$ miles. The newly occupied area is calculated using Eq. 2, and contains ΔY square miles, with $K\Delta Y$ animal units. If the newly encountered animal units exceed the deficit, $(N - GM)Y$, the advance stops. If not, R is increased in steps of 10 until either sufficient prey is encountered or the 3 million square miles are covered.

Suppose sufficient prey is found in a new area of ΔY. Then a quarter circle, apex at Edmonton, of ΔY square miles is evacuated of people and is devoid of prey. The radius of this circle is $D_1 = (4\Delta Y/\Pi)^{1/2}$. After evacuation of this northern quarter circle, the people are now found in a band or "front" of width $W = D + R - D_1$. The area of this band at $t + 1$ is the same as that of the previously occupied quarter circle (radius D) at t. The human density in this band at time $t + 1$ is the same as the density in the previously occupied quarter circle. The prey biomass at $t + 1$ is $(1 + A)$ times the biomass surviving predation.

After the initial jump, there is a populated quarter-circular ring or

front of width W. As long as there is sufficient prey within this area, then smooth advances occur and the width of the front W is increased. But suppose that at time t the outer perimeter of the ring is at distance D from Edmonton and the ring has width W and occupies area Y. If prey is again depleted, another jump occurs. In this jump the entire ring is moved southward $R = 20$ miles, keeping the ring-width, W, fixed. The new area swept by this front in passing is $Y_4 = (\Pi/4) R(2D + R)$. The increase in area occupied by the front itself (still W miles wide) after sweeping this new area is $\Delta Y = (\Pi/2) WR$. The prey deficit in animal units is $(N - GM) Y$, and the number of newly encountered animal units is $K Y_4$.

If sufficient prey has been encountered, the advance stops. If prey is insufficient, then, as with the initial jump, R is increased in steps of 10 miles until sufficient prey is found or until there is no further room for expansion. The biomass in the front at $t + 1$ is $[(1 + A)((N - GM)Y + K Y_4)]/(Y + \Delta Y)$ and the human density at $t + 1$ is $MY/(Y + \Delta Y)$. As long as the advance R is smaller than W, the front width, it is possible to think of a cleanly swept herbivore population, with little or no "leakage" of herbivores into unoccupied areas behind the front.

One mathematical result can be demonstrated for our simulation model. For example, extinction of prey will occur if and only if

$$L \geq AK/G^*$$

where $G^* = (1 + A)G$. Only if the human population attains the "critical density" AK/G^* will the prey be eliminated.

In one of our simulations we use a destruction rate which is a function of prey biomass. Following Murdoch (1971), we consider a destruction rate $G(N) = G_1(1 - e^{-DN})$, where $G_1, D > 0$. The term *monomolecular* is applied to this function by Medawar (1945), who uses it as a growth function. (It is the one-hit curve of bioassay; Cornfield 1954.) Here the destruction rate decreases as prey density decreases. In another simulation, we change the "within-year" occurrence of predation, letting all prey repro-

Table 1. Simulation with conditions of moderate biomass, heavy kill, and fast growth (see Table 8 for summary of conditions and results for prey and hunters)*

Features of the front

Years after arrival	Distance from Edmonton	Width	Human population	Human density
20	100.2	100.2	199	0.025
60	101.1	101.1	788	0.098
100	104.7	104.7	3,119	0.362
140	329.8	61.3	8,459	0.294
180	614.0	65.6	20,690	0.346
220	1,018.1	69.6	41,168	0.383
260	1,502.0	73.5	71,385	0.422
293	1,954.4	76.2	100,696	0.439

* More detailed versions of all tables are available from the authors on request.

duce before predation. There we use the replacement equation $(1 + A) N - GM$, rather than $(1 + A)(N - GM)$.

Simulation results

Using the present tense, we describe various strategies that lead to extinction and one that does not. The first strategy involves a moderate biomass, a heavy kill, and fast growth (Table 1). In our first simulation we consider the fate of a Pleistocene megafauna of 75 million animal units spread over 3 million square miles, or an average of 25 animal units per section. This is equivalent to the biomass found in many African game parks. Twenty-five animal units of Pleistocene megafauna could be made up of species ranging in size from extinct antelope to imperial mammoth and would only coincidentally total 25 individual large animals per section. We allow the herd to replace lost biomass at a geometric rate of 25 percent annually.

We introduce 100 Paleoindians at Edmonton. The hunters take an average of 13 animal units per person per year. One person in a family of four does most of the killing, at an average rate of one animal unit per week, which is more meat than can be eaten; at least 50 percent of the meat is wasted.

The hunting is easy; the tribe doubles every 20 years until local herds are depleted and fresh territory must be found. In 120 years the Edmonton population grows to 5,409. It is concentrated on a front 59 miles deep at a density of 0.37 persons per square mile. Behind the front, the megafauna is exterminated. By 220 years, the front reaches northern Colorado in the position shown in Figure 1. Its density is virtually unchanged; the total human population is just over 41,000. In the final 73 years, the front advances the remaining 1,000 miles, attains a depth of 76 miles, and reaches a maximum of just over 100,000 people. Assuming an average life expectancy of 25 years, the total number of persons in the sweep from Edmonton to the gulfs is less than 300,000. Average population growth is 2.4 percent annually. The front does not advance more than 20 miles in one year. In 293 years the hunters destroy a megafauna of 93 million animal units.

The hunters move south through the region of radiocarbon-dated kill sites (UP in southern Wyoming to Lehner in southern Arizona; see Fig. 1) in 60 years. It would be very difficult to detect so slight an age difference by radiocarbon dating. The amount of cultural debris left by the brief but explosive passage of the hunters would be limited. Unless conditions for burial of camp or kill sites were extremely favorable, it is not likely that much evidence of the human invasion can be hoped for. With the possible difficulty of a narrow front, perhaps one that permitted some leakage of prey from south to north, this simulation appears to satisfy the major conditions for a sudden overkill. We regard it as a basic scenario.

In the second simulation, characterized by high biomass, moderate kill, and fast growth (Table 2), we assign the animals an initial density of 50 animal units per square mile, or a total biomass of 15×10^{10} pounds in the area of the United States. This biomass, about twice the size of that used in the first simulation, is about equal to the present U.S. biomass of all livestock and wild game equal to or larger than a Virginia deer (*Odocoileus virginianus*).

We increase the geometric rate of biomass recovery, making it equivalent to that of Virginia deer under heavy hunting pressures, i.e. 40

Table 2. Simulation with conditions of high biomass, moderate kill, fast growth

Features of the front

Years after arrival	Distance from Edmonton	Width	Human population	Human density
20	100.2	100.2	199	0.025
60	101.1	101.1	788	0.098
100	104.7	104.7	3,119	0.362
140	117.9	117.9	12,349	1.131
180	196.5	94.9	45,644	2.054
220	613.3	111.7	90,822	0.929
260	1,012.1	130.5	187,041	0.963
300	1,527.9	146.3	313,359	0.938
329	1,954.4	155.4	412,634	0.901

percent annually, and we reduce the kill rate from 13 to 7 animal units per person per year. If the edible half of all carcasses were consumed, the kill rate would provide an average daily ration of 10 pounds of meat per person. While such a value may seem excessive, it is close to the frontier meat ration of 150 years ago in regions where meat alone constituted the daily diet (Wheat 1972, pp. 108–09).

In 120 years the Edmonton population grows from 100 to about 6,200, at a rate of 3.5 percent annually, a density of 0.7 persons per square mile. The megafauna sustains its losses without extinction. By year 180 the human population of 46,000 attains a density of 2.1 persons per square mile on a front 95 miles in width. Extinction begins. By the 260th year, a population just under 190,000 is located along a front at the latitude of Denver (as shown in Fig. 1). In the final 69 years the front advances the remaining 1,000 miles, attains a depth of 155 miles, and supports a population of 410,000 at a density of 0.9 persons per square mile.

The total number of persons in the sweep from Edmonton to the Gulf of Mexico is 1,190,000, at an average population growth of 2.6 percent annually. In 329 years the hunters destroy a megafauna of 209 million animal units. Extinction occurs in 149 years. The mammoth sites dated by radiocarbon are overrun within 60 years of each other.

This simulation takes 36 years longer to complete than the first; more than twice as many animal units are killed by more than four times as many people. More artifacts should have been discarded, but archaeological visibility would still be poor.

Deevey (1960) and Haynes (1966) considered much lower rates of increase for Paleolithic people. Haynes's low rate gives an increase of 1.2 times in 28 years, or an annual rate of 0.653 percent. Incorporating this slow growth factor with high biomass and heavy kill, and beginning with the same founding population of 100, we allow it to consume 13 animal units per year from a megafauna of the same size as used in the first simulation.

Table 3. Simulation with conditions of high biomass, heavy kill, slow growth

		Features of the front		
Years after arrival	Distance from Edmonton	Width	Human population	Human density
20	100.0	100.0	114	0.014
100	100.1	100.1	192	0.024
300	101.0	101.0	705	0.088
500	103.9	103.9	2,594	0.306
700	233.1	63.1	9,176	0.459
900	779.0	69.0	28,307	0.351
1,100	1,645.8	75.8	78,685	0.411
1,157	1,954.4	77.9	102,764	0.438

In 500 years the Edmonton population grows to 2,600 people, with a density of 0.3 per square mile (Table 3). The megafauna replaces its losses. Local extinction and the development of a front 62 miles in width occur in year 680, when the human population reaches its maximum density of 0.84 per square mile. The front now begins to sweep southward with increasing speed, covering the last 1,200 miles in 257 years. The total number of persons in the sweep from Edmonton to the gulfs is 800,000. In 1,157 years, 260 million animal units are destroyed; extinction occurs in 477 years.

One difficulty with this model is the long time—700 years—required to build the front in the vicinity of Edmonton. The local fauna has an opportunity to adapt to the new predator and to learn resistant behavior that should make hunting increasingly difficult. But the sweep across the lower half of the continent is rapid. The mammoth kill sites in southern Wyoming and southern Arizona are overrun within 170 years of each other.

Another simulation is based on moderate biomass but preferred prey. Here we assume that American elephants, both mammoths and mastodons, are preferred over all other big game. One hundred hunters arrive at Edmonton and increase at Haynes's (1966) "fast rate" of 1.2 percent annually. Each consumes 7 animal units (about 1.5 elephants) annually from a population averaging one elephant per square mile, or 15 million animal

units overall. African elephant biomass replacement is known to be slow—about 5 percent per year (Petrides and Swank 1965); we apply this recovery rate to the mammoths and mastodons.

In 140 years the Edmonton population grows to 519, with a density of 0.05 persons per square mile (Table 4), and occupies a front 54 miles wide. All elephants within 100 miles of Edmonton are eliminated. In 380 years the front supports 6,000 people and is almost 1,000 miles beyond Edmonton. Hunter population density remains low. In the next 100 years, the region enclosing the radiocarbon-dated mammoth kill sites is overrun. The sweep from Edmonton to the gulfs takes 532 years; 94,000 hunters destroy 3.3 million elephants, exterminating all herds north of Mexico.

In the last year, there is a population of 20,000 on the front. If we allow 7,000 of them to continue their elephant hunting into Central America, the remaining 13,000 must find a new food source or starve. Stretching the geometry of our model somewhat, we consider a returning wave emanating from the southeastern U.S. Regrouping 13,000 people in a quarter circle with a radius of 300 miles, with its center at Gainesville, Florida, we now simulate predation on the less preferred prey on a return sweep north (Table 5). In the absence of elephants, prey biomass is allowed to increase to 25 animal units per square mile (75 million units overall) and to replace losses at 30 percent annually.

Table 4. Simulation with conditions of moderate biomass, preferred prey: Mammoth

Features of the front

Years after arrival	Distance from Edmonton	Width	Human population	Human density
60	100.2	100.2	206	0.026
140	160.6	54.1	519	0.046
220	361.0	54.6	1,203	0.042
300	601.6	55.1	2,724	0.055
380	942.2	55.7	5,809	0.073
460	1,403.0	56.5	11,523	0.094
532	1,954.4	57.3	19,552	0.113

Table 5. Simulation with conditions of moderate biomass, preferred prey: Non-mammoth

Features of the front

Years after arrival	Distance from Gainesville	Width	Human population	Human density
20	301.9	301.9	16,532	0.231
100	315.6	315.6	43,237	0.553
200	1,156.2	238.8	92,185	0.237
279	1,954.4	244.4	147,302	0.209

Table 6. Simulation with destruction rate dependent upon prey biomass (monomolecular: $G = 13$, $N = 25$; $G = 6.5$, $N = 5$)

Features of the front

Years after arrival	Distance from Edmonton	Width	Human population	Human density
40	100.5	100.5	396	0.050
80	102.3	102.3	1,568	0.191
120	128.8	60.1	5,997	0.643
160	317.0	68.2	17,420	0.575
200	567.1	78.4	45,644	0.702
240	976.4	87.7	90,822	0.707
280	1,407.8	99.1	174,605	0.826
319	1,954.4	107.6	263,840	0.821

Extinction of the less preferred mammals takes 279 additional years at the hands of a total population of 760,000 people: 133 million animal units are destroyed. Including the elephant hunters, a total of 850,000 people consume 150 million animal units in 811 years.

This model would gain chronological support if horse, camel, and ground sloth extinction proved to be slightly later than mammoth or mastodon extinction. We assume that preferences in prey were observed locally, with larger, more easily killed, or tastier animals hunted first. But we doubt that preferred prey were hunted exclusively for hundreds of years as postulated in this extreme case.

Thus far we have kept the rate of destruction constant. However, the destruction rate may be expected to decline with a decrease in prey. We next ran simulations in which the destruction rate decreased according to the monomolecular function. The parameters of Table 1 are repeated, but with a monomolecular destruction rate of 13 animal units per person per year at prey biomass 25, and 6.5 animal units per person per year at prey biomass 5 (Table 6).

In 120 years the Edmonton population grows from 100 to 6,000, at a density of 0.6 per square mile, and occupies a front 60 miles wide; local extinction begins. By 240 years the front has reached northern Colorado, in the position shown in Figure 1. The density is 0.7 persons per square mile, and the population is over 90,000. In the final 79 years the front sweeps the remaining 1,000 miles, attains a depth of over 100 miles, and contains 264,000 people. The total number of persons in the sweep from Edmonton to the gulfs is 734,000. In 319 years 97 million animal units are destroyed. The hunters pass by all radiocarbon-dated mammoth sites within 70 years.

If the same simulation is run with the monomolecular curve adjusted to give a destruction rate of 13 animal units at prey biomass of 25 per square mile and 6.5 animal units at 10 per square mile, then a total population of 2.3 million is required for the sweep and its destruction of 95 million animal units in 348 years. With destruction rates declining as prey becomes scarce, a much larger and archaeologically more visible population of hunters is generated. But extinction still occurs rapidly in these two examples.

The simulations we have discussed are performed in discrete time. In any given year, predation is scheduled to occur prior to reproduction of both prey and predator. If we let all reproductive increases in prey biomass occur prior to predation, the situation is more favorable to the prey. Reasonable models in continuous time should give results somewhat higher than those of Table 1. If we repeat the simulation of Table 1 with all annual increase in prey biomass occurring *prior* to predation, extinction occurs in approximately 300 years. A total population of 366,000 completes the sweep from Edmonton to the gulfs, destroying 95 million animal units. This adjustment has little effect on our basic scenario.

We sought limiting conditions. As noted, extinction will not occur if human population density does not exceed a critical value. If held below the critical value, population growth slows before a front forms. In effect, there is a conservation strategy, which enables a large population of meat-eaters to crop the megafauna on a sustained-yield basis.

For example, under our second simulation (Table 2), the critical human population density is 2.04 persons per square mile. If the human population is held to 1.95 persons per square mile, there will be no front. Growing steadily at 3.4 percent annually, the hunters reach the gulfs of Mexico and of California in 329 years. A total of 8.7 million hunters consume 1.5 billion animal units (Table 7). This is 7 times the number of people and potential kill sites which could be expected under our second extinction scenario and 30 times more people than the number generated in our basic scenario (Table 1).

Further growth in the 3 million square miles now occupied is impossible without risk of swift extinction. Just under 6 million people may eat as much as 10 pounds of meat daily as long as they wish, provided they control their numbers and maintain a careful schedule of age- and species-adjusted cropping. If maintained 1,000 years, this system would have supported a total population of 234 million people consuming 4,016 billion animal units—an effective demonstration of its high potential archaeological visibility.

Had the invaders been able to adopt such a strategy of sustained yield, the prehistory of the New World, not to mention the fate of the native fauna, would have been radically different from the one we know. The megafauna would have survived, and the yield of Paleolithic-type artifacts and of kill or camp sites would be vastly greater than archaeologists report.

Table 7. Simulating survival

| | *Features of the front* | | | |
Years after arrival	Distance from Edmonton	Width	Human population	Human density
20	100.3	100.3	199	0.025
100	109.4	109.4	3,119	0.332
200	271.0	271.0	97,290	1.686
300	1,389.2	1,389.2	2,941,063	1.940
329	1,954.4	1,954.4	5,839,204	1.946

In the advancing-front model, the hunters not only eliminate the large mammals they prey upon but also systematically reduce the area available for surviving prey to live in. This reduction in area is an essential feature of our simulations. Suppose no front is established, but 100 people, with geometric growth at 3 percent annually, are simply injected into 3 million square miles with an initial (and ceiling) prey biomass of 25 animal units per square mile and a prey replacement rate of 25 percent annually. With a destruction rate of 7 animal units per person per year, extinction occurs in 350 years and requires a population of just over 4 million people. With a destruction rate of 13 animal units per person per year, extinction occurs in 330 years at the hands of a population of over 2 million. These figures are mathematically derived, not simulated. Extinction occurs swiftly, but the size of the human population is many times larger than the one able to destroy the megafauna under the assumptions we make in our basic simulation.

To review our results briefly, we find that in our basic simulation, a total of 290,000 people destroy a megafauna of 75 million animal units, plus recruitment—93 million animal units in all—in 293 years. To do so, one person in four must kill an average of one animal unit (1,000 lbs) per week. The human population increases at an average of 2.4 percent annually. A megafauna of 150 million animal units plus recruitment, preyed upon half as heavily as the fauna in the basic scenario, is obliterated in just 329 years (Table 2). This simulation should yield twice as many kill sites and support a human population four times larger than the first.

If we follow Haynes (1966) and consider the fate of a human population increasing at an average of 0.6 percent annually, 1,157 years are needed to overwhelm a rich megafauna (Table 3). Even under this condition, the front of hunters moves from southern Wyoming to southern Arizona in less than 200 years, which may be fast enough to account for the apparent similarity in age of the radiocarbon-dated mammoth kill sites.

If mammoth and mastodon were selected as preferred prey, a remarkably small number of hunters, slowly increasing to 90,000, could destroy a hypothetical North American elephant herd of 3.3 million animals (Table 4). Allowing this hunter population to continue growth at a maximum rate of 1.2 percent per year, other large prey would vanish in less than 300 years (Table 5).

If predation intensity is reduced when prey density drops, following a monomolecular distribution, a larger number of people and a somewhat longer time interval are needed before extinction occurs. But the number of animals destroyed is barely affected (Tables 6 and 8), and the basic chronology is not radically changed.

Finally, a strategy that will not lead to extinction is one in which the hunters manage to regulate their own density and develop a conservation program (Table 7). The result is a steady state population of almost 6 million people and 150 million animal units. This

Table 8. Summary of simulations

| | Conditions | | | | | | Results | | | | |
| | Prey | | | Hunters | | | Prey | | Hunters | | S. Wyoming to S. Arizona (yrs) |
	K	A	L	C (%)	M	G	Total a.u. consumed × 10⁶	Years to extinction	Total people × 10⁶	Mean C (%)	
Table 1. Mod. biomass, heavy kill, fast growth	25.0	0.25	4.0	3.5	.0127	13.0	93	293	0.29	2.4	55
Table 2. High biomass, mod. kill, fast growth	50.0	0.40	4.0	3.5	.0127	7.0	209	329	1.19	2.6	59
Table 3. High biomass, heavy kill, slow growth	50.0	0.25	4.0	0.65	.0127	13.0	260	1,157	0.80	0.6	170
Table 4. Preferred prey, mammoth	5.0	0.05	4.0	1.21	.0127	7.0	17	532	0.09	1.0	120
Table 5. Preferred prey, non-mammoth	25.0	0.30	4.0	1.21	.1839	7.0	133	279	0.76	0.9	—
Table 6. Monomolecular, ½ G at N = 5	25.0	0.25	4.0	3.5	.0127	13.0	97	319	0.73	2.5	64
* Monomolecular, ½ G at N = 10	25.0	0.25	4.0	3.5	.0127	13.0	95	348	2.31	2.6	62
Table 7. Simulating survival	50.0	0.40	1.95	3.5	.0127	7.0	1,518	(fauna survives)	8.68	3.4	40

* Not given as a table.

group would yield abundant evidence of artifacts associated with megafauna. Such evidence does not appear in the fossil record, and thus this strategy can be rejected.

Archaeological visibility

All simulations are summarized in Table 8. Our purpose was to learn more about how overkill might have happened if it were caused by human interference. At issue is the question of archaeological visibility. The 1.2 million people required to bring about extinction under the conditions presented in Table 2 might seem enough to guarantee reasonable archaeological visibility. But this is not the case. The front of hunters averaged 118 miles in width, advanced about 10 miles per year, and supported about one person per square mile. It would pass through most localities in about 12 years. To find evidence of its passage, the archaeologist would have to detect 11,000-year-old artifacts discarded by one person per square mile *within an interval of 12 years only*. These artifacts must be discriminated from all others left in the next 11,000 years by all later cultures. If the hunters destroyed the fauna according to the schedule presented in Table 1, they would be even less visible archaeologically.

To pursue this analysis further,

Paleoindians hunting bison persisted in the High Plains from 10,500 to 8,500 years ago, or later. Even if these hunters maintained a population of only 0.1 persons per square mile, they would still constitute a prehistoric population 16 times larger, and therefore presumably that much more visible, than that of the big game hunters in their sweep of the same area as simulated in Table 2. If site preservation were equally probable between 11,500 and 8,500 years ago, the associations of early postglacial bison with artifacts should be far more numerous than Paleoindian associations with the extinct genera. According to Hester (1967), such is the case. At first it seems that the millions of animal units removed by overkill in our simulations must surely provide numerous kill sites for the paleontologist to discover.

The 260 million animal units slaughtered in 3 million square miles represent an average of 87 animal units per square mile (Table 2). Letting one animal unit correspond to one individual from the extinct megafauna, then 87 large animals are candidates for fossilization and subsequent discovery in each square mile swept by the front.

But this number is dwarfed by that

obtained for even a brief part of the late Rancholabrean—say the 10,000 years immediately prior to passage of the front. Again letting one animal unit correspond to one individual, an average biomass of 50 individuals suffering natural annual mortality of 20 percent would generate 10 individual carcasses each year on one square mile. In 10,000 years, a total of 100,000 carcasses per square mile are available for fossilization. Such an abundance of fossils is unknown, although it may be hinted at in the unusual case of tar pits such as Rancho la Brea, California, and Talara, Peru. The point is (paleontologists will not be surprised) that fossils are rare.

If we assume the probability of burial, fossilization, and discovery to be the same in the 10,000 years preceding extinction as it was during the period of slaughter, then the probability that any late Rancholabrean bone comes from a slaughtered animal is about one in one thousand. In other words, while an archaeologist or geologist searching outcrops of full- and late-glacial age may have a good chance of finding extinct animals, he has a very poor chance of finding one that might have been destroyed during the period of overkill. Add to this the well-known hazards affecting the likelihood that artifacts and bones will be preserved in association, and we conclude that the dozen well-documented cases of human artifacts associated with extinct mammoths may be a rich, not a poor, record of extinction by overkill.

Even if as many as 200 million large animals were destroyed by hunters, the remains of those dying from natural causes should be much more abundant. So should the remains of bison hunted after the time of the major extinctions. Expecting the fossil record to yield *abundant* fossil evidence of herds of game animals swiftly hunted to extinction over 10,000 years ago turns out to be unrealistic.

Simulations can prove nothing about prehistory. In ours, we attempt to show how, under conditions we believe are ecologically reasonable, large numbers of large animals might be destroyed rapidly by hunters alone. To explain extinction, it is unnecessary to invoke a combination of coincidental circumstances—the effects of ice-age climatic change, the possible introduction of new animal diseases, the appearance of new competitors, the hypothetical decline in genetic vigor among the large mammals (senescence), *and* the invasion of hominid predators. By prehistoric blitzkrieg, 300,000 hunters in North America could wipe out 100 million large animals in 300 years.

We find that fossil evidence of overkill, even of an abundant fauna, need not be easy to detect. The paleontologist must discriminate bones of animals killed by hunters in one or two decades from the vastly larger number contributed to the fossil record by natural mortality of the same species in previous millennia. The archaeologist must discriminate the artifacts produced in a decade or two during passage of the hunters through any one region from the vastly larger number contributed to the prehistoric record by later cultures in following millennia. To demonstrate human predation, he must find artifacts in situ with the bones. In these terms, it may be easier to understand how the late-glacial fossil record of America could be so rich in extinct genera of large animals and so poor in kill sites. In our model, overkill is almost invisible.

References

Birdsell, Joseph B. 1957. Some population problems involving Pleistocene man. Population Studies: Animal Ecology and Demography. *Cold Spring Harbor Symposium Quant. Biol.* 22: 47–69.

Budyko, M. I. 1967. On the causes of the extinction of some animals at the end of the Pleistocene. *Izvestiya Akademii Nauk SSSR seriya geograficheskaya* no. 2, pp. 28–36. Also *Soviet Geography Review and Translation* 8(10) 783–93.

Budyko, M. I. 1974. *Climate and Life.* N.Y.: Academic Press. 508 pp.

Caughley, Graeme. 1969. Eruption of ungulate populations, with emphasis on Himalayan thar in New Zealand. *Ecology* 51:53–72.

Colbert, E. H. 1937. The Pleistocene mammals of North America and their relations to Eurasian genera. In *Early Man*, ed. G. E. MacCurdy. London: Lippincott.

Cornfield, J. 1954. Measurement and comparison to toxicities: The quantal response. In *Statistics and Mathematics in Biology*, ed. O. W. Kempthorne. Ames: Iowa State College Press. pp. 327–44.

Deevey, E. S., Jr. 1960. The human population. *Sci. Am.* 203(3):194–204.

Eiseley, Loren C. 1943. Archaeological observations on the problem of post-glacial extinction. *American Antiquity* 8:209–17.

Haynes, C. Vance. 1966. Elephant-hunting in North America. *Sci. Am.* 214(6):104–12.

Haynes, C. Vance. 1970. Geochronology of man-mammoth sites and their bearing on the origin of the Llano complex. In *Pleistocene and Recent Environments of the Central Great Plains*, ed. W. Dort, Jr., and J. K. Jones, Jr. University of Kansas, Department of Geology spec. publ. 3:77–92.

Hester, James J. 1967. The agency of man in animal extinctions. In *Pleistocene Extinctions: The Search for a Cause*, ed. P. S. Martin and H. E. Wright, Jr. New

Haven: Yale University Press. pp. 169–92.

Krantz, Grover S. 1970. Human activities and megafaunal extinctions. *Am. Sci.* 58:164–70.

Long, Austin, Richard M. Hansen, and Paul S. Martin. 1974. Extinction of the Shasta ground sloth. *Geological Society of America Bulletin* 85:1843–48.

Martin, Paul S. 1967. Prehistoric overkill. In *Pleistocene Extinctions: The Search for a Cause*, ed. P. S. Martin and H. E. Wright, Jr. New Haven: Yale University Press. pp. 75–120.

Martin, Paul S. 1973. The discovery of America. *Science* 179:969–74.

Medawar, P. B. 1945. Size, shape and age. In *Essays on Growth and Form*, ed. W. E. le Gros Clark and P. B. Medawar. Oxford: Clarendon Press. pp. 157–87.

Murdoch, W. W. 1971. The development response of predators to changes in prey density. *Ecology* 52:132–37.

Petrides, G. A., and W. G. Swank. 1965. Estimating the productivity and energy relations of an African elephant population. *Proc. 9th International Grasslands Congress*, Sao Paulo, Brazil. pp. 831–42.

Pielou, E. C. 1969. *An Introduction to Mathematical Ecology* N.Y.: Wiley-Interscience.

Reed, C. A. 1970. Extinction of mammalian megafauna in the Old World late Quaternary. *Bioscience* 20(5):284–88.

Simpson, G. G. 1961. *Horses.* Natural History Library Edition. Garden City: Doubleday. 323 pp.

Wendorf, D. F., and J. J. Hester. 1962. Early man's utilization of the great plains environment. *Amer. Anthro.* 18:159–71.

Wheat, Joe Ben. 1972. The Olsen-Chubbuck site: A paleo-indian bison kill. *Memoirs of the Society for American Archaeology.* 26(1).

Zaret, Thomas M., and R. T. Paine. 1973. Species introduction in a tropical lake. *Science* 182:449–55.

"Some of us endangered species are getting together Saturday night for one last fling at the water hole."

Index